EDUCATIONAL POLICY
AND
THE MISSION SCHOOLS

Contributors

BRIAN HOLMES

R. E. BAIN

T. R. A. RUBERU

GRACE GEORGE

S. Z. AHMED

J. H. SISLIAN

P. K. PERSIANIS

P. E. B. INYANG

EDUCATIONAL POLICY
AND
THE MISSION SCHOOLS

Case Studies from the
British Empire

edited by
BRIAN HOLMES

LONDON
ROUTLEDGE & KEGAN PAUL
NEW YORK: HUMANITIES PRESS

First published 1967
by Routledge and Kegan Paul Ltd.
Broadway House, 68-74 Carter Lane
London, E.C.4

Printed in Great Britain
by C. Tinling & Co. Ltd.
Liverpool, London,
and Prescot

S B N 7100 6002 5

CONTENTS

PREFACE

J. A. LAUWERYS
Professor of Comparative Education, University of London

IN his analysis of the reasons which led to China's troubles and miseries, Chairman Mao attributes great importance to the 'cultural imperialism' of the missionary movement. Like many other ardent nationalists in Asia and Africa, he believes that this movement received full support from home governments, desirous of enslaving and exploiting weaker nations. But, in fact, is he right? What is the evidence? Is it true that missionaries did more harm than good? Would it have been better, as some Western liberals tend to think, not to have interfered with patterns of culture and religion?

What one thinks about such questions determines political attitudes and, yet, how hard it is to find answers based on facts. What is the truth? I can hope only that the present volume will be a modest contribution to the investigations that should be made. The case-studies presented were prepared by former students in the Department of Comparative Education of the University of London Institute of Education. Each has written about his own country: which means that, at the start of his work, he was handicapped by ethnocentrism and national prejudice; inclined to see things—particularly the British administration—in harsh black-and-white terms. One outcome of scholarly activity was the moderation of pre-misconceptions and of snap assessments. Everyone came to see that the government of human beings is a terribly complex and muddled affair, that policy is made by fallible men, seldom altogether good or altogether bad and usually short-sighted, that chance and expediency are powerful factors when decisions have to be taken.

The research that had to be done involved the need to consult first-hand sources. Happily—unhappily perhaps for the workers! —there is an immense store in the archives and libraries of the missionary societies in London while the Public Record Office is

vii

rich in material bearing on British colonial policy. The librarians in these institutions displayed warm-hearted generosity, sparing neither time nor kindness: it is truly pleasant to have this opportunity of expressing to them the gratitude both of the students they helped and of the department.

It may cause mild surprise that detailed historical studies of one country are part of research in Comparative Education. The point, however, is that the reaction to educational problems arising under broadly similar conditions displays similarities. Case-studies then help to identify the specific dimensions of common problems. The idea of comparison is both to note what is alike and what is different, interpreting and explaining both. In addition, detailed case-studies throw light on the general process of educational development and on the way in which contextual differences affect the final outcome.

There is another point to be noted: often in education the problems of today cannot be understood without taking full account of the way in which they were generated: the historical dimension is essential to the analysis. This is particularly true in the evaluation of missionary effort: policy decisions were taken in the very early days and institutions created. The effects were permanent and persist. For this reason, our students paid much attention to beginnings. Their interest, however, was always pragmatic: history, yes, but not for the sake of antiquarian devotion; mainly in order to illuminate present conflicts and disputes.

Modest and tentative conclusions can be drawn from the work already accomplished. First, there really were educational policies which can be stated and examined. Each missionary society debated anxiously why missionaries should be sent and what aims should guide their work. Quite often, detailed instructions were given, for instance about the importance to be given to the task of converting non-Christians. The societies did not always agree on such matters as the content of school curricula, language policy, selective or universal education. But none of these differences were, in the last instance, as decisive regarding what was done as were the circumstances under which the missionaries worked in the field. Anyway, the results achieved were never exactly those aimed at: they are related to but distinct from the stated intentions. Much of what the missionaries hoped for came to pass but nearly always entirely unexpected and unforeseen results also followed.

Preface

The policies of the British Government tended to change as the years went by, largely under the pressure of interested parties: trading groups like the East India Company, the West Indian planters, philanthropists and humanitarians like Wilberforce. For much of the nineteenth century it was more or less 'laissez faire'. The intention was to play a political role as modest as possible in the affairs of colonial territories. Then, too, the particular relationship of the local authorities to the Home government affected the practical working out of major decisions. In some instances, the local governor had great freedom to pursue policies in the light of his own beliefs, elsewhere he was closely controlled from London. Or it might happen that he was much influenced by local pressure groups. Yet, in spite of these interesting variations it is possible to detect a steady government policy and to show how it changed during a century and a half.

The missionaries were never entirely free to do as they wanted: the British authorities supported them when it suited their purpose and placed restrictions on them when this seemed necessary in the light of their own aims. Colonial governments were always very sensitive to indigenous religious traditions. In the West Indies and Nigeria it seems they were not regarded as worthy of preservation: indeed some practices in Nigeria were condemned outright. Under such circumstances, the missionaries were given a free hand. But where Buddhism or Islam were encountered, the British authorities were very cautious and usually discouraged the missionaries from attempting to proselytize.

Among the general results of the missionary activities, shaped as they were by religious and humanitarian purposes but deeply influenced by the cultural background from which they drew nourishment and largely controlled by an administration not always sympathetic, we would stress above all the political consequences. Most of the new leaders in the colonial territories were educated in Mission schools, which also trained administrators, bureaucrats and clerks. Social differences, hallowed by tradition and religious authority, were frequently upset. Then also those who attended English-medium schools gained economic advantages. Independence movements were frequently inspired and sustained by the products of mission schools: but after independence the unity of indigenous élites frequently broke down in part because of the ways in which European-type education divided along new lines, not related to traditional stratification. The extent to which in various colonial territories differential advantage was taken of missionary schools exacerbated many of today's political conflicts. The examples of Ceylon and Nigeria spring to mind. Some of these consequences could have been foreseen, and perhaps ameliorated, by comparative study. Indeed, some of the predictions made in the present volume have already happened— events have outrun publishing schedules.

Two chapters in this book may appear out of place: those on Cyprus and on Egypt. In Cyprus, the British missionary societies did scarcely anything to develop education. But it is fascinating to see how British colonial policy was adapted to meet conditions in which it faced a strong, active, aggressive religious group, the Greek Orthodox Church, firmly rooted in the European tradition and with powerful friends in the West. The case-study on Egypt discusses some of the problems which arose from the clash of British and French cultural and political interests in that country— a clear example of the way in which out-of-date concepts and battles fought long ago can thwart and bedevil sensible action.

The responsibility for preparing this volume is that of Dr. Brian Holmes. He drew up a splendid scheme and structure which was accepted by each of the authors. The studies they present are new, though based on material they gathered for their theses. Because of the structure, comparative analysis becomes possible. Without making exaggerated claims, it will be evident that, as a result, prediction of the results of educational development is possible. One sees how some of the social consequences of action through the schools could be foreseen. In addition, light is thrown on the results of Imperial rule during the nineteenth century and on the nature of the impact of Western education in Asia and Africa. Almost incidentally the naïve Marxian view—that missionaries were agents of commercial and political imperialism—is shown simply to be wrong. The missionaries, so often misguided and short-sighted, were in fact pioneers of modernization, of science and of freedom. Dr. Holmes deserves our gratitude for this contribution to scholarship, which would not have appeared without his work and devotion.

Institute of Education, University of London
December 1966

ABOUT THE CONTRIBUTORS

THE authors of chapters 2–8 undertook the major part of their research as students at the University of London Institute of Education. Their work for research degrees in the department of Comparative Education was supervised by Professor J. A. Lauwerys, Professor of Comparative Education, and Dr. B. Holmes, Reader in Comparative Education in the University of London.

MRS. SAJADA ZAMIR AHMED was born in Srinagar and was educated at the Lahore College for Women, Punjab, and at a Kashmir Teacher Training College, from which institutions she received B.A. and B.T. degrees. She had nine years of teaching experience, including a period as headmistress of a Srinagar High School. She came to England as a Government Scholar in 1955 and completed her M.A. at the University of London Institute of Education in 1958. Mrs. Ahmed has now returned to Kashmir where she is Principal of a Teachers' Training College.

MR. R. E. BAIN received his education at Government High School, Nassau, University College, Hull, and the University of London Institute of Education. He obtained a Professional Certificate of Education at the London Institute in 1946, a B.A. London degree in 1949, a Teacher's Diploma in 1950 and an M.A. (with distinction) in 1957. He was an assistant teacher in the Bahamas (1938–9) and then the head teacher of a village school (1939–45). From 1950–6 Mr. Bain was a Supervisory Head teacher and in 1956–7 Acting Principal of the Bahamas Training College. He became an Education Officer in 1959 and has been Deputy Director of Education in the Bahamas since 1962. For a year 1963–4 Mr. Bain was Acting Director of Education and Permanent Secretary and was attached to the Inspectorate for a short time in 1961. During the Academic Year 1965–6 he followed a course in Administration and Planning at the University of London Institute of Education. He was recently appointed Director of Education in the Bahamas.

About the Contributors

MRS. GRACE GEORGE obtained her B.A. and B.T. degrees from Indian universities and registered at the University of London Institute of Education in 1955, where she obtained her M.A. During her stay in England Mrs. George gained considerable practical experience as a teacher. On her return to India, she was appointed Director of Studies in a private college in Hyderabad, Deccan, her home town. Later she was Director of St. Mary's Institute there for two years. Mrs. George then took up a post as senior teacher at the Sultan Omar Ali Saifuddin College, Brunei Town, under a three-year contract with the Government of Brunei. She is now working on aspects of general and technical education in Sabah, Sarawak and Brunei States.

MR. P. E. B. INYANG was born in Ikot Nkim, Iwawa, Nigeria and received his secondary school education at St. Patrick's College, Calabar. He attended the National University of Ireland from 1953–6 and obtained a B.A. degree. At the University of London Institute of Education he studied for an M.A. degree which was awarded to him in 1958. At the University of Wisconsin he studied for two years (1964–6) and was awarded an M.S. degree. Mr. Inyang has taught in a mission primary school and been a headmaster. He served as tutor and senior tutor in St. Augustine's and St. Mary's teacher training colleges respectively before going to the University of Nigeria, Nsukka in 1961. After a year as tutor at the University of Wisconsin (1965–6) Mr. Inyang was appointed Lecturer at the University of Nigeria.

MR. P. K. PERSIANIS was born in Cyprus and from 1950–4 studied ancient and modern Greek literature at Athens University. In 1959 he was granted a scholarship by the Greek Government to study education. At the University of London Institute of Education he obtained his M.A. after submitting a thesis entitled 'The Contribution of the Greek Orthodox Church of Cyprus to Cyprus Education during the British Administration'. He is Deputy Headmaster of the Pancyprian Gymnasium in Nicosia, Cyprus. Mr. Persianis has written a series of articles on the educational problems of Cyprus in the official educational magazine of the Ministry of Cyprus Education.

DR. T. RANJIT RUBERU graduated in science with honours at the

University of Ceylon in 1952. He taught for several years after graduation and joined the University of Ceylon as Lecturer in Education in 1956. He studied in England between 1957 and 1961 and obtained the Post Graduate Certificate in Education in 1958, the Academic Diploma in 1959 and his Ph.D. in 1961—all at the University of London Institute of Education. He has made several research contributions to learned journals and is author of several publications about the history of education and teaching methods in Ceylon. He is author of *Education in Colonial Ceylon*, Kandy (1962), and was promoted to Senior Lecturer in Education at the University of Ceylon in 1966.

MR. JACK HEINZ SISLIAN was born in Cairo, Egypt. He is German but was educated at the English Mission College, Cairo and obtained his first degree in education from the American University, Cairo and his M.A. at the University of London Institute of Education. He commands several languages and has translated articles for the *World Year Book of Education*. His special field of interest, school and society in the Middle East, is based on a first-hand knowledge of the region. He has studied the educational systems of many countries and is well acquainted with American, French, English and German scholarship. Since 1955 Mr. Sislian has been attached to the German Educational System and has been lecturing in Adult Education in Germany. He now works as lecturer in comparative Education with Professor Dr. G. Hausmann, who is Director, of the Institute of Education and Department of Comparative Education, Hamburg University.

Editor's Note

FATHER JOSEPH THAIKOODAN was born in Cochin. He graduated from St. Joseph's College, Trichinipoly, subsequently studied philosophy and theology and was ordained in 1949. Father Thaikoodan has taught chemistry in a high school and at a college and has been headmaster of a lower secondary school. He studied at the University of London Institute of Education from 1961 to 1965. On his return to India he worked on *The Kerala Times* particularly in the field of education. Some information from his thesis has been incorporated in Chapter 4.

REFERENCES AND ABBREVIATIONS

THE chapters in this volume are based, for the most part, on research carried out in the archives of various missionary societies, church organizations, and Government Departments. Most, but not all, the manuscript material is in London and Edinburgh. The addresses of the most frequently used libraries and the abbreviation adopted in the text and references are given below.

Mission and Church Libraries

Baptist Missionary Society (BMS), 93 Gloucester Place, London W.1.

Church Missionary Society (CMS), 157 Waterloo Road, London S.E.1.

Church Mission to Jews (CMJ), 16 Lincoln's Inn Fields, London W.C.2.

Church of Scotland (C of S)
Offices: 121 George Street, Edinburgh 2.
Library: St. John's Library, 352 Castle Hill, Edinburgh.

Lambeth Palace Library (LPL), Lambeth Palace, London S.E.1.

London Missionary Society (LMS), Livingstone House, 11 Carteret Street, London S.W.1.

Methodist Missionary Society (MMS), 25 Marylebone Road, London N.W.1 (includes archives of Weslyan Methodist Missionary Society (WMMS) and the Primitive Methodist Missionary Society (PMMS)).

The Society for Promoting Christian Knowledge (SPCK), Holy Trinity Church, Marylebone Road, London N.W.1.

The United Society for the Propagation of the Gospel (USPG), 15 Tufton Street, London S.W.1.
(Archives of the Society for the Propagation of the Gospel in Foreign Parts (SPG) are kept here.)

Official Papers and Documents
Most of the material is available either at the Public Record Office
(P.R.O.), Chancery Lane, London W.C.2. or among the State
Papers, British Museum (BM), London W.C.1. The following
abbreviations have been used:

C.O.	Colonial Office Papers
F.O.	Foreign Office Papers
C	
Cd	
Cmd	Parliamentary Papers
Parl. Papers	

The Missionary Register contains an abstract of the proceedings of the
principal missionary and Bible societies throughout the world. It
was published in London in 43 volumes during the years 1813–55.

INTRODUCTION

FOR many years the object of British imperial policy was to prepare each of the dependent territories for self government and eventual independence. In cultural matters a general policy of *laissez faire* did not prevent the British authorities from attempting to protect and maintain indigenous institutions. Educational policy was designed, in the main, simply to create a corps of suitably trained locally recruited minor officials and clerks for the colonial service.

Under these conditions the mission societies moved in where they could, with the main purpose of converting people to Christianity or of improving the quality of the faith where it already existed. The agencies through which conversion was to be attempted were the church, the school and the hospital. Sometimes local opposition made it necessary to open a hospital first. Frequently the school preceded the church and in some cases it was impossible to open a church at all. Understandably, schools were seen by some local leaders as the agents of British imperialism and Christianity.

The mission schools were, naturally, modelled on those familiar to the missionaries at home—the charity schools and the English public or grammar schools. The monitorial system which was widely used was to some extent a product of colonial conditions. The initial acceptance of a foreign institution depended on local politics; its survival, development, and growth were related to its ability to adapt to local needs. The reception given to the mission schools by the political and religious leaders of the society into which they were introduced was an important determinant of survival. Their subsequent popularity helped to determine their long-range influence. The force of this impact was closely related to the power structure of the country or region where the schools operated. Progress was very difficult in societies where power was centralized and the leaders were hostile. When they were friendly— a rather rare situation—centralized control greatly benefited the

B

work of a small, well-organized minority group. Generally the devolution of power favoured such a group of missionaries.

Policies had to be adapted to circumstances. Thus, while several mission societies set out with the intention of providing education in the vernaculars for the masses they were soon running prestige English medium schools. Attempts to provide vocational or technical training usually failed because an articulate minority demanded the prestige curriculum of English or European schools, i.e. a heavily literary one. The political determinants of the policies followed are of considerable interest and in this volume have been examined in selected historical settings.

Of even greater interest are the political outcomes of missionary educational policy. It has not been possible to assess these with the same care, but of major concern is the contribution they made to the forces of unification or disintegration inherent in the different colonial territories. Among the divisive social forces language, religion, kinship ties and caste rank high. Geographical conditions also influence the possibilities of unifying a nation, or holding together a federation. Many colonial territories were not delineated by natural boundaries. Language and religious differences should be viewed against this kind of background.

Undoubtedly the English language gave some unity to a small but influential élite. Members of it provided the new political leaders and a corps of competent bureaucrats and technologists. New methods of recruiting political leaders through education did not always ensure that the socializing power of traditional institutions was replaced by more appropriate ones. The seeds of political conflict between the educated and the non-educated (in a European sense) and between generations were sown.

English education was accepted or rejected on religious and linguistic grounds. Any group which rejected it tended to develop a greater sense of communal identity and thus national unity was weakened. Groups which accepted English education had conferred upon them advantages which were resented by groups which rejected it. This gave rise to communal competition rather than co-operation. Competition for support between the mission societies was another source of social disintegration. Under certain circumstances it helped promote communalism.

These outcomes of missionary educational activity help to explain the ambivalence shown towards the mission schools when countries in the British Empire became independent. No systematic attempt (except for example in Cyprus when it came too late) had been made by the British authorities to Anglicize and Christianize the native populations. After independence English political institutions had to be run by people whose value system contained many elements from both the old and the new traditions. Attitudes towards mission schools have been reflected in post-independence legislation. The reaction of the Protestant churches to these moves to increase Government control have been different from that of the Roman Catholics. In many cases the future of the missions schools is uncertain.

It is with the historical background to these problems that this volume of case studies is principally concerned. With the exception of Chapter 1 each contribution is based upon a thesis prepared in the Department of Comparative Education at the University of London, Institute of Education. Each has been prepared by an educationist who was born and has worked for many years in the country about which he or she writes. The views are those of the authors but it is hoped that the comparative analysis will make some contribution to a wider and general understanding of the politics of education. Certainly not all the data are strictly comparable but the problems were sufficiently common to encourage the formulation of some general conclusions about the impact of missionary education. These have been stated very tentatively in this brief introduction.

THE EDITOR

University of London
Institute of Education,
December 1966

BRITISH IMPERIAL POLICY
AND THE MISSION SCHOOLS

Brian Holmes

AFTER the Second World War socio-political changes gathered momentum. The victors from western Europe were soon called upon to liquidate their colonial empires. Over the years, either as a matter of policy or after bitter struggles, Britain, France, Belgium and the Netherlands granted independence to their dependent peoples. Pre-war British policy of evolution to responsible self-government was implemented at a vastly accelerated rate. India and Pakistan became independent in 1947. Ceylon, already by 1940 an example of responsible local government, became fully independent in 1948. During the fifties the process continued. The withdrawal of British troops from Egypt after a period of over seventy years was completed in 1956. After years of agitation and a period (1955–9) of open rebellion in Cyprus a settlement was reached in 1959 which restricted Britain's direct influence in the island's affairs to small enclaves for defence. In Africa one territory after another established independent régimes under new constitutions: Nigeria celebrated independence in 1959; of the islands in the Caribbean the Bahamas had in fact long enjoyed a very considerable measure of self rule. Except for rather small changes the Constitution written in 1729 remained substantially the same until a new one was drawn up in 1964 which gave complete control over internal affairs to the Bahamian Government.

The new constitutions were based on the assumption that democratic self government would be possible. In most cases the institutions of Government were derived from British models; Parliamentary procedures were copied from Westminster and concepts of local government found expression in a devolution of certain powers. In short, the theory and practice of Government in the newly independent territories reflected British democracy. Unfortunately some of the hopes for the tranquil transition from colonial rule to successful self government have been thwarted.

So too have other post-war expectations. Not all the much publicized human rights in the United Nations Universal Declaration have been realized in practice. Among the thirty articles listing these rights and liberties, the twenty-sixth dealt with education. It said that everyone had the right to education which at the elementary stage should be free and compulsory. Technical and professional education should be generally available and higher education should be open to all on the basis of merit. The constitutions of many newly independent nations either anticipated or closely followed this declaration of intention; for example, Article 45 of India's constitution provided for free, universal and compulsory education within ten years.

Similar provisions were included in major post-war educational legislation. The details varied from one country to another, to be sure, but until the late fifties and early sixties education laws reflected the concept of education as a human right with the corollary that democracy could not survive without a system of universal primary education. The difficulties of meeting this demand by providing a school place for every child were soon apparent. Studies in the economics of education helped to reorientate educational policy in the light of economic considerations. Manpower needs in relation to economic resources suggested that priority should be given to secondary and higher education and to technical and professional training.

No doubt many observers hold the imperial powers responsible for the difficulties of developing education either as a human right or as a form of economic investment in many newly independent countries.

THE POST-WAR SITUATION

Certainly the situation at the end of the war was very unpromising. Crude illiteracy figures from Unesco sources reveal one aspect of it. In 1944 the percentage for India was 85, for Egypt 88 and in 1946 Cyprus reported an illiteracy figure for people over fifteen years of age as 22 per cent. In that year the percentage in Ceylon was 37. These figures may be compared with a 15 per cent illiteracy of the over five year old Bahamian population in 1953. A Unesco report in 1950 estimated that three out of every four humans could neither read nor write.

The reasons for this state of affairs are complex. It was nevertheless easy to argue that the provision of education in the pre-war British colonies had been restricted to a small minority of the population and that too little money had been made available for education.

In fact the local governments (with some encouragement from Britain) had not been unmindful of the need to promote education. Laws about compulsory education have been on the statute books in the West Indies since the 1880s. By 1900 education in the Bahamas was free and compulsory up to the age of fourteen. The 1908 Act made it available to the remotest village. Compulsory education laws were passed in Ceylon in 1906 (Town Schools Ordinance No. 5) and 1907 (The Rural School Ordinance No. 8). Clause 19 of the National Constitution of 1923 made school attendance in Egypt compulsory for children between the ages of six and twelve.

Two processes were at work during the twentieth century. As a matter of policy education was becoming the responsibility of local governments in which elected representation was increasing. The second aspect of policy was that there was a growing devolution of function. Regional and local authorities were being given more and more responsibility for education. The Government of India Act 1919 introduced dyarchy in the Provinces under which education was transferred to popular control. By 1937 Indians had obtained almost complete control of education. By 1923, too, the Ministry of Education in Egypt had passed into purely Egyptian hands. In Nigeria the educational codes of 1926, which referred to the Northern Provinces (ordinance No. 14) and the Southern Provinces (ordinance No. 15), remained in force, virtually untouched, until after the Second World War. When Nigeria became a Federation in 1954 under a new constitution, there was a devolution of functions of the Central Authority on Regional Directors and Regional Boards. In the Eastern Region the Education Law of 1952 established local education authorities and in 1954 it was proposed to introduce free and universal primary education by 1956.

The Cyprian case is special. After 1931 laws were passed with the

7

intention of giving the British authorities a greater measure of centralized control. They attempted to promote secondary as well as elementary education under the provisions of the Elementary Education Law of 1933 and the Secondary Education Law of 1936. In 1935 the English School Law was passed to strengthen the position of English. Mr. Persianis claims that the motives were political.

A policy of decentralization needs to be sustained by popular demand for education, and Mr. Bain's point is that in the Bahamas there was relatively little demand for the kind of education provided under the compulsory education laws. Elsewhere in the thirties the economic situation was such that there were few openings for educated people. The growth of literacy depends very considerably on motivation which turns on the evident benefits which literacy confers on those who possess it. Government service was an obvious attraction. Evidently the extent to which local communities were prepared to support educational development depended upon economic circumstances and the priority given to education.

The vicious circle was not broken by the assistance provided by the British Government. From 1929 under the U.K. Colonial Development Acts only technical and economic projects qualified for assistance. Little attention was paid to social welfare schemes, including education. The economic crisis of the thirties had disastrous effects on the economies and planned development of many colonial territories. Consequently opportunities to benefit from the money invested and from whatever education was provided were restricted by the slowness of industrial and commercial growth. Only after the war did social welfare schemes qualify for aid.

By that time few of the non self-governing territories in the British Empire had achieved universal primary education let alone mass literacy. The responsibility of the colonial Governments for this state of affairs will not be analysed. Except in Cyprus it was the British missionaries (and in Egypt the British and French) who had, with the assistance of Government grants, shouldered the burden of providing whatever education these countries possessed by the time they became independent. In some cases the missionaries had done little more than introduce European schools. In other cases they had accepted responsibility for the provision of most of the schools at one level or another. In the Bahamas nearly 25 per cent of the primary schools in 1951 were denominational and were attended by over 30 per cent of the pupils. There was one Government high school enrolling little more than 12 per cent of high school pupils. In 1949–50 of the 279,309 educational institutions in India over 100,000 were managed by private bodies. A fifth of the schools in Kerala were managed by Christian organizations. In Ceylon the privileged position of the mission schools had been questioned for a long time but as late as 1958, under a dual system of control, roughly 53 per cent of the 7,674 schools were owned by the Government and 47 per cent by private bodies. The Dike Report on the educational system of Eastern Nigeria pointed out that in 1962 the voluntary agencies owned more than 80 per cent of the schools in the Region. Indeed nearly 50 per cent of all schools were owned and controlled by the Roman Catholics.

The contribution of the mission schools was obvious. For example, in Nigeria literacy rates were highest in the provinces in which the missionaries had been particularly active. In Ceylon the standards among Christians were higher than among Buddhists or Hindus. In most countries the prospects of the Government's building up a system of universal primary schools without missionary help were slight. But post-independence debates have frequently centred round the position of the mission schools. The reason is not difficult to find—they represented a dual threat to indigenous institutions. In the first place the policy of the missionaries was to convert people to Christianity, and the school was one agency of conversion. Young people and parents were brought into contact with Christians and natives could be trained as catechists and priests. The reception given to this policy depended upon local circumstances and in particular on the religious beliefs of the people. It was rejected, resented or accepted, and so the missionaries were not always able to follow a policy of proselytization. Everywhere, however, by design or chance, they introduced a second threat by introducing the English language. Even where Christianity was rejected, the mission schools attracted pupils from groups in the community who saw the value of English in commerce, education and politics. Elements of British or English secular education including political ideals were inevitably taught, if incidentally.

The education provided in mission schools was thus feared (or

9

resented) by some and in great demand from a small minority group. An understandable ambivalence towards missionary education lies at the heart of the politics of education in many developing countries. Its development and the form it has taken have been investigated by the various contributors to this book.

THE POLITICAL FRAMEWORK OF MISSIONARY EDUCATION

Because local conditions determined so much of what the missionaries could do each contributor has followed his own line of analysis within a broadly conceived framework. Three themes, however, run through each chapter. The first is how and under what political conditions the missionaries first established schools. The next theme relates to the educational policies pursued and how far they succeeded. Finally attempts have been made to estimate the consequences of mission schools in the societies where they were set up. These careful studies of the origins of mission schools make it possible to understand the ambivalent attitude towards them. Moreover, some vague dimensions of educational problems in newly independent countries may be clarified. In short, the intention is that these articles, although heavily historical, should illuminate some aspects of the dilemmas facing educational statesmen today.

The case studies examine the socio–political circumstances under which the mission schools were first established in selected countries. British political influences came from home and were also present in the local environment. Traders at home and overseas were interested in the role of the mission schools. The British Government and its representatives in the colonies were also involved. Finally British public opinion and the supporters of missionary endeavour exercised a profound influence on this work abroad. Indigenous political forces operated through the rulers, the priests, and the parents. Inevitably the missionaries became involved in politics. Sometimes they supported a Governor against directives from home. At other times they sought to influence the home Government against the policies of the colonial Government. In the long run their success depended upon their ability to win the support of the political power groups in whatever country they tried to work.

A general sequence of events throughout the British Empire can be described. The traders usually arrived first, then the missionaries. They set up schools. Then later the British officials came along and gradually secularized the control of education. The timing varies but the denominational battles and the process of removing education from clerical control tend to follow those which went on in England.

During the eighteenth century the commercial value of the West Indies made them the heart of the Empire. Since sugar was by far the most important crop in the islands the planters dominated political life. They filled most of the public offices—colonial secretary, attorney general, provost marshal—and were appointed from England. The position of the Bahamas was unique in that they depended less than the other islands on a plantation economy. Once piracy had been brought under control and constitutional Government had become increasingly possible trading interests dominated policy. The arrival from America of Loyalists strengthened the power of the colonists against the Home Government. During the first quarter of the nineteenth century, the great issue between the planters and influential groups in England was, of course, slavery which had been introduced during the sixteenth and seventeenth centuries. When the missionaries arrived they depended very much on the attitudes of the planters towards their work. In the islands dependent on sugar the planters were hostile. They feared the political consequences of allowing the slaves to meet together in church.

Even in the Bahamas the Society for the Propagation of the Gospel (SPG) was unable to do much work among the slaves because of the attitude of their owners. It was the Baptists and Methodists who arrived much later, around 1800, who helped the Negroes—slaves, freemen and indentured servants—and Dr. Bray's Associates who opened a school for free Negroes in 1793. The attitude of the Government is reflected in the legislation passed against the Methodists in 1816 during a period when the West Indies lost a good deal of their cotton trade with Britain to the U.S.A. There can be little doubt that the subsequent deterioration of the economy was another reason why the Bahamian Government failed to implement its Education Acts.

In the East, of course, the East India Company was the dominant British influence for many years. A succession of Charters from 1600 gradually modified its role but not until the India Act of 1784 were the powers of the Proprietors effectively curtailed. In 1813 the Company lost its monopoly of Indian trade, twenty years later it was prevented from restricting the entry of British subjects into India. Its patronage was reduced when in 1853 all posts to the Indian Civil Service had to be thrown open to competition. It remained influential until the Government of India Act of 1858 transferred its powers to the Crown. Consequently, at a time when British missionaries began to reach India during the first quarter of the nineteenth century, their success depended upon the attitude of the East India Company.

For many years the Court of Proprietors in England had maintained a policy of strict neutrality towards religion. In 1792 it opposed Wilberforce's proposal to add to the Charter Act clauses to send schoolmasters out to India. Subsequently, Charles Grant, a director of the Company, urged upon his colleagues the need for education in India. These proposals and Wilberforce's expressed aim to get Christian missions established in India caused a split among the directors prior to the 1813 Charter which, in fact, required the Company to allocated 100,000 rupees to education, literature and science.

In 1812 the Company's representative refused to allow American missionaries to remain in Calcutta, ordered them to leave, and declared that they were unacceptable in any of the territories over which the Company had jurisdiction. Under their leader, Samuel Newell, the American missionaries left for Ceylon where after a violent rebellion in 1802 British rule as a Crown Colony had been established. Henceforth political power was not directly in the hands of the representatives of trading interests. In the Crown colonies the attitude of the Governor towards the missionaries was of great importance.

The situation in the Near or Middle East was again somewhat different. The East India Company, however, recognized the vital importance of the overland route to India. In order to protect this line of communication and subsequently the Suez Canal Britain took a great interest in Egypt and Cyprus. But after the fall of Napoleon English traders were also searching for commercial openings. In fact, a number of them subscribed to missionary society funds and at the same time suggested how the missionaries could further British commercial interests in the Mediterranean. It is not without interest that one-third of the members of the first committee of the CMS were merchants, bankers and brokers. Political rather than economic factors, however, were more relevant to the success (and lack of it) of the British missions in Egypt.

In Eastern Nigeria the traders and missionaries were at first allies. The latter were opening up the country. It was MacGregor Laird who, in 1832, first organized the navigation of the Niger from its mouth to a point above its confluence with the Benue. In 1854 he fitted out a steamer which carried the Reverend Crowther (later Bishop) on his successful missionary expedition up the Niger and Benue rivers. Later the expansionist policies of Sir George Goldie through the United Africa Company, which received a royal charter under the Royal Niger Company, heralded a new kind of imperialism. In 1900 the political rights of the company were transferred to the Crown.

In the early days Crowther regarded the success of the West Africa Company as vital to his own mission's success. In fact, collaboration was mutually beneficial. Mission workers were often agents for the company and used their local influence on behalf of the traders. Crowther was also interested in the possibilities of establishing links with England through a cotton industry. But as the scramble for markets increased and more and more traders with fewer scruples arrived the trade connection became a source of embarrassment to the missionaries.

Many traders, merchants and planters were either neutral or hostile to the missionaries because they feared the political consequences of missionary education. To be sure there were exceptions. The East India Company's Resident Colonel J. Munro, for example, welcomed the missionaries to Kerala and helped them a great deal. Certainly the presence of a sizeable Christian group favoured the missionaries but Munro's help in the establishment of schools should not be underrated.

When British officials took over from the traders a fairly well-defined pattern of authority was followed. These agencies of Government in the Empire were modified but not radically altered until independence. The British Parliament was the supreme legislative and executive authority for the dependencies. Colonial affairs were looked after by the Colonial Office in London. Laws passed were enforceable where expressly relevant to a particular territory and could be altered by Parliament or by the local legislature. Laws passed by a local legislature could not be declared invalid on the grounds that they did not conform to English law. Pressure groups in England could attempt through Parliament to influence policy and events in the Colonies. The power of the local government to resist Parliamentary pressure varied: at the same time the British Government could effectively veto legislation with which it did not agree.

Thus in the Bahamas the local legislature was able to resist the Bishop of London's advice that instruction should be provided for Negroes. By the turn of the century the British Government was in a position to support the missionaries and to disallow certain local laws passed in the West Indies. A bill passed in Jamaica in 1802 restricted the activities of preachers among the Negroes which the Secretary of State thought too harsh. In 1807 a clause objected to by the Wesleyans in Britain resulted in the Act's being disallowed. Certainly the abolition of the slave trade in 1808 and emancipation in 1834 indicate the extent to which political pressures in England affected the colonies. However, in the West Indies, not until the nineteenth century was Parliament able to play a regular part in the working of the 'old representative system'. It decayed in most of the British West Indian colonies, but not entirely in the Bahamas.

The Crown Colonies developed a common form of government. The executive was effectively under the Secretary of State for the Colonies. Usually there were Executive and Legislative Councils over which the Governor presided. In carrying out his duties, however, he was bound to consult the Executive Council which consisted of *ex officio* heads of departments and official and unofficial members nominated by the Governor. This Council gradually assumed the role of a cabinet. The proportion of unofficial members grew and they were appointed on the nomination of the representative bodies. This evolution is significant because, as stated, education became the responsibility of the local governments.

The composition of the Legislative Councils varied from one colony to another. They included *ex officio* heads of principal departments, nominated official members and unofficial members who were nominated or elected. The powers of these councils were wide and the sphere of authority to legislate became less and less restricted, subject to the Governor's power of veto and the Imperial Government's overreaching power to legislate for the

Colony. Eventually, in practice, there was parity or a majority of unofficial members. The basis on which they were nominated or elected varied. Property qualifications ensured that white Bahamians occupied a far larger proportion of the voting list than their numbers warranted. Representation was not on a communal basis since the tribal structure of society had been destroyed by slavery. Indeed a measure of unity among the Africans was achieved through a common language, a single legal code and one religion—Christianity. In Ceylon, on the other hand, some of the most serious consequences of communal representation were condemned in 1931, by the Donoughmore Commission as 'the canker on the body politic'.

In India the Government of India Act of 1858 created an India Office by amalgamating the East India Company's Board of Control and Court of Directors. The Council of India under a Secretary of State for India controlled affairs in London subject to Parliament. Executive Councils were established in various parts of India and a legislative council, largely of elected members but with a minority of nominated members, was the local Parliament. The system effectively concentrated authority at the centre, gave the executive control over the legislature and gave the British Parliament responsibility for the whole of Indian Government. Nevertheless the central Government of India played a greater role in the development of education between 1854 and 1900 than did the Home Government. This system lasted until 1919 when dyarchy decentralized authority in accordance with general British policy.

The great problem was to achieve the transition in government from communal to territorial representation. It has involved many difficulties. Certainly by 1950, when many territories were on the way to responsible government through a majority of unofficial members in the legislative councils and membership of executive councils the prospects of achieving this transition were uncertain. Events have revealed some of the problems of maintaining self-governing federations in the West Indies and West Africa. The dangers of provincialism in India are apparent. Communalism in unitary states such as Ceylon has given rise to political violence. This volume shows how and to what extent missionary education helped to widen existing social and political divisions and created new ones. Parenthetically, one hypothesis worthy of closer examination is that decentralized systems of educational control are more vulnerable than centralized systems to the domination of well organized minority groups—in these case-studies the mission societies.

The policy of laissez-faire

Under this system of government whatever the policy of the Home Government and the political pressures upon it, the political strength of the Governor greatly affected the success or failure of the missionaries. If he agreed with the policies of the Secretary of State he put them into operation immediately. Dr. Ruberu illustrates this point by referring to the application made in 1823 by the American mission to establish a college in Ceylon. The Home Government was adamantly against it—for political reasons—and Governor Barnes, who from the start of his administration had shown hostility towards the American mission in Jaffna, had no hesitation in refusing the request. Earlier, Governor Brownrigg had welcomed American and English missionaries alike. And Governor North at an earlier date (1803) had been slow to carry out the instructions of the Secretary of State to reduce very drastically expenditure on education.

The same point is illustrated very vividly by Mr. Persianis. In Cyprus political, not economic considerations, determined British policy. The island was assigned to Great Britain in 1878. It was part of a defensive alliance made with the Sultan against the threat of Russia. Although the occupation of Egypt in 1882 made the defence of the Suez Canal from Cyprus unnecessary the British stayed and when Turkey entered the First World War on the side of Germany, strengthened their hold. But for a period of almost fifty years the policy of the Home Government towards education was one of *laissez faire*.

The evolution of policy was decisive. Persianis classifies the Governors as colonial-minded, illiberal and liberal. He maintains that the colonial-minded governors failed to recognize the difference between Cyprus and the British colonies in Africa and Asia. The illiberal governors were extremely intolerant of any pro-Greek propaganda. As early as 1902 Sir H. Smith proposed to make schools participating in political propaganda ineligible for Government grants. The liberal-minded governors in fact followed the Home Government's policy of not interfering with the education of Greek Cypriots. The point at which the Home Government exercised its authority is made clear in Persianis's chapter. After the

1931 riots no Governor was free to follow his own policy. Each had to attempt to integrate and assimilate the several communities into a Cypriot nation loyal to Britain. Education had to be geared to this purpose and it was no longer possible to pursue a policy of non-interference.

In general a somewhat *laissez faire* attitude towards education was not unusual. It was frequently accompanied by a desire to avoid cultural clashes which might lead to political troubles. Officially the need for schools which would train local people for posts in the administration was recognized. But the vital role education might play in peaceful political evolution was perhaps not as clearly appreciated until it was too late for any policy to be effective.

Frequently British colonial policy was based upon the belief that the occupation of a country would be a purely temporary measure designed to protect British interests until the external threat to them disappeared. The anomalous position of the British in Egypt illustrates how events forced local officials into a position for which sound educational policies had not been devised. After the occupation in 1882 British officials were servants of the Egyptian Government. Their Consul General was only one of the accredited representatives of foreign powers and theoretically was in the same position as the others. The presence of a British Army was almost accidental and a policy of withdrawal from Egypt was announced as early as 1883. Yet Cromer effectively controlled Egypt for nearly a quarter of a century.

Lord Lloyd suggests in *Egypt since Cromer* that Cromer regretted the general policy of the Home Government to preclude any direct attempt to establish in Egypt the influence of British culture. By 1904 (during his period of office) finance and public works came directly under the control of his officials. The departments concerned with social and moral life did not. There was a general feeling in Government circles in England at the time that a general scholastic education had some magical power that would achieve political success. Cromer could do little. He made no attempt to awaken in Egyptians any sentiment of loyalty to the British Empire. Under an Egyptian Minister of Education and a Scottish adviser a literary form of education developed which, as it did in India, simply turned out more and more people who were fitted for nothing else other than to be Government officials. Cromer thought that the occupation would have been much more successful had the

British taken over responsibility for education. If he had had his way El Azhar, the symbol of Muslim academic traditions, would have been reformed. Widespread elementary education based on the three Rs and industrial training would have been introduced. Secondary education would have been carefully channeled to supply the technical and professional needs of the country.

In contrast, French educational policy in Egypt was aggressively nationalistic and Catholic, as Mr. Sislian's chapter reveals. French culture and language were allowed to gain a firm hold in Egypt. In 1882 after a period of dual control French influence was used to obstruct British policy. Very many young Egyptians went to France to be educated. In their own country they received an education which frequently presented an anti-British point of view. Whether or not more positive support for the English mission schools in the early part of the century would have significantly altered the sequence of political events, is a question which cannot be answered. In Cyprus the policy of anglicizing the Greek Cypriot schools certainly failed to prevent the outbreak of violent anti-British nationalism. It could be inferred that this policy was adopted too late to be successful.

English or vernacular schools?
Ambivalence towards the anglicization of dependent peoples through education is to be found in other places. Between 1813 and 1833 one great debate in colonial educational policy turned on the relative emphasis which should be given in the schools to English. Against those who urged in its favour as a medium of instruction and as a foreign language to be studied were ranged the supporters of the classical or vernacular languages. In the context of India the supporters of the classical languages maintained that the money granted under the 1813 Charter had been intended to promote an interest in oriental literature, language and science. They also worked to protect oriental institutions of learning. Macaulay's famous Minute of 1835 was one of several official recommendations in support of English. His arguments were that the classical languages, Arabic, Persian and Sanskrit were not very widely used and that the vernaculars were not well developed. The claims of the vernaculars were not pressed by either side. As President of the Committee of Public Instruction Macaulay's views were influential and Wood's despatch in 1854, prepared for the

Directors of the East India Company, laid down educational policy on purely Western lines.

In retrospect this general policy of promoting English education is difficult to reconcile with the stated intention of Government spokesmen that the indigenous schools should not be abolished and cultural institutions should not be destroyed. It seems to have been assumed that English could be introduced without seriously interfering with local institutions. To be sure the issue was seen to have wide implications. The question was, should education in the colonies make people English in speech and outlook? Should it raise them from superstition, slavery, exploitation and ignorance? Apparently yes, provided it did not touch the religion of the people. No doubts were expressed in Macaulay's writings about the superiority of European and in particular English culture in the field of ethics, aesthetics, politics and science. But at the same time he wished to abstain, and hoped others would, 'from giving any public encouragement to those who are engaged in the work of converting the natives to Christianity'. This unhappy compromise, which often amounted to *laissez faire*, in the long run satisfied no one and the issue recurs again and again in debates on colonial policy in territories where a world religion other than Christianity flourished.

Where there were few Muslims, Buddhists or Hindus the Home Government did little to protect local beliefs and institutions. It encouraged the missionaries in the West Indies to convert the slaves and freed Negroes to Christianity. Only in the Muslim north were the missionaries in Nigeria dissuaded from proselytizing. Wherever there was a large proportion of Muslims the attitude of the British officials was unambiguous. Missionaries who found themselves in trouble with the Muslim authorities could expect no help. In North Africa, French and Russian consuls were prepared to protect converts to Catholicism or the Orthodox Church. British consuls were expressly forbidden to extend the same protection to British missionary converts. Some indication of official British policy is given in Lord Dalhousie's order of 1854 forbidding European visitors from remaining in Kashmir during the winter. Some time later the Reverend Clark received no encouragement from the Earl of Elgin when he pleaded that he should be granted, as the nationals of other Governments were, freedom to 'give the Cashmerees the Gospel of Christ'.

19

In Ceylon the position of Buddhism dominated British policy. Article 5 of the Kandyan convention of 1815 stated that the Buddhist religion was inviolable and that its rites and places of worship would be maintained and protected. Several writers have examined the extent to which the British subsequently honoured this clause—the Ven. H. Ratanasara in an unpublished Ph.D. thesis, Dr. K. M. de Silva during the period 1840–55, and the Buddhist Committee of Inquiry which published its report *The Betrayal of Buddhism* in 1956. This report claims that until the last quarter of the nineteenth century no positive Government support was given to Buddhist education. On the other hand de Silva shows how strongly opposed church opinion in England and Ceylon was to the implicit recognition of Buddhism in the Kandyan Convention both at the time it was signed and during the 1840s.

Evidently official neutrality was more a reality in Ceylon than in Kashmir or Egypt. It enabled the mission schools to establish themselves and did not prevent a revival of Buddhism and Buddhist schools towards the end of the century. The changes in emphasis between 1815 and 1900 are not surprising in view of the evolution of educational policy in England. Denominational struggles were followed there by a greater measure of non-sectarian control. A similar trend can be discerned in Ceylon. But as in England the influence of the churches persisted and inevitably nationalists tended to view Christian schools as agents of British Imperialism— as indeed in one sense they were.

It was not that the missionaries played a direct part in the Government in the dependencies through membership of the Executive or Legislative Councils. At the same time there is plenty of evidence to show how they could act as a powerful pressure group. The control they were able to exercise over education came through the executive branch of the Government. When a School commission was set up in Ceylon on the recommendation of the Colebrooke Commission it was composed of the archdeacon and clergy of the island, agents of the Government in the districts and some senior officials. The Buddhists were not represented. C. Godage, in an unpublished thesis, has examined the extent to which the archdeacon attempted to make it an instrument of Anglican policy. By 1863 membership of the educational department (constituted in 1841 as the Central School Commission) was still overwhelmingly representative of church interests. By 1932 the situation was transformed. On the executive committee for education of the State Council of Ceylon there were no Christians—but in 1946 there was one.

There is evidence to suggest that under certain circumstances the denominations manoeuvred for control of education through these executive boards. In the Bahamas the period between 1836 and 1847 was such a time. An Act in 1836 established a Board of Public Instruction with more than sixty members. In 1839 the Board was made interdenominational but this system soon proved to be unworkable and in 1841 a small Board of five appointed members was established. A secretary with inspector duties to perform was appointed but no clergyman could be a member. The dispute continued. The 1847 Act forbade sectarian teaching in the Board's schools. In 1864 it was decreed that the Board should consist of the Governor and five members of the legislature. A secretary was to be chosen from among candidates at the Institute of the British and Foreign Society at Borough Road. The subsequent role of the Secretary-Inspector in the development of education was very great. It was matched by officials and their staff in other dependencies.

Although clerical control was weakened the continued appointment of senior British personnel was enough to ensure that English educational policies would be followed in the colonies. Civil servants in the Colonial Service were, it is true, increasingly recruited in the territories so that by 1950 some 96 per cent of them were in this category. The senior posts, however, continued to be held by persons recruited in Britain. It was these permanent officials rather than the elected assemblies who began to dominate policy-making in education. No doubt in many territories it was a source of considerable resentment not only among nationalists but among those who found their road to the top blocked by a succession of expatriates. Independence was frequently quickly followed by policies designed to 'indigenize' the bureaucracy.

In general neither the transition from clerical to secular control in education nor the transfer of effective power to officials recruited locally had been fully accomplished by the time most of the territories became independent. The association of clericalism and imperialism was bound to be close in the minds of many nationalists. British *laissez faire* effectively placed responsibility until fairly recently in the hands of the missionaries in the same way that it allowed denominational control over English education. In the debates about Colonial educational policy the missionaries took part. In the language controversy their early interest was in the possibilities of using the vernaculars as media of instruction. Language policy was incidental to their main purpose, conversion to Christianity. On the whole they received little direct support for this policy from the Home Government when political trouble was likely to result. To meet parental demand the missionaries opened English schools and inevitably introduced European ideas, attitudes and knowledge. After 1835 the Home Government undoubtedly approved any policy which, in promoting English education, increased the supply of clerks and minor officials. The response to these policies varied, depending upon local circumstances. Certainly knowledge of English made it possible for those who possessed it to read not only Christian literature but the political and social theories of anti-clerics, secularists and so on. For those who were educated in mission schools the acquisition of some aspects of European culture was inevitable. Equally apparent is the desire and determination of many of them to retain aspects of their own cultural heritage. Among these language and religion loom large.

Local groups and missionary policy
Within the broad and general evangelical basis of all missionary policy each society directed its attention towards somewhat different groups of people and adapted its policies to particular circumstances. The church, the school and the hospital were the institutions through which each of them worked. Frequently the demand for education or for medical services made it expedient to establish schools and hospitals in the hope that conversion would follow. Faced with the hostility of the Maharaja and lack of support from the British authorities the CMS missionaries in Kashmir were isolated from the community. Medical work offered a chance for them to reach the people. Policies followed in the first mission school in 1880 were designed to give no offence to the ruler or his subjects. Only after 1894 was the school changed in a way that made few concessions to local customs.

The Methodists in Egypt set out to convert the Muslims but, in the face of determined official opposition, turned their attention to the Greek children in Alexandria. The relentless opposition of the Jewish ecclesiastical authorities in Egypt and the lack of consular protection for converts defeated the evangelical efforts of the Christian missions to the Jews and the Church of Scotland mission whose first object was to convert Jews to Christianity.

For centuries in Ceylon there has been a close connection between the State and Buddhism. When members of the missionary societies which became permanent arrived—Baptists 1812, Wesleyans 1814, American 1816 and CMS 1818—British authority was in the process of being extended from the Maritime Provinces to the whole of the island. Sir Robert Brownrigg was Governor (1812–20) at the time. As a friend of Christianity he welcomed them and supported their efforts to promote Christianity and education. He was fortunate to receive positive support from the Government in England. The fifth Article of the Kandyan convention was an embarrassment to him. Influential citizens in England protested. But the Government and Brownrigg were able to interpret the clause as allowing education to be extended into the Kandyan areas with the eventual downfall of Buddhism but attempts by mission societies to enter the Kandyan territory were resisted by Brownrigg. Early missionary activity was thus confined to the coastal regions where the influence of Christianity had been felt for over 300 years. The hostility of the non-Christian groups towards the missionaries always existed but was never violent. Dr. Ruberu's account reveals the influence the Buddhist clergy was able to assert on attendance even during Brownrigg's period of office. But the absence of national Buddhist or Hindu organizations made it possible—in spite of local opposition—for the mission schools to prosper. The utilitarian value of education—and particularly English education —was recognized and accounts for the spread of mission schools. Even so many of them were established in the Tamil areas and the Hindus made more use of them than the Buddhists, thus gaining differential advantages which were later resented.

A similar situation developed in Nigeria. Little was known of the animist religions of the West African tribes in the southern part of the country. Moreover, there was little appreciation among British officials in the early period of their administration of the close connection between religion and politics. The overt manifestations of control: juju, human sacrifice, the poison ordeal, twin murder and the fattening ceremony were abhorrent to the missionaries. So. too were the secret societies, but they performed very real functions In the Cross River area the Aro people established a combined religious, judicial and economic ascendancy over a very large area. Although relatively few in number they dominated the slave trade, dispensed justice and possessed a powerful oracle known as 'the long Juju'. The Ekpe (or Egbo) operated in the Calabar area. Its political functions were well developed and conducted through a single organization which brought together the leading, but not necessarily the oldest, men from each of the local communities.

Rejection of and failure to understand many of the indigenous African institutions accounts for the initial failure of the British authorities to use them to build up their own administrative organization. It also explains why the missionaries were free to proselytize among the peoples of southern Nigeria. Not so in the North. The Emirates were theocracies. Crowther found that although he was at first warmly received in Rabbah the suspicions of the Muslim leaders were soon aroused. The British authorities actively dissuaded the missionaries from penetrating into the northern region and establishing schools. In the south education rather than Christianity was in demand. Within the limitations set by communications and finance, mission schools flourished In the process of Anglicization, or Europeanization, the north was left behind. At the time of Independence the extent of education in the Western and Eastern Regions was greater than in the North. There were more qualified candidates for white collar jobs from Eastern Nigeria than the Northern peoples liked.

Some missionary societies set out with the intention of helping special groups. In Egypt the CMS hoped to revive the Coptic Church. The missionaries were well received, the British authorities had no objection to their working among the Copts. But they could not gain the confidence of the Coptic clergy and so concentrated on educating the young Copts. The Coptic communities, moreover, were difficult to enter because of their isolation from European contacts. Many Egyptians thought the missionaries were bound to be agents of the British Government. The Catholics threatened to excommunicate Copts who were converted and finally the demand for the kind of education provided by the missionaries was limited. Certainly it was used by many Copts to obtain clerical jobs. From a purely evangelical point of view the CMS missionaries failed. Their work had the effect of consolidating the Copts' sense of community—culturally, religiously and ethnically.

In Kerala the policy of the CMS was to work with the Syrian

Christians and to improve their conditions so that they would then be able to diffuse Christianity more widely. The treaties between the East India Company and the Rajas of Travancore and Cochin placed internal administrative responsibility in the hands of the Rajas. Colonel Macaulay was able to invite an LMS missionary to work in Travancore without asking for official permission to do so. Munro, his successor, wrote to Madras asking for two Anglican missionaries. He had strong views on the value of a Christian education and persuaded the young Ranee to appoint a number of Syrian Christians to official positions. One object of this policy was to create support for the British and to extend Christianity. Thus there was no opposition to the CMS when they arrived. Only in 1836 did a split between the CMS and the Syrians open up. But a pattern of institutions had been founded in Kerala by the missionaries which was copied elsewhere in India. The conditions under which it was established could hardly have been more propitious.

Once established the missionaries had to face certain educational issues. They had to decide on a medium of instruction. Were they to provide schools for an élite or for the masses? Should the curriculum be general or vocational in its orientation? In practice there was a measure of agreement among the missionaries on these issues, but again they could only do what was possible under particular circumstances.

EDUCATIONAL POLICIES

The common purpose of spreading Christianity or improving the existing standards was shared by all missionary societies. Where conversion was the objective opposition was expected and schools or medical services preceded the church. The first and most important aim of education, therefore, was to make conversion possible. It could be done only if the Scriptures could be understood and preferably read. Bible study was the central aim of all Protestant missionary education. Local circumstances determined whether the pursuit of this policy was immediately possible and, if it was, how. Knowledge of the Bible had to be provided either by means of translations or English versions.

At the beginning of the nineteenth century the English missionaries had rather few models from which to choose in establishing schools. Charity schools had been set up at home and abroad. The

Society for the Propagation of Christian Knowledge (SPCK) was created in 1699 and worked to establish them for the poor in England. The Society for the Propagation of the Gospel (SPG), set up in 1701 worked largely overseas. An outcome of the 1698 Charter Bill was that the East India Company had similar schools for European and Anglo-Indian children living in the company's possessions. Later in the century the Sunday school movement grew up in England particularly after Robert Raikes had worked its practices out afresh and set them out in 1873.

The aims of the charity schools were simple. Children were to be taught to read, know and understand the catechisms. They were to learn the principles and duties of the Christian religion in order to make them faithful servants of God and loyal members of the Church. As such they would grow into good people and useful members of society. The poor, thus educated, would lead subsequently industrious, upright and self-respecting lives.

In some cases writing and arithmetic were added to the curriculum and schools might also be coupled with technical institutions. Girls were taught to knit and sew and in some cases a rudimentary form of teacher training began. Later in fact the monitorial system of teaching, developed by Bell—supported by the Church of England—and Lancaster—whose supporters were Dissenters—was introduced into a number of charity schools.

The other type of school was the English grammar or public school. During the nineteenth century, particularly after Arnold's reforms at Rugby, it was modified but its emphasis on character training was strengthened. The qualities and moral values of the Christian English gentleman epitomized this concept. The chapel was the focus of boarding school life. The curriculum was heavily academic and emphasized classical studies. Extra mural-studies were important and increasingly centred round team games. The denominational public schools, set up or remodelled during the nineteenth century, were copied, as far as possible, by the local authority's secondary schools of the twentieth century.

A number of problems had to be faced by the missionaries when they attempted to transplant the uniquely Anglo-Saxon type of school in a foreign environment. Perhaps the first difficulty was one of language. In the West Indies the issue was not in doubt. English was taught to Indians and Negroes as a medium of conversion. Elsewhere there seems to have been fairly general agreement among the English Protestant societies that, at least at first, the vernaculars should be used.

This policy meant that the missionaries were expected to learn the local languages. The first Baptist missionary in Ceylon, the Reverend J. Chater, learned Sinhalese and other languages in order to spread Christianity. When the Wesleyans arrived in 1814 they agreed to use the native languages—Tamil in the north, and Sinhalese in the south. In Egypt the first Methodist and CMS missionaries tried to learn Arabic—not without difficulty it seems. Even after Macaulay's Minute many missionaries thought it was necessary to learn the language of the people with whom they worked. The Reverend Clark maintained that any missionary who hoped to succeed in Kashmir had to know Kashmiri. From another viewpoint Bishop Crowther stressed the need to know the vernacular if true meaning was to be given to the Scriptures. In many Eastern Nigerian schools the vernaculars were used to teach English, to be abandoned as soon as a child could construct a few sentences in English.

The second aspect of this policy was that the missionaries were expected to translate the Bible, catechisms, prayer books and other Christian literature. In Kerala Munro asked the early missionaries whom he welcomed as agents of Christianity and British power to translate the Bible into the vernacular. A great deal was done to develop the Malayalam language in a uniform and independent manner. One consequence was to help unify the Christians of Travancore, Cochin and Malabar. These provinces were helped incidentally by the establishment in 1821 of a press. Other examples of this kind of work occurred in Nigeria. The pioneering missions codified many Nigerian languages in Roman characters. The CMS missionaries did this for Yoruba and other languages including Hausa. The Methodists translated the Bible, catechism and prayer books into the Idoma languages and Scottish Mission Society workers did much the same for the Efik language.

The vernacular policy was particularly appropriate for the native or village mission schools. These schools were in many cases the backbone of missionary activity. Frequently they were similar to the indigenous school with the addition of religious instruction. This was the policy of the LMS and the CMS in Kerala. By 1824 the CMS could claim that there was a parochial school wherever at least fifteen children could be brought together. In Ceylon the

Wesleyans attempted to provide mass education from the start. By 1820 they had seventy-two village schools in different parts of the island in which the medium of instruction was the mother tongue. The intention was merely to prepare the majority of children for the simple routine of life. Usually provision was made to select the abler children for further education. As a matter of policy, where circumstances permitted, a condition of admission to the village school was that the children should receive religious instruction. One condition of grant to mission schools in 1843 in Ceylon was that only a limited part of the day school should be given to religious teaching which should be non-sectarian. In some instances, as in Egypt, compulsory religious instruction resulted in parents withdrawing their children and in most cases the schools became increasingly unacceptable to local nationalist and religious leaders.

Even before Macaulay's Minute English had received pride of place in the post-primary schools set up by the missionaries. The Anglicist-Orientalist controversy raged between 1813 and 1835 and once it had been decided in favour of English British official policy encouraged the growth of English medium schools. However, prior to the formalization of this decision several missions had established English schools. As early as 1813 the CMS opened Kottayam College for Syrian Christians in which English took pride of place. The LMS followed with a similar post-primary school. In 1827 the Wesleyans opened an English Academy in Ceylon for respectable natives and children of Europeans.

These schools were in practice, if not deliberately, for the élite. Mental ability and ability to pay determined admission. In most cases room was found for worthy and capable village school pupils. For the most part they were for children from well-to-do homes or of European descent. They spread, perhaps sometimes in spite of missionary policy, for the very obvious reason that knowledge of English was a prerequisite of Governmental service. Where they were in a position to do so, British officials encouraged English schools. The Colebrooke Commission report in 1831 on education in Ceylon, for example, argued against vernacular schools. It recommended that missions should be the sole authority in vernacular education. Although neither Kerala nor Kashmir were crown colonies the demand for an English education which would lead to an official position was strong. In Kerala the

Maharaja announced in 1844 that for public office preference would be given to those educated in English schools. Throughout the century the debate smouldered. Missionary leaders, although providing English education in face of the demands, were not entirely convinced that English should be the medium of instruction, particularly at an early age. Policy fluctuated. Often pressure was brought to bear on the mission schools by officials, such as the first English school Inspector in Eastern Nigeria in 1882. About this time in Ceylon Anglo-Vernacular schools were set up by the Government to meet criticism of the lack of English provision and at the same time to allay the suspicions of Buddhist leaders.

The secondary schools were undoubtedly fashioned after the image of the English public schools. Many of them were boarding schools. Frequently the headmaster was a clergyman and every effort was made to ensure that the teachers were Christians. The curriculum was typically English—classical languages, mathematics, some science, geography, history and English literature. In addition, in some schools in Ceylon, Sinhalese, Pali, Tamil and Sanskrit were part of the curriculum for candidates preparing for Indian and English university examinations. The success of the secondary schools in Nigeria was often measured by the number and percentage of General Certificate of Education passes gained by pupils. Achievement in sport was another criterion. The healthy athleticism of the CMS school in Kashmir under Biscoe is an example of the way in which the same kind of extra-curricular activities as those cherished in England were introduced into the local schools.

The emphasis in education was on literature. The possibilities of industrial, commercial or agricultural schools developing were remote, firstly because in most colonies manual labour was despised more than in England. Equally important, however, was the fact that most colonial economies during the nineteenth century could not absorb many well-trained skilled workers. Some efforts were made to introduce elements of the English 'schools for industry'. The LMS in Kerala proposed opening industrial and bazaar schools and in the Girls' Seminary some profitable skills were learned. But embroidery and sewing were valued, as in Egypt, more as social accomplishments than vocational skills. After 1834 little was done in Kerala to develop technical education and even in the twentieth century the proportion of technical institutions was never more than 2 per cent of the whole. In Ceylon there were no specifically vocational schools until the twentieth century. Attempts made at Oron Boys High School in Nigeria to introduce some agricultural education received little priority. Certainly the failure to develop a vocational school tradition reflects the attitudes and outcomes of debates among English educators during the nineteenth century.

Support for the Mission Schools
Somewhat similar patterns of education on mission foundations were built up in the dependencies. In order to survive, the mission schools had to be supported either by the Government as a socially needed service or by parents. They needed equipment, buildings and personnel. The rather brief histories of some of the British mission schools in Egypt indicate some of the problems of survival. Mohammed Ali granted the missionaries free land and buildings for their educational work but both the Methodists and the CMS were unable to find satisfactory teachers from among the local Muslim or Coptic communities. Many other examples of the difficulties of finding and training suitable personnel can be found. In the early days Crowther in Nigeria had to be content with very inferior men. Europeans could not or would not work in many places along the Niger. Africans recruited from Sierra Leone and Lagos also found conditions very difficult, so they left and painted such a grim picture that their fellow countrymen would not volunteer for work in that area. The Roman Catholic mission was also short of staff. In 1906 there were ten priests per 1,000 pupils in the Omertu and Ogboli schools alone. The teacher-catechist was poorly trained and most missions had to use the post-primary schools to prepare school teachers. There were rarely sufficient English missionaries and on occasions, such as in the early days of the CMS school in Kashmir, non-Christians had to be employed.

Mohammad Ali's economic support was not sufficient to ensure mission school success in Egypt because the missionaries failed to arouse a sufficiently strong and consistent sympathy for education in the communities they attempted to penetrate. Parental demand for useful education was often discouraged by ecclesiastical teachers who feared that proselytization would occur. Kerala and Ceylon show somewhat different features. Very important to the success of mission schools in Kerala was the practical support of the local rulers who on the advice of Munro made land over to them. The Ranee's declaration that education should be supported by the State set a precedent which was followed by succeeding rulers so that private agencies have always received generous gifts of land and money from the Government, and a contribution to teachers' salaries. Differences arose between the CMS and the Syrian Christians in the 1830s but there was no powerful ecclesiastical resistance. In the first period the missionaries in Ceylon met little opposition. General Government support found practical expression in a grant-in-aid system which started in 1841. It was a tremendous factor in the growth of mission schools which was only seriously resented by Buddhist and Hindu leadership later in the century. In Eastern Nigeria it seems that the missionaries were able to gain the support of many village leaders and tribal chiefs. Mr. Inyang describes how some of the early missionaries were received and how land and buildings were given to them for a mission centre. The impression gained is of a demand for education promoted by chiefs and shared by parents. There seems to have been little organized resistance. Examples of such opposition no doubt could be found, but the powerful positive influence of women is instanced at Emekuku when they insisted that an impasse between the Catholic fathers and local landowners should not prevent the founding of a mission school in their town.

If the attitude of the indigenous leaders helped to determine the ability of the missionaries to establish schools, parental demand kept them going. In order to analyse the outcome of missionary educational activity it is necessary to see which members of society were attracted to the schools. The position of such people in the social and political structures of society should also be investigated. The chapters in this volume give some indication of the patterns of recruitment to the mission schools. The evidence is not conclusive but illuminating, since education undoubtedly became the main determinant of social mobility and of the chances to achieve an enhanced political status. The fact that in the Colonial Empire there were two groups into which educated persons could move strengthened the position of education. One group formed the national political parties. Members of the other groups worked as permanent officials in Government agencies. To a much greater extent than in Europe and North America a person's level of education determined his chances of entering these groups. The mission schools offered opportunities of upward social and political mobility, and they were obviously attached to the agencies of British power. The consequences of mobility were profound. Of interest are the social origins of the new leadership groups in the light of traditional principles of leadership recruitment. Possibilities exist of one group of the same generation usurping the position and power of another. Equally possible is the creation of a younger generation group wishing to and able to challenge the authority of the older generation leadership group. A third issue for consideration concerns the influence on communalism and its political implications. Frequently in fact there are several élite groups which may or may not compete with each other.

The socio-political consequences of missionary education
The structure of a society determines the distribution of power within it. In a monarchy or aristocracy power is inherited; the caste system ensures a more rigid and sharp differentiation than is to be found in a class society and, in some societies, age is the defining factor. This crude classification is intended to suggest that a fuller comparative analysis of social structures needs to be made in order to examine the influence of British educational institutions on political recruitment.

The Indian and Ceylonese case studies exemplify some aspects of the relations between caste and education One or two principles may be stated. In general it may be argued that the higher castes—Brahmins and Kshatriyas—were more conscious of their Hinduism than members of the lower castes. Members of the highest castes were not easily converted to Christianity. On the other hand they tended to be the persons who took most advantage of English secondary education. It can hardly be disputed that the traditionally privileged groups in India were strongly represented in educational institutions. The underprivileged were poorly represented especially at the higher levels. One reason was that the post-primary mission schools charged fees. Nevertheless mission and Government schools during the British period offered some opportunities to ameliorate caste differences.

In a rather straightforward caste system education tended to reinforce the processes of political leadership recruitment. Indeed the transfer of British power in India enabled caste to assume political functions. After Independence some castes had their own constitution printed and distributed. The Constitution safeguarded backward sections of the community and in a sense gave a new lease of life to caste. Some indication of the close relationship between education, caste position, and political leadership is found in the fact that in 1956 of the Indian Council of Ministers 46·4 per cent were Brahmins and all but two of them were graduates of colleges or universities. Of the Cabinet members 93·7 per cent had attended institutions of higher education. Up to 1950 all the general secretaries of the Indian Communist Party had been educated in college. On the other hand the fact that a non-Brahmin political movement grew up in the twentieth century is some evidence of the wider appeal of English education. The non-Brahmin movement was, incidentally, decisively beaten by Congress in the 1936–7 elections.

Caste systems are never simple. In Kashmir in a largely Muslim area it was the upper caste Hindus, the Pandits, who were attracted to the CMS schools, to some extent strengthening the hand of the rulers. Kerala's social composition was, of course, mixed. Even when the English Protestant missions arrived there were many Christians. Some were Syrian Christians, others had been converted by the Portuguese. There were also some Muslims. The Hindu caste system was rather unusual. The dominant caste among the Hindus were the Nayars who occupied many educational, administrative and political positions. Their rivals were a backward caste, the Ighazars, not the Nambudris, who in Kerala were Brahmins among Brahmins. Unlike their fellow caste members in the eastern and northern parts of the country the Nambudris did not take advantage of western education. Thus in Kerala, as in no other state in India up the the First World War, the Brahmins did not dominate the administration and the liberal professions. The Christians had a long history of protection. The Syrians educated by the mission schools entered public service and by 1818 a lot are reported to have been in office. In 1951 the major election clash was between the Hindus and Christians. Claims were made that the Christian schools preached against the National Congress. There is no doubt that the élite on both sides came from English schools.

The other side of the coin was, of course, that members of the lower castes sought protection from the British. They attended school and were often converted. The LMS in Travancore in 1806 first appealed to the Shanar community which was very poor and ignorant. The society made a special effort to attract the low-caste boys. There is evidence to suggest that the schools provided a refuge for the dregs of society. For the LMS seminary, however, clever children from the village schools were selected to be trained as native teachers and schoolmasters.

Caste in Ceylon has not been regarded as vicious in its effect as in India, but it certainly affected the running of mission schools. Its influence increased as Hindu Tamils came into the country. The caste system of the Hindu groups was peculiar too. Caste systems varied throughout the Island but there was always a trace of the Brahmins and Kshatryas. The highest caste were the Goyigamas or cultivators and some 50 per cent of the Hindus were members of it. The majority of the population were Buddhists whose caste system is such that some priestly orders are open to members of all castes. A small minority of Christians were left after the Portuguese and Dutch occupations.

Mission schools appealed to Buddhist and Hindu in spite of resistance. The secondary schools charged fees and catered for urban people on the whole. A majority of the urban school children embraced Christianity. They went into Government offices, the liberal professions or entered politics. A new élite group of Tamils were over-represented—no doubt because of missionary activity in the provinces where they lived. Ventures into the Kandyan territories were discouraged by the authorities and no doubt Buddhist opposition to mission schools was stronger than Hindu resistance. There can be little doubt that mission education helped to strengthen a communalism which was overtly recognized in Government representation.

There is plenty of evidence to show that distinguished political leaders were educated at mission schools. In Kashmir, a Prime Minister and a Minister of Education were products of Biscoe's school. In 1964 the President and at least one minister of the Indian Government had been educated at Madras Christian College, another minister was a product of St. Xavier's College, Bombay. The first Prime Minister of independent Ceylon was at school at a very famous Christian school, St. Thomas College. Missionary education in India and Ceylon (where it loosened the political hold of Buddhism) was an important agency of recruitment to positions of political leadership.

This was the case in Nigeria too. A glance at R. Segal's *Political Africa 1961* shows that many prominent ministers attended mission schools. A considerable number of federal and regional ministers were products of them. In the north several ministers had attended Katsina College and had been teachers. It seems that the missionaries promoted Africans from the lowest strata and according to Kirk-Greene in 'Bureaucratic Castes in a Traditional Milieu' (*Education and Political Development,* edited by Coleman) a very high proportion of the new élite was from common stock. Of greatest significance to the tensions within the political structure is the fact that the new educated élite are young men. In Eastern Nigeria within a complex system of extended family, kindred groups and town or village groups age is often the most important criterion of traditional leadership patterns. In the larger groups a senior family might exercise leadership. Certainly among the Ibo there were thousands of small groups. When the missionaries gained access to them the aged and responsible members were seldom open to their influence. Even if politically the younger men were unwilling or unable to overthrow their elders the newer educated groups were the technocrats, bureaucrats and specialists with European training and knowledge. The possible sources of tension in these older younger generation differences in educational background are obvious. At the same time the expansion of mission schools in the southern regions and the slow development of English schools in the north gave differential advantages at the bureaucratic level to southerners and especially those from Eastern Nigeria.

All the educated leadership groups were similar in that before independence at least they were the promoters of national consciousness and in the forefront of anti-British activity. It was, incidentally, a culturally unifying force too. Those in England who at the end of the eighteenth century had argued that Christian education would carry with it riches of liberty and freedom which would give rise to political agitation were correct. English education introduced West Indians, Indians, Ceylonese, Egyptians and Africans to political ideas and ideals which they used in their fights for independence.

These ideals were taken from European literature and found expression in political theories ranging from *laissez faire* liberalism through socialism to communism. Overriding all of them was a sense of democracy. These theories were frequently a far cry from those put forward by traditional socializing agencies—extended family, tribe and caste. Moreover, the extent to which they had been absorbed into the thought processes of these peoples is problematical. To be sure, the acceptance of certain political theories did not necessarily mean that associated social or economic theories were acceptable. Nor were the scientific theories of the new technologies always able to oust completely the science of the Vedas, the Koran or the Pali texts. Political socialization was inevitably somewhat incomplete when judged in the light of British patterns.

On the basis of selection processes through education, political and bureaucratic élites were established. The case studies show the different ways in which divisions in society were maintained or widened. Selective education meant that the gap between the élite and the masses widened. In one sense this was a gap between the literates and the illiterates, or between the Christians and non-Christians. Again mission education in particular tended to perpetuate and intensify the divisions among ethnic, regional and parochial groups. In short, the disintegrating effects of education in colonial areas are all too readily apparent.

COMPETITION BETWEEN MISSION SOCIETIES

Another aspect of missionary work which should be considered from this viewpoint is the extent to which the various missionary societies competed with each other. Evidently in Egypt and in Kerala the CMS set out with the intention of working among groups of Christians. The Church missions to the Jews and the Church of Scotland mission in Egypt hoped to convert the Jews to Christianity. Under such circumstances competition between the missions was unlikely to be acute. In Ceylon the LMS, whose missionaries arrived in 1805, were appointed by the Government. Each missionary was sent to a different part of the island. When the party of Baptist missionaries arrived they were allowed to reside in Colombo and make it the central station of the mission. Soon they moved into the Sinhalese areas. The mission remained small and appears to have catered largely for the down and out Portuguese population in the area. The Wesleyans quickly opened many schools in two areas—Jaffna in the north and along the south-west coast from Negombo south through Colombo, Kalutara, Galle and Matara. By 1850 these southern towns were connected by road. Three stations some miles inland had nearly 1,100 children enrolled in school in 1833. The American missionaries arrived two years after the Wesleyans. With Governor Brownrigg's permission they established themselves in the Jaffna district. Growth was rapid but by 1834 all the stations were exclusively situated in the Jaffna district where the number of children in Wesleyan schools amounted to about 1,000 at that time. The American mission village schools enrolled over 3,000 children. The first four CMS missionaries who arrived in 1818 were assigned to Colombo and Galle, in the south-west and Mannar and Jaffna in the north-west. The Mannar station was soon closed and that at Galle moved out to a village twelve miles away possibly because the Wesleyans were already there. The CMS sought and finally received permission to work in the Kandyan areas. By 1833 there were four stations, Kotte in Colombo, Nellore in Jaffna, Kandy and Baddegama near Galle and there were nearly 2,000 children enrolled in the village schools. There were very few private Roman Catholic schools (some sixty-three) with an enrolment of less than 1,500 but they too were in the same coastal centres, namely Colombo, Negombo, Jaffna and Mannar. They also had a school at Kalutara—a large centre of Wesleyan activity. Official Roman Catholic activity commenced much later in the century.

The Wesleyans, Americans and CMS had native and English schools. One or two of the latter were usually attached to a mission station and were in effect central schools or schools for children of European descent. The institutions of secondary education were usually boarding schools. The Wesleyans established an Academy or seminary at Colombo which had a somewhat chequered early career. The Americans hoped to establish a college or seminary in Jaffna. Governor Barnes turned their plan down in 1823 and they developed a less ambitious scheme to cater for promising youngsters. The CMS had three boarding schools or seminaries in Jaffna, Colombo and at the station near Galle. The numbers enrolled there in these schools were small.

The distribution of these early mission schools indicates that they would compete for pupils. There was the chance that the missionaries would compete politically. Ruberu claims that until the 1880s there was goodwill and co-operation between them. The conflict between the High Church Anglican establishment and the reformist Evangelicals and Governor MacKenzie's attempts to deprive the Anglicans (not the CMS missionaries) of their near monopoly of the School Commission have been examined in

K. M. de Silva's *Social Policy and Missionary Organization in Ceylon 1840–1855*. The 1840s were years when the missionary societies were united in opposing any link between the State and Buddhism. Interpretations of the Kandyan Convention were again debated with vigour. It was during this period that the mission societies used their influence in England to persuade the Colonial Office to dissociate British power from Buddhism. The missionaries felt themselves fortunate to have an official in the Colonial Office fighting their case so strongly. The period, however, marked the start of a long and at times bitter struggle by Buddhist groups against mission schools. A partial success was when the Government recognized all religious schools for grants. But official Roman Catholic schools multiplied, quickly creating a new and persistent source of tension between Buddhists and Christians.

The competition between missions in Eastern Nigeria gave rise to somewhat different consequences. Communication difficulties probably helped considerably to create conditions under which the various missions appealed to the same children or different children in the same family or kinship group. Movement was at first possible only in the Delta, along the coast and round the Cross River estuary. Later, from centres along the Niger, missionaries moved out to nearby towns and villages. It was not unusual for more than one missionary society to make its headquarters in the same town. Onitsha, for example, was the centre of CMS and Roman Catholic missionary activity. Calabar was a Scottish Mission Society centre and the Roman Catholics were also active. The concentration of the missionaries in areas in which kinship ties were close and extended to many members doubtless resulted in the inter-familial tensions described by Inyang. The fact that denominational issues were often meaningless to the Africans probably added to their surprise that Christians, far from collaborating were in competition. One result had been to proliferate the sects in Nigeria.

Efforts to reduce this disintegration among the Protestant churches began at the beginning of the twentieth century. In the Eastern region the Methodists, Anglicans and Presbyterians agreed not to trespass on each other's territory. Conferences took place between the African Church leaders, but only those of the three named churches seemed really prepared to consider establishing a Church of Nigeria. From 1950 they ran Trinity College at Umuahia as a joint enterprise to provide teacher training. A joint women's training college was established in the same town. Another form of co-operation was created through the Christian Council of Nigeria, the purpose of which was to give the missions a common educational policy. Collaboration at the national level was not matched by the local congregations.

Bitter conflicts between the Protestant Churches and the Roman Catholics had died down by the early sixties. The attitude of the Roman Catholics to the secularization of all schools is quite different from the more permissive attitude of the Protestant missions. The Dike report on education in Eastern Nigeria issued in 1962 pointed to the differences of policy between the Catholics and Protestants. Only clerical control could satisfy the former. It was also reported that the Nigerianization of the schools had not taken place to the same extent as in the Protestant schools. The differences between the churches weakened the position of teachers as a profession.

The general thesis put forward here is that in many countries the mission schools had a devisive effect on society. Traditional forces of authority were weakened and attitudes to them modified. Radical political concepts were developed through the schools but were not sufficiently widespread to make the running of western political institutions possible. Where the missions attracted the lower classes of society the political structure was modified. Where traditional leadership groups took advantage of the mission schools, as often happened, the gap between the privileged and under-privileged widened. Religious objections to mission schools which resulted in the non-participation of members in the mission education left them disadvantaged (except politically in democratic societies). Nevertheless the leadership groups of most of the colonial dependencies owed much to the mission schools. Another group benefited from military training. This frequently cut across tribal and caste lines. In India after the mutiny heterogeneous regiments were formed in which all castes were included. One consequence was that the higher castes took over power. The army was an agent of social mobility. Frequently the attitude it developed was somewhat different from the liberal Christian views inculcated by the mission schools. In many British territories the mission-trained leaders took over the reins of office when independence was gained. Army-trained groups moved in when the divisions in the new societies threatened to destroy them as units.

The success of the mission schools is difficult to assess. In terms of their main purpose, conversion, they can hardly be said to have made a tremendous impact, except in the West Indies and particularly the Bahamas. But in Ceylon less than 10 per cent of the population is Christian, in Nigeria there are only 3½ million Christians in a total population of 55 million and no headway has been made in the North. In India the percentage of Christians out of a population of more than 450 million is low at around 2·5. Hence the percentage in Kerala is unusually high at nearly 20 and is, of course, explained by the presence of Christian groups for many centuries. Among the British missions the Roman Catholics have met with the greatest success. Of the Christians in Ceylon 90 per cent are Catholics and in Eastern Nigeria where nearly half the population are Christians the majority of these is Catholic.

This success is reflected in the educational achievements of the missionaries. The extent to which mission schools dominated the educational systems of territories about to become independent has been mentioned. The freedom of the mission schools to proselytize had been reduced by Government legislation in many cases, particularly in Ceylon. But the number and quality of these schools made the new nations very dependent on them. Many nationalist leaders had received an education at one or other of them some of these men had been converted to Christianity. The mission schools were viewed with suspicion for two main reasons. In the first place they threatened indigenous institutions. Secondly not all the mission societies were prepared to hand control of their schools over to the new government. The threat was cultural and political. The English language and Christianity introduced by the mission schools represented cultural challenges to indigenous traditions which were regarded as agencies through which a sense of national unity could be built. In multi-cultural societies such as Nigeria, Ceylon and India the breakdown of Imperialism imperilled national unity and gave rise to communalism, based either on religious or linguistic differences, or both. As a major social service, education politically controlled by organizations inherited from the Imperial power, was unacceptable. Independence meant freedom to control all aspects of national life. In practice the possibilities that the Christians would engage in politics were soon realized. The Christians were in most situations members of a small minority group which possessed considerable educational advantages. Under the British these had helped them to gain positions of power and status in the bureaucracy and professions. Political action by them was resented.

POST-INDEPENDENCE LEGISLATION

After independence the ambivalence shown to mission schools was resolved in various ways. The threats to indigenous language and religion had to be removed. In the newly dependent territories language policy debates involved choice of official language and the medium of instruction in the schools. These two issues became closely connected with attacks on mission schools as agents of imperialism and Christianity.

Certainly India's language problems are among the most difficult in the world to solve. After independence there was a wide measure of agreement that English, as the *lingua franca* of an élite, should be replaced by a truly national language. But which of the 845 languages or dialects spoken should be chosen? Which of the main ones should be the official Union language? The Constitution laid down that it should be Hindi, spoken by some 150 million people. The position of English and the claims of other vernaculars created many difficulties. A decision to retain English as the subsidiary official language for as long as was necessary was based more on expediency than on ideological grounds. The rival claims of some vernacular languages were still pushed.

As for the medium of instruction prior to 1937 English had been a compulsory subject and the medium of instruction in secondary schools. Subsequently, the mother tongue or the regional language became the medium of instruction. During the fifties the need to strengthen national unity through Hindi was stressed but by 1961 a committee on national integration was set up which pointed out that the English language had evoked a sense of unity and 'Indian-ness'. The committee's view was, however, that regional languages in education rather than any of the languages used by intellectuals—Sanskrit, Persian and English—would help bridge the gap between the masses and the intellectual élite.

The rival claims of Hindi, English and Malayalam in Kerala were complicated by the clash between the Congress and Communist Parties. The latter, in line with general policy, opposed English, was lukewarm to Hindi and favoured Malayalam. The

Communist Party was firmly opposed to the continued influence of the mission schools. In office it passed an Education Law (6) in 1959 which effectively placed control of all Government and aided schools under the Government. The appointment of teachers to mission schools could be made only through a Public Service Commission. Teachers were to be paid directly by the Government or through the headmaster of the school and the Government had power to take over the management of any aided school. The Bill was referred to the Supreme Court for an opinion on its constitutionality. The crux of the issue was whether or not minorities had the right to establish and administer schools of their choice and receive Government aid without the imposition of conditions. The Catholics vigorously opposed the Bill. The situation in Kerala became so tense that the President of India proclaimed the dissolution of the Legislative Assembly in 1959. Amending Acts 8 and 35 made it once more possible for the managers of aided schools to appoint teachers.

In Ceylon these issues were debated no less fiercely. In 1944 basic decisions had been taken that Sinhala and Tamil would become the official languages in place of English. Soon after independence the parity issue took a serious turn. In 1956 a new Government which had depended heavily on Buddhist Sinhalese support at the election passed an Act which made Sinhala the one official language (Act No. 33). Opposition mounted and culminated in violent riots in 1958. As regards the medium of instruction a commission's report in 1926 had recommended that instruction in the vernaculars should be compulsory. In 1947 an amendment to the 1939 Education Act made Sinhala and Tamil the medium of instruction in all schools. Later this policy was extended to apply to the universities. Among the issues of the 1956 election were the disadvantages which teachers in Sinhalese schools suffered compared with those in English schools. In effect the Swabasha policy and the decision to make English a compulsory subject increased the extent to which Sinhalese and Tamil children attended different schools and helped to strengthen communalism.

The history of the religious issue covers a period of over 100 years, but the clash between Buddhists and Hindus and the Christians sharpened during the last quarter of the nineteenth century. The Wace Commission in 1905 suggested modifications to the conscience clause. An ordinance in 1920 was intended to prevent undue duplication of mission schools. It also gave the Director of Education power to enter assisted schools and a measure of control over the teachers appointed. The Roman Catholics in particular have opposed attempts to reduce their control over their schools. Again one consequence of this struggle was that children began to group together as Christians, Hindus and Buddhists.

The 1939 ordinance increased the State's control over assisted schools. In 1960 the Assisted Schools Education Act No. 5 gave rise to violent opposition. It states that all primary and secondary schools except collegiate could be taken over by the Government. The Roman Catholics violently resisted entry into their schools by public officials. A second Act—No. 8 of 1961—strengthened the hand of the Government by making it possible for the authorities to take action against persons forcibly resisting entry into a school. It also prohibited the establishment of schools without official approval. After this Bill was passed all the assisted schools with the exception of some at the collegiate level accepted the earlier ruling. The situation is, however, fraught with unresolved difficulties.

In Eastern Nigeria the kind of hostility witnessed in parts of India and in Ceylon to the threat of English and Christianity was not so apparent. The Dike report on education in Eastern Nigeria showed how dependent the system was on mission schools but indicated how these in turn needed Governmental aid. The duplication of facilities because of denomination differences was noted. It resulted in innumerable half-filled schools. Suggestions that the relationships between mission schools and Government should be examined with a view to establishing a publicly owned and operated system working side by side with a voluntary agency system revealed that the Catholic and Protestant positions differed. On the Government's plan to introduce universal primary education the Protestants agreed but questioned the timing; the Catholics regretted the policy. The Methodists and Church of Scotland were willing to withdraw from the provision of primary schools and concentrate on keeping a few good secondary schools. The Anglicans were prepared for a planned state system of education. One aspect of this transition concerned the Nigerianization of education. The process had not taken place to the same extent in Roman Catholic as in Protestant schools. The crux of the matter was, and is, whether a true education can be provided outside the framework of a Christian value system. The Roman Catholics argue that it cannot, that it is not simply a question of religious instruction but the whole atmosphere and ethics of the school. To create these, control must remain with the Church so that control alone will satisfy the Catholics. These different positions are, of course, reflected in Church policy towards education in England under the 1944 Act. The issue becomes highly charged and deeply political.

The Cyprus case study, of course, shows how education was used as a weapon by both sides in a violent political conflict. It shows how closely language, religion and nationalism can be linked and suggests that anti-colonialism was perhaps a stronger force than anti-Christianity in many cases. If this is the case it seems likely that the mission schools in the Colonial Empire have been under pressure more because of their connection with imperialism than because they wished to convert people to Christianity.

Evidently the anomalies associated with the provision of education by the missionaries have not yet been resolved. It seems unlikely that many countries could afford to dispense with the facilities they provide. It is equally certain that few Governments are prepared to assist denominational schools financially unless they are able to obtain a considerable amount of control over teacher appointments and salaries, and over religious teaching. The Protestant churches seem disposed to compromise, but the Roman Catholics are committed to a view of education which makes it impossible for them to relinquish many aspects of control without destroying the schools. In the long run it seems certain that the State authorities will prevail; the question is under what conditions. There is an obvious need in many newly independent countries for a system of education that will be truly national in that it will develop national attitudes and loyalties rather than tribal and communal loyalties. There seems little chance that as representatives of a minority group (whether indigenous or not) the mission schools can perform this function. Perhaps in the immediate future the pressing need is to work out policies which will make it possible for aided and Government schools to co-exist. This can only be done if the Christian schools offer no threat to the development of indigenous languages and religions. Both Church and State face dilemmas in educational policy none of which are easy to resolve, as subsequent chapters in the book very clearly show.

SELECTED BIBLIOGRAPHY

In addition to Chapters 2–8 in this volume the following are among the books most frequently consulted in preparing this chapter:

Ajayi, J. F. A., *Christian Missions in Africa 1841–1891* (London 1965).
Almond, G. A. and Coleman, J. S., *The Politics of the Developing Area.* (Princeton 1960).
Anene, J. C., *Southern Nigeria in Transition 1885–1906* (Cambridge 1966).
Bahamas, *Report on Education 1951* (Nassau 1952).
Burns, Sir Alan, *History of Nigeria* (London 1963) (6th ed.); and *History of the British West Indies* (London 1965) (2nd ed.).
Christian Council of Nigeria, *Building for Tomorrow, A pictorial History of the Protestant Church in Nigeria* (an independence souvenir).
Coleman, J. S. (Ed.), *Education and Political Development* (Princeton 1965).
Craton, M., *A History of the Bahamas* (London 1962).
Cromer, Earl of, *Modern Egypt* (London 1908).
Eastern Nigeria, *Report on the Review of the Educational System in Eastern Nigeria* (Official Document 19 of 1962) (Enugu 1962). (The Dike Report.)
Ezera, K., *Constitutional Developments in Nigeria* (Cambridge 1964).
Farmer, B. H., *Ceylon, A Divided Nation* (London 1963).
Flint, J. E., *Sir George Goldie and the Making of Nigeria* (London 1960).
Forde, Daryll (Ed.), *Efik Traders of Old Calabar* (London 1956).
Garrett, T. D. and Jeffery, R. M. C., *Unity in Nigeria* (London 1965).
Gordon, Shirley C., *A Century of West Indian Education* (London 1963.)
Gratiaen, L. J., *The Story of Our Schools. The First School Commission 1832–1841* (Colombo 1927).
Hill, Sir G., *A History of Cyprus* (Cambridge 1949).
H.M.S.O., *Nigeria 1954* (London 1958).
Hogben, S. J. and Kirk-Greene, A. H. M., *The Emirates of Northern Nigeria* (London 1966).
Lacouture, J. and S., *Egypt in Transition* (London 1958).
Lewis, L. J., *Education and Political Independence in Africa* (Edinburgh 1962).
Lewis, L. J. and Loveridge, A. J., *The Management of Education* (London 1965).
Lewis, W. A., *Politics in West Africa* (London 1965).
Lloyd, Lord, *Egypt since Cromer* (London 1933).
Mayes, S., *Cyprus and Makarios* (London 1960).
Mendis, G. C., *Ceylon under the British* (Colombo 1952).
Menon, K. P. Padmunabha, *History of Kerala* (Ernakulam 1924).

Murray, D. J., *The West Indies and the Development of Colonial Government 1801–36* (Oxford 1965).

Newman, P. A., *Short History of Cyprus* (London 1953) (2nd ed.).

Nurullah, S. and Naik, J. P., *A History of Education in India* (Bombay 1951) (2nd ed.).

Le Page, R. B., *The National Language Question* (London 1964).

Panikkar, K. M., *A Survey of Indian History* (London 1964) (4th ed.).

Park, R. L. and Tinker, I. (Eds.), *Leadership and Political Institutions in India* (Princeton 1959).

Parry, J. H. and Sherlock, P. M., *A Short History of the West Indies* (London 1956).

Peggs, Deans, *A Short History of the Bahamas* (Nassau 1951).

Perham, Margery, *Native Administration in Nigeria* (London 1937).

Philips, C. H., *The East India Company 1784–1834* (Manchester 1961).

Powell-Price, J. C., *A History of India* (London 1955).

Refaat Bey, M., *The Awakening of Modern Egypt* (London 1947).

Ruberu, Ranjit, *Education in Colonial Ceylon* (Kandy 1961).

Safran, W., *Egypt in search of Political Community* (Cambridge, Mass. 1961).

Segal, R., *1961 Political Africa* (London 1961).

Seton, M. C. C., *The India Office* (London 1926).

de Silva, K. M., *Social Policy and Missionary Organisation in Ceylon 1840–1855* (London 1965).

Spicer, E., *The Peoples of Nigeria* (Nigeria 1962).

Srinivas, M. N., *Caste in Modern India and other Essays* (Bombay 1962).

Stahl, Kathleen, *British and Soviet Colonial Systems* (London 1951).

Sundkler, B., *Church of South India: The Movement towards Union 1900–1947* (London 1954).

Wriggins, W. H., *Ceylon, Dilemmas of a New Nation* (Princeton 1960).

2

MISSIONARY ACTIVITY IN THE BAHAMAS, 1700-1830

Rodney Bain

IN his Report[1] on Education in the Bahamas, 1958, Mr. H. Houghton states that there was no demand for education. A number of Bahamians would not have taken exception to this statement if they had understood what Houghton meant. The critics pointed to the hundreds of students who attended evening classes established by the Department of Education, as evidence for the demand.

The purpose here is not to deny that there was, and still is, a strong desire to pass examinations (mainly commercial and academic) with a view to improving the job status of the candidates, some of whom, according to their teachers, suffer from a naïve faith in the teacher to 'get them through' the examination without much effort on their part. It is important also to note that this desire indicates a motive force which could be harnessed and guided; but whether it constitutes a demand for education is another matter. Cultural and recreational classes have not been successful, and tended to be supported mainly by expatriates.

A demand for education is an inherent demand, rising out of the social and economic situation, and is so compelling a force that it permeates the whole country and becomes a vital consideration in the formation of national policy. It is imposed from without but arises from within; it is not a wish or a desire, but positive action based on social and national needs; it is not a naïve faith in a magic called education, but a pragmatic approach to the art of living.

The aboriginal inhabitants of the Bahamas, the Arawaks,[2] were too primitive to know schools as we understand them today. But they knew the practical advantage of mastering their environment which was dominated by the sea. This was a real demand for education—a demand for the knowledge and skills which the

47

life of an Arawak in the Bahamas made necessary and desirable.

During the periods of piracy, privateering and wrecking in the Bahamas there was a similar demand for seamanship; yet it is hardly likely that the best seamen had much schooling, as the few schools which existed failed to provide the kind of training required.

A study of Bahamian education today would reveal these important elements:

(a) On the whole the schools offer a literary kind of training by formal methods which tend to enshrine learning by rote. The monitorial system which was introduced in 1817 is still going strong, although it has altered somewhat. The percentage of qualified teachers is less than 30 (including expatriates), but the percentage of illiteracy is less than 20.

(b) Religious knowledge appears prominently on the time-tables of religious as well as secular schools, and it is traditional to begin the day with a simple act of worship. All Bahamians are Christians; religion has a significant place in their lives and the Bible is highly revered.

(c) The work done in the schools bears but token relationship to the life of the society outside school. The text books in use were intended mainly for English children and only in 1963 was serious consideration given to Bahamian studies and the production of text books for the Bahamas.

(d) The schools fall under these headings:

(i) Maintained schools, including one high school and four secondary modern schools.

(ii) Aided schools, all run by religious bodies, with fees—high schools with primary departments.

(iii) Independent schools, mainly run by religious bodies with fees. They include a number of small nursery and primary schools, but the best known are religious high schools and one independent high school.

Religious and independent bodies account for a quarter of the total school population.

ORIGINS OF EDUCATION AND PRESENT TRENDS

How did this come about? The simple answer is not difficult to find. The missionaries and early settlers brought with them ideas of education from England direct or via America. In part the same ideas were taken to America and the Bahamas in the seventeenth and eighteenth centuries. But whereas in America, the external religious demand for education resulting from the work of the missionaries soon gave way to the real national internal demand relevant to the strong economic and social growth of the country, in the Bahamas, the economy was never strong nor constant enough, neither was the population stable nor large enough to support an internal development and demand. Thus Bahamian education has remained more or less stagnant, depending for such development as there has been on imitation and even transplantation from the United States, the home of the early settlers and key Government officers.

Government participation in education came quite early. The first Education Act was passed in 1746. The constitution of the Bahamas which dated from 1729 and remained substantially the same until the present constitution of 1964 was a survival of the representative system of the first Empire and has been described as representative but not responsible government. Under the bi-cameral system a large measure of local control rested with the Bahamian legislature, subject to the prerogative of the Crown. So it was that a number of Education Acts have been passed by the Bahamian Legislative since 1746, but none of them could be described as comprehensive or as setting out any clear guidance on policy until the Act of 1962, which is itself based on the 1944 Education Act in England.

Constitutionally, the Bahamian Government has been in a position to formulate its own policy in education since 1729. However, this was never done on account of the absence of social and economic motivation. The booms and slumps which have characterized the economic history of the Bahamas did not provide a suitable foundation on which to build a system of education.

The colony has therefore leaned heavily on the missionaries and the churches not only for a policy in education but also for the provision of schools. After one unsuccessful attempt to establish a high school in Nassau in 1808, the Bahamas Government made no further effort at this level until 1926 when the Government High School was established. It is still the only maintained high school, some eight others being owned and operated by religious bodies and one of them an independent body. Four are grant-aided. On the whole, religious and independent schools account for about a quarter of the total school population. Thus, up to 1926 the high school education was only available to a small élite who could afford the fees of the religious high schools which existed, or who could afford to send their children abroad; and this small élite tended to be synonymous with the local white population who have maintained political and economic power from the start.

The result of all this has been a strange mixture of apparently progressive elements unrelated to local problems on the one hand, and on the other hand, an indifferent tardiness. Following the English example, education has been free and compulsory in the Bahamas since before 1900, at first between five and thirteen years of age and since the Act of 1908 available to even the remotest villages; reorganization according to the Hadow Report was introduced in the 1920s. But the Government did not establish a high school until 1926; a Director of Education was not appointed until 1946 and all Government effort in Education came under the same authority only in 1962. Despite earlier attempts a training college for teachers was not finally established until 1950, and a technical institute came only in 1962.

Recent developments would seem to favour a positive policy in education, based on local national needs. The present economic prosperity has been sustained on an ever improving rate over the past twenty years. Under the new Constitution 1964, the Government has complete control over internal matters and it has obtained affiliation with the University of the West Indies which is deeply concerned with solving social problems in the area. With the downward filtration of the fruits of prosperity, high school and university education have become more available to more and more Bahamians, though the element of the élite remains on account of the strong influence of vested interests and the scattered Out-Islands where half the total populations of under 140,000 live, and where no high schools exist. The existence of an independent sector makes it possible for the upper strata of society and especially parents with political and economic power to avoid the maintained schools where conditions tend to be less favourable than those in independent schools at the primary and secondary modern level, as opposed to the high school level. As a result the maintained schools suffer from a lack of direct interest, as well as a large element of vested interest.

Unfortunately, prosperity is still based in the main on industries which can be seriously effected by agencies outside the colony. Reference is made to the tourist industry, off-shore companies and banking and commercial firms. It is easy to bring personnel from outside the colony to fill key posts in these industries as in the service of the Government. But current signs point to the training of local men and women, and indeed the Government has committed itself to a policy of giving preference to qualified Bahamians, which may well be translated into real terms of planning in due course.

If the present prosperity continues these industries and their ancillaries could form the basis of an educational system extending from primary school to university. The difficulties are considerably eased by a long-standing tradition of primary schools, literacy and Christianity, and for this Bahamians owe thanks to the early missionaries.

Early missionary work
Formal education came to the Bahamas after the expulsion of piracy in 1718, and was an external religious demand. Under instructions from the British Government, governors of the Bahamas encouraged schools for the preservation of order and morality, and the propagation of Anglican orthodoxy, and encouraged the conversion of Negro slaves. But as the colony was too poor at first to attract ministers and schoolmasters from abroad, successful appeals were made to the Society for the Propagation of the Gospel in Foreign Parts (SPG), but even after the local government took an active part in education much depended on the interest of SPG ministers.

From the Minutes of the Standing Committee of the Society for the Promotion of Christian Knowledge (SPCK) for Tuesday, 17 March 1772,[3] it appears that one Thomas Cox 'of Providence' who 'has liv'd there seven years' attended a meeting of the Committee on that date to ask for help for the Bahamas. It is possible that he had in mind the moral and religious desolation of the Bahamas when he approached the SPCK. But that was not the only reason for his appeal to a religious body. He had little choice because at that time, the SPCK was one of the only two organized sources of help that could be tapped for education in the colonies. On Tuesday, 3 April 1722, the SPCK Committee 'agreed upon the Contents of a Packet for the Bahama Islands' to the value of £5, and at the next meeting a week later was informed that a packet of books would be sent by the Society and 'Mr. Jackson said it would be recommended to Governor Finey to address the Government for a Minister or Chaplain to be sent to the Garrison at Providence'.[4]

The other organized source of help was the SPG, sister organization to the SPCK, and founded in 1701 with the overseas field as its province. For the SPG the employment of missionaries, catechists and schoolmasters in the colonies was a chief concern, and its interest in the Bahamas continued throughout the eighteenth century. By 1731 there already existed communication between the SPG and the Bahamas. Captain Woodes Rogers in his second term of office as Governor of the Bahamas had written to the Bishop of London on 13 October 1730,[5] that, despairing of the arrival of a minister from Carolina which he had been expecting for the past year, he was appealing to his Lordship for help. He assured the bishop that the people of New Providence, whom he estimated at about 140 families, were willing to contribute to the support of a minister; he had also written to the Secretary of War, urging the need for a chaplain to the garrison, and he envisaged a single incumbent for both offices in order to make the appointment financially worth while.

Alternatively, he suggested that the bishop,[6] (if he thought it advisable) should recommend to the SPG that a clergyman and a schoolmaster be appointed by the society with the usual allowances, to each of which the Bahamian people would add suitable amounts. He stressed the great need of a clergyman, to whose absence could be ascribed the paucity of settlers and the discouragement of the few who did arrive.

The following year, while Woodes Rogers was in Carolina for his health, he made the acquaintance of the SPG missionary, the Reverend William Guy whom he persuaded to accompany him on his return to the Bahamas where no minister had officiated for some years. Arriving on 12 April 1731, Guy spent two months in the Bahamas, performing the offices of a minister in all the inhabited islands.[7]

In his report to the SPG in July, Guy observed that all the inhabitants professed to be of the Church of England and were very desirous of having a minister; he believed they would contribute to a minister's support to the best of their abilities; but he recommended that 'as they were in general very poor it would ... be a very great charity to send a Missionary to them'.[8] In the same letter, Guy remarked that the people had 'very thankfully received' the Bishop of London's Pastoral Letters for promoting the conversion of the Negroes. Accepting this recommendation, the SPG at its meeting on 21 April 1732 agreed that an allowance of £50 per annum be made to a missionary to be sent to New Providence, 'who is also to officiate in the other islands'.[9]

A memorial[10] from the President, Council and Principal Inhabitants of the Bahamas considered on 16 March 1733 reinforced Guy's recommendation; but a house and £40 per annum towards the support of a clergyman proving inadequate, a resident minister could not be retained. The Reverend Hooper had stayed for only twelve months, then left for Maryland and a more attractive cure.

Recalling their decision of 21 April in the previous year, made on the condition that the people provided £50 sterling per annum according to Woodes Rogers's letter, the SPG agreed that in view of the 'dearness of provisions'[11] in Providence, £60 would be allowed to the missionary there if the people continued to contribute £40.

The first SPG missionary to be appointed to the Bahamas arrived in 1733. He was the Reverend William Smith. In 1735 the SPG considered a letter[12] from Governor Fitzwilliam, Rogers' successor, in which he revealed that he had succeeded in persuading the local Assembly to pass legislation forming all the inhabited islands into one parish and settling £50 on a clergyman, but he had failed to secure a salary for a schoolmaster. The Governor pleaded, 'That there is no place in his Majesty's American Dominions, where a Schoolmaster is more necessary than in that Government, by want of which their youth grow up in such Ignorance (even of a Deity) and in such immorality as is most unbecoming'.[13] Immediately it was agreed that the society would make a grant of £15 per annum for a schoolmaster if a suitable one could be found there, and the Governor was requested to inform the society 'what number of poor children such a Schoolmaster should teach gratis'.[14] Considerable difficulty in finding a local master for the school delayed its opening until 1738.

One of the Bishop of London's Pastoral Letters, distributed by

Guy, suggested that time could and should be spared for Negro instruction. If the missionaries owned Negroes themselves, they should set the example. But this point of policy[15] was not implemented in the Bahamas until the opening in 1793 of the Associates' School for free Negroes financed by the Associates of Dr. Bray. The schools in the Bahamas associated with the SPG catered for white children, especially poor white children, and a small proportion of free Negro children. Some of the slaves received spasmodic religious instruction whenever the minister visited and the masters could be persuaded to acquiesce; but no sustained effort along these lines was attempted until the early nineteenth century, and not by the SPG missionaries although a few of them like the Reverends Gordon at Exuma, and Moss, Dixon and Robertson at Harbour Island in the 1790s took an interest in the Negroes. Also the opening of Sunday schools for Negroes was discussed in letters between some of the missionaries and both the society and the Bishop of London, at the end of the century.[16]

However, not only was each schoolmaster in the Bahamas required in his half-yearly *Notitia Scholastica* to give the number of Indian and Negro children taught; each missionary had also to submit in his half-yearly *Notitia Parochialis*, the number of heathen and infidels in his parish and the number of those made converts during the past six months. The ministers invariably distinguished between white and black children baptized, the total number of coloured baptisms was always very small in comparison.

When Guy observed in 1731 that the people of the Bahamas all professed to be of the Church of England, he had a most important aim of the SPG in mind. It is necessary to note at this point that no small amount of the zeal for missionary effort in the eighteenth century was generated by denominational rivalry and religious conflict in England. It was feared that the advance of Dissenters and Papists, checked by legislation in England, would flourish in the colonies to the exclusion of an indifferent Established Church.[17] However, there was no need to fear either opponent in the Bahamas. The Papists were practically non-existent during the eighteenth and early nineteenth centuries, and although there were several families of Presbyterians as early as the middle of the century, these attended the Church of England as they had no church of their own, and the non-conformists presented no problem to the established Church until the Methodists and Anabaptists immigrated from America in the 1780s and 1790s.

Each SPG missionary was supplied on his appointment with a library worth £10 and a supply of books for distribution worth £5.[18] The books selected were, with the exception of spelling books, all religious and moral. In addition he received the Annual Reports of the society including the Anniversary Sermon, and any special publication such as the Bishop of London's Letters. These were practically the only books to be found in the Bahamas until the arrival of the Loyalists. All missionaries had small personal libraries, but as Bray pointed out,[19] it was the poor clergy who went to the colonies, with limited means for buying books. The library served to occupy the leisure hours of the ministers, to keep them supplied with doctrinal arguments and to keep them mentally alert. The reading books in the schools were religious books, the distribution among the inhabitants serving also as a means of retaining what literacy there was. The annual reports and sermons kept them in touch with the work in other colonies and the latest statements of policy.

It appears that Smith was selected with a good deal of care. This was generally true of all appointments, although the men sent to the Bahamas were not all ideal missionaries. In fact, one was dismissed for bigamy on his own confession, another turned to be a restless adventurer, and a third was dismissed shortly after his transfer to America. But on the whole the method of selection was satisfactory. Testimonials accompanying applications were required to testify to a knowledge of age, condition of life (i.e. married or single), temper, prudence, learning, sober and pious conversation, zeal for the Christian religion and diligence in his holy calling, affection to the present Government, conformity to the doctrine and discipline of the Church of England.[20] Testimonials had to be signed by the applicant's Diocesan or by three members of the communion of the Church of England known to the society,[21] and 'In the examination of candidates, special regard was had to their reading, preaching and pronunciation, which were submitted to a practical test'.[22] Several lists of instructions indicated how they should behave. One very important order pointed out that they should not offend the local authorities by meddling in 'Affairs not relating to their own Calling and Function'.[23]

Aims of SPG

The aim of the society being, briefly, religious indoctrination for moral and orthodox purposes, the importance of schools could hardly be overlooked as strategic centres of control and activity. The charity schools were the channels for the diffusion of Christian and moral education among the children of the proletariat. Whatever else was taught, was a means to that end. The English language was imparted to Indians and Negroes as a medium of conversion;[24] in SPG schools, spelling was taught as an indispensable preliminary to reading, necessary to participation in the Church services and an understanding of the Bible and books like *The Whole Duty of Man* which was supposed to ensure an enlightened proletarian bulwark against the superstitious ignorance of popery. In 1761, after eleven years as a missionary in the Bahamas, the Reverend Robert Carter attributed the absence of religious observances in Eleuthera to a lack of what he called 'The First Foundations in Literature'. He said, 'a greater progress in their spiritual Instruction might be expected, if the way for it was prepared, by the knowledge of the first Elements of Learning—without which they must continue still in darkness'.[25] It is true that subjects like writing, arithmetic, casting accounts and even navigation sometimes formed part of the curriculum in SPG schools; however, the purpose remained moral and religious, as these subjects were moral in their utilitarian[26] aspect and religious in that their inclusion answered the challenge of the non-conformists who taught similar subjects in their academies. Qualifications for schoolmasters according to SPG orders were similar to those required of missionaries. The character and religious view of the schoolmaster were at least as important as those of the clergyman, for besides having the duty of fashioning the moral and religious bias of the children, he was often called upon to act as locum for the missionary in districts so widely dispersed as in the Bahamas. As resident guardians and promoters of SPG religious educational policies in the Bahamas, the missionaries played an important role, enhanced considerably by their official status in Government.[27]

Personnel

Between 1731 and 1807, the year in which the SPG ceased for a time to support a clergyman in the Bahamas, no less than twenty-four incumbents served in this field. Except for the Reverend

D. W. Rose, a white West Indian with family connections in the Bahamas, they all originated in the British Isles, and so were familiar with the organization and administration of the charity schools of the time. Some of them may even have attended one.

Doubtless economic and social class considerations motivated many of them or reinforced their missionary zeal. But the threat of wars and piratical raids often materialized to the discomfort and even hardship of missionaries and inhabitants alike. These problems, joined with isolation in tiny island communities, suggest that the men who were prepared to travel through some 4,000 miles of dangerous waters to meet them had some higher motive than that of economic gain. Two missionaries on their way to the Bahamas, the Reverends Henry Jenkins and Rose, were actually taken, though later released, by French privateers. There was yet another deterrent. News of the untimely death of several predecessors was surely known to applicants for appointments overseas. The missionaries agreed with the other Europeans in erroneously ascribing the high rate of mortality to the climate and the inability of the white man to become readily acclimatized to the conditions of a warm environment. Some of them had leave of the Governor at various times to seek restoration of their health in some cooler more northerly American colony. Undoubtedly the change did them much good. But the explanation is no more reliable than the modern suggestion that Europeans are unsuitable for work in the tropical colonies. In fact the climate was only a contributory agent to the unsanitary conditions of an eighteenth-century port, and the lax social habits of a shifting population—all of which combined to aid the rapid spread of disease, especially in the warm summer months. The health of the reverend gentlemen suffered further from the enervating effects of a monotonous diet of salted food, because fresh meat, fruit and vegetables were seldom obtainable from a community which relied upon imports, and despised agrarian cultivation.

Seven of the twenty-four clergymen had a university education, but only three of these graduates remained in the Bahamas any length of time, and as it happens all three served as schoolmasters. That the other seventeen were quite well educated can be gathered not only from their selection by the SPG but from their letters, always well written and full of comments on contemporary conditions and topical events. There can be no doubt that the mission-

aries were all capable of discharging the duty of superintending
the work of the charity schools and advising the schoolmasters in
the Bahamas.

The impression is formed that the missionaries were all men of
mature years; yet little is known about them before they entered
the service of the SPG. Perhaps many of them had been schoolmasters like the Reverend William Smith.[28] Two were secretary to

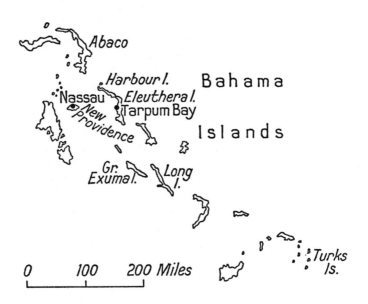

a governor before adding to their duties pastoral work, which was
performed with doubtful zeal. Since most of the appointments
involved *ad hoc* ordinations, scarcely one-third of the total number
of clergymen boasted previous experience of pastoral work as
curate, chaplain or minister; and only two of these had seen service
in a mission overseas. The missionaries were 'generally pious
good men',[29] as an agent for the Bahamas said, but their work was
hindered by lack of time, most of it being absorbed by a dearth of
personnel, brief terms of office and the perennial problems of the
geography of the colony. In 1767 an Act of legislature[30] divided
the colony into two parishes: New Providence, and Harbour
Island and Eleuthera with provision for two ministers. This
number was not increased until 1787, after the American War of

Independence which caused the withdrawal of the SPG from the rebel colonies. The society was then in a position to expand its activities in the Bahamas where a growing population of refugees on formerly uninhabited islands increased the need for missionaries who were always kindly received by the population. The Harbour Islanders[31] stood a little aloof from the Reverend Moss until they knew that they would not be required to maintain him, and they petitioned against the Reverend Gordon who also became involved in a couple of legal disputes, as J.P. But these cases are exceptional.

Each missionary through his conversations, sermons and discourses proclaimed the existence of a moral and religious standard of behaviour to be aspired to. At the same time, and especially in the isolated settlements of the Out-Islands with their transportation difficulties, he formed a means of communication with the world outside. Also the very fact that he catechized the children in church and school and conducted services which required response from the congregation provided a motive for the acquisition and maintenance of literacy.

Control of schools

In addition to his missionary appointment each minister had an official status. Not only was he head of his parish as established by law for purposes ecclesiastical as well as civic, he was often a J.P.[32] in the Out-Islands, and also a member of council if he were stationed in New Providence. The Education Acts named him a member of the trustees or commissioners of the schools, with responsibility for the appointment and supervision of the schoolmasters as well as the regulation of the activities of the schools. Undoubtedly, the work fell almost entirely upon the shoulders of the ministers who, after all, were better qualified for it and could easily include it in their pastoral duties. The other members were either Government officials or politicians for whom public service was spare-time occupation. Thus, the clergy controlled schools supported by the SPG as well as Government schools, partly because they represented the Established Church, but also because there was no one else to do it. The religious bias of the teaching in the schools was assured and even to this day it is commemorated in most Bahamian schools by the prominence of religious knowledge in the curriculum.

There was another way in which the influence of the missionaries could make itself felt, namely among the slaves. The SPG missionaries, however, did little work among the slaves because of opposition from the owners. Some tried[33] and the Methodist missionaries were especially concerned about the education of Negro slaves.

In 1787, four years after the flow of loyalist refugees began to settle the other islands of the colony, and before the Bahamas Government considered either the social or political welfare of the new arrivals, the SPG appointed a third missionary to the colony with headquarters on the newly inhabited island of Exuma. The first incumbent, the Reverend Twining, left in 1788 on account of ill health; but his successor, the Reverend William Gordon, who arrived the following year is worthy of note. He was easily the most energetic of the SPG missionaries of the eighteenth century. He is interesting as the first minister to serve the new settlers for any length of time, and he is alone in having earned an unsolicited gratuity from the SPG in recognition of his services. Not only did his long informative letters contain helpful suggestions for the improvement and expansion of the SPG ministry in the Bahamas; they also commented copiously on current social problems; and above all he took a special interest in education in both its broader and narrower interpretations. His whole mission was an educational effort.[34]

The society went further than accepting one of his recommendations, to appoint a missionary to Long Island: a Committee was set up to take 'under their particular consideration the state of the Bahama Islands respecting the Religious Instruction now afforded and to make an arrangement on a more extended plan than the present'.[35] The recommendations of this Committee, made in 1791, were not implemented until the Parochial Act of the Bahamas House of Assembly in 1795 which divided the whole colony into Parishes and made provision for building churches and maintaining ministers.[36] The fact that the parishes were civic as well as ecclesiastical units further emphasizes the extent to which the Bahamas Government depended upon the initiative and cooperation of the promoters of religion.

Two religious groups helped the Negroes—slaves, freemen and indentured servants—to endure and partially overcome the social handicaps inherent in their situation. They were the Methodists and the Baptists. Both sects were introduced from America by coloured men at the end of the eighteenth century. These preachers were men of some education who went to minister to the Negroes with whom they were able to make physical and spiritual contact more easily than a white man could. Unfortunately, the moral behaviour of the earliest Methodists left much to be desired. They clashed with the police and had to return to America. The Baptists did better, and stayed in the Bahamas long enough to introduce the sect well known today as the Native Baptists.

THE METHODISTS

In 1800 the Reverend William Turton arrived, the first representative of the Wesleyan Missionary Committee who sent him in answer to an appeal from one of the small groups into which the Methodists divided after the departure of their preachers. Both Baptists and Methodists conducted day schools for children and Sunday schools for children and adults. But they are of special interest on account of their evangelical work among the Negroes. Their respective doctrines and modes of worship gave to the Negro the opportunity to express some of the emotions which his social circumstances forced him to repress for most of the time, while the democratic organization of both groups offered to individual members some scope for participation and self-realization essential to human dignity but normally denied to Africans in a slave society. Readings from the Bible and the explanations or homilies which followed were often given by laymen whose language, though imperfect, was more intelligible to the hearers than that of a trained minister was likely to be. In addition, members of the congregation were themselves encouraged to give accounts in oral English under conditions which stimulated a desire for literacy, oratory and correctness. The regular evening and early morning services also provided a form of recreation. For these reasons, Baptist and Methodist meetings were popular among the Negroes who attended in large numbers.

However, the Methodists did not serve the Negroes exclusively. They preached to all who would listen, though they paid particular attention to the religious instruction of Negroes. Thus the society always had a majority of black members; but with a significant minority of white members the society served racial relations and education by bringing white and black people together on terms other than master and servant or owner and slave. Methodist day schools, evening classes and Sunday schools in New Providence and the Out-Islands (Eleuthera, Harbour Island and Abaco) were nearly always mixed. These and the class meetings around which much of the work of the Methodist Church was organized, were able to tap for instruction to Negroes, the services of white men and women that were otherwise unavailable.

Both the minister and his wife taught the three Rs and religious instruction to poor children—black and white—in day schools; the work in Sunday schools was confined to spelling, reading and religious instruction, though classes in arithmetic were not unknown. Sunday schools were attended by children and adults alike, and many Negroes owed their literacy to the zeal and dedication of Methodist ministers and their wives. One special advantage of the Sunday school was that it did its work without disturbing the economic and social order. This was exactly what the Methodists wanted to achieve. Traditionally, most slaves had Sundays off, and some had Saturdays as well. Thus Sunday schools in the Bahamas in the nineteenth century were as economically convenient as their counterpart in England.

The Bahamas Government, far from showing gratitude for the excellent social work of the Methodists, actually legislated against them in 1816[37] under the influence of the Anglicans who were alarmed by the progress which the non-conformists had made since 1800. Meetings were restricted to daylight hours when the people whom the Methodists wanted to reach were at work. But the Sunday schools continued and even increased in numbers. In 1817, there were two Sunday schools in New Providence with rolls of 100 and 50. When the offending Act was disallowed in 1819 partly as a result of a protest from the Methodist Conference in London,[38] the missionaries in the Bahamas were able to carry on their good work as before, with pleasing results.

Dr. Bray's Associates

The SPG was not the only English charitable organization to take an active interest in Bahamian education during the eighteenth and early nineteenth century. The other was the Associates of Dr. Bray, which opened a school in Nassau in 1793. Separate consideration of the Associates' School is not intended to imply that it was materially different from the SPG or Government schools in curriculum and organization, nor that the two societies did not co-operate in the implementation of essentially similar charitable objectives. In fact the SPG minister of Christ Church was inspector for the Associates' School, and the records of the Associates are to be found in the SPG archives; not to mention that the common founder of the two groups was the Reverend Dr. Thomas Bray. This pious man of vision and missionary zeal begot three brain-offspring, sisters with family characteristics but of distinctive individual features. The eldest, the SPCK, organized charity schools in England and distributed literature at home and over-seas; the second sister, the SPG, propagated the Gospel through schools and missionaries abroad; the purpose of the youngest sister, the Associates, was to educate the Negroes and maintain libraries in the West Indies and America.

The aims of the Associates were not unlike those of the SPG. In the case of the Associates, the approach originated in England. On 23 May 1788[39] the Secretary of the Associates wrote to Governor Lord Dunmore sending two boxes for distribution and enquiring about the number of Negroes in the Bahamas. In 1792 the Associates agreed[40] to open a school for the instruction of thirty Negroes in Nassau. Apparently the original intention was to open more than one school because letters were written to the Reverends Richards and William Gordon[41] to establish Negro schools, and a packet of books for the purpose was dispatched. When he acknowledged receipt of the letter, Richards mentioned the establishment of two schools.[42] However, the only reference to such a school made by Gordon is a remark in 1796 that Tarpum Bay would be a good location for a Negro school, 'if such a one was to be established'.[43] Such a one was not opened in an Out-Island, unless it was the Sunday school at Turks Island.[44] The Associates opened one day school in Nassau on 25 March 1793.

Perhaps the intention of opening the Out-Island school was abandoned as a result of Richards' letter of 18 March 1793 that there were more free blacks in New Providence than anywhere else in the Bahamas.[45] In the same letter, the minister made what is considered an important statement of policy, to which the Associates raised no objection, as, in any case, they placed complete confidence in the discretion and advice of their Inspector. Still referring to the 'free Blacks', Richards said, 'they are perhaps greater objects of attention than the slaves; for if the masters of slaves are well disposed (as numbers of them are) they will get the children instructed themselves; if they are of hard-hearted natures, they will not send the children to school, though free of expense'.[46] This policy was invoked thirteen years later by the Reverend Richard Roberts who succeeded the former Inspector of the Associates' School. He suggested that according to the former rules of the school, which he thought were the ones that ought to be followed, free Negroes should have preference over slaves for admission.[47] Therefore he had ordered the names of five slaves whose owners could pay for their instruction to be struck off the roll and he promised that he would strictly enforce a priority for the admission of the poor and destitute.[48] The Reverend Dr. Stephen, the next Inspector, replying to queries in 1811 said that only children of free Negroes were admitted to the school, the attitude being that masters could afford to pay for the schooling of their slaves if they wished them to have it.[49] Thus, the Associates' School was a charity for poor free Negroes only, as the Government or SPG school was a charity for poor white and a few poor free Negro children. The rest of the population was considered capable of paying for the education of their children, the slaves being the responsibility of their masters.

The Associates' School had a continuity which no other school of the time in the Bahamas enjoyed. It provided classes in Nassau without serious interruption from 1793 to 1844 when they transferred their support to the school at Carmichael, which was a Negro village about seven miles west of Nassau. The school came directly under the superintendence of an Inspector appointed by the Associates, who, in the Bahamas, was always the Rector of Christ Church Parish and so the SPG minister—until the SPG withdrew their support of any clergyman in the Bahamas about 1807. The only detailed directions given to the Inspector are suggested in the following quotation and are specific to the general policy of religious teaching without a change of condition. Worthy Inspectors were to see that 'the Children are properly instructed in the Principles of Christianity, and that the great and necessary Duties of Obedience and Fidelity to their Masters, and Humility and Contentedness with their Condition were duly impressed on their Minds'.[50] Richards boasted that the pupils of the Associates' School were the best disposed Negroes in New Providence.[51]

The religious bias was determined by the books which the Associates supplied; but even without them, it was assured by current practice and the policy of the SPG already discussed, which the inspector would naturally follow; for the Associates depended wholly on his discretion for the administration of the school. He appointed and paid the schoolmaster, issued the books supplied by the Associates; and undoubtedly he also advised on the day-to-day running of the school. So it would be strange indeed if the Associates' School was very different from any other Bahamian elementary school of the time except in racial characteristics.

With the possible exception of the schoolmaster at New Guinea appointed by the Reverend Carter and any who may have succeeded him, all the schoolmasters before the loyalists were white men. The teachers of the Associates' School, however, were all Negroes. Of course it would have been an outrage to place a Negro in charge of a Government or SPG school which accepted a majority of white children. But there were two points in favour of such masters at the Associates' School: it received only Negro children and by 1793 Negro teachers were not abundant, but available, for although the black loyalists were generally poor ignorant people, several had a vocation and could read, write and understand the scriptures. They had been taught by missionaries in America. Indeed, some of them had proceeded to the Bahamas as professional Methodist or Anabaptist preachers[52] sent by religious societies in U.S.A. to expound their respective doctrines to their 300 to 400 Negro followers. These preachers were popular with neither the Established Church nor the Government;[53] nevertheless, there was one society[54] of Negroes, dissenters from Methodism, who used the Anglican Prayer Book and attended services at Christ Church and who were, therefore, acceptable to the Anglican community. This group was led by Mr. Joseph Paul, the first master of the Associates' School which owed a good deal of its success to the fidelity of the family of which he was head. He died in 1802.

THE MADRAS SYSTEM

After his death Joseph Paul Jr. became master at the school, followed by a younger son, William Paul. Informing the Associates of the death of Mr. William Paul in 1813[55] Dr. Stephen said that he knew of no one willing or able to fill the post of master of the Associates' School. He would keep on trying to find a recruit; but he wanted the Associates to consider whether in the circumstances they wished to continue the school at Nassau. The Associates must have been pleased with the work of their school, because the Secretary replied with a firmness born of conviction of the worthiness and ultimate success of a cause to be prosecuted with unswerving resolution. The letter is worth quoting at some length. After regretting the death of Mr. Paul, the Secretary said:

> I have the satisfaction to assure you that the Associates entertain no intention of withdrawing their aid from the School at Nassau. On the contrary they are desirous, provided the Measure be in your opinion practicable, of extending the Benefits of religious and useful Instruction to every Negro Child resident in that Town. They have therefore desired me to suggest for your consideration, whether it would be desirable to introduce into the School at Nassau, the Madras System of Education. Upon this System, almost any Number of Children may be educated by one Master or Mistress, at a comparatively small expense. The Excellence of this System is now fully recognized in England.[56]

The letter continued to explain that to learn the system required no high standard of intellectual attainment on the part of the teacher, and if Stephen agreed to the proposal he would be supplied with the publications of Dr. Bell and 'Complete sets of School Books recommended by National Society for educating the Poor in the Principles of the Church of England', to enable him to instruct the schoolmaster.

The reasons for introducing the Madras system in the school are not far to seek. One has already been touched upon: the Associates were so satisfied with the former progress of the school, that they were willing to expand a work pertinent to their aims, and showing such hopeful signs of success, despite a lamentable dearth[57] of the human and monetary resources indispensable to such an extension. Fortunately, the latest teaching device resolved the problem of expansion within scarce means, by offering cheapness and expedition through a system that applied the mechanical methods of the factory to the school. This was none other than the Monitorial System then at the height of its popularity in England, and which was itself the product of similar problems of scarcity of funds and teachers that was threatening the Associates' School as well as the other schools in the Bahamas.

There was yet another reason for the action of the Associates. It was denominationalism. The introduction of the monitorial system in England had developed into a politico-religious feud between the British and Foreign School Society founded in 1810 and representing the non-sectarian views of Joseph Lancaster and the Non-Conformists; and the National Society founded in 1811, adhering to the doctrines of the Established Church and inspired by Bell. Of course, the Associates wanted Bell's system practised in their school. But the progress of the Methodists and the Baptists among the Negroes in the Bahamas since 1800 made the case rather urgent. When he wrote on behalf of William Paul, the leader of the coloured Anglican group, in 1810, Stephen showed how strong was denominational feeling in the town. He said, 'I am the more anxious to obtain something of this kind for him as he was tampered with . . . by a wild Methodist Missionary in this place who offered to procure him a maintenance from their Society in England, provided he and his People go over to them . . .'.[58]

Immediately the Secretary, who seemed as anxious as Stephen, promised to apply to the SPG and to the Society for the Conversion of Negroes for financial help for Paul; the Associates granted books and a small gratuity of £5 and the Secretary himself donated some books—all intended to keep the group within the Anglican fold and to 'prevent this good man's yielding to the artful solicitations of sectarian Missionaries'.[59] The Madras system was to assist this purpose by communicating 'religious and useful Instruction' according to the National Society's method of educating the poor in the Principles of the Established Church on a wider scale.

The Associates appointed a Committee[60] to find a teacher; and it was this committee which eventually selected Mr. William Cooper,[61] whose appointment, according to agreement,[62] was to cost the Associates £86 13s. 4d. sterling, and the Bahamas Government £233 6s. 8d. It was also agreed from Associates' funds to provide Cooper with enough cards, slates and elementary books 'as recommended in the Report of the Central National Society' to introduce the Madras system to 500 children.[63] For his 'own use' he received *The Scholar Armed* and *The Churchman Armed*.[64] With these and a packet of SPCK tracts for the rector to distribute, Cooper left England in October 1816 and arrived at Nassau on 14 December of the same year.

In a letter[65] of 10 January 1817, Dr. Stephen outlined the revised arrangements for the introduction of the Madras system. They show that the Assembly had assumed control of the Associates' proposals. Said Stephen, 'It has been found proper and convenient to open only the White School at first, where all the former Masters attend to learn the System, and to take an active part in Teaching; and when that School is fully organized, and the Masters in some degree qualified to conduct it, it is intended to open the Black School'.[66]

This is the first occasion on which the Assembly or any branch of the Bahamas Legislature applied a clear racial distinction to the schools. A resolution of the House passed on 23 January 1817 provided £800 to remunerate a 'fit and proper person as may undertake the management of a School and teach the white children of the island of New Providence according to Dr. Bell's System of Education . . .'.[67] The post was offered to Cooper, but he left the Bahamas in disgrace early in 1818, for his moral character fell far short of expectation,[68] and he was succeeded by John Malcolm. As far as is known he never taught in the Associates' School, in which case he spent about a year in the white school; and so the introduction of the Madras system originally intended to benefit the Associates' School and the Negro children of Nassau, was used by the Assembly for the greater advantage of the white children. The Associates' School was even closed for six months while Watkins, its schoolmaster, was in training. The House of Assembly did provide rent for the Negro school, but it was not until the Act of 1821 that the schoolmaster received the promised annual stipend from the Government. This discrimination is significant in view of the hostile attitude adopted by the Assembly towards the emancipation movement that was then gaining momentum. It also poses the question whether, by establishing a school for Negroes only, the Associates did not assist the development of the idea of separate schools. Under the circumstances the policy was, prejudice apart, sensible.

The Associates of Dr. Bray did two things. They provided education for poor Negro children and adults and they introduced the Madras system of education. All the inspectors of the Associates' School agreed that the effect on the behaviour of the pupils as children and later as adults was favourable. So the religious and moral ends of the Associates must have been attained, although the Reverend Hepworth was not satisfied with the children's attendance at church and threatened that he would have to turn away the more negligent from the school as a warning to the rest.[69] Even so, he reported in 1822 that:

> the good Work of the Associates in giving Education to the poor black and coloured Population of this Island, already shows itself in the more orderly Demeanour, the more regular Attendance upon public Worship, of those who have been instructed by the late Mr. Paul and now by Mr. Watkins, than in any other of the numerous Sects with which this place abounds.[70]

Economic conditions

Education in the Bahamas in the eighteenth and early nineteenth centuries was handicapped by a shortage of schools and qualified schoolmasters. For this there are several reasons, some already suggested. In the first place a scattered colony required more schools and teachers than a compact community. Secondly, the economy so closely wedded to maritime activities produced either the poverty of peace which could not afford schools or the ephemeral prosperity of war which could do without them. Thirdly, there was a lack of demand for schooling. Except for a little 'Casting of Accompts' and navigation, the lessons taught in such schools as there were bore but distant relationship to the life of the colony; moreover, the future merchants and clerks who would benefit from a course in book-keeping were restricted in number and confined to Nassau, while the skill of navigation, particularly that essential to a seaman in Bahamian waters, could be acquired better through apprenticeship.

The poverty of the eighteenth century looked for help from outside. An absence of strong internal motivation left the way clear for the transplantation of an external artificiality taking the form of moral and religious motives linked closely to the purpose of organized bodies in England like the SPG and the Associates of Dr. Bray. Hence the fourth reason: a dependence on some external source of supply for a motive, a system and teachers. All contemporary writers testified to the ignorance and illiteracy which existed among the old inhabitants of the Bahamas who were innocent of any desire for learning, so there was no local reservoir to tap for a supply of schoolmasters. To some extent the loyalists who became schoolmasters can be described as outsiders also. The moral and religious motives were kept alive by colonial officials steeped in the eighteenth-century views about the poor and, of course the missionaries whose duty it was to spread the Gospel and to supervise the work of schools not according to a system prescribed by the Bahamas Government, but according to SPG policy and conveniently laid down. When the Reverend Moss wanted guidance for the schoolmaster at Harbour Island, he applied to the SPG for a copy of its rules,[71] although three local Education Acts had already passed the Bahamas Legislature.

The SPG and Government schools can be considered under one heading—the free schools. They were partly financed by the generosity of the English public through the agency of the SPG, and in part by the Bahamas Government. Books were supplied by the SPG, and each schoolmaster was required by law to provide the poor children with 'proper books, pens, Ink and Slate'—out of his salary in some cases. On one occasion the SPG sent a quantity of stationery to the schoolmaster at Harbour Island.[72] The books were overwhelmingly religious in character and included catechisms, Prayer Books, Bibles, Testaments and spelling books, and books of homilies and discourses like the *Whole Duty of Man*—more or less the same books intended for the churches.[73]

The free schools were full-time co-educational schools catering for ages five or six to about twelve, under the control of separate boards of commissioners among which the church was well represented. The organization was nothing more than a collection. There was no system and, except for two attempts, no central administrative body. Thus, were it not for the SPG missionaries, the SPG instructions to ministers and schoolmasters, and the Associates of Dr. Bray, there would have been no uniformity of method and indeed no clear purpose.

Legislation

Bahamian Governmental policy before emancipation is reflected to some extent in the sixteen Education Acts passed between 1746 and 1823. Before 1746 the Government did not even assist the SPG. Only in 1729 was a legislature set up and until 1740 it was beset with administrative problems. Certainly it was too poor and unsure of itself to provide education although in 1729 instructions from England to Governor Woodes Rogers[74] envisaged the establishment of schools. The first Education Act of the Bahamas was passed in 1746. It proposed that enough money should be raised for one schoolmaster. The school was to serve the well-to-do whites, poor whites, and free Negroes. It was, in effect, a charity school. Under this Act the Government entered into partnership with the Church, but in fact policy remained in the hands of the SPG.

The next Education Act was passed in 1763. It differed in detail rather than in spirit from the previous Act. More attention was paid to the qualifications of the teacher and more power was placed in the hands of the trustees. The next significant change occurred in 1774 in an Act in which some responsibility was accepted for providing education for a wider range of young people. Two schools were established. The Act of 1774 did not differ in any essentials from its predecessor and in broad outline was renewed up to 1789. By this year the impact of the new settlers from America was being felt. A bill was introduced to establish public schools in the several islands, but it was rejected. So another was presented in 1790. No further bill came up for consideration until 1795[75] when an Act to provide schools and qualified teachers was passed—perhaps under some pressure from the Home Government. The Act of 1799[76] brought few changes but placed the schools in each of eight parishes definitely under the control of the Established Church.

For a short time during 1804 the Act of 1746 was again in force, a new Act,[77] however, re-established the parochial schools in that year. It was renewed in 1809,[78] amended in 1811,[79] and reviewed in 1816[80] for ten years. Before it had run its course an Act was passed in 1821[81] which was a direct result of the stimulation provided by the Madras system. It set up machinery for regular school inspection and central administrative control. Some elements of the present machinery can be traced back to it. A central school was set up in Nassau on the Madras system. In rapid succession between 1821 and 1823 four[82] Education Acts were passed, the last of which indicated that no advantages had been gained from the schools. So in primary education the wheel came full circle back to the position established by the 1746 Act.

A High School Act was finally passed in 1804.[83] It survived until 1811 but was not renewed and can hardly be regarded as a success. The school was intended for the children of wealthy Bahamian parents who in more prosperous times would have sent their children to England for their education. It offered a traditional, classically orientated curriculum. It was slow to open, fees were high and it failed.

Policy was not very clearly formulated at any stage. The Government accepted responsibility for the education of poor whites, and took some interest in the training of other white children. It legislated for the slaves but placed responsibility for their instruction with the owners. Since many of the masters ignored the Act of 1797 many slaves relied on Baptist and Methodist missionaries for instruction. The training of indentured African servants was left entirely to their masters and no laws referred to the education of free Negroes, and without the schools opened by the Associates of Dr. Bray they would have fared little better than the slaves and the indentured servants.

The introduction of the Madras system extended education but, as elsewhere, in retrospect produced rote learning, a cruel discipline and little direct contact between the schoolmaster and his pupils. Unfortunately the monitorial system, in a modified form, remains to this day an unhappy feature of education in the Bahamas. Nevertheless it focused attention in the early days on the need for teaching training and on professional as well as moral religious qualities. It revealed the importance of grading, the value of equipment and the advantages of centralization. The 1821 Act made the Madras system the official mode of education and for the first time placed all Government schools under one central authority. When the time came to organize education for emancipation there existed a recognized system on which to build and an important minority of literate Negroes to assist in the running of it.

NOTES

1. Houghton, H., *Report on Education in the Bahamas*, C.O. (1958).

2. Herrera, Antonio de, *General History of the Vast Continent and Islands of America 1601*, trans. Capt. John Stevens (London 1740).

3. SPCK Standing Committee 17 March 1772, Minutes, vol 4, pp. 95–6. The meeting was held at St. Dunstan's Coffee House, London. Members present included Sir John Philips, Mr. Chamberlayne, Mr. Shute, Mr. Tillard, Dr. Bray, Lord Percival, Mr. Beale, Mr. Mayo, Mr. Boehm.

4. *Ibid.*

5. Lambeth Palace *MSS*, Fulham 5, *Bahamas 39*.

6. This letter was read to a meeting of the SPG on 19 March 1730, see SPG *Journal*, vol 5, p. 290 (USPG archives).

7. Pascoe, C. F., *Two Hundred Years of the SPG* (London 1901), p. 210; also SPG *Journal*, vol 6, pp. 20–1.

8. Pascoe, p. 217.

9. SPG *Journal*, vol 6, p. 21.

10. *Ibid.*, pp. 75–6.

11. Pascoe, p. 217.

12. SPG *Journal*, vol 6, p. 260.

13. *Ibid.*

14. *Ibid.*, p. 262.

15. When Pascoe (p. 770) wrote that primary schools for Negroes were started in Barbados in 1712 and in the Bahamas in 1738 he was stating a point of policy.

16. Lambeth Palace *MSS*, Fulham 5, Bahamas 40. Robertson to the Bishop of London, 1790. Also letter from Rev. Gordon 1796 (SPG 'B' *MSS, West Indian Papers, Bahamas 1760–99*).

17. The efficiency and missionary zeal of the Roman Catholic Church was envied, see Thompson, H. P., *Thomas Bray* (London 1954), p. 36.

18. SPG, *A Collection of Papers* (London 1788), p. 34. Standing Orders VII; Orders relating to Missionaries Nos. III and IV.

19. Anon., *Publick Spirit, illustrated in the Life and Designs of the Reverend Thomas Bray, D.D.* 1846. Reprinted with additions by Rev. H. J. Todd (London 1908), p. 7.

20. Pascoe, p. 837.

21. *A Collection of Papers*, p. 35. Standing Order VII; Orders relating to Missionaries No. VII.

22. Pascoe, *ibid.*

23. *A Collection of Papers*, p. 12. The missionary was in part supported by the local government and was placed under the direct supervision of the Governor from whom he had his licence.

24. Bishop of London's Pastoral Letter No. 1, LPL.
25. SPG *MSS*, B6/3.
26. See 'Instructions for Schoolmasters' in Pascoe, pp. 844–5.
27. Two secretaries to the Governor, for example, became ministers.
28. For an account of his career see SPG 'A' *MSS*, vol 24, pp. 70–3.
29. The description by George Chalmers, Agent for the Bahamas, Lambeth Palace *MSS*, Fulham 5, *Bahamas 44*.
30. See C.O. 25/4, No. 51.
31. SPG *MSS*, B6/31.
32. Rev. Gordon's letters of 5 Sept. 1793, *Bahamas 1760–99*.
33. SPG, *Journal*, vol 6, p. 261.
34. See letter dated 27 Aug. 1795, *Bahamas 1760–99*.
35. SPG, *Journal*, vol 25, p. 400.
36. See Minutes of the Council 22 Aug. 1792, C.O. 23/32; Also Report of the SPG Committee, 1791 Journal of House of Assembly for 2 Dec. 1795, C.O. 23/31.
37. C.O. 25/16, No. 640.
38. Misc. E. Protest by the Methodist Conference to Lord Bathurst, dated 26 Feb. 1817, C.O. 23/66. Also Dispatch of President Munnings in reply to Lord Bathurst's letter of 4 Sept. 1818, C.O. 23/67, No. 49.
39. Dr. Bray's Associates, *Bahamas Papers*, Lord Dunmore's letter of Aug. 1788 (SPG *MSS*).
40. Dr. Bray's Associates, *Minute Book 1768–1808*, p. 189 (SPG *MSS*).
41. SPG, *Abstract of Proceedings of Dr. Bray's Associates for 1792*, II, p. 34.
42. *Minute Book*, p. 203.
43. Rev. Gordon's Letter of 16 April 1796, *Bahamas, 1760–99*.
44. *Abstract of Proceedings*, p. 34.
45. *Minute Book*, p. 203.
46. *Abstract of Proceedings 1793*, p. 30.
47. *Bahamas Papers*. Rev. Roberts' Letter of 14 Feb. 1806.
48. *Ibid.*, 9 Oct. 1806.
49. *Minute Book 1808–22*, p. 84. Dr. Stephen's letter of 19 April 1811, pp. 83–6.
50. *The Designs of Dr. Bray's Associates*, 1821, p. 13.
51. *Bahamas Papers*. Rev. Richard's letter of 3 July 1796.
52. Rev. John Richard's letter of 30 April 1791. SPG *MSS*, *West Indian Papers, Bahamas 1726–1843*.
53. Section II of 'An Act to prevent the resort of Rogues, Vagabonds and other idle and disorderly persons . . .'. See C.O. 25/10, No. 318 of 1799.
54. Minutes of District Meeting 1807. MMS *MSS*, *West Indies, 1803–13*.

55. *Minute Book*, pp. 133–5. Dr. Stephen's letter of 27 Aug. 1813.

56. SPG Associates' *Letter Book 1808–16*, p. 154. Letter to Dr. Stephen, dated 26 March 1814.

57. *Minute Book*, pp. 218–22. Meeting of 5 July 1816.

58. *Bahamas Papers*. Dr. Stephen's letter of 24 April 1810.

59. *Letter Book 1808–16*, pp. 74–6. Letter to Dr. Stephen dated 3 Sept. 1810.

60. *Minute Book*, p. 240. Meeting of 5 July 1816.

61. *Ibid.*, p. 244. Meeting 1 Nov. 1816.

62. *Ibid.*

63. The free Negro population of New Providence under fifteen years of age was about 463 in 1810. See C.O. 23/59 dispatch No. 1 of 16 July 1812.

64. *Minute Book*, pp. 249–50. Meeting of 1 Nov. 1816.

65. *Bahamas Papers*. Dr. Stephen's letter of 10 Jan. 1817.

66. *Ibid.*,

67. Votes of House of Assembly, 1816/17, C.O. 26/14.

68. When he departed from the Bahamas for the U.S.A. he left a reputation for dishonesty in money matters, neglect of his family in England whom he tried to make the responsibility of the Associates, and marital infidelity.

69. *Minute Book* 1822–35, pp. 142–4. Meeting of 3 Dec. 1824, Rev. Hepworth's letter of 2 Oct. 1824.

70. *Ibid.*, p. 9. Meeting of 8 Nov. 1822, Rev. Hepworth's letter of 4 June 1822.

71. Rev. R. Moss's letter dated 7 March 1775, also his letter B6/43, 20 Dec. 1773, *Bahamas 1760–99*.

72. See SPG *Journal*, vol 25, p. 384.

73. *Op. cit.*, p. 288. Rev. Robertson's letter of 26 March 1790, see also *Journal*, vol 9, p. 24.

74. Instruction to Governor Woodes Rogers, 13 May 1729, C.O. 24/1.

75. C.O. 25/9, No. 250.

76. C.O. 25/10, No. 305.

77. C.O. 25/12, No. 425.

78. C.O. 25/14, No. 536.

79. C.O. 25/15, No. 558.

80. C.O. 25/16, No. 650.

81. C.O. 25/17, No. 661.

82. C.O. 25/17, Nos. 661, 690, 700 and 701.

83. See Council Journal, 1802, C.O. 23/43.

3

MISSIONARY EDUCATION IN CEYLON

Ranjit Ruberu

IN the year 247 B.C.[1] an event of great significance occurred in the history of education in Ceylon. Buddhism was introduced, and it was introduced by the greatest Buddhist missionary ever known—the Venerable Mahinda. He successfully converted a large proportion of the people and Buddhist traditions have been cherished now for over two thousand years, remaining an integral part of the island's culture and a guide to educational thought today. This situation is by no means unique; for Buddhism can with justice be regarded as the first missionary religion in the world:

> Centuries before Jesus sent out his twelve disciples 'to the lost sheep of the house of Israel' Sakyamuni (Lord Buddha) had sent out sixty disciples to announce the message of salvation to the whole world. Hundreds of years before Paul started on his missionary journeys in Palestine and the neighbouring countries, the Buddhist church had sent out Theras (Buddhist monks) to preach the Dharma (the Doctrine) in every part of Asia.[2]

A detailed description of the Buddhist system of education would be out of place here, but some awareness of its existence is necessary if the work of the Christian missionaries is to be understood. When the Christians arrived in Ceylon there was in existence a formidable force ready to oppose their work. The extent to which it was able to withstand missionary activity will be discussed later. Suffice it to say that in the Buddhist system the temple or monastery was the centre of learning and monks were the teachers. The temple school provided a predominantly religious education but there was always some secular instruction for lay students. Higher education, imparted in Pirivenas, included subjects which were of value to the laity of the time.[3]

The close connection between the State and Buddhism is clearly evident. The State always recognized that the latter had responsibility for education. Whenever a system of schools existed it always received the ready patronage of royalty. Indeed, a well-organized educational system would not have been possible without State support and the fact that under the domination of foreign rulers the Buddhist educational system degenerated is evidence of its dependence on the native kings.

On the other hand the influence of the Buddhists was never destroyed completely. Many of the problems the missionaries faced were due to the fact that Ceylon was not a virgin field for them to work as they wished. They met stern resistance. The opposition was sustained chiefly because an indigenous educational system existed which could be revived at an appropriate time.

PORTUGUESE AND DUTCH MISSIONS

The Roman Catholic domination of Ceylon started when the Portuguese conquered the maritime provinces and remained there from 1505 to 1656. In these parts of the island missionaries successfully converted a substantial number of the inhabitants—a state of affairs which has justified the view that the 'Portuguese were much more successful than any other Christian missionaries who came to the Island later'.[4] Roman Catholicism has made a permanent contribution to the life of the country. For example, under the Portuguese education was the responsibility of the Roman Catholic missionaries, the 'pioneers of Western education'.[5] The first of them were Franciscan priests who started work in 1541.[6] These were followed by the Jesuits,[7] the Dominicans, and the Augustinians.[8]

The Franciscans organized two kinds of school—parish schools and colleges. Parish schools were established in every parish (or village) that came under Portuguese rule and gave rudimentary instruction in the three Rs and Roman Catholicism. The Franciscan seminaries provided a Catholic education for Catholic pupils. The Jesuit missionaries who commenced work in 1602 paid special attention to 'secondary education', particularly in Colombo. Elementary schools were, however, found wherever there was a

Jesuit mission station. They taught the 'three Rs in the mother tongue' and in addition, good manners and Christian doctrine.[9] The Jesuit colleges were always established in the important towns. The largest of its kind was the college of St. Antonia in Colombo with about 150 children of the Catholic faith in attendance.[10]

The pioneer Protestant missionaries came to Ceylon when the Portuguese surrendered to the Dutch East India Company in 1640.[11] The Dutch Reformed Church then took over responsibility for education, but they used it as a State monopoly to persecute Roman Catholics and convert others to the Dutch Reformed Church or Calvinism. Enforced attendance[12] at Protestant schools maintained by the Government was the chief means of conversion. Attendance was secured by a system of fines. Births, baptisms, marriages and deaths were registered by the schoolmaster which together with a system of rewarding Protestants with Government posts helped to ensure acceptance of the State religion. The well organised Dutch school system was inherited by the British whose first Governor[13] was so impressed by it that he accepted it 'as a working basis'[14] for the educational reforms he was later to introduce.

Under both the Portuguese and the Dutch the Christian missionaries had an indispensable role to play but they were never given complete freedom in the educational field. Only when a British Government[15] committed to a policy of delegating responsibility for education to the Church[16] was established in Ceylon did the Christian missionaries really succeed in achieving their educational aims. The British period was one of enormous missionary activity, and its achievements in education have been a powerful force in the evolution of the country's affairs.

THE FIRST BRITISH MISSIONS

During the British period the London Missionary Society (LMS)[17] provided the 'first non-Roman missionaries to come to Ceylon'.[18] On their arrival on 4 February 1805 the four missionaries[19] were 'cordially welcomed' by the British Governor[20] who 'rejoiced at the arrival of these experienced and worthy men'[21] and expected to employ them to great advantage in the colony. The Governor sent them to different parts of the country to work for the Government and gave them an allowance for it. The missionaries neglected the duties entrusted to them in London and their preoccupation with Government schools led the directors of the Mission in London to withdraw aid so that the Ceylon branch of the LMS came to an untimely end. R. Lovett speaks of this mission 'as an early example of the unsatisfactory result during the first twenty-five years of the Society's history of attempting too soon to make missionaries locally self-supporting'.[22]

The Baptist mission[23] began work in Ceylon in 1812 when James Chater and his wife, Ann, arrived. The Governor, Sir Robert Brownrigg,[24] was a great supporter of Christian missionaries and allowed Chater to reside in Colombo and establish his central mission station there.[25] It has been the headquarters of the mission ever since. Chater's desire to spread Christianity motivated him to learn the languages of the people, and his ability to speak and even to preach in these languages (particularly Sinhalese) helped him to extend his influence. It is on record that the early missionaries of the Baptist mission could preach in four languages including Portuguese and Dutch.[26] This work continued and under the leadership of A. M. Ferguson and G. B. Leechman the long-cherished ambition of the mission to become independent of the parent committee in London was achieved in 1874. Today, as with other missions in the country, the Baptist mission is maintained by local means and resources.[27] It has always been the smallest of the missions in Ceylon.

In 1813 a group of missionaries from the Wesleyan Methodist Missionary Society[28] set sail for Ceylon under the leadership of the Reverend Dr. Thomas Coke who died on the voyage. The remaining members of the mission arrived on 29 January 1814, two years after the Baptists had established their mission.[29] The Wesleyans received the same encouraging Governmental support, and immediately concentrated their activities in two areas, one in the north, the other in the south. The division was based on the languages spoken in these two areas, Tamil and Sinhalese respectively. At their first synod it was agreed to use the native languages for missionary work.[30] Further comments on missionary language policy will be made later, but it should be noted that the Wesleyans from the start recognized the advantages of employing native languages in their work, and the mission remains active in the country even now. At the time when the American missionaries[31] embarked on their tour to India in 1812 the attitude of the English East India Company towards missionaries was still hostile. When the Americans landed in Calcutta the company ordered them to leave and declared them as unacceptable in any of the territories over which it had jurisdiction.[32] Since no place in British India was likely to receive them, their leader, American missionary Samuel Newell, embarked for Ceylon—by this time a British Colony no longer under the East India Company. Here the missionaries found favourable conditions for their work: primarily because of the encouragement and support they received from the Government.[33] The American Board of Commissioners sent a second batch of missionaries out in 1816 in order that 'the people of the Island might receive the benefits of Christian Instruction'.[34] Brownrigg gave the American mission every protection It remained in the northern district of Jaffna and is still active today.

From its inception the Church Missionary Society (CMS)[35] had considered the possibility of establishing a mission in Ceylon, but the difficulties of recruiting suitable men caused considerable delay.[36] The first contingent of four missionaries[37] was despatched from England in November 1817. They arrived during Brownrigg's terms of office and received every assistance from him and his Government. The mission opened four mission stations at first[38] and others later.

The CMS was joined in 1840[39] by the Society for the Propagation of the Gospel (SPG). The missionaries of the Society for the Propagation of Christian Knowledge (SPCK) also associated themselves with this work. The SPG was not able to continue indefinitely since it was needed in other parts of the Empire. In 1929 it withdrew its grant from Ceylon,[40] but left as a memorial to its work the St. Thomas College, Mount Lavinia, as the foremost Christian institution in the country.

The Church of England Zenana Mission was founded in Ceylon in order 'to bring Christian Education to girls in a more organized manner' than hitherto.[41] Two English ladies, Miss Mellerby and Miss James arrived in 1889 and a year later commenced work in the villages of Kandy (the hill country) by converting a bungalow called 'Hillwood' into a boarding school[42]—the origin of the Hillwood of today. The first training school for girls was founded by the CEZM in 1903.

In 1930 the Diocesan Board of Missions was formed which

transferred the responsibilities of the CMS in Ceylon to a local body. In this way, after more than a century of work, the CMS was reconstituted as the Church of Ceylon, an autonomous branch of the Church of England.[43]

Mention should also be made of the Salvation Army which began missionary work in 1885. Its concern was evangelical and with the social services, and no educational activity has been recorded. The Indian Christian mission and the Pentecostal mission were also engaged in evangelical work.[44]

One important point stands out from this very brief account: all the missionary societies which became permanent were established between 1812 and 1815. There is no doubt that the attitude of the Government at that time had much to do with their early success. Brownrigg's enthusiasm for and support of the Christian cause made the country attractive and profitable. His sympathy for these missions is evident from his own observation that '. . . it has been a matter of peculiar satisfaction to me that I have seen under my government Wesleyans, Presbyterians and Baptists, working with regular clergy of the Church of England'.[45] The political climate of the country favoured all the missionary societies and not only one or two of them. They were all able to gain a permanent place in Ceylon and to exercise a hold over educational development.

In some parts of the island the structure of society was also helpful. Early missionary activity was confined to the coastal regions where the influence of Christianity had been felt for over three hundred years. The population did not exceed 750,000 and was very cosmopolitan. Several European and Eurasian races[46] lived together with the Sinhalese and Tamils. Then, as now, the Sinhalese occupied the southern and south-western parts of the island and the whole of the hilly country which did not come under British rule until 1815. The Tamils were in the north and north-eastern parts. The Europeans and Eurasians concentrated in the towns. A few Moslems were also found in the towns.[47] In these territories where the British missionaries first worked a large proportion of the population was Christian. The second largest group were the Buddhists (unconverted Sinhalese) and then the Hindus (unconverted Tamils). Consequently the missionaries found a population, the majority of which was well disposed to their cause.

Moreover, other subtle changes had occurred in the society as a result of the occupation of the Portuguese and the Dutch. This was the case particularly in those communities which considered themselves fortunate to have been able to acquire some knowledge of a new language. They had also learned to imitate the governing class in matters of dress, names and religion. This new social class offered considerable advantages to the foreign missions.

Policies of the missions and the Government
All the missions had the same or similar aims and objectives. Consequently they tended to pursue similar policies. Proselytizing was the chief goal as is evident from policy declarations and from their activities. The Baptist mission declared as its objective 'to diffuse the knowledge of the religion of Jesus Christ through the whole world beyond the British Isles, by the preaching of the Gospel, by translation and publications of the Holy Scripture and the establishment of schools'. The Wesleyan methodists were 'sent from England in order to convert the natives from Heathenism'.[48] Similarly the American mission was 'anxious for the conversion of the heathens'. The objectives of the CMS were expressed by the parent body in London in the following manner: 'There are two objectives which you will ever keep in mind as forming the great design of all your labours. The revival of true Christianity in the hearts of the natives who at present only nominally profess it.'[49]

The success of the different missions varied considerably since it depended on factors such as the resources at their disposal, the availability and enthusiasm of personnel, the attitude of the people and above all the relationship they had with the Government. The Government's attitude, to be sure, was really an expression of its policy and it is very relevant to discuss this in the light of what happened during the period when the missionaries were attempting to establish themselves.

Governmental policy found expression at two levels. The Home Government pursued the same policy towards the missionaries in all the colonies which remained effective throughout the period of British rule. Domestic politics certainly changed the emphasis, particularly as far as education was concerned. The nineteenth-century denominational battle for control of the schools in England had repercussions in the colonies. Each colony was to some extent unique, and each governor could influence the application of general policy to a considerable extent. The local government very often acted in accordance with his wishes. Although in

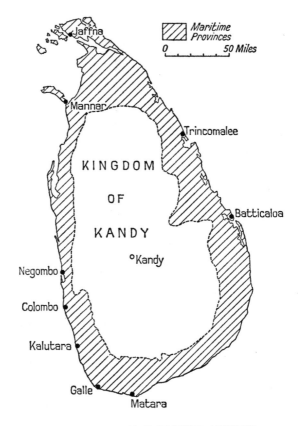

Maritime
Provinces

0 _____ 50 Miles

Jaffna

Mannar

Trincomalee

KINGDOM

OF

KANDY

Batticaloa

°Kandy

Negombo

Colombo

Kalutara

Galle

Matara

CEYLON WHEN THE BRITISH ARRIVED

Ceylon there was never an open conflict between local policy and the wishes of the Home Government, subtle differences of opinions were evident. Sometimes a governor applied colonial policy very strictly, at other times much less attention was paid to it. Generally the educational policy followed in Ceylon was characteristic of British policy during the nineteenth century. The Government's *laissez faire* attitude left education in the hands of voluntary

84

agencies—chiefly the churches. Consequently the missions were left with the task of providing education for the people.

In Ceylon transference of responsibility was not unconditional. From the start of British rule the policy of the Home Government was to promote the interests of the Established Church. This was attempted by restricting the activities of non-English missions and by promoting the welfare of English missions. There is evidence of restrictions against foreign missions in the declarations of the Secretary of State. At the time the only one in Ceylon was the American mission whose entry to the island has already been mentioned. That it was allowed to do so as a result of Brownrigg's personal wish seems evident from comments made somewhat later by the Secretary of State when in a letter to Governor Barnes he wrote:

> ... had the question indeed been now to be decided, whether an establishment of foreign missionaries should be formed in the Island, I should have had no difficulty in withholding my consent. But . . . permission to these gentlemen to reside had originally been given without the previous sanction of His Majesty's Government.[50]

The motives of the Home Government were largely political. It was feared that foreign missions would 'foster political objects' as the following remarks by the Secretary of State in a letter to Brownrigg make clear:

> As it is most desirable not to admit the subjects of a foreign state to situations in the British Colonies, in which they must necessarily acquire considerable authority and influence over the inhabitants . . . Lord Bathurst[51] does not consider it either necessary or expedient to encourage or admit missionaries proceeding from foreign states.[52]

The same view found expression in the restrictions placed on the admission of additional American mission personnel. On this occasion the Secretary of State observed '. . . There are, however, such serious objections to the unlimited admission of foreign missionaries to a residence in the British possessions, and it is difficult to make an exception in favour of any particular nation'.[53]

These comments certainly reflect general policy towards foreign missions at the time. Was it therefore in violation of policy when Brownrigg allowed the American missionaries to settle in Ceylon? No definite answer based on documentary evidence is possible. Perhaps Brownrigg's enthusiasm for missionary activity made it impossible for him to distinguish between the different missionary societies. On the other hand it could be said that prior to his allowing them to enter Ceylon the Home Government had given no indication to him as Governor on the treatment of foreign missions. Policy was stated only after the American mission's dispute with Brownrigg's successor, Governor Barnes.

The vehement opposition of Barnes towards the American mission is obvious from his remarks in a letter to the Secretary of State. He wrote: 'I cannot contemplate the necessity of having recourse to a foreign nation for the instruction or conversion of our Indian subjects . . . nor do I think it expedient or prudent to allow subjects of a foreign state to gain that influence over the minds of the natives'.[54]

The case of the American mission illustrates the extent to which individual governors differed in their interpretation and implementation of Home Government directives. Evidently governors were not expected to put their own policies into practice without the prior approval of the Home Government. Their own opinions and enthusiasms counted for a great deal when policy was not clearly enunciated and directives were not given. They also determined the strictness with which Home Government policy was implemented. The privileges the American mission enjoyed under Brownrigg can be regarded as primarily due to his character. By the same token the strict application by Barnes of Governmental directives throws light on his own attitudes and policies.

Among these were those relating to the various denominational missions. There is evidence that the Governments in England and Ceylon discriminated between the various Christian missions. The Home Government held that 'the religious wants of Ceylon should be supplied by ministers of the established church'.[55] Barnes agreed:

If the present establishment of Church missionaries (and such are the only missionaries he would wish to see employed in the Island) are proved to be insufficient in point of number, the Lieutenant-Governor is persuaded that time will have the salutary effect of removing the difficulty, especially as Wesleyan missionaries are readily increasing.[56]

In short only English missionaries were acceptable to the Government and of these those of the Established Church were preferred.

In practice the *laissez faire* policy of the Government towards education helped all the missions. Until the last quarter of the nineteenth century the mission schools and their control over education remained virtually unchallenged. The Christian mission were accepted and received Government protection and support.[57] Even later when the State became more actively concerned with the control and finance of education the mission schools still enjoyed a privileged position and can be said to have done so until the end of British rule in Ceylon.[58]

The attitudes of indigenous groups

Generally the attitude of the non-Christian groups towards the Christian missions was hostile, but opposition from the Buddhists and the Hindus was never violent. There is no record of religious riots, in spite of the religious persecution of all the foreign rulers. Support for this is found in the views of H. J. Charter, a Baptist missionary, who wrote: 'Buddhists have severely opposed and persecuted their own people for embracing Christianity, but the opposition that missionary societies have met has been intellectual and political and nationalistic'.[59] The formation, during the closing years of the nineteenth century, of Buddhist and Hindu organizations[60] to spread education should be regarded as an attempt to oppose the foreign Christian missions. British policy facilitated this revival.

At first, during the early years of British rule, Buddhist and Hindu parents had little choice but to send their children to Christian schools; towards the end of the century they realized the disadvantages of this situation, perhaps as a result of the protests of Buddhist leaders. There was a growth of criticism from the national leaders. One example of it will suffice. A former President of the Buddhist Theosophical Society observed:

> Let me frankly admit that in this respect (i.e. education) Christian missionaries have rendered much service to the country . . . let us not be blind to the benefits they have conferred on the Sinhalese through their schools, and let us give them every credit

87

for the good they have done in offering the people an opportunity for intellectual improvement at a time when theirs was the only agency existing for the purpose. . . . But on the other hand the benefits of missionary education have been to a very large extent counterbalanced by greater evils of no less magnitude which could not possibly be separated from a proselytizing policy such as the Christians pursued.[61]

Hindu leaders expressed similar feelings. For example, a Hindu member of the Special Committee on Education[62] protested against the education of Hindu children in Christian schools by saying:

Our people cannot be expected to realize the objectionable nature of the education of their children in Christian schools, as their religious spirit has been sapped by the religious slavery to which they have been subject for three centuries, first under the Portuguese and Dutch Governments and then in Christian schools.[63]

These rather mild statements of opinion were uttered towards the end of the British period and contrast rather sharply with the earlier, more severe forms of hostility. At the local level the opposition of the Buddhist clergy was always a factor to be reckoned with. They persuaded Buddhist parents not to send their children to Christian schools for fear of conversion. A CMS missionary, the Reverend James Selkirk, records how a Buddhist priest reacted to an attempted conversion. He wrote to the secretary of the CMS in London in 1828 thus:

The boy who attends our English school and whose uncle is a Buddhist priest . . . I have now and then mentioned in my Journal, is, I believe, surely desirous of believing in Christianity of Jesus. . . . The circumstances, however, in which he is placed are much against him. He is living with a Buddhist priest . . . they are afraid of losing him and therefore do all they can to make him think ill of Christianity, and despise Christianity. Christianity they tell him is a pack of lies and the missionaries are vagabonds. The boy is obliged to hear these insults.[64]

Again children were prevented from attenting Christian schools regularly. A report from the Reverend T. Browning of the CMS described the situation in this way: 'The schoolmaster came as usual. On inquiry of one of them the reason why his children did not attend more regularly, he said that the priests[65] had been persuading them not to attend, telling them that it would not be good for them to hear other religions'. The work of the schools was disrupted by parents withdrawing their children. In 1833, Selkirk reported to the CMS in London:

> It is very discouraging when we have been instructing our children almost daily throughout the year in the truths of Christianity, to find their parents and relations step in between us and then say to them 'you must now come with us to worship Buddha' and this is very frequently done.[66]

Hindu parents also prevented their children from attending Christian schools. In a letter home, the Reverend T. Squance of the Wesleyan Methodist mission commented on this by declaring that '. . . The *Brahmins* do all in their power to prepossess the minds of the people against us, as their influence is great, they find no difficulty in succeeding. . . . They are a most deceitful set of men'.[67]

If conditions had reinforced it the presence of such hostility at the local level would have seriously curtailed missionary activity in Ceylon. In fact the mission schools prospered. Why? In the first place there were no effective national organizations able to compete with the missionaries until towards the end of the nineteenth century when Buddhists and Hindus at last undertook to organize themselves into active groups and to establish schools. Lack of competition alone does not explain the unrivalled educational success of the mission schools. Two main reasons can be advanced for this: the financial assistance the missions received from the Government and the utilitarian value the people attached to the education of their children.

Financial aid to the mission schools originated in 1842 when the Central School Commission[68] decided to make grants to the missionary societies. This grant-in-aid system was expanded year by year and the mission schools were able to increase rapidly as a result. In 1866 (the year in which the Buddhist Theosophical Society was formed) except for a few private schools not in receipt of aid and a few Government schools, the majority of schools were aided Christian mission schools.[69] Ultimately under the Denominational School System the schools of every religious denomination were included, but in the early period the grant system benefited the Christian missions since they alone maintained schools. The grant met a large part of the costs of running the schools, and with fees provided adequate funds. Financially the missions were well off under the scheme.

The policy of Anglicizing education also helped the missions to consolidate their position. The progress of western education induced people to judge education mainly in terms of its usefulness for social advancement. Colebrooke's recommendations in 1831[70] had set the seal on English medium schools as the agency through which Government posts could be obtained. One proposal was that 'a competent knowledge of the English language should be required in the native functions' and another was that a college should be established in Colombo to train teachers and public servants with preference given in the curriculum to English. Parents set great store by an education in English because it offered the greatest material prospects. English was the language of Government and commerce and some knowledge of it was required of all who wished to seek employment in these spheres of activity. It was also the gateway to higher education. The missions came forward to meet the demand for this kind of education by establishing English schools all over the country.

A change of Governmental policy in 1884 further consolidated missionary hold on English education. In that year the Government proposed that its few English schools should be maintained by local authorities with the assistance of a grant.[71] Opposition to this suggestion included that from the missions and the proposal to raise an educational tax by local authorities was abandoned. All the Government English schools except the Royal College and a few English elementary schools, were handed over to the existing mission agencies who were willing to accept them.[72] One consequence of this transfer was that the Christian missions gained even more control over English education in Ceylon. They retained this position until the administration of education was unified by legislation passed in 1960.[73]

But to return to the original point: the attitudes of the indigenous people towards the mission schools were ambivalent. The hostility of Buddhist and Hindu leaders did not check the spread of mission schools throughout the island. Of all the other factors which helped to secure the position of the missions the utilitarian value of the education they provided was probably the most important. In the long run this feature of educational provision dominated all aspects of policy. Success depended on the extent to which the kind of education the mission schools provided was in demand.

Élitism versus mass education

In general the policy of the missionaries everywhere was to teach the younger generation to read and write. In countries like Ceylon where most of the population were non-Christians the task took on a special significance. All the missions considered the schools as a means 'to convert the natives from Heathenism'.[74] They were more than places where children could be brought together to be instructed in reading, writing and the Scriptures. Through the Christian schools the missionaries hoped to discover 'gradual openings to preach the Gospel to all'.[75] Through the children it was hoped that the adults could be reached and anti-missionary prejudice reduced. A Baptist missionary, for example, observed: 'As a means of introducing the Gospel we have had our thoughts on schools for a long time'.[76] The CMS recognized the 'importance of the education of children in subserving the diffusion of Christianity'.[77] And for the Wesleyans 'the chief prospects of success of the mission in the Island rested in the "formation of schools and their vigorous support" '.[78]

Mass education with a particular purpose was attempted from the start. The following extracts from original documents of the Wesleyan missions in Ceylon make the position very clear. In 1820 two misionaries wrote:

> As our great object is to instruct the natives in the principles of Christianity, we endeavour to make all our pursuits subserve this desirable end . . . we are sensible that this change can only be accomplished . . . by the regular diffusion of instruction among them. This persuasion led us sometime back to resolve upon the establishment of Christian schools . . . and while we endeavour to make the rising generation acquainted with the first rudiments of learning, we try at the same time to accompany these instructions with such others of a religious kind, as we are convinced will answer the design of our mission. . . . We have so far succeeded in these attempts, as to have established in different parts of the Island about 72 schools. . . . From this

system of schools, conducted on such plans, the most moderate calculations will be in favour of their proving greatly beneficial.[79]

The Wesleyans considered it a duty bestowed on them by God 'to convert the natives' and 'to extend the advantages of education' to such converts and make them 'understand their duty to God'.[80] Their achievements are recorded in the Report of the mission for 1827 which stated that '. . . the missionaries have the pleasure to state to the friends that at no period in the history of the country was so extensive a system of schools in a more active and energetic states of operation than are the Wesleyan schools'.[81] The earlier comments of Brownrigg confirm this self-assessment. He wrote to the Wesleyan Methodist missionaries in 1820 in the following terms:

> The numerous schools established under the vigilant superintendence of your mission forming a most extensive system of public education, cannot fail to produce a most beneficial effect upon the morals and habits of the rising generation . . . when our observation is turned to that large part of the native population, which yet wanders in heathen darkness, the superior advantage of early education is still more striking and apparent.[82]

For the converts at that time a rudimentary form of education was needed chiefly in the language of the people so that they could read the Scriptures in translation. On this question some comments of the Wesleyan missions are relevant. 'We do not aim at making the natives learned men, but to impart to them such a power of acquiring useful knowledge through the medium of their own language as will enable them to understand the duty to God'.[83] These views in fact reflect the general purpose of the mission schools. To achieve it the medium of instruction in the native or village schools (which were set up by all the missions) was always the mother tongue. The Wesleyans record that their free schools were the most widely distributed and were founded for the 'benefit' of the 'middle and lower classes of native children'.[84] Similarly of all the American mission schools in Jaffna the most widely distributed and successful were their village schools. The purpose of this mission was 'the raising up a reading population' which could afterwards be 'addressed and instructed through the Press'.[85] The purpose of the CMS village schools was similar.

There is evidence to suggest that the missionaries, at least, gave to these schools the greatest importance. The president of the Wesleyan mission in Ceylon made this clear when he said, 'the principal strength of the missions . . . is employed on the native schools'.[86] The American missions guarded the development of their village schools by placing them 'under the immediate care of a missionary' at the station.[87] In addition the schools were examined at frequent intervals by the chief missionary. The teachers were paid according to the number of children who were taught and this arrangement probably helped to check any decline in attendance. The incentive to attend was not very great. These schools did little more than provide rudimentary instruction. As a Wesleyan missionary put it, they were 'purely Native' and prepared children 'for the common routine of life'.[88] Nevertheless scripture figured prominently in the school timetable and the Bible was read as a class textbook.[89]

Enough has been said about this category of school to show to what extent the Christian missions emphasized mass education, particularly for the poorer sections of society. The village schools did not provide a very ambitious programme but rather a form of cheap education in humble schools for the bulk of the population. The children were taught free of charge, which accounts for the relatively high level of attendance. There is little doubt that through these schools the missionaries hoped to achieve their aim of spreading Christianity among the ordinary members of the population.

Undoubtedly the Government's policy, established during the time of the Central School Commission, of granting aid to the mission schools helped them very much. The Administrative Report of the Director of Public Instruction for the year 1889 gives some idea of the extent to which education was available in Ceylon at that time and the degree to which it was provided by the missions. At the end of 1889 the total number of schools was 1,752. Of these 489 were Government schools, 120 Buddhist and 1,143 mission schools. The Buddhist and the mission schools were recognized for the purpose of grant aid.[90] Others managed by the missions were not in receipt of grants from the Government. The figures show to what a large extent the missionaries were in control of mass education at the beginning of the twentieth century.

There is evidence to show that rhe press also helped to spread elementary education. The first printing press in Ceylon was established by the Dutch and after their power declined printing remained a monopoly in the hands of the British Government until about 1814 when the Wesleyan mission set up a press in Colombo. Most of its publications were ecclesiastical tracts, scriptures and translations of the Bible. Later the American mission in Jaffna and the CMS in Colombo established presses. The Bible Society founded in 1812 and the Tract societies which followed all contributed to the spread of mass education by providing printed material. The work of the Wesleyan Mission press was commended by Brownrigg in these words:

> The great influence of the press is exercised with more or less effect over every civilized country in Europe; but here where it was so much wanted, it was utterly unknown. It was rare that any publications ever appeared in a language intelligible to the people, except a Regulation of Government. The children had nothing to learn, their parents had nothing to read. But the Wesleyan missionaries have established a press from which there is a continual issue of elementary works of devotion, morality and science, that the native population is at length gradually admitted to a participation in the richness of European knowledge.[91]

The education of an élite was another matter. It was provided in English in rather better mission schools. It strengthened the position of the privileged groups in society. Only an English education could produce an élite and only members of the existing élite could avail themselves of the kind of education provided. These conditions gave to English education a position of dominance in the country. The British Government encouraged it because there was need for a corps of local men who could help in the running of the country. An English education ensured employment in the public and private sectors of the economy. The recent report of the Commission on Higher Education presented in 1956 shows how readily English education was accepted.[92] It said:

> The Sinhalese and the Tamils too eagerly took to the study of English. It must be stated that neither the Sinhalese nor the Tamils nor the Dutch had any compunction, national, emotional or otherwise in neglecting their own respective mother tongue

for the sake of learning a completely foreign language. The national emotional and educational factors were overlooked by them when the question was a matter of success in the race for positions and office. The prosperity for a knowledge of English was a passport to such a privileged position at that time.[93]

Under the British élitist education remained an education in English. The fact that the missionaries were the only people competent to provide it made them the leaders in this field too. At first they provided this kind of education for a very limited clientele which in missionary terminology included only the children of 'well-to-do natives' and those of 'European descent'. But as time went on these restrictions were difficult to maintain, largely because so many people began to appreciate the value of an English education. Evidently the missions not only recognized this demand but were prepared to meet it. For example, the Academy of the Wesleyan mission established in 1827 had as its limited aim the provision of a 'superior education exclusively appropriated to the English language' to the 'children of Europeans and respectable natives who are to pay the masters for their instructions'. It was also to be a 'graduation school, for native children who have conducted themselves well in other schools' of the mission.[94] Similarly one of the main objectives of the college established by the American mission in Jaffna was 'to give native youth of good promise a thorough knowledge of the English Language'.[95] The Christian Institution of the CMS admitted as well as the rich who could pay fees, children of native families of average or good means who were 'distinguished both for their piety and capacity'[96] and who could profit from this kind of education. Ability to pay and ability to profit were the two criteria used to admit pupils. Such policies the missionaries envisaged would result in the growth of a new élite.

Its expected characteristics are apparent from the curriculum and general ethos of the schools. The Wesleyan Methodist mission aimed at 'a complete education in the Classics and Mathematics as well as in English Literature' with prominence given to Theology.[97] The object of the education offered in the mission college of the American mission was 'to open to them the treasures of European Science and Literature'. In addition, 'a thorough knowledge of the English language' was expected to bring the learning of the west to the east.[98] Evidently the missionaries hoped that the members of the new élite would be Europeanized. A report from the Wesleyans in 1827 made clear that more than the learning of English was intended. It included this sentence:

> It would be desirable to increase the number of schools, the advantages resulting from such instructions being very great, but, it is not merely the acquirement of English which is to be looked to, though it is of great importance but in schools where English is taught, it is necessary to appoint a man acquainted not only with English language but also European ideas and modes of thinking and activity.[99]

These missionary colleges, in fact, imitated the English public schools and established these traditions in Ceylon. They were residential boarding schools very often, with missionary principals. The Roman Catholic colleges which developed later were similar, but always had a large number of religious teachers.

The colleges also offered opportunities for higher education. Many of them were either affiliated to one or other of the universities of Madras, Calcutta and Bombay or prepared candidates for examinations run by them, particularly during the period prior to the time when English university examinations were conducted in Ceylon. Cambridge, Oxford and London examinations were introduced in the 1860s and many colleges began to prepare their students for them.

Once recognized, the colleges received Government grants but they also charged fees which only wealthy parents could afford to pay. From this viewpoint they were exclusive schools meeting the needs of an élite even though a few exceptional scholars were admitted to them. Moreover they catered primarily for the urban folk but their reputation spread to the remote villages and children of rich parents in the rural areas flocked to the schools in order to learn English. All these young men and women learned something of the art and science of the west. A majority embraced Christianity. A great many teachers, doctors, lawyers and civil servants were educated at the mission colleges and thus a new élite of learned men and women, the majority of whom were Christians, was created by the end of the nineteenth century. It was an influential group with considerable wealth and prestige.[100] Further reference to it will be made when the social consequences of missionary activity are discussed.

In summary, it can be said that the Christian missions in Ceylon endeavoured as a matter of policy to provide an education both for the masses and for an élite. The ordinary mission schools aimed at mass conversion and gave converts rudimentary instruction in the language of the people. The colleges and English schools provided for the needs of the élite.

English versus the vernaculars as a medium of instruction
In view of the success of the policy outlined in Macaulay's famous Minute of 1835 it is well to review the attitude of the missionaries to the vernaculars as media of communication with the people. They all knew that until they mastered these languages, namely Sinhalese and Tamil, their influence on the people of Ceylon would be limited. The CMS committee in London instructed its missionaries by stating that 'the acquisition of the languages spoken in the Island claims your earliest attention'.[101] In a letter to the CMS secretary the Reverend Joseph Bailey wrote: 'I am fully convinced that the first step which a missionary should take after he arrives at the scene of his labours, if he has no means of doing it before, is to acquire the native languages'.[102]

A convincing account of missionary policy regarding the vernaculars is given in H. J. Charter's book, published in 1955. He wrote:

> The Baptist Missionary Society has a good language record in its various fields both for speech and translation. The Society wisely insists on its missionaries giving the first two years almost exclusively to language study. It is essential to be able to talk to the people and preach the Gospel to them in their own language even if they have some knowledge of yours . . . in a country like Ceylon where parents often cannot speak English, but want their children to learn it because it opens so many doors and is so advantageous in the matter of employment . . . you must know the people's own languages.[103]

The value of learning the native languages had also been recognized by the Portuguese and the Dutch. From the moment they arrived in Ceylon the Jesuit missionaries applied themselves to the

H   97

mastery of Sinhalese and Tamil. H. A. Wyndham states that 'as early as 1545 a Sinhalese Catechism was produced at Goa and other works in the same language followed'.[104] Similarly, the Dutch priest Baldaeus learned Tamil and was a strong advocate of the vernacular. Wyndham considers that 'He took the line that it was more reasonable to ask one man to accommodate himself to many than to expect the many to adjust themselves to him'.[105]

The objects of all the missionaries who learned a native language and employed it in their day-to-day work were the same. They wished to popularize the native languages through translations of the Bible, prayers and other scripture into Sinhalese and Tamil. The publication of tracts, pamphlets and books provided the missionaries themselves with useful material in these languages and offered the vernacular schools necessary reading matter. Whatever their differences of opinion on other matters the missions were agreed that emphasis should be given to the vernaculars and the spread of vernacular schools was a significant outcome of their joint efforts.

Government policy immediately after the Colebrooke Report of 1831 was rather against the development of vernacular schools. The report criticized existing Government schools as places where 'nothing is taught . . . but reading the native languages and counting in the native character'.[106] It further recommended that the Government should not spend money on vernacular schools but should concentrate on promoting English education. At the same time Colebrooke recommended that the missionaries should be the sole authority in the field of vernacular education. Until there was a change in Government policy in favour of vernacular schools the missionaries remained indisputed leaders in the field.

It can be concluded that this was the kind of education in which they were most interested. At first they were concerned with English in a small way and only when the demand for it grew did they organize a system of English schools. A post Second World War writer summed up the policies of the missionaries in the following way: '. . . It was only in response to a spontaneous demand in the country that education in English was seriously undertaken . . . the emphasis in the early years . . . was on education in the vernacular'.[107]

Liberal versus vocational education

In a broad general sense liberal education may be academic and yet not aimed at preparing students for a particular occupation. Today it is sharply contrasted with vocational education and takes as its aim the education of the whole person. In spite of its merits such a form of liberal education can be followed by only the few for whom the material benefits derived from education are of secondary importance. In the nineteenth century an education intended to improve the cultural development of pupils was less important to the average Ceylonese than one which prepared him for future employment. Education, however, whatever its stated purpose was the chief agent of social mobility and a better life, and for this reason it was favoured by the mass of people, whether it was academic or not.

In fact only an education in English really offered material benefits, and the prestige it enjoyed is perfectly understandable. It was academic in the sense that education in the grammar and public schools of England was academic, but it was in demand. The missionaries perhaps realized this when they set up schools in the image of the secondary schools of England, and imparted a form of education which would be regarded today as highly academic but hardly 'liberal'. The content even in the best schools fell far short of what might be termed a liberal curriculum. It was narrow and specialized and there is no substantial evidence to indicate that the missions ever attempted to provide an education solely for the purpose of liberalizing the individual except that the treasures of European science and literature would be opened up to him.[108]

Nevertheless the kind of education given in the mission schools broadened the outlook of those who received it. Generally the curriculum included subjects such as Latin, Greek, some western classics, science, philosophy, mathematics, history and geography. The indigenous languages such as Sinhalese, Tamil, Pali and Sanskrit found a place later when the colleges began to prepare candidates for Indian and English university examinations. In short an education which prompted many pupils to follow it for its utilitarian value also succeeded in liberalizing them to some extent.

In the same way the vocational education provided in missionary schools was not such as to prepare girls and boys for a specific occupation in industry, commerce or agriculture. There is no evidence that the missionaries attempted this at any stage by setting up special vocational schools. It is not difficult to find reasons for this policy. A special committee on education reported in 1943[109] that 'even by 1910 there was no higher technical or professional education in the Island except in law and medicine'.[110] There was no real need for special vocational training because the foreign rulers had made no great effort to promote industry, commerce or agriculture. Vocational education in Ceylon is a product of the twentieth century. Indeed the foundations of it were laid as recently as 1943 by the special committee. The education given in the ordinary schools prior to this was sufficient to meet most occupational needs. The failure of the mission schools to provide specialized vocational training simply reflects the country's economic position.

An exception to this general policy is found in the few Church supported schools for physically disabled children such as the deaf and the blind in which the education provided had a vocational bias. The CMS school for the deaf and blind had a programme of the following kind:

> The outside activities of the school are well provided for. The boys have a Scout troop and Cub Pack, and the girls a Guide company with Brownies. They indulge in both indoor and outdoor games and the deaf boys have done a great deal in food production. There is a Coir Centre in charge of a government teacher where the blind boys make coir yarn, door mats, etc., and these find a ready sale. . . . In the deaf section both boys and girls make baskets and boxes out of palmyrah leaves. . . . The aim in view of the boys in these Industrial Homes is to make them self-supporting,[111]

In general it would be unwise to make a sharp distinction between liberal and vocational education in the system organized by the Christian missions. There was not the same need as there is now for vocational education. For the most part, education was academic and though not vocationally orientated, prepared young people for employment.

Evangelism versus ancillary services
The *raison d'être* of any missionary society is evangelism. In non-Christian countries the Christian Church could hardly expect people to come to it voluntarily. Missionaries sought to influence

people who by tradition and up-bringing would not as a matter of course be attracted to Christianity. Particularly in a country like Ceylon with an established religion evangelism permeated every aspect of missionary education. In the early mission schools Biblical studies were important. The Bible was often read as a textbook, and for non-English speaking children it had been translated into the local languages. The task is made clear in F. Lorenz Beven's *A History of the Diocese of Colombo* in which he writes:

> The early missionaries who opened schools in the villages, had, in addition to finding teachers and founding schools, to provide suitable textbooks for the use of children both in English and vernacular schools. It is not easy for us to realize at this time what a stupendous task this meant. The Bible had first of all to be translated into *Sinhalese* and *Tamil*, then books of moral instruction and readers. All this was done in those early days by the missionaries themselves, with the assistance of faithful Christian teachers.[112]

The function of Bible classes, which were held at regular intervals, was to 'emphasize the value of Bible reading by helping children to form that habit' and they were a common feature of the early missionary mission schools. One account of the situation was in the following words: 'some elder scholars willingly came to weekly Bible classes which my *Sinhalese* colleagues and I held and three were baptized along with a young woman on last Sunday'.[113] The work was often conducted by specially appointed Bible teachers.

The proselytizing achievements of the Christian missions can be attributed to their schools. Later this very success was to undermine the prestige of the missions as some comments of the late Sir D. B. Jayatilaka (one-time president of the Buddhist Theosophical Society) indicate. In a diamond jubilee souvenir of the Society he wrote:

> Their schools are avowedly for the purpose of spreading Christianity among the 'heathen'. Subordinating every other consideration to this purpose, the missionaries used the unique position they held for a length of time as the sole educators of the youth in the villages with an amount of reckless bigotry, which

while helping them to swell the number of so-called converts, tended to weaken, if not destroy, the moral sense of the children who came to them for education. Inducements, by no means spiritual, used to be fully offered by mission agents to win over young minds to Christanity. Children, Buddhists by birth and persuasion, were induced or compelled to study the Bible, attend Sunday classes, and take part in Christian services and ceremonies in the same manner as Christian boys and girls.[114]

It did not take the Buddhists long to realize that 'the real danger to Buddhism lay not in the open conversion of adults, but in the wholesale perversion of Buddhist children attending missionary schools'.[115] Very soon the conviction grew that 'so long as the education of the Buddhist children was in the hands of the Christian missionaries, the Buddhist faith ran the risk of extinction'. It was to remove this threat that the Buddhist leaders (many of whom were ironically the products of the mission schools) organized the Buddhist Theosophical Society. Ever since its formation it has been a formidable opponent of missionary educational work.

There is reason to believe that when the Government finally accepted a policy of religious neutrality it looked with suspicion on the evangelism found in missionary schools and made attempts to curtail such undemocratic activities. After 1900 educational legislation was designed to curb Christian influence throughout the country. Success came some fifty years later. The Wace Committee of 1905[116] can be regarded as the first of these official attempts.[117] In its report it revealed that it had grasped the situation quite clearly:

The schools which are under Christian Management fall roughly into two classes; those which are Roman Catholic and those which are not. In the Roman Catholic schools it is generally the case that the majority of children—often a large majority—are Roman Catholics. In the other Christian schools it is generally the case that a large majority of children are not Christians at all; in fact cases are not unknown in which every child in a school under Christian management is either a Buddhist or a Saivite. The Roman Catholic schools are the only considerable body of Christian schools of which the main object is to provide an education for children of their own denomination. The main object of the other schools under Christian management is to convert to Christianity the non-Christian children attending them.[118]

There can be little doubt that all the mission schools in Ceylon used their schools for evangelistic purposes. Indeed they were the very centres of this kind of activity.

THE IMPACT OF MISSIONARY ACTIVITY

Government educational policy based on the Colebrooke Commission's recommendations of 1831 helped to promote the mission schools. The Commission pointed to the growing demand for English and recommended that the Government vernacular schools should be closed down. The contribution of the American mission to the progress of English was praised and the lack of effort by the English missions in this field was roundly criticized. The commission also recommended that the principal native functionaries should have a competent knowledge of English and that opportunities to learn it should be offered. In short, the Government should promote English education in order to qualify Ceylonese for Government appointments. These recommendations encouraged in varying degrees the Baptists, the Wesleyans, the Americans, the CMS, the Presbyterians and the Roman Catholics to promote English education. This was virtually the start of a well-organized system of English schools.

The Colebrooke Commission downgraded vernacular education and as a result the missionaries took it over. Only during the last decades of the nineteenth century did the Government reverse its policy regarding vernacular schools. Then the missions were in such a strong position that the Government had to move with considerable caution. Governor Torrington described the situation in a letter in which he wrote:

the expansion of vernacular education by Government is also rendered somewhat delicate in consequence of the field being to a considerable extent occupied by missionary schools . . . in consequence of which a good understanding with the various missionary bodies may be considered to be indispensable to success; for it has been found as the result of experience that government schools, though conducted at a much greater expense cannot compete successfully with missionary schools in the same field.[119]

The Government's position was given by the Morgan Committee in 1867 when it reported that the value of the vernacular schools had been recognized by the Christian missions and that they had achieved a great deal but that Government vernacular schools were found only in the western province of the island.[120] This committee was responsible for a clear statement of policy that 'vernacular education could not be left entirely in the hands of the missions by the Government only aiding them with grants in aid'.[121] Previously the general conclusions of the Colebrooke Commission had not gone entirely unchallenged. In 1839, for example, Governor MacKenzie pointed out that '. . . before English shall be taught each scholar should learn to read his native language'.[122] Such opinions did not mean that the Government was prepared to do more than aid the missions in running vernacular schools. Even after the Morgan Committee report grants-in-aid were made to the vernacular schools run by the missions.

By the 1870s the missions had many vernacular schools, and a few English schools. The reverse was the case with Government schools. One reason for this state of affairs was that the English schools were expensive. Another was that the vernacular schools served the purposes of the missions well. The general demand for schools, however, resulted in a new type of school. These Anglo-vernacular schools were solely for native children who desired to learn English. They differed from the purely English schools in that the vernacular languages were used for teaching up to standard three. The Anglo-vernacular schools were less costly, which perhaps explains why most of the missions had more of them than they had English schools. Statistics for the year 1877 show the position clearly.[123] The Roman Catholics and the Presbyterians preferred English schools to Anglo-vernacular ones.

	CMS	American	Baptist	Wesleyan
English	6	1	1	13
Anglo-vernacular	25	12	7	14
Vernacular	111	111	21	118

	RC	SPG	Presby-terian
English	21	13	1
Anglo-vernacular	3	6	0
Vernacular	146	43	2

Two factors explain the growth of the Anglo-vernacular schools —expense and politics. L. J. Gratiaen explains the situation in the following manner:

> The political troubles of the sixties prejudiced English education in the eyes of the authorities. The remedy was more education, but in *Sinhalese* and *Tamil.* English education had few friends. Government's care was now for the extension of vernacular education in the villages. But the people's desire for English was too strong to be easily refused. There already existed also a large English-speaking population for whom an education in English was necessary. Government was less willing than before to maintain comparatively expensive English schools.[124]

Torrington, who was Governor from 1847 to 1850, had in fact advocated this kind of policy in a letter to the Home Government when he wrote that:

> English education has now been extended as far as there is legitimate demand for it, thus leaving the Government free while it merely provides for the efficiency of the present English educational establishments, to direct its efforts towards the extension of education in the vernacular schools.[125]

The existing English establishments were provided for by the system of grants-in-aid to the mission schools.

Naturally the missions were in favour of this kind of support. It grew out of the provisions contained in a Minute dated 27 March 1841, from Governor MacKenzie which authorized the Central School Commission[126] 'to grant sums in aid of any private schools which they may consider deserving of encouragement, but, always on condition that they shall have full right of inspection and examination'.[127] In 1843 grants-in-aid were extended to non-Government schools which complied with the Department's requirements[128] and made provision 'for the education of boys and girls through the medium of English'.[129] To be eligible for a grant the mission schools had to meet the following conditions. Only the first hour of the day was to be used for religious work—teaching or worship. Religious instruction was to be confined to simple explanations of the Bible and the leading tenets of Christianity. They were to be given in a spirit which would not exclude any scholar on the grounds of denominational teaching. Any child whose parents or guardians objected to religious instruction was allowed to withdraw from the class during the period.[130] There was, however, no obligation on the part of the school to ask parents whether or not they wished their children to attend such classes.

The missions found the conditions 'strict' and objectionable. The Reverend T. J. Stephen, vicar of Jaffna, criticized as 'insufferable' the Government's 'attempt at regulating the nature and the mode and at limiting the amount of religious education to be given'.[131] Yet in spite of this kind of objection the missions accepted Government grants and were prepared to abide by the conditions laid down from time to time. In Jaffna the grant system first 'took root' when the Wesleyan and American missions received grants from the start of the scheme. It gradually spread to other parts of the country and became indispensable to missionary effort. Indeed it led to the expansion of the English mission schools. At present all the leading English schools which previously belonged to the missions were established after the grant system was started. Buddhist and Hindu aided schools were started at the same time but neither group was able to match the privileged and well organized Christian missions.

The provision of public funds to schools which gave religious instruction to children of another faith was open to criticism. The conscience clause previously mentioned placed responsibility on parents. The Wace committee of 1905 pointed out that in many Christian schools a hundred per cent of the children were non-Christians, yet a primary aim of the schools was to convert to Christianity the children attending them. The extension of grants to mission schools was held to be anomalous in that 'funds raised by taxation were used to support a movement for changing the religion of those taxed'.[132] The Commission thought it doubtful whether 'public opinion will permanently allow the payment of a grant, unless it is coupled with some guarantee that religious instruction shall not be given to those who disapprove of it'.[133] Indeed in any multi-religious country like Ceylon there is need in a compulsory system of education to safeguard the religious beliefs of the people.

There was, however, vehement opposition to the incorporation of a new conscience clause as a condition of paying grants-in-aid. Events forced one to be introduced. The earlier clause dating back to 1841 had been somewhat negative. A more positive approach was introduced in the Education Ordinance No. 31 of 1939, as a result of which the Christian schools were prevented from giving religious instruction to non-Christian children without the written consent of their parents.[134] The regulations for assisted schools were brought up to date and brought under greater Governmental control the activities of the mission schools which continued to receive assistance provided the rules were kept.

One outcome of these early financial arrangements was that education was promoted by private and denomination bodies rather than by the State. The Christian missions monopolized English education and as foreigners virtually controlled the whole educational system. This power did not go unchallenged during the nineteenth century but it was not until towards the end of it, when the position of the Church in the running of the schools in England changed, was any very great attempt made to place educational policy firmly in the hands of a Government department. After 1870 there was a weakening of church control over education in Ceylon. But effective State influence over this denominational control really dates back to the State Council period of government (1931–47) under the Donoughmore Constitution.[135] A universal franchise placed more power than previously in the hands of elected representatives and the educational reforms during the period, and particularly those introduced by the Special Committee on Education of 1943,[136] led to varying degrees of State control over mission schools. In principle the denominational institutions were recognized as constituting a separate system working side by side with that of the State, but the grant system gave the Government effective control over them.

Independence in 1947 created a need for a national system of education in keeping with the national and cultural aspirations of the people. A denominational system in which the majority of schools were conducted by Christian missions could not be justified in a country where over 90 per cent of the population was non-Christian. During the fifties the Government considered the feasibility of absorbing all denominational schools into the State system. Justification for this policy can be found in the fact that all denominational schools were built with the help of the State.

The final chapter was written when the Assisted Schools and Training Colleges (supplementary Provisions) Act No. 8 of 1961 made the Director of Education the manager of all assisted denominational and private schools. This takeover by the State virtually brought to an end the Christian mission school system. Hardly any Christian schools now exist in Ceylon[137] and the foundations of a national system of education have been laid to provide for the growing needs of independent *Lanka* (Ceylon).

Social and political consequences
Before Ceylon came under the influence of the mission schools its social system and school organization was geared to Buddhist thought. Nevertheless, as a close associate of India, the Hindu influence was also evident. Judged on the literature of the country, it can be assumed that education in Ceylon in the pre-Christian era had been well developed. Over twenty-five centuries the Buddhist educational system had cherished its original aims and yet had undergone subtle changes in face of the changing needs of the country. The secular learning provided in recent times in the Pirivenas is indicative of such adaptation. Somehow or other Buddhist education has always kept pace with changing social conditions. Only when the influence of Christian education was most strongly felt was this ancient Buddhist social and religious matrix loosened. The arrival of foreign educators—the Christian missionaries—initiated the breakdown of Ceylonese society and laid the foundations of a new one.

Although they did not organize a system of education the way of life of the Portuguese and the importance they gave to the learning of their language were sufficient to undermine the cultural and social heritage of the people. A few of them were converted so successfully by the Portuguese that they were able to withstand severe persecution from their foreign successors, the Dutch. The very elaborate Dutch system of education was, to be sure, aimed at the mass conversion of Catholic and non-Christian children to the Protestant faith. The English missions were not very different in that their intention was to convert people to their own faith. One important difference between English and Dutch Government policy was that while the English missions received no official State sanction the Dutch missions had the official support and approval of their Government.

An immediate impact of the missionaries was spiritual, and a significant proportion of the people changed its religion. Yet today only some 10 per cent of the population are Christians so that it cannot be said that three centuries of missionary work has been outstandingly successful as far as the spiritual conquest of Ceylon is concerned. On the other hand its influence on the social norms and the social structure of the island has been very considerable. Permanent changes have been brought about, for example, in the caste system, one of the most important institutions in Ceylon when the missionaries arrived. In ancient and medieval Ceylon a person's place in society, the education he received, and his vocation in life were decided by the caste to which he belonged. It was 'an institution which keeps together a community of people by not allowing its members to marry outside their group. It further prevents its members mingling freely with those of other castes by forbidding them to take meals in common with anyone outside their caste'.[138] The spread of Hinduism in Ceylon led to an extension of the caste system.

Caste influenced occupational patterns which 'formed the corner-stone of the economic and social life of the country'.[139] The type of occupation a man followed 'determined not only the income of a particular community, but also its social status'.[140] Occupations seem to have been considered hereditary so that the 'people had no choice of occupation'.[141] Perhaps it was considered 'wrong to abandon the hereditary occupation in pursuit of another even though this might be more lucrative'.[142] Hence the caste to which a person was born decided his destiny.

The Christian mission schools helped to reduce caste conscious-ness, ameliorated the plight of the underprivileged, and in general emphasized the ideal of equality. The provision of educational facilities in the remotest parts of the island gave the backward communities opportunities they would not otherwise have had. The caste barriers which prevented free intercourse between the different social groups within the community were weakened. Moreover the secular education provided in mission schools pre-pared members of every caste for employment. Occupation began to be determined less by caste and more by educational qualifications. Education became the ladder of social mobility. There can be little doubt that this radical change benefited the country.

At the same time a new social structure was created. A new, previously unknown, class of people came into being. Members of this new middle class 'lived chiefly in the towns and had a good knowledge of English which was very necessary for government jobs and mercantile services. From this class of people . . . many of whom received their education in English in mission schools . . . also came a great number of teachers, doctors, lawyers and clerks'.[143]

Christian education initiated certain cultural changes too. A review of them cannot be attempted here but some observations of an ethnologist writing about cultural changes in Ceylon under foreign domination may be appropriate. He pointed out that change was a common feature of all Asiatic lands, but added that such

> . . . changes have been more profound in Ceylon, than for example in our neighbour India. For, as a small geographical unit, the changes have gone far more deep into social life in Ceylon and because of the unbroken succession of westernizing influences, from the time of the coming of the Portuguese in 1505 the cultural changes have been both intensive and extensive. The changes beginning with the coastal cities have permeated, though in varying extent, to the villages.[144]

The influence extended to domestic institutions such as wedding customs and funeral rites even among non-Christians. The westernization of bride and groom has occurred through the acceptance of foreign attire and the 'modernizing of the wedding feast which even in villages will not be complete without intoxication, cakes and patties; for it will not be up-to-date to entertain the guests on the traditional confectionery'.[145]

Another consequence of missionary education has been the creation of a group of people, often described as westernized and denationalized, who are regarded by some as aliens in their own country. This 'class of people eager for Western knowledge' by their 'excessive admiration of the West, coupled with an increased necessity for education in English in order to enjoy the best fruits of Western culture, tended to ignore their own national culture'.[146] Sometimes the blame for this deculturization is laid 'at the door of

Christianity'[147] but those who defend the Church against such a charge consider that change was inevitable and 'would have taken place whether there was Christianity or not'.[148]

The greatest influence of the mission schools was on social mobility. It benefited Christians and non-Christians alike although the former were often at an advantage because of the prestige they enjoyed. An English education helped to raise the status of all those who could benefit from it. There is some truth in the claim made by Christian leaders today that 'the present national consciousness itself is due to the English education received in the mission schools by Christians as well as non-Christians'.[149]

Particular attention should, of course, be paid to the influence of the mission schools on the emancipation of women. Through it the quality of family life was greatly improved. To a large extent social change depends for its success on the participation in social affairs of enlightened women with opportunity and responsibility. The Christian missions always recognized this and 'the instruction of females was one of the first subjects to attract their attention'.[150] At the beginning of the twentieth century, there were girls' schools in every part of the country preparing some girls, at least, for higher education in the universities, others for professions such as teaching, the law, medicine and clerical work and still others for domestic service. The time is near when they will enter more fully into the administrative service of the country. Already Ceylon is proud to have produced the first woman Prime Minister.

The political consequences of missionary education need not be stressed because the social revolution which it initiated was in turn the cause of political change. The cry for political independence grew out of the social conscience of an educated minority. Movements for constitutional reform originated among the English educated middle class of Sinhalese and Tamils who, after learning about the politics of the west, fought for the freedom of the nation. It is perhaps sufficient to recall that a majority of the elder statesmen of the country came from this new middle class. As a matter of fact, the first Prime Minister of independent Ceylon, the Hon. Mr. D. S. Senanayake, received his education at St. Thomas College, the foremost Christian institution in the country.

Ranjit Ruberu

NOTES

1. See *The Mahavamas or the Great Chronicle of Ceylon* (trans. by Wilhelm Geiger and published for the Pali Text Society, London 1934), pp. 54–61.
2. Jayatilaka, Sir D. B., 'Christian Methods of Conversion' in *Diamond Jubilee Souvenir of the Buddhist Theosophical Society of Ceylon, 1880–1940* (Colombo 1940).
3. For more information on Buddhist education see: Rahula, W., *History of Buddhism in Ceylon* (Colombo 1956); and Ruberu, R., *Education in Colonial Ceylon* (Colombo 1962), pp. 1–15.
4. Perera, L. H. Horace, *Ceylon under Western Rule* (London 1955), p. 58.
5. Perera, S. G., *Historical Sketches* (Jaffna 1939), p. 70.
6. de Queyroz, Fernão, *The Temporal and Spiritual Conquest of Ceylon* (trans. S. G. Perera, Colombo 1930), vol 1, pp. 235–6.
7. The Ceylon Mission of the Society of Jesuits was established in 1602. Perera, S. G., *Jesuits in Ceylon in the XVI and XVII centuries* (Madura 1941), p. 30.
8. The Dominicans arrived in 1544, Queyroz, p. 257.
9. Perera, S. G., 'Jesuits in Ceylon in the Sixteenth and Seventeenth Centuries' in *Ceylon Antiquary*, vol II, p. 7.
10. *Ibid.*, p. 34.
11. Dutch East India Company. Founded in 1602 and obtained authority from the State General of United Netherlands for the monopoly of trade in the East Indian seas. This commercial company became a political power and conquered extensive territories in the East.
12. Under Dutch laws of compulsory attendance children were expected to remain at school until the age of fifteen. On leaving school they were expected to be present at school on a part-time basis for four more years to receive instruction in religious knowledge.
13. Frederick North, 1766–1827, Governor of Ceylon from 1796 to 1805.
14. Turner, L. J. B., *Collected Papers on the History of the Maritime Provinces of Ceylon* (Colombo 1923), p. 162.
15. British administration in Ceylon commenced with the subjugation of the Dutch territories in the country in 1796, which made the British the rulers of them. In 1815 the remaining parts of the island were also captured, leaving the British sole rulers.
16. This was the policy pursued by the nineteenth-century British, and was nothing new to Ceylon.
17. LMS: Founded in 1795 for the sole purpose of 'spreading the knowledge of Christ among the heathen and unenlightened nations'.

See Lovett, R., *The History of the London Missionary Society 1795–1895* (London 1899), vol 1, p. 20.

18. Fernando, C. N. V., 'Christian Missionary enterprise in the early British Period', in *Ceylon University Review*, vol VII, p. 198.

19. Palm, J. D., de Vos M. C. C., Ehrhardt, J. P., Read, W.

20. Frederic North was Governor at the time.

21. Letter of North to the secretary of the LMS, 8 April 1805 (LMS archives).

22. Lovett, vol I, p. 21.

23. The BMS was founded in 1792 with the chief object of 'diffusing the knowledge of Jesus Christ through the whole world beyond the British Isles, by the preaching of the Gospel, the translation and publication of the Holy Scripture and the establishment of Schools'.

24. Sir Robert Brownrigg, 1759–1853, Governor of Ceylon from 1811 to 1820. His affection for the missionaries becomes evident from the fact that all Christian missions established themselves in the island during his administration.

25. BMS, *Periodical Accounts relative to the Baptist Missionary Society*, (Clipstone 1800–17), vol V, p. 141.

26. Charter, H. J., *Ceylon Advancing (An Account of the History and Development of Baptist Missionary Work in the Nineteenth Century* (London 1955), p. 55.

27. *Ibid.*, p. 58.

28. Wesleyan Methodist Missionary Society—founded in 1814.

29. Tebb, R., 'The Wesleyan Mission', in Wright, A. (Ed.), *Twentieth Century Impressions of Ceylon* (London 1907).

30. *Ibid.* p.276

31. The American mission in Ceylon consisted of missionaries of the American Boards of Commissioners for Foreign Missions. This was founded in 1812 by the General Association for Massachusetts for the propagation of Christianity in Asia.

32. *Missionary Register* 1815, p. 137.

33. The mission's gratitude to the Government has been expressed in letters sent by the missionaries to the Governor. See C.O. 54, Series 59.

34. Letter from Brownrigg to Secretary of State on 27 March 1816.

35. CMS, founded in 1799 as a result of the Evangelical revival in England. The spread of Christianity in Africa and Asia was the chief objective of the mission.

36. Stock, E., *The History of the Church Missionary Society, Its Men and its Works* (London 1899), vol I, p. 216.

37. These included Samuel Lambrick, Robert Mayer, Benjamin Ward and Joseph Knight.

38. Colombo, Galle, Mannar and Jaffna.

39. Latourette, K. S., *A History of the Expansion of Christianity* (London 1947), vol VI, p. 132.

40. *Ibid.*, p. 144.

41. *Ibid.*, p. 156.

42. *Ibid.*, p. 157.

43. Fernando, C. N. V., 'The History of Christianity in Ceylon' in de Soysa, H. (Ed.), *The Church of Ceylon, Her Faith and Mission a Centenary Book* (Colombo 1945).

44. de Soysa, p. 129.

45. Harvard, W. M., *History of the Church Missionary Society* (London 1830), and *Missionary Register*, 1819, Letter 25 June 1818.

46. Europeans included the English and the Eurasians, the descendants of the Portuguese and the Dutch.

47. Bertolacci, A., *A View of the Agricultural, Commercial, and Financial Interests of Ceylon* (London 1917), p. 42.

48. Crozier, G. M. (Ed.), *Report of the Wesleyan Methodist Mission in Ceylon* (Colombo 1895), address of the President, 4 Dec. 1827.

49. Instructions of the Home Committee to the Ceylon Mission, 8 Oct. 1817 (CMS archives).

50. Letter of Secretary of State to Governor Barnes, 25 Aug. 1821 C.O. 55, 66.

51. Lord Bathurst was Secretary of State for the Colonies.

52. Letter of Secretary of State to Governor Brownrigg, 27 March 1816, C.O. 54, 59.

53. Letter of Secretary of State to Governor Barnes, 18 June 1820, C.O. 55, 63.

54. Letter of Governor Barnes to Secretary of State, 10 Oct 1820., C.O. 54, 77.

55. Observations of the Secretary of State, 27 March 1816, C.O. 54, 59.

56. Letter sent by the Governor's Secretary to the American mission, 22 Sept. 1820 (CMS archives).

57. Observations of the Secretary of State in a letter to Brownrigg, 20 Oct. 1813, C.O. 55, 63.

58. British rule ended in 1947.

59. Charter, p. 122.

60. The Buddhist Theosophical Society was formed in 1880 to spread Buddhist education by establishing schools and colleges. The corresponding Hindu Society—*Saiva Paripalana Sabha*—was founded in 1880 for a similar purpose.

61. Buddhist Theosophical Society—*Diamond Jubilee Souvenir*, address by the President, Dr. A. D. Silva.

62. *Report of the Special Committee on Education (Ceylon)*, Sessional Paper XXIV (Colombo 1943).

63. *Ibid.*, p. 136.

64. Letter of Rev. James Selkirk to Secretary of CMS London, 1 April 1828 (CMS archives).

65. Buddhist monks.

66. Letter of Rev. James Selkirk to Secretary of CMS, 14 May 1833 (CM.S archives).

67 Letter of Rev. T. Squance to Secretary of CMS London, 12 Nov. 1817 (WMMS archives).

68. The Central School Commission was appointed in 1841 as the body responsible for the administration of Government schools.

69. *Report of the Special Committee on Education.*

70. Colebrooke Commission *Report.* See Colebrooke–Cameron Papers, C.O. 54, vol 122 (London 1832).

71. Ordinance 33 of 1884.

72. *Report of the Special Committee on Education.*

73. This refers to the *Assisted Schools and Training Colleges (Special Provisions* Act No. 5 of 1960 by which the Assisted denominational schools were taken over by the Government and placed under the management of the Director of Education.

74. Comments of the President, Wesleyan Methodist Mission in Ceylon at a meeting held 4 June 1827 in Crozier.

75. Letter of Rev. Knight and Rev. Ward to Secretary of CMS, 11 Jan. 1820 (CMS archives).

76. *Missionary Register* 1819, p. 9.

77. Letter of Secretary of CMS to Rev. Lambrick, 12 Aug. 1822 (CMS archives).

78. Letter of Rev. Robert Newstead to Secretary of WMMS, 30 Oct. 1817 (MMS archives).

79. Letter of the Wesleyan Missionaries B. Clough and G. Erskine, 25 Jan. 1820, C.O. London Records 54/60.

80. Observations of Rev. D. J. Gogerly of the Wesleyan Methodist Mission, *Colombo Journal* (Colombo, 16 Feb. 1833).

81. WMMS, *The Tenth Report of the General Wesleyan Methodist Missionary Society* (London 1827).

82. Letter of Governor Brownrigg to the Wesleyan Methodist missionaries, 30 Jan. 1820, C.O. London Records 54/60.

83. *Colombo Journal*, 16 Feb. 1833.

84. WMMS Archives *MSS, Native Schools Report* 1818.

85. Letter of American mission sent to the Colebrooke Commission, 2 Dec. 1833, C.O. 416, 6.

86. WMMS *Report 1827*. Address of the President of the Mission in Ceylon, 4 Dec. 1827.

87. *Columbo Journal*, 16 Feb. 1833.

88. WMMS, *Native Schools Report*, 1818.

89. *Colombo Journal*, 16 Feb. 1833.

90. Director of Public Instruction, *Administration Report* (Colombo 1900).

91. Letter of Governor Brownrigg to the Wesleyan mission, 30 Jan. 1820, C.O. London Records 54/60.

92. *Final Report of the Commission on Higher Education in the National Languages* (Sinhalese and Tamil), Sessional Paper, X, (Colombo 1956).

93. *Ibid.*

94. *Minutes* of Committee meeting, 4 Feb. 1824 (WMMS archives).

95. Statement concerning a mission college for Tamil and other youth in Jaffna, 1823.

96. Foundation of Institution Proceedings, 8 Nov. 1828 (CMS Archives).

97. WMMS *Report 1818*, p. 112.

98. Statement concerning the Mission College for Tamil and other Youths in Jaffna, 1823.

99. WMMS *Report 1827*, p. 112. The word 'college' was employed for English schools which gave instruction beyond the sixth standard. Earlier they were known as 'superior schools'.

100. Although the colleges of the missions were responsible for the education of this group, it should be mentioned that from about 1870 onwards Buddhist colleges also came into existence and later followed Hindu colleges as well.

101. Instructions of Home Committee, 8 Oct. 1817 (CMS archives).

102. Letter of Rev. J. Bailey to Secretary, 8 Dec. 1821 (CMS archives).

103. Charter, p. 262.

104. Wyndham, H. A., *Native Education: Ceylon, Java, Formosa, the Philippines, French Indo-China and British Malaya* (London 1933), p. 19.

105. *Ibid.*, p. 24.

106. Colebrooke Commission *Report*, see Colebrooke–Cameron Papers, C.O. 54, vol 122, London 1832.

107. de Soysa, account of boys' schools by Rev. R. S. de Saram.

108. Chelliah, J. V., *A Century of English Education* (Colombo 1922), p. 9.

109. *Report of the Special Committee on Education.*

110. *Ibid.*

111. Beven, F. L., *A History of the Diocese of Colombo, A Centenary Volume* (Colombo 1946), p. 163.

112. *Ibid.*, pp. 315–16.

113. Charter, p. 84.
114. Jayatilaka.
115. *Ibid.*
116. *The Commission on Elementary Education in Ceylon*, Sessional Paper XXVIII (Colombo 1905) (Wace Committee Report).
117. What the Wace Committee recommended was the introduction of a conscience clause into educational legislation. For details see later.
118. Wace Committee Report, p. 4.
119. Letter of Governor Torrington quoted in Barrow, Sir George, *Ceylon Past and Present* (London 1857), p. 164.
120. *Sub-committee of the Legislative Council appointed to inquire into the state and prospects of education in the Island*, Ceylon Sessional Paper, VIII (Colombo 1867) (The Morgan Report).
121. *Ibid.*, p. 13.
122. Governor Mackenzie's address to the Legislative Council, 24 Dec. 1839.
123. Director of Public Instruction *Administration Report for 1877*, p. 142 C.
124. Gratiaen, L. J., *Government Vernacular Schools in Ceylon, 1870–1900* (Colombo 1933), pp. 2–3.
125. Letter of Torrington to Home Government quoted in Barrow, p. 163.
126. This was the central body organised under Mackenzie in 1841 for the administration of Government schools.
127. Minute of Governor Mackenzie, 27 March 1841.
128. Resolution of the Central School Commission, 18 Sept. 1843.
129. *Ibid.*
130. Other requirements included the attendance of a minimum number of children, the appointment, payment and dismissal of teachers, according to the rules of the Central School Commission, and schools to be open for inspection.
131. Rev. T. J. Stephen's evidence to the Morgan Committee.
132. Wace Committee *Report*, p. 4.
133. *Ibid.*
134. The full text of the Conscience Clause of 1939 is: No child belonging to a religious denomination other than that to which the proprietor or manager of an assisted school belongs shall be permitted to attend any Sunday school or any place of religious worship or to attend any religious observance or any instruction in religious subjects in the school or elsewhere unless the parent of the child has expressly stated in writing his consent that his child shall attend such place of religious worship or receive instruction in religious subjects in the school. Under this constitution a State Council formed of elected

117

members with both legislative and executive powers was introduced in 1931.

135. Under this constitution a State Council formed of elected members with both legislative and executive powers was introduced in 1931.

136. *Report of the Special Committee on Education,* Ceylon Sessional Paper XXIV (Colombo 1943).

137. The exception to this is found in a small number of Christian schools which have decided to remain independent. Although they are independent they have to follow State educational practices and policies.

138. Ariyapala, M. B., *Society in Mediaeval Ceylon* (Colombo 1958), p. 285.

139. *Ibid.*, p. 329.

140. *Ibid.*

141. *Ibid.*

142. *Ibid.*

143. Thillayampalam, E. M., 'The Influence of the Church on Social Life', in de Soysa, p. 184.

144. Raghavan, M. D., 'Sinhalese Culture', in *The New Lanka* (Colombo 1949), vol 1, p. 85.

145. *Ibid.*, p. 86.

146. Fernando, p. 126.

147. *Ibid.*

148. *Ibid.*, p. 126.

149. Thillayampalam, p. 184.

150. Pridham, C., *An Historical, Political and Statistical Account of Ceylon and its Dependencies* (London 1849), vol 1, p. 431.

4

MISSIONARY ACTIVITY AND THE SYRIAN CHRISTIANS IN KERALA*

Grace George

THE State of Kerala[1] was established under the States Re-organization Act of 1956. In 1957 a Communist[2] Government was voted into power in a free election. Presidential rule was proclaimed in 1964 and maintained when the election of March 1965 proved indecisive. The finely-drawn balance of power between the Congress Party and the Communist Party of India in Kerala is not, however, the only unique feature of a state which, in drawing together Travancore, Cochin and Malabar recreated a political unit which had, according to tradition been a prosperous little kingdom called Chera, ruled by the Perumals from the third to ninth century A.D. Its beauty is legendary,[3] but the Western Ghats running the length of the country from north to south and varying in height from 2,500 to 8,000 feet do more than add grandeur to the scene: in the past[4] they effectively cut Kerala off from the rest of India. The 340 miles of coastline connected in some places by canals to an extensive system of waterways parellel to the coast offer more than the charm of lagoons and backwaters; they have made access to Kerala from the sea easy. Pepper, spices and ivory attracted a succession of foreign traders, some of whom established colonies. Isolation from the rest of India and a rich admixture of foreign settlers are important factors which have contributed to Kerala's present position as the most literate state in India.

In 1961 the literacy rate in Kerala was nearly twice the national figure. The percentage of literate women compared with the national figure was even more impressive, being more than three

* The Editor and Mrs. George wish to thank Father J. Thaikoodan for allowing them to incorporate in this chapter information drawn from his M.Phil. thesis.

times greater. This situation was not very different from that which existed in 1900 although, of course, literacy rates have risen everywhere in India since that time. Another indication of the high level of education in the state is the fact that in 1960 nearly 100 per cent of the school age population[5] between six and eleven was in school; for the eleven to fourteen group the figure was 48 per cent; and for the fourteen to seventeen group over 23 per cent. Facilities were available for an even larger proportion of the middle age group. Finally, in terms of finance the Government of Kerala claims to spend more on education than any other Government in the world. Certainly in 1960 the expenditure of over 33 per cent of the total budget[6] on education in Kerala far surpassed that of any other Indian state. Rajasthan, with a percentage of almost 25, came next.

Paradoxically Kerala is a poor state.[7] To be sure in the fifties 3·4 per cent of the national income of India came from a state whose area represented only 1·2 per cent of the whole. Industrial growth has not, however, kept pace with population expansion. The result is a high level of unemployment and a lower *per capita* income than the all-India average. Two reasons have been advanced for this situation in a state where the density of population is amost three times that of India as a whole. The first reason is the continuance of small scale economic units in the form of cottage industries. The second reason advanced is political instability.

Evidentally any explanation of the present educational, economic and political situation in Kerala would have to take account of a great many historical and present-day factors. Of particular interest here is the fact that among the most advanced communities in the State are the Syrian Christians who number some $3\frac{1}{2}$ millions compared with $10\frac{1}{4}$ million Hindus and 3 million Muslims. The history of the Syrian Christians dates from the first century A.D. when, according to them, an apostle of Christ,[8] St. Thomas, landed near Cranganore and converted many of the foreign community of Jews as well as many high-caste Hindus, among whom was the Chera king's nephew. A knowledge of the subsequent political and social status of these Christians is important in attempting to understand what made it possible for the English missionaries to begin their educational work in the nineteenth century.

The Perumals[9] welcomed them and gave them an honourable place in society. The unusual caste system in Kerala made it possible for them to be assigned the role of the merchants (Vaishya caste) along with the Jews and the Mohammedans. The Brahmins of Kerala were called Nambutiris[10] whose special concern was the study of religious rites and practices, and education. Since there was no warrior caste (Kshatriya) this role was assigned to the Nairs—members of an inferior Shudra caste. The weakness of the family system among these military men and the extent to which it strengthened their system of education particularly in the arts of warfare are of interest because it undoubtedly influenced the kind of education provided for the Syrian Christians; two aspects of whose position prior to the arrival of the British are very significant. For centuries the local leaders helped them by giving them grants, raising them to the position of independent merchants and making them rulers of certain principalities.[11] By the time the Portuguese arrived in 1502 the position of the Syrian Christians had declined during nearly six centuries of feud and anarchy. Their religious zeal and teaching had waned. The Portuguese, partly through a desire to convert the Christians of Malabar to Catholicism, offered the Syrians protection, indeed some of the members of the community met Vasco Da Gama[12] to seek it. The next Portuguese governor, Albuquerque, inserted in a treaty with the Rajah a clause designed to ensure that the ancient rights of the Syrians should be reviewed. Other evidence of this protection is found in the fact that the Christians of Cochin[13] were given a place among the high court judges by the Portuguese. The latter established elementary parochial schools, orphanages, Jesuit colleges[14] for higher studies and seminaries for theological students. Attempts made at the turn of the sixteenth century to bring the Malabar Church into line with the Roman Catholic Church through the autocratic actions of a Jesuit who was made official head of the Church resulted in a dramatic demonstration of independence[15] and the withdrawal from this church of a large number of Syrians. One reason for the failure of the Portuguese in India has, in fact, been attributed to their antagonism towards the non-Catholic section of the Syrians in Malabar.

The protection offered to the Christians in Cochin was, however, transferred to the Dutch during their period of occupation (1663–1766) and to the British. Between the eclipse of Portuguese power and the arrival of the English missionaries in 1806 other missionaries from Europe were treated well by the Rajahs, the Dutch and the British and there was no opposition to them from the non-Christians.

The existence of a group of Christians which for the most part had from early times enjoyed the political support of the ruling authorities goes a long way towards explaining why conditions in Kerala were congenial to missionary educational work in the early nineteenth century. Their own education had been influenced by the traditional education in Tamil-speaking Southern Travancore. They had imitated to some extent the education of the high-caste Hindus, i.e. the Nambutiris, and the military emphasis given to the education of the Nairs. The Jews[16] and Muslims[17] had their own liturgical schools and each group as traders felt the need for education. Traditions, therefore, existed which were certainly not antithetical to the introduction of a European pattern of education. Political conditions ensured that the mission schools had the support of the British authorities when they were established.

Treaties[18] between the East India Company and the Rajahs of Travancore and Cochin made the Company responsible for protecting them from external attack but placed internal administrative responsibility in the hands of the Rajahs. In these matters the Resident could only offer advice. Thus Colonel Macaulay was able to invite a missionary to work in Travancore without seeking official sanction. An attempt to assassinate Macaulay when he was Resident failed. The Rajahs of Travancore and Cochin sued for peace and a new treaty in 1809[19] established British control over the internal administration of the States. In 1810 Colonel Munro replaced Macaulay and was instrumental in the following year in having the young Ranee installed as ruler.[20] After helping her as unpaid prime minister to settle the affairs of the temples Munro was able to turn his attention to the missions. He appealed to the Church Mission Society (CMS) for help through the Corresponding Committee in Madras. Two missionaries were sent to help the Syrian Christians, the first of whom, the Reverend Norton, arrived in 1816.

Meanwhile the situation generally had improved for the missionaries. In 1813 Grant's observations, written in 1792 at the instance of Wilberforce, were published. He introduced a resolution into Parliament 'to promote the interest and happiness of the inhabitants of the British Dominion in India'.[21] It is not necessary here to assess the influence on the Company of Grant's observations on the conditions of the Asiatic subjects of Britain, suffice it to say that in the new charter granted to the East India Company in 1813 educational activities were encouraged and the first educational grant was made. Previously in 1808 the Court of Directors had declared a policy of strict religious neutrality.[22] The new charter, without specifically mentioning the missionaries, gave encouragement to them. Certainly for some twenty years the Company was not loath to let the missionaries provide a basis of education for the Indian population. By 1835 when Macaulay's Minute virtually decided the English-vernacular issue in favour of Anglicizing education many aspects of the pattern of education had already been established. It is with the significance of this period of development in Kerala that this chapter is principally concerned.

During these crucial years of missionary educational activity it is important to remember that the region now known as Kerala consisted of the two native states of Travancore in the south, Cochin in the centre and the British district of Malabar in the north. The character of missionary educational activity varied from region to region partly because of local conditions and also because the two major missionary societies, the London Mission Society (LMS) and the CMS worked in different regions, had somewhat different policies and before 1836 at least, did not really compete against each other.

The LMS[23] worked principally in southern Travancore among a mixed population, the majority of whom were Tamils. Much of the mission's activity centred around Nagarcoil and Trivandrum. Until 1836 the policy of the CMS was to work with the Syrian Christians. The centre of activity was Kottayam but some work was carried on in Alleppy on the coast among a mixed population of French, Portuguese, Italians, Syrian Christians, Roman Catholics, Muslims and Soodrans.[24] Further north in Cochin[25] and Cranganore[26] the CMS opened schools for Jews.

Two reports[27] influenced the missionary societies in their decision to send workers to Kerala. At the request of Lord William Bentinck, Governor of Madras, the Reverend Dr. Kerr was sent to Malabar in 1806 and reported on conditions there. In the same year the Governor General Lord Wellesley sent Dr. C. Buchanan to enquire into the position of the Syrian Christians. Support was needed, however, from English people at home and the officials of the East India Company in India, whose policy of strict non-interference in religious matters had prevented the Company from helping the Syrian Christians. The interest of Macaulay, the Resident to the Court of Travancore according to the treaty of 1795,

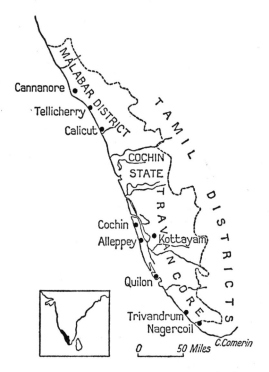

KERALA IN THE MISSIONARY PERIOD 1806–34

was aroused by the reports and he supported the LMS missionary,[28] the Reverend Ringeltaube when he arrived in 1806. Munro was to offer even more direct assistance. Indeed early in 1815 he wrote to the Madras Corresponding Committee[29] requesting the services of two Anglican missionaries.

At the turn of the eighteenth century the Christians in Malabar were divided into four sects, the Syrian Christians, the Romeo-Syrians, the Latin Catholics and the Protestants.[30] The Christians had long enjoyed a social status second only to the Brahmins. The Arabs arriving in the ninth century challenged the commercial supremacy of the Christians and by the beginning of the nineteenth century the increasing influence of the Arabs, the indifference of the Dutch, and the extermination of the Christians during the Mysore conquest of Malabar had contributed to their lowly position. The Syrian Christians were reported by Buchanan to be ignorant, all around he perceived 'symptoms of poverty and political depression', and the Church was in decline. Yet they received some sort of education and evidence of the standard reached by some members of the community can be found in the number of Christians employed in various departments of the two native states. The policy of the CMS was that their help should be exclusively for the Syrian Christians with the intention of improving their conditions and using them as instruments for the wider diffusion of Christianity.

Role of the Residents

The support the missionary societies received from the Residents Macaulay and Munro was evidently of great importance to their success. Equally significant is the extent to which both men were able to influence the local rulers and persuade them to give the missions direct help.

In Travancore, where the Reverend Ringeltaube[31] made a fresh start after his earlier experiences in North India, neither the Dutch nor the Danish missionaries had made any serious attempt to convert the local inhabitants. The Brahmins and the Nairs dominated the scene and Ringeltaube's mission attracted members of the Shanar community most of whom were ignorant and extremely poor. In addition there were a few Muslims, some Catholic and a few Protestant converts from the neighbouring Tamil country. Colonel Macaulay was able to help Ringeltaube to enter Travancore and defrayed some of his expenses but he was unable to persuade the Rajah and his prime minister to allow a church to be opened. After the attempt on his life Macaulay's position was stronger and permission to build a church was granted. At first, therefore, education received high priority. Even so the main aim was religious because, as Ringeltaube pointed out in a letter to London in 1813, 'It is vain to print and distribute Bibles if there are none who can read them'.[32] A year before his departure he gave an account in 1815 of the activities of the schools he had helped to establish. Although his schools were mainly for the children of converts he had allowed pupils from other communities to attend.

The three Rs formed the basis of instruction, with some religious teaching for Christians. There is no mention of English as the medium of instruction. By the time he left, Ringeltaube had seven schools, seven schoolmasters, and nearly 200 boys in attendance. No girls came. Among the aspects of these schools which justify the claim that they laid the foundation of modern education in Travancore were the building of schools as such, the replacement of cadjain leaf books by printed books, the regular payment of salaries to teachers, and the bringing together in the schools of members of various communities. On these foundations two LMS missionaries, the Reverends C. Mead and C. Mault, built.

By the time they arrived Colonel Munro had taken over from Macaulay as Resident. His régime is looked upon as a golden age. One reason for this was the influence he had on the Ranee—he had helped to gain power—and her successor. He had very strong views about the value of Christian education and as soon as he became Dewan of Travancore and Resident of the two native states[33] he persuaded the Ranee to take a considerable number of Syrian Christians into public service, so that in 1818 it was reported[34] that more than 200 Syrian Christians were employed as judges, collectors of revenue and so on. Munro concluded from his enquiry into the conditions of the Christians that education should be provided for the clergy, the Bible should be translated into the vernacular, the Government should support education by making appointments and providing grants, and that the improvement of education should be placed under the control of the missionaries. He was able to help both the LMS and the CMS in their attempts to build on the early foundations. In this he was greatly helped by the Charter of 1813 which allowed missionaries to come to India and authorized the first grant of money by the British Government for education in India.

When Munro arrived in 1810 communal strife and lawlessness were common. Indeed conditions had dissuaded missionaries from coming to Kerala. With the support of the State Governments Munro employed vigorous methods of rewards and punishment to effect change. Throughout he held to the view that native governments should be retained and that well-paid positions of dignity and trust should be given to the local inhabitants. Finding the Syrians divided among themselves Munro came to a decision which had far-reaching consequences. Each of the two divided

Syrian Christian groups claimed the right to draw on the interest on investments deposited by Macaulay. Asked to decide, Munro came down on the side of the Syrian Christians on condition that a college was established for the education of the community. Kottayam College was the outcome. The management of it was entrusted to the CMS. More money was needed and the Ranee was induced to give a site of sixteen acres. A small grant of money[35] was made and building materials for the construction of the seminary were donated. A further gift helped the missionaries to build a chapel attached to the college. Just before Munro left for England in 1818 two large donations from the Ranee, Rs. 20,000 and 2,000 acres of land known as Munro Island, helped to make the college self-supporting.

He was also able to help the LMS establish a post-primary school similar to that set up by the CMS at Kottayam in 1813. He hoped, before leaving for England, for 'something like a college with a printing press to be established in Nagarcoil'.[36] Considerable assistance was provided by the Ranee through tax reductions, monetary grants and materials. The influence of these two post-primary schools was of course widespread. The fact that the British Resident was able to win not only the acquiescence but the active and generous support of the local rulers is important to any understanding of the educational role these schools were able to play.

Evidently there was more than one motive behind Munro's policy of getting the CMS to help the Syrian Christians in their civic and religious affairs. He saw that in doing so he could anticipate their support in establishing without opposition the power of the British authorities. At the time there was hostility, and the hope that British power would weaken was common. A Minute to the Madras Government makes Munro's aims clear:

Our first objective is to put the Syrians upon a respectable footing. . . . We shall afterwards be able, if a sufficient number of missionaries can be obtained, to lay a foundation for the gradual extension of Christian knowledge among other classes of the people . . .'.

THE LMS

The first English LMS missionaries, the Reverends Mead and Mault, envisaged four kinds of school, a seminary or college, a girls' school, a school for industry and a bazaar school.[37] They were designed to meet the needs of Christians and non-Christians. Mead arrived in 1817 to find a few primary schools established by Ringeltaube. These village mission schools continued to form the backbone of the educational effort. They were not very different from other village schools except that religious instruction was provided and the teachers were paid by the mission. Apparently they were popular with the villagers except the Brahmins. To meet the religious objections of these Hindus and the Mohammedans a bazaar school was set up in Nagarcoil and in 1822 Mault reported that of the fifty boys in attendance some were Brahmins. As far as possible the British system of teaching was introduced but the breakdown of rote learning was not easily achieved.

When Mead arrived the need was for some form of post-primary school. One began to take shape in 1819 and, as the seminary, quickly took pride of place among the LMS schools. Regulations drawn up in 1828[38] make the objects of the seminary clear. Promising youth connected with the mission were educated as native teachers and schoolmasters. The curriculum was based on theology, useful knowledge and languages. Clever students learned Greek in order to read the Bible in that language. Subjects such as chemistry, mathematics, astronomy, geography, history and music provided useful knowledge. High standards were reached in Tamil, Malayalam, Sanskrit, English and Greek. A succession of distinguished principals—Mead, Mault, J. Roberts and O. J. Whitehouse—raised the level of education provided.

Associated with the seminary in the early years was a daring experiment in girls' education. In 1819 it was reported that the seminary contained forty boys and a few girls.[39] A boarding house for them opened in 1820, developed into a separate school in 1823. Both Mrs. Mead and Mrs. Mault were associated with it. Their efforts were in the face of fierce opposition to the education of girls and under conditions of wretchedness and degradation for many of them. Some were slaves, many were orphans. The intentions of the missionaries were to improve the social position of the girls and provide them with marketable skills and to Christianize them. Mrs. Mead started another girls' school in Nayoor in 1828.[40]

Trade schools also were started by Mead. His intentions were rather simple. Since he could not rely upon Hindu workers during the construction of mission buildings he proposed to become independent of them 'by raising up a class of Christian artisans in this country'.[41] Apparently children attended school for part of the day and worked the other part. They were taught by natives working on the mission's premises and not by the missionaries themselves.

Growth of facilities

Some indication of the growth of educational facilities during the first quarter of the nineteenth century can be gained from reports that in 1819 the number of mission schools had risen to fifteen. By 1827 the total number of schools had reached fifty-nine; they were attended by nearly 2,000 pupils[42] and employed ninety-five schoolmasters. Some assessment of the catalytic effects of these schools is, however, desirable. As for the educational outcomes the gradual introduction of new methods of teaching which broke down rote learning was among the most important. Perhaps Whitehouse[43] gave most attention to this aspect of education. It was he who pressed for more modern methods of training teachers. In 1846[44] he wrote that there were many men who called themselves schoolmasters but few of them could teach. The reason, he thought, was that too little attention had been paid to the distinction between knowing and ability to teach. The girls' schools also introduced a system of teacher training, in the first instance rather like the monitorial system. A number of the girls were sent out to villages to start girls' schools there.

The social effects were evident as well. The girls learned profitable skills and helped defray the mission costs. More important perhaps was the influence of mission education on the caste system. The presence of non-Christian teachers encouraged non-Christians to attend the seminary. By 1844 the principal was able to report that in the English class there were Christians, Brahmins and low-caste Hindus. In fact most of the students were selected from among the lower castes and in order to keep poor but promising boys at school thirty free boarding places were provided. At another level the trade schools also attracted converts from the poorest community—the Shanars. They learned trades which had previously been the prerogative of certain other castes and thus helped to break down the rigid system which was based upon birth and occupation. As for the seminary several of its pupils reached eminent positions in the service of the State.

Yet in 1851 Whitehouse assessed the success of LMS education in Travancore in somewhat despondent terms. The mission had served as a place of refuge for the oppressed outcasts and dregs of society. In meeting the needs of these people the education of persons who could have benefited more from it was neglected.[45] Perhaps the concentration of effort by the CMS on the Syrian Christians paid more handsome dividends.

THE CMS

The first batch of four CMS missionaries arrived towards the end of Munro's period of office. The Reverends T. Norton and B. Bailey reached Travancore in 1816, J. Fenn in 1818 and H. Baker in 1819. They were all instructed to place themselves at the disposal of Munro, whose policies for education have already been mentioned. Though brought principally to serve the needs of the Syrian Christians Norton established his mission outside the Syrian sphere at Alleppy where there was a very mixed population. The other three went to Kottayam. Munro asked them to train the clergy, translate the Bible and undertake the teaching of English as a way of promoting the Protestant faith. He also used them as intermediaries in his dealings with the Syrians. He attempted to bring them together by arranging meetings between the Metropolitan of the Syrians and the missionaries. Norton succeeded in persuading the Metropolitan that his mission was intended to help the Syrian Church and people. The missionary was received as a deliverer and protector sent by God. Munro also ensured that Norton would occupy a key post in Alleppy by having him appointed judge in the civil court as soon as he knew enough Malayalam. Norton was able to preach in the streets and in his own church in this language.

His educational role was to open an evangelistic school. He started an English charity school in 1817 with 35 scholars divided into 4 classes and an orphanage for 26 children supported by local contributions. By 1827 he had 7 schools with nearly 100 children in them; figures soon to rise to 11 schools with 300 boys and 57 girls. There were boarding houses for boys and girls on the original site and by 1829 his wife had established a separate girls' school. The work of the other three missionaries is of greater interest. Tasks were allocated to them as follows: Bailey was to devote himself to the education of the clergy and the translation of the Bible; Fenn was to manage the college and the grammar schools, and Baker was to be in charge of the parochial schools. Each brought to his task special gifts of scholarship and character and because their spheres of educational activity were fairly clearly delineated the role of the CMS in education can best perhaps be appreciated through brief accounts of the activities of these three men—the 'Kottayam trio' or the 'Travancore Triumvirate'.[46]

The Reverend Benjamin Bailey and his wife arrived in Travancore in 1816 and stayed there for thirty-four years until 1850. Prudent and persevering, Bailey was greatly loved and in return loved those among whom he worked. His pastoral concern and that of his wife extended far beyond the spheres of religious instruction and education. Marriages were arranged for girls and, where necessary, dowries provided. Women were helped during their confinements and illnesses. Help was also extended to the non-Christians. During his only furlough in 1834 Bailey devoted his time to superintending the cast of a new fount of Malayalam type. Indeed the Kottayam printing press is one of the outstanding monuments to his work.

Munro had taken a lead which was accepted by the missionaries. They wrote to London for a printing press which arrived in 1821.[47] It was brought out to print the scriptures in Malayalam. Bailey had not only to make adequate translations but had also to make his own type. He set out to do so depending for information on books and the knowledge of local workmen. The first serious printing of the Bible was made in 1829 with an edition of 5,000.[48] Other publications were produced, including textbooks. Among the problems Bailey faced was the lack of patterns of graded learning the tradition being of rote memorization. He based his textbooks on some of those produced in Tamil by the Tranquebar mission. So important was regarded the production of textbooks that in 1868 soon after the Government had begun to take a direct interest in education, a textbook committee was set up. The Kottayam printing press contributed to education in three ways: it helped develop the Malayalam language in a uniform and independent manner; it helped to minimize the differences between the dialects spoken in various parts of Kerala each of which had a rich admixture of foreign words (the development of a common language evidently acted as a powerful unifying force among the Christians of Travancore, Cochin and Malabar—an influence not without political significance); finally, it made a great contribution to the success of literacy campaigns and, in so far as it did, can be regarded as one of the determinants of Kerala's high literacy rate at present.

An assessment of Bailey's achievements is found in Baker's report to the CMS in 1850:

> The Church built by Rev. Bailey who has just returned home after many years' labour is, without doubt, the largest and most handsome in Travancore. Rev. Bailey has also built a neat and plain schoolroom near the Church. . . . The Printing Press, under my charge was next to the translation of the Scriptures, which Rev. Bailey himself made and printed at it. . . . Mr. Bailey's great work which must have cost him much labour. . . . The workmen, all natives, are thoroughly acquainted with each his own work, which they do with neatness and accuracy that does them credit.[49]

Henry Baker first presented himself to the CMS in London in 1814. He brought with him a letter of introduction from the Reverend John Bull of Colchester, another written by himself and a legacy of £1,400 which he was due to receive when he came of age. The CMS accepted his services but not the legacy. He was sent to Tanjore in Southern India where he married the Reverend Jasper Kohloff's niece who was also the granddaughter of an early missionary, Balthazar Kohloff. In 1819 they came to Travancore and made Kottayam their headquarters. Their popularity among the people is evidenced in a CMS report:

> Their name has become a synonym for generosity and friendliness. Of the early missionaries, Rev. Baker who was in charge of a number of parochial schools throughout Travanacore, had the greatest opportunity of coming in contact with all classes of Syrians while as a result of the educational work carried on by Mrs. Baker for many decades, she became intimately acquainted with several generations of Syrian women rich and poor alike. Their intimate acquaintance with the vernacular of the country enabled them to converse freely with the people. They have settled in this country happily. . . .[50]

Baker's letters throw great light on the dignity and restraint of his character, and on his eagerness to serve the mission. His son, Henry Baker junior, left school in England to take up missionary work in Travancore and to learn the vernacular. The feelings of the father towards his work in Travancore are well summarized in a letter to the Reverend Josiah Pratt of the CMS:

Rev. and dear sir,

. . . Intelligence respecting our mission at Kottayam you receive through the Madras Corresponding Committee. I am happy to say that we are proceeding steadily on in our labour and not without evident blessing of God upon them. We meet with great encouragement from the attention which the boys pay to the instructions given them and from the progress they are making. The Syrians are becoming dearer to us every day and we likewise to them and we have reason to believe that some are truly blessed of God. On those accounts, you may sir, rejoice with us. . . . We ourselves have been hitherto highly favoured. We have had comparatively no sickness among us. Living in such a climate as Travancore among interesting people as the Syrians and altogether under such circumstances as we find ourselves we cannot but proceed cheerfully and happily in our work. . . .[51]

Growth of schools

Baker took charge of the schools. It appears that the Syrians had no parochial schools when the CMS missionaries arrived.[52] Religious instruction was the responsibility of the Church and the scattered nature of the dwellings, the dangers due to wild animals and prolonged monsoon made the churches and schools inaccessible. One of Baker's first tasks was to visit the parishes to study local conditions. Enthusiasm for education did not run high. The practical difficulties were shortage of teachers, funds and pupils. He proposed a seminary for the training of teachers, meanwhile appointing Hindu teachers. One reason for the shortage was that Syrians were being appointed to all departments of the Government. Nevertheless progress in the establishment of parish schools was substantial. A year after he came to Kottayam he reported that in 1820 there were 10 schools, that by the next year the number had risen to 35 and by 1824 to 50 with 1,300 scholars. In that year he claimed:

there is not strictly speaking a school to every parish, but there is not a place where fifteen children can be brought together to which a schoolmaster has not been appointed.[53]

As the grammar school developed it provided some of the needed teachers.

As for finance, when requests from Munro to the Madras Government for assistance were turned down the bishop was asked to support the schools by paying the salary of a teacher—Rs 5 per month. Reluctance to pay on the part of many parishes resulted in the closing of several schools. Additional support came from the Madras Corresponding Committee and in spite of difficulties Baker was able to raise the level of expenditure on schools by the CMS from Rs 600 in 1821[54] to Rs 3,130[55] in 1825. In order to attract and hold children an honorarium was paid either to parents or teachers. Many of the former were suspicious of an education provided through books, having been used to palm leaf strips written upon by an iron stylus.[56] One of Baker's most daring actions was to appoint two Nairs as inspectors of schools. Their duties were to visit schools regularly and check on attendance, supervise studies and asses the progress of pupils. They helped reduce the suspicion of the Hindus by teaching them to appreciate that the three Rs and other subjects as well as religious education were provided in the village schools. When Baker realized that there was no prejudice against Christian schools he closed down some redundant parochial schools and opened schools under Nair management in their place, encouraging Christian children to attend them. Thus the differences between the secular elementary schools and the mission schools were reduced. When the Governments entered the field of education they merely extended this system of missionary and secular schools.

Baker also appreciated that the need for central schools to which promising boys from the parochial schools could go and saw where the best of these could be made into teachers. His idea was to start three so-called grammar schools, one at Kottayam, one at Cacarb in the north, and the third at Munro Island in the south.[57] Apparently only the one at Kottayam made any progress. It was, unlike the parochial schools, built and maintained by the CMS. By 1825 the annual expenses of this school of 60 boys amounted to about Rs 2,000. The grammar school sent able boys on to the college and helped solve the teacher shortage. Indeed some former students opened schools of their own. The curriculum was orientated towards the preparation of teachers. Baker's connection with the grammar school changed. At first Fenn was in charge but it was soon transferred to Baker's supervision and he remained in control until 1825 when the Reverend Ridsdale took over. Baker resumed charge of the school again in 1827 at a time when only a few boys remained, the rest having been transferred to the college. This policy was followed in 1834 as well so that the new principal of the grammar school was very disappointed at the standard reached by the boys. Two years later came the split between the CMS and the Syrian Christians. The CMS was forced to start a new college to which nearly all the boys from the old grammar school were transferred and in 1838 it came to an end as a separate institution.

It had always been used to feed the college which was intended to educate religious and lay leaders. Fenn remained in charge of the new college for eight years after his arrival in the country with his wife in 1817. He took over from teachers who were 'the most learned and zealous priests of Malabar'[58] and for a time ran this school for thirty boys single handed. An appeal to Madras for help resulted in the arrival of two assistants, Ryan and Roberts, and two English masters, Jones and Hamilton. After Fenn left, broken in health,[59] continuity at the head of the college was not achieved until the Reverend Peet was appointed Principal in 1833 and served for five years.

Under CMS management the college admitted students for the ministry (as before) and lay students. To the task of training clergymen was added the role of training teachers. The Resident made provision for 45 free boarders and the CMS made a quarterly grant. Numbers rose slowly, in 1820 there were 42 students, 48 in 1826, 50 in 1829, and 95 in 1831. The impact of the college was very considerable however. A succession of visitors reported on the excellence of the students and the quality of the education provided. Thanks to Munro, English received pride of place in the curriculum and according to W. S. Hunt was the first missionary college in India to teach through the medium of English. The Government was anxious that the college should train boys for the public service and for this reason introduced secular subjects such as history and chemistry into the course of studies. A heavy bias towards religious instruction remained, but even in 1820 Fenn reported that the students were studying English, Malayalam, Sanskrit, Latin, Syriac and arithmetic. During Peet's régime in 1836 the curriculum included arithmetic, astronomy, geography, Syriac, Sanskrit, Malayalam, English, Greek, Indian History, conic sections and optics. Only the very able studied all these subjects and promotion from one class to the next was according to ability and not age. Many Nair students were outstanding but the general level of work and effort was always high. The tone of the college could perhaps be compared with that hoped for in an English public school; mental and physical training were regarded more highly than subject specialization.

Mrs. Fenn helped Mrs. Baker to run a school for girls. They taught sewing and a little English.[60] Essentially an attempt was made to provide an education which would produce suitable wives for priests and schoolmasters. The Syrian girls at Kottayam, however, enjoyed far better social and economic positions than those who attended the LMS school in Nagarcoil. Social accomplishment rather than economic independence was the aim of the CMS's educational endeavour. The Baker Memorial School, started in 1822, became in later years one of the best English high schools in Travancore and thousands of Syrian girls have been educated there. It stands as a memorial to the effort of the early missionaries to break down the determined opposition of the people of Kerala to the education of women.

SYRIANS AND CMS SPLIT

The success of the work of the CMS to improve the lot of the Syrian Christians should be seen against a background of dissension between the Romeo Syrians and the Jacobite Syrians. A dispute about four churches at Piravam, Changanacherry, Kottayam and Alleppy occurred in 1819. They were jointly owned by the Romeo Syrians and the Puthenkoor Syrians. The missionaries made considerable efforts to return these churches to the latter for their exclusive use. Fenn made clear in his letter to Munro's successor how anxious he was that the political and social security of the Puthenkoor Syrians, in particular, should be protected. In fact the British Resident warned the Romeo Syrians not to provoke trouble and placed the churches at Kottayam and Parur under the Syrian Metropolitan. He also informed Baker that the Ranee intended to restore the four churches at Government expense. Evidently the Syrians were of great value to the Travancore Government and although Munro's successor, Major Dowall, had no wish to use the missionaries as intermediaries between himself and the Syrians, his correspondence with the missionaries reveals the high regard in which they were held.

After the 1836 split between the CMS and the Syrians, the missionaries were able to work with the less fortunate communities of central Travancore, yet they did not abandon their efforts on behalf of the Syrians. Nevertheless a new phase in the work of the CMS in Kerala had opened.

There can be little doubt that during the early period the political and social conditions in the states facilitated the acceptance of the missionaries. The close alliance between the British Resident and the Ranees made possible not only acceptance but a considerable amount of financial support. Munro's firm determination to support the missionaries as agents of Christianity and British power gave an impetus to missionary work under favourable conditions. Again the somewhat unusual caste system in that part of the world gave the Nairs a position of importance which such a caste would not ordinarily have. In the case of the two inspectors the situation was brilliantly exploited by Baker. Finally the fact that the CMS's first object was to serve the Syrian Christians must be taken into account. Their long history of service in the states and the willingness of the Ranee to employ them again in positions of some authority meant that although the missionaries' institutions certainly appealed to lower caste Hindus and converts they also educated persons who reached high office in the Government.

To be sure there were differences of opinion regarding policy. Any proposed change gave rise to a great deal of correspondence between the CMS governors and the Corresponding Committee. Three issues were particularly important. English as the medium of instruction was not entirely acceptable to the leadership of the CMS. Most of the correspondence on this matter deals with Travancore and Cochin and is about the Syrians. The British officials were anxious to introduce English and Syrian and Hebrew slowly gave way to the vernacular and English. Secondly there was the issue of proselytization. Some missionaries sought to influence the higher social classes while others wished to appeal directly to the masses. Again some favoured a policy of expansion while others argued that their efforts should be concentrated on chosen portions of the vast field that lay before them. All these problems were, of course, mingled with those which arose as a result of the generally low position of the Syrian churches and the divisions and disagreements between them.

At first the attitude of the Syrians towards the missionaries was cordial. They were conscious of the need for spiritual and material help from outside and took to education as a means of achieving greater self-sufficiency. Changes in the affairs of their Church however turned them against the missionaries. They were opposed to the admission of low caste converts and some Syrians joined the Anglican Church. The turning point in the relations between the missionaries and the Syrian Church occurred after the departure of Fenn. The Syrian bishop suddenly refused to allow the missionaries to use his churches. Several attempts were made by the CMS to improve relations but the bishop, recognizing the danger to his Church if many of its members became Anglicans, urged the Syrians to sever their connections.

As for education, the Syrians claimed equal rights with the Anglicans over schools started with Government money. The Syrian bishop, the missionaries and the Travancore Government appointed a committee to arbitrate on the distribution of properties previously held in common. The dispute dragged on until 1840 although the formal split had occurred at the Synod of Mavelikara in 1836. The Committee assigned certain properties to the missionaries at Kottayam and set up trustees. The Reverend W. S. Hunt visited Travancore and praised the patience shown by the Syrians but remarked that after twenty years, 'The end of the experiment was hailed with relief on both sides. Yet it was sad because there was no small mutual affection between the Syrians and the Missionaries.'[61]

As for English as a medium of instruction, the controversy between the Anglicists and the Orientalists dragged on until 1835 when Lord Macaulay, President of the General Committee of Public Instruction, penned his famous Minute in favour of English. Bentinck, then Governor General, agreed with Macaulay and issued a resolution stating 'that the great object of the British Government ought to be the promotion of European literature and science among the "natives" of India'.[62] The decision 'gave a decided bias to the whole trend of education in the western direction, discouraging education through their mother tongue. It caused a great intellectual ferment, bringing about an "Indian Renaissance" an era of unprecedented social, moral, industrial and political progress, conducive to national unity . . .'.[63] Be this as it may there can be no doubt that the first half of the nineteenth century witnessed an advancement of western education in many of the native states in India. The institutions founded by the missionaries in Travancore and Cochin represented an ideal prototype which was copied in other parts by the Government. Certainly in Travancore there were English high schools and colleges as early as the third decade of the century and teachers of English were not difficult to find. Even so by 1911 in Travancore only 87 persons in 10,000 could read and write English. The figure rose to 190 in 1931 giving a total of some 97,000.

Regarding expansion, progress was slow and it was not until Wood's Despatch in 1854 that a comprehensive programme for education was promulgated. The Despatch recognized that the interest in education of the Court of Directors of the East India Company had been to raise the intellectual and moral level of those who were likely to receive positions of trust in India. Many observers have noted that the downward filtration theory of education was retained almost until India became independent. The extent to which progress towards universal primary education was held up as a matter of deliberate policy or because of economic difficulties is debatable. Certainly it could be argued that British educational practice in India resulted in the creation of a small English-speaking élite from among whom the post-independence leaders of India were drawn.

Policy regarding religious teaching and conversion can more easily be described. The missionaries saw their role among the Syrians in Kerala as one of moral and material uplift. Education was a useful agent. The British Government accepted, as in England, Church educational policies, but gradually secularized them. The religious element in western civilization was removed. Indians copied the social and educational institutions of England but not its religion. The role of the British Government is summed up in R. N. Cust's reply to a CMS circular:

The educational system of India is entirely based on the educational charter of 1854, written by Sir Charles Wood (Viscount

Halifax). Strict regulations regarding religious neutrality were written in 1854, before the Sepoy mutiny. In 1858 Lord Stanley, Secretary of State for India, reviewed the whole subject with reference to the allegation that this educational matter had been among the causes which led to the mutiny. The missionary Bodies then proposed to move her Majesty's Secretary of State for India, to withdraw from the work of higher education in India on the ground that education without religion is not complete education.[64]

In a memorial to the Queen in 1858 the CMS religious policy of the British Government and the opposition of the native Governments are referred to. The policy of neutrality was rejected by the society, with some success. In Travancore, for example, it was reported that:

> Mr. Roberts was at the head of a superior school supported by the Rajah of Travancore, which was commenced at Trivandrum in 1834. At first there was a prohibition of the Bible in the school except for Christian children. But after four years Mr. Roberts proposed to the Rajah and the native authorities that the Bible should be generally introduced. The restriction was then removed and a grant of two hundred and fifty rupees was made from the public funds for the purchase of Bibles and testaments to be used in schools.[65]

The slow growth of mission schools and the gradual incorporation of them into the state system paralleled developments in England, and in India was achieved on the basis of a number of grant-in-aid codes. Among them were regulations relating to technical and industrial schools. The initiative of the LMS in the first quarter of the century was not maintained. Though Wood's Despatch clearly imposed on the Government a duty to provide 'education of such a character as may be practically useful to the people of India in their different spheres of life' little happened in technical education during the next thirty years or so. No doubt the historic proclamation of the Maharaja in 1844 helped to reduce interest in technical education. This announcement stated that in public offices preference would be given to those educated in English schools. Against this should be weighed the establishment in Kerala between 1820 and 1870 of some six printing presses which provided training and a desirable form of employment for many converts to Christianity. A school of art was established in 1862.

The slow pace of industrialization probably helps explain why the education of Indian women made such slow progress. According to the Hartog Committee report in 1928 by 1894–5 there were less than 30,000 girls in the whole of India attending schools and colleges. While the movements for the emancipation of women in Europe had their effect in India they did not take the same aggressive and militant form; doubtless in part because the rate of industrialization was itself very slow. The position of women in the Syrian community was such as to offer greater possibilities of Western education than were available to most other groups. Even so, women's education was not popular. The role of the missionaries for the advancement of education for women should certainly be seen in terms of the extent to which they initiated policies rather than in quantitative terms.

In summary, by the turn of the nineteenth century it may be said that in Travancore a number of events provided a measure of educational advance. Among them may be noted: the establishment of English, Malayalam and Sanskrit schools; the opening of the art school; the award of scholarships to students to continue their studies in England and other foreign countries; the establishment of technical schools; the introduction of a grant-in-aid system; the provision of free primary education for deserving members of the backward classes; and the encouragement of women's education. The estimated literacy figure in Travancore was about three times that for India as a whole.

Improvements in literacy rates during the twentieth century give some indication of the quantitative impact of education in Kerala. In 1901 some 15 per cent of the Travancore and urban populations was literate; in 1931 the figure was 30 per cent; by 1951 it had risen to 46 per cent; and by 1960 the figure had reached 47 for the whole of Kerala. To be sure the changing definitions of literacy and the difficulties of establishing reliable figures should warn readers not to do other than see more than a general—but nevertheless substantial—improvement.

TWENTIETH-CENTURY REPORTS

A propos types of education the reports of two twentieth-century committees might be mentioned. Under the chairmanship of Mr. Statham a State Reorganization Committee was set up in 1930.[66] In general it criticized the literary type of education provided and proposed improvements in technical education. Detailed proposals included: the abolition of overlapping mission and private schools where there were Government schools to cater for the population of the town; the creation of five instead of four primary classes; the expansion of teacher training facilities; the setting up of a separate university for Travancore; the establishment of a college of technology; the revision of school curricula with more emphasis on social and athletic activities; and the rejection of compulsory education. Some of these proposals gradually found their way into the system.

The next educational commission under the chairmanship of Mr. Papworth recommended that universal free and compulsory education should be introduced into the state. This recommendation was accepted by the Government and the Primary Education Act was passed in 1946. Another proposal of the Papworth commission was that the organization of the school system should be: primary—five years, secondary—three years, high school—three years.

The Syrians, too, have not been inactive during the twentieth century. The Romeo Syrians, the Jacobites and the Marthomites have constantly been adding to the number of English schools and have modified methods of imparting instruction to a generation with changing ideas and ideals. The majority of the English schools and colleges in central and north Travancore and Cochin were managed by Christians of the Syrian Church. The only daily newspapers were run by the Jacobites. The Marthoma Syrians maintained seminaries in Kottayam and Thiruella. Two high schools and eighty-seven vernacular schools were also run by them. The very popularity of these English schools resulted in the establishment of a Commission on Christian higher education which submitted its report in 1931.[67] Its task was to enquire into the existing colleges and advise the authorities on the possibilities of improving and furthering the spread of Christian education.

Questionnaires were sent out enquiring into the relationships between the colleges and the Christian community, their financial position and their freedom to experiment. The principals of the Christian colleges co-operated very well.

One matter of great concern was the absence of adequate teacher training facilities for Christian teachers. The fact that there was no training college for them should be viewed against the fact that there were 500 Christian high schools and colleges. St. Christopher's training college in Madras was a college for women. In a memorandum to the Commission a group of Syrian Christians maintained that a Government teachers' training college could not provide adequate training for Christian teachers. The request for better facilities was appreciated by the Commission but was not immediately granted. It suggested the establishment of a teacher training college jointly by the Syrians and the Governments of Travancore and Cochin at Thiruella or some other suitable centre where a residential Christian high school could be used as a practising school. Three proposals were made by the Commission to meet the shortage of Christian teacher training. Hostels should be maintained for students attending non-Christian colleges. The Ashram method of education should be encouraged, and Christian literature should be produced and distributed.

The Commission also recommended that a Christian university should be created on the pattern of the Hindu university in Benares and the Muslim university at Aligarh. It was stressed that such a university should be of the unitary type and should avoid the ambiguity of purpose from which many of the Christian colleges suffered. The political situation in India during the thirties was partly responsible for the fact that these advanced ideas and proposals did not take practical shape. A number of interesting institutions reflect the general attitudes of the Syrian community towards education.

The Union Christian College at Alwaye in Travancore, for example, represents an undertaking of one group designed to awaken the missionary spirit of the churches and unite their members in the service of the nation. The 'brotherhood' which guides the college have set themselves ideals of self-sacrifice and dedication. This 'Alwaye settlement' started as an experimental village scheme of social uplift. Students from the Union Christian College took care of outcast children under better social conditions and in a homely atmosphere. They were taught a trade when they were old enough. A remarkable achievement has been that all caste barriers were swept away.[68]

The Nicholson Syrian Girls' High School was founded in 1910 by Mrs. Nicholson who was one of the principal workers of the International Police Association in Liverpool. At the request of the Reverend Gregson she came to India to start social work among the Syrians of Malabar. After spending a few years there she felt the need for a girls' school. In 1904 she was joined by Mrs. McKibbin and together they selected a site for a residential school at Thiruella. It opened in 1910 with sixty boarders. During the first fifty years of its existence thousands of girls were educated there.

Balika Madham at Thiruella and Christava Mahilalayam at Alwaye are also residential schools for Christian girls. The Syrian Christian Seminary and English High School for boys, founded by the Marthoma Syrian Christians at Thiruella, is another institution with a long-standing reputation. It has a college and teacher training college attached to it.

The Mar Grehorius Memorial English High School at Thiruella was started by the Jacobite section of the Syrian Christians. The Anglican Church too, opened a number of educational institutions in Thiruella such as Bethel for girls and an orphanage where girls are taught a trade. (There are similar institutions all over Travancore and Cochin meant for unwanted children of the backward classes.) The fact that there are so many educational institutions in Thiruella is due to its central position in Travancore.

In general a fairly recent picture of the educational scene is of a system in which the Syrians play a very important role. According to the census report in 1947 there were nearly $2\frac{1}{4}$ million Syrians of whom more than $1\frac{1}{2}$ million were Romeo-Syrians. Of the six thousand educational institutions 2,716 or 45·5 per cent were managed by the Government and 3,309 or 54·5 per cent were under private management. Of these 70 per cent were Christian institutions. In the north of Kerala most of the private schools are run by individuals. In Cochin and Travancore the Christian churches and Nair and Muslim organizations are in charge. In 1947 the following educational institutions were run by Syrian Christians:

Institutions	CMS	Roman Catholics	Jacobite	Marthoma
Seminaries	—	3	1	—
Colleges	1	4	—	—
High Schools	18	46	12	9
Community Schools	—	45	—	—
Other Schools	168	551	125	201

In 1957–8 of the 72 colleges in the state, including arts and science teacher training, Sanskrit, medical and engineering colleges, some 13 were managed by Christian bodies. The university of Kerala was established in 1958. A significant fact should finally be mentioned: of the 10,000 educational institutions of all types in Kerala only 200 are technical and vocational institutions.

Social consequences

This tiny proportion of technical schools reflects in Kerala a situation which is widespread throughout India. The vast majority of the population in the State is too poor to continue education beyond the prescribed minimum. These people are also indifferent to proposals to change existing ways of life and labour. A sudden technological revolution in agriculture or industry is beyond the bounds of possibility. The middle-class population is the one which might adapt itself to technological change. Farming and manual labours are not attractive to the younger generation of landowners. Their sole aim, after leaving high school or college, is to move to a city in search of white-collar jobs. Industrialization is slow due to lack of resources such as coal, and to a dearth of finance and technical personnel. Unemployment among a young educated élite is a source of great discontent.

There is more to the problem than this. Urbanization, a necessary concomitant to industrialization involves dislocation of patterns of ideals and social life. The solution must include an education which helps young people to be conscious of the ambiguities of scientific and technological processes and to discern the proper dialectical relationship between these processes and human values. Among these values are those associated with caste and class differences. In the present situation in Kerala the Churches have an important role to perform. They can make a contribution to the peaceful development of greater social justice during a revolution in which both the aristocracy and the masses will be involved. To some extent this task suggests that the Churches, through education, should more consciously continue to work towards some modification of the class structure of society. Throughout the nineteenth century one of the most important influences of the missionaries was in promoting social mobility.

The close correlation established by sociologists between education, social status and social mobility applies to the Hindu and Christian communities in Kerala. To be sure individual socioeconomic mobility on a scale of occupational prestige is not an ideal measure for an agrarian population like that of Kerala. But a general analysis of mobility among the Hindu and Christian communities during the second half of the nineteenth century is not without interest. Between 1850 and 1900 there was considerable upward mobility. The lowest level of mobility was from the upper-middle to the upper class but the figure for movement from the lower to the lower-middle class would not be much higher. A middle class was automatically created by the upward mobility of lower-middle class members. An estimated percentage for this new group would be 18 by 1900.

The caste system influences rates of movement. For example the speed is checked in the case of the Malayalies. Again although some 20 per cent of the Syrian, Hindu and Muslim groups could be said to fall into the lower class on the socio-economic scale the Syrians and high-caste Hindus in this group have higher living standards and a richer cultural background than scheduled caste members who also fall into this lowest class. Moreover the Nairs, Syrians and Brahmins are more easily able than other people in Kerala to move up the socio-economic scale. Nevertheless the social distance between the lower and the lower-middle strata has been reduced. Social snobbery has in many instances replaced the barriers of caste. In the slow process of transition from a caste to a social class system the missionaries undoubtedly played an important part.

Family patterns have also been influenced. The passive, non-interfering Indian woman has certainly become much more demanding, ambitious and efficient both inside and outside her home. Whether her head has been turned by the introduction of Western ideas of freedom is a matter of opinion. All such role changes have their advantages and disadvantages. In Kerala the measure of freedom for women that has been introduced has meant an increased demand from them for higher education and higher earning potentialities. For many centuries women of the Syrian communities have enjoyed freedom in matrimonial and financial matters, but their sphere of activity was restricted to the community. Now with modern English education and western ideas available to them the women of Kerala are more liberal minded and less critical than formerly of changes going on around them. The joint family system is fast disappearing due to the greater possibilities women now have to supplement the family income. Thousands of them in Kerala work, but thousands of them though highly educated still remain housewives and impart their knowledge to their children within the family circle.

As for political change the Syrian community is ambivalent. It has always been progressive but is somewhat hostile to modern socialist tendencies which, according to some members of the community, may eventually destroy the bases of solidarity among the land-owning class. The majority of Syrians belong to this group. Essentially a religious group with long traditions, members of it are committed to the enterprise of modernization. It is a movement from which there can be no return. Many old customs and ways of life will vanish and it remains to be seen whether the influences of the missionaries in Kerala will help the people to move on by evolutionary rather than revolutionary processes.

NOTES

1. Logan, W., *Malabar* (Madras 1887), vol I, p. 2; Panikkar, K. M., *A History of Kerala 1498–1801* (Annamalinager 1960), p. 2.

2. Zinkin, T., *Reporting India* (London 1962).

3. Hunt, W. S., *The Anglican Church in Travancore and Cochin, 1816–1916* (Kottayam 1920), vol II, p. 48.

4. Segal, R., *The Crisis of India* (London 1965), p. 25.

5. Mukerji, S. N., *Administration and Education in India* (University of Baroda 1962), Chart 12.

6. *Ibid.*, Chart 6.

7. National Council of Applied Economic Research and Technology, *Techno-Economic Survey of Kerala* (New Delhi 1962), pp. v, 8–9, 261.

8. Moraes, G. M., *A History of Christianity in India* (Bombay 1964), vol I, and Brown, L. W., *The Indian Christians of St. Thomas* (Cambridge 1957).

9. Moraes, pp. 78–9.

10. Srinivas, M. N., *Caste in Modern India* (Bombay 1962) p. 63.

11. Rae, G. M., *The Syrian Church of Kerala* (Edinburgh 1892), p. 372 and Potham, S. G., *The Syrian Church of Kerala* (London 1963).

12. Cherian, P., *The Malabar Syrians and the CMS 1816–40* (Kottayam 1935).

13. Menon, A., *Cochin State Manual* (Ernakulam 1911), p. 153.

14. Cherian, pp. 43–4.

15. Ritcher, J., *A History of the Missions in India* (Edinburgh 1908), p. 84.

16. Rae, p. 51.

17. Logan, p. 198.

18. Hacker, I. H., *A Hundred Years in Travancore* (London 1907), p. 11.

19. Menon, P. Shungunny, *The History of Travancore* (Madras 1878), pp. 339–43.

20. Ramanath Aiyer, S., *A History of Travancore* (Madras 1938), p. 67.

21. Mohamood, Syed, *History of English Education in India 1781–1893* (Aligarh 1923), p. 15.

22. Mayhew, A. I., *Christianity and the Government of India* (London 1929), p. 61.

23. Books on the LMS are: Agur, C. M., *Church History of Travancore* (Madras 1903); Lovett, R., *History of the LMS, 1795–1895* (London 1899), vol I; Goodall, N., *A History of the LMS 1895–1945* (Oxford 1954)

24. *Missionary Register* (1818), p. 100.

25. *Ibid.*, p. 109.

26. *Ibid.*

27. Hunt, p. 67.

28. Mateer, S., *The Land of Charity* (London 1871), p. 414.

29. Stock, E., *History of the CMS* (London 1899), vol I, p. 232.

30. Logan, vol I, p. 199.

31. Mateer, p. 258.

32. LMS, *Report of the LMS* (London 1814), vol I, p. 564.

33. See Rev. Fenn's address before the Mavelikkara Synod (1818) in *Missionary Register* (1819–20), p. 428.

34. *Ibid.*

35. Cherian, p. 88.

36. LMS *MSS*, 11 January 1819. The idea of a college was not new to Munro because it was he who was responsible for the Kottayam College started in 1813 for the Syrian Christians.

37. *Quarterly Chronicle*, vol II, p. 200.

38. LMS *MSS* (1828).

39. *Ibid.* (1819).

40. Agur, pp. 881–2.

41. *Madras Christian Instructor*, vol III, p. 52.
42. Agur, pp. 809–10.
43. LMS *MSS* (1843).
44. *Ibid.* (1846).
45. See *ibid.*, Mr. Whitehouse's report, 11 Sept. 1844 and 15 March 1845.
46. See Cherian, p. 144; and Stock, vol I, p. 232.
47. CMS, *Proceedings of the CMS for the years 1821–2* (London 1822), p. 150.
48. Thomas, P. J., *Malayala Sahityavum Kristyanikalum* (Kottayam 1961), p. 185.
49. CMS archives, Folio I Report 1850 and letters written by Rev. H. Baker, Sr.
50. *Ibid.*
51. *Ibid.*
52. *Missionary Register* (1817), p. 103.
53. *Missionary Register* (1823–4), p. 148.
54. *Ibid.* (1821).
55. *Ibid.* (1825).
56. Hunt, vol II, p. 70.
57. CMS, *Proceedings of the CMS 1821–2*, p. 165.
58. The Syrian priests of Malabar were known as Kattanars, and the bishop as Metran. In this study, however, they are referred to as priest and bishop.
59. Hunt, vol II, p. 77.
60. *Missionary Register* (1827), p. 605.
61. Hunt, vol I, p. 90.
62. Howell, A. P., *Selections from Education* (Calcutta 1872).
63. *Ibid.*
64. *Papers on India*, vol II, p. 218 (CMS archives).
65. Memorial to Her Majesty the Queen, 1858 (CMS archives).
66. Travancore State Manual, *Progress of education in India*, 10th quinquennial Review (1931).
67. CMS, *Report of the Commission for Christian Higher Education* (CMS Library 1931).
68. Crowley, E., *Travancore Then and Now* (London 1957).

5

THE CHURCH MISSIONARY
SOCIETY IN KASHMIR

S. Z. Ahmed

A T the end of the seventeenth century Kashmir stood as a pioneer of progress and a beacon of enlightenment to the surrounding territories. From this position, it declined under the tyrannies and extortions of subsequent rulers, until, by the early years of the nineteenth century, the cultural glories of its past had disappeared, and it was known abroad chiefly for the desolation of its land and the misery of its people.

To the faith of the Christian missionaries knowledge of these conditions presented a clear challenge, to their humanity they presented a duty and an opportunity. Coming to Kashmir in the middle of the century they found that such had been the destruction there were no educational institutions on to which they could build. Starting afresh they founded schools through which the Gospel might be propagated and want and misery mitigated. Lacking native models, they built upon the only prototypes they knew—those of the West. Slowly, disinterestedly, but thoroughly and in time they completely organized a system of education. Its schools had all the administrative, curricular and social characteristics of the schools of the West. But cultural penetration was not a deliberate aim. They were concerned only to give to Kashmir the best they knew. In the event, the educational system which the missionaries thus established, was copied by state and local enterprise.

In this article the growth of missionary educational activity in the second half of the nineteenth century will be examined against the contemporary background. Some of the far-reaching and enduring social consequences to which that activity gave rise will be analysed. Since all current education in Kashmir originated with the missionaries, the link between education on the one hand and culture and social improvements on the other is peculiarly close, as in few other countries in the world, and its study may be uncomplicated by extraneous factors.

EARLY CONTACTS WITH THE WEST

Kashmir remained unknown to Europe until the late sixteenth century. Thereafter, in gradually increasing numbers, a succession of men from the West whose courage, curiosity, or love of adventure exceeded that of their contemporaries, penetrated to its beautiful but remote valleys.

The first real contact with the West came as a result of the Treaty of Amritsar in the year 1846. When this beautiful valley was 'transferred and made over, for ever to Maharaja Gulab Singh' by the 'British Government in exchange of 75 lakhs of rupees, and in token of the supremacy of the British Government was to present annually to the British Government one horse, twelve perfect shawl goats of approved breed (six male and six female), and three pairs of Kashmir shawls'. On its part the British Government agreed to 'give its aid to Maharaja Gulab Singh in protecting his territories from external enemies'.[1]

The missionaries also knew the history of Kashmir very well. They knew that it was formerly a great missionary centre for Buddhism, as much as Iona and Lindisfarne were missionary centres for Christianity in Scotland and Northumbria. They knew that Kashmir at one time sent 500 Buddhist missionaries to convert Tibet, and Buddhism penetrated from there to Kandahar and Kabul. So they hoped that if its people were won for Christ, they might become great evangelists in Asia.

The same view was shared by Moorcroft who visited the valley in the early nineteenth century. He said, 'I am convinced that there is no part of India where the pure religion of the Gospel might be introduced with a fairer prospect of success than in Kashmir'.[2]

This knowledge of the religious history of Kashmir gave hope to the Christian missionaries. In those high valleys in the past had flourished successively, Hinduism, Buddhism, Saivism and Islam. Might not Christianity receive an equal welcome from the people? Might not the Gospel there fall on fertile soil? Such at least was their hope.

Besides this the very instructions of the CMS committee stated that opportunities for expansion should not be missed. So Kashmir was to provide its one station.

The first but not the least important cause was a moral one. The deplorable condition of people had been clearly depicted by many who had visited the valley. Not only had Kashmir suffered through the iron hand of despotic rulers, but there was in addition, ignorance, disease, a degradation of morals and poverty. It was a call missionaries could not resist. According to the Reverend R. Clark:

Kashmir is not paradise, the population are but the enfeebled and diminished remnant of what they once were. Oppressed for centuries by the iron hand of despotic rule, they are impoverished and degraded in the midst of productive capabilities. Numerous but ruined villages were scattered over the surface of this once thickly-peopled district. Many of the houses were tenantless and deserted, the fruit was dropping unheeded from the trees, the orchards were overgrown with a profusion of wild hemp and wild indigo, and the graveyards still covered with blue and white iris flowers, which are always purposely planted over them, partly for the sake of ornament, and partly because the roots, by being matted together, prevent the turf from falling in. There is yet enough to show that the villages were once the very *ne plus ultra* of snugness and rusticity.

Where was the Sikh rule ever found to exercise a beneficial influence? But that rule has passed away. The sceptre has fallen into the hands of others. Let it be our prayer and hope that the same ameliorating influences which are abroad in the Punjab, may gladden, also this lovely spot, where God has wrought so much of good, and man so much of evil.[3]

Policy of the missionaries
Such were the causes which brought the Christian missionaries to Kashmir. Their aim was to win the country for Christ, and they further sincerely believed that the spread of the Gospel would provide a remedy for the sufferings of the people. Their policy was to extend the knowledge of Christianity and they saw in Kashmir a duty and an opportunity. But to make use of this opportunity and to fulfil the duty was not an easy task, there were serious obstacles in its way.

Kashmir was not directly under the British Government, but under a Maharaja, so it was decided by the CMS committee, as a matter of policy, that a preliminary tour should be conducted in order to survey the ground for the work of the missions. In the summer of the year 1854 Clark, accompanied by Colonel Martin, visited Kashmir.

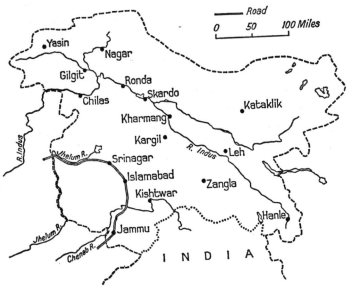

KASHMIR

At a time when missionaries wished to open a mission in Kashmir the general situation in India was not very propitious. The efforts of those who generally wanted to serve were doubted and looked upon with suspicion. It was the time of the Indian Mutiny, which had wrought great damage on the Christian communities in the North. In it about thirty-eight British and American chaplains and missionaries perished with their families.[4]

The second difficulty was due to the general lack of material and human resources. Financial difficulties within the CMS helped prevent any determined missionary activity immediately after 1854. The third obstacle was that of language. As already pointed out by Clark in his letter, 'any missionary who is to work in Kashmir has to know Kashmiri'. So time was needed.

The fourth obstacle was the lack of a good road between the Punjab and Kashmir. The journey had to be made on horseback or on foot. But to missionaries this seemed no obstacle as Clark reported, 'the journey is a rather difficult one, but it is often performed even by English ladies'.[5]

The last and one of the most serious obstacles was a political one. It hindered the growth of missionary activity for a long time. When the Punjab was annexed to the British Empire, the leading spirit of the country was Maharaja Gulab Singh. He was the greatest of Ranjit Singh's nobles and a powerful chief of the Dogras. Though he was outwardly a friend of the British he was at heart opposed to any Western penetration in Kashmir. A special order was issued in 1854 by the Governor-General, Lord Dalhousie, at the request of Maharaja Gulab Singh, forbidding European visitors to remain in Kashmir during the winter. He laid down that Europeans were to be admitted to Srinagar by prescribed routes only and from the time of their entrance to their exit, they were to be under vigilant supervision and were not to be allowed to mix with the people.[6] For an ordinary visitor, who wanted merely to spend the summer amidst the natural beauties of this lovely spot, this presented no difficulty. But for missionaries it was a serious obstacle. They were not allowed to rent a house in the city of Srinagar, where they could carry out the mission work. Under no circumstances could a European or a British subject own landed property in the dominions of the Maharaja. Guest houses were built outside the main city for the convenience of European visitors, and a special quarter in the environs of Srinagar was set apart for them. Agents were appointed to supply their wants, and all business was transacted through a *Babu*, deputed for that purpose.[7] Thus the isolation of Europeans from the people of the country was complete. This presented a serious difficulty for the missionaries, whose work lay with the masses and whose success depended upon close and constant contact with the people.

This deliberate isolation was prompted by the understandable fears of the Maharaja, his officials and his great landowners. The Maharaja did not wish the missionaries to take back to British India details of his treatment of a people in whose welfare he showed little interest. To the British he owed his throne, and upon their tolerance he depended. He feared that they might investigate further should the manner of his rule become known. The

Maharaja's fear was not without foundation. By 1862 and 1863 when Clark revisited the country the opposition of the Maharaja had hardened and conditions had deteriorated. In fact the writings of missionaries regarding the misrule and harsh treatment of the people was one of the causes of the land reform which took place in the state in 1880 under Sir Walter Lawrence.

Under these circumstances initially the missionaries could hope for no more than to obtain leave to remain in the country and hope that their work and attitudes would overcome the people. Thus, though their ultimate policy and aims remained unchanged, the lines on which it was implemented were modified by local conditions. The importance of the political situation is clearly stated in. Clark's letter to the Earl of Elgin, Viceroy and Governor-General:

> I cannot ask a Hindu prince to be permitted to preach the Gospel of our Saviour in his dominions, but I do humbly ask, My Lord, that our Christian Government will not recall me, should I otherwise be enabled to remain. I will obey the laws of this country and show all respect to the authorities in it. I will act entirely on my own responsibility, and be content to bear all opposition from either native Government or people, which I may meet with in my endeavour to remain. I merely ask for the same liberty which is continually granted by other foreign Governments under similar circumstances—the liberty which has ever been willingly given by the Indian Government to so many travellers along its frontier states in the present time, as well as in the years gone by—the liberty which is already allowed in Cashmere itself, to every Sikh, Afghan, Persian, and Tartar, Tibetian and Hindu. I ask for no help, but simply that I may not be turned back by our own Government. If the Cashmere Government obliges me to leave, I will be content to do so.

> I will not attempt to dwell on the present state of the Cashmerees, but it is evident that, spiritually at least, they need our deepest sympathy. Very many people, in both India and England, are desirous to impart both their sympathy and help as has been shown by the remarkable manner in which this mission has been commenced. I am sure, My Lord, that the endeavour to give the Cashmerees the Gospel of Christ will be attended with the greatest blessings, both to them and to ourselves. There are some reasons which render the acknowledgement of our religion

peculiarly important in a country where much evil exists, and which is yearly visited by so many countrymen of our own. But independently of these, we know that the favour of God ever rests upon the people from whom such efforts emanated, and on their Governments too. I trust, My Lord, that the vast import-ance of this subject will be accepted as my apology for writing this letter, and that your Lordship will give a favourable con-sideration to the very earnest request which it contains. It is simply this, that our Government will not require me to relin-quish, for a part of the year, the work which I have been sent by our own countrymen to perform. Should the native Govern-ment enforce it, I will, after using such means as I am able, retire quietly into our own territories for the winter months.[8]

On returning from Srinagar Clark went to Peshawar. At the beginning of the winter of 1865 he returned to Amritsar. Here his main task had been strongly to state before the mission authorities the claims of what at the time was considered to be startingly novel approach to missionary work—medical missions. He was now fully convinced that this was the only way to gain a footing in the Vale of Kashmir. In a way this was not new. The obstacles of 1864 were the same as those already faced during the preliminary tours of 1862–3. As early as 1862 it was felt that in Kashmir the policy to establish a mission must be a 'combination of healing with preaching'. The subject was brought forward at the Lahore Conference, during Christmas 1862. Kashmir was especially alluded to in the general resolution, as being a country where 'medical aid is not available and where deep prejudices may be removed by this means'.[9]

The immediate result of this conference was that the Lahore Committee for the medical missions was formed. The establish-ment of a mission in Kashmir was thus the culmination of a long process of sustained effort.

Educational policy

In its earlier years the CMS school was run and organized on an indigenous model. The only unique feature the CMS school had was that the missionaries held regular, compulsory, Christian scripture lessons. Indigenous schools in Kashmir were always connected with the temples and mosques. Their main aim was to impart religious instruction, and the main stress was on the language of the sacred books. In temple schools the emphasis was on Sanskrit so that the boys might be able to read the sacred Hindu books. In the mosque schools the stress was on Arabic, so that children could read the Koran. To these two languages, Persian was added as it had been the court language since the dawn of the Muslim era. After the seventeenth century, this system of education was dealt fatal blows by the oppressive rule of the Afghans. Those who were interested in education continued it in the home. It is very difficult indeed to find evidence of a single school in the Valley of Kashmir in the first half of the nineteenth century. They seem to have been completely eliminated.

The first to start again in 1868 was a State school (an Arabic school). By the end of the nineteenth century we see a small sprinkling of them. These schools were, in a way, an indirect result of missionary activity. At the beginning of the second half of the nineteenth century the demand seems to have been for an indigenous type of education. The State schools were founded on a traditional model and the missionaries too, at first, adopted the same pattern though at regular intervals new subjects and various activities such as games were introduced. The missionaries adopted this approach for many reasons.[10]

The difficulties and official hostility encountered by the missionaries were slowly overcome by a combination of tact, goodwill and determination. In this process the policy changes which followed the abandonment of the Kashmir mission school in 1864 and which emerged from the deliberations of the Lahore Conference were of vital importance. Their immediate consequence was the establishment of a state dispensary in 1867 and the commencement of a State-aided Arabic school in 1868. In the long run the years of devoted service by the medical missionaries, in a land where pestilence was common, served both to win the confidence of the people and to undermine the hostility of the authorities. The beneficial results of the medical work were clear even to the most illiterate and they could not be denied even by the most bigoted. But amidst these activities the missionaries never forgot their prime aim—the propagation of the Gospel. Their healing skill brought them into contact with the people and opened their homes to them. And on every occasion while ministering to the body they did not omit to care for the spiritual welfare of the patients as well by providing a knowledge of Christianity. Thus to the intellectually starved land of Kashmir there came a little knowledge, medical and religious. These small beginnings, however, served to stimulate the demand. The delight in physical vigour, and the love of learning which centuries of calculated oppression had almost extinguished, revived among the Kashmiri people. The way was thus open for the foundation of schools.

As the climax of long endeavour and as a triumph over difficulties and discouragement, the first mission school was started on the hospital premises in 1880. Since then Christian education has enjoyed an unbroken existence in Kashmir. Conscious of how precarious was the foothold that they had gained, for the first twelve years the missionaries sought to run the school on lines that would give no offence to the people and local authorities. At the end of that time they realized that a policy of propitiation, while weakening the effective educational work of the school served not to disarm but rather to strengthen official opposition which was encouraged by the appearance of weakness in the missionaries.

The new school
After 1894, therefore, policy changed and the school was remodelled on lines that it subsequently retained. The new aims and structure of the school made little concession to local customs and the essential model was that of a good secondary school in nineteenth-century England. Education was conceived as a process affecting the body, mind and soul of the pupils. The work of the school was thus directed to instilling some accurate information, to producing healthy bodies and to building characters based on the Christian virtues of modesty, charity and service.[11] For pupils who believed that they were superior by right of birth, who despised sport as a waste of time, and who, if they did not actually abhor it, shared with Aristotle the belief that manual work was suited only to slaves, this aims was not easy to realize. That in these circumstances the school survived the difficult early years is high tribute to the ingenuity and faith of those who guided its destinies and taught in it. Its success and the influence which it came to exert is a monument to their endeavours and a memorial which they themselves would have most wished for.

Thus the foundation of Kashmir CMS School was laid by the Reverend Hinton Knowles[12] in 1880 on the hospital premises.

From 1880 to 1883 it was under the Reverend J. S. Doxey and from 1883 to 1894 under Knowles, its founder. In 1890 he was joined by Cecil Tyndale Biscoe who had the great and congenial task of helping the former to develop the school in Srinagar. In 1894 Knowles handed the school over to Biscoe who remained its Principal and supervised its branch schools for the next fifty years.[15]

In its early years this school had to face all those problems which every educational system faces. The initial economic one of how the essential resources for the educational enterprise are to be acquired is almost overwhelming in its magnitude. Buildings, books and teachers are all expensive; money, manpower, and space must be devoted to the cause. If an educational system is to be supported by the country a relatively high standard of living is necessary; and philanthropic support from outside bodies points to a strong belief in the worth of education. The early difficulties of the missionaries arose from the fact that in Kashmir neither of these desiderata was present.

The first, and basic problem was that of a school building. It was mainly due to this difficulty that Clark's first school was abandoned in 1864. From 1864 to 1880, due to the kindly and humane services of the Kashmir medical mission, good relations and understanding had been built up among the people. But in official circles there was little change of attitude. The orders prohibiting the missionaries from renting a house for a school building were still in existence. The only alternative for the missionaries was to start the school on hospital premises. Doxey thus used the same building which was used as an orphanage by Dr. Downes during the famine of 1877–9. Along with this he sometimes used his own room to instruct his pupils.

In 1880 there were five pupils. Accommodation was a great problem. Pupils could not be attracted in large numbers because the hospital buildings were outside the city, and those who attended complained of the distance. To overcome this difficulty the missionaries obtained in 1883 a building at Sheikh Bahg—in those days a place close to the city of Srinagar. This act aroused opposition. Knowles wrote:

During the past year the mission school has been terribly opposed by the Government of this country. The reason for the increased opposition was our renting a large house by the city, and transferring our school there. H.H. the Maharaja will not permit any person to rent a room or possess a stick in the valley.[14]

Biscoe gave another reason for this increased hostility:

One of the pupils has been seriously ill with typhoid and was of course weak from after effects. Mr. Knowles, therefore, kindly lent this boy his own horse to ride to and from school. As soon as this fact became known tales were spread that the boy was a convert, and pressure was brought to bear upon his parents to take him away from the mission school.[15]

In 1883 the number of boys on the school roll fell from 47 to 30. Knowles complained that this fall was due to nothing but distance:

There are 47 names on the roll, and we shall not have a larger number, I am afraid, until His Highness the Maharaja allows us to build in the city, or follows his more favourite plan of giving us a building. The only spot of ground one can obtain at present in this land to call one's own is just a few feet in the Sheikh Bagh Cemetery should necessity demand. There are many boys who wish to come but complain of the distance.[16]

The impossibility of renting a suitable school building in the city persisted until 1890. In that year the missionaries were granted permission to move the school down to the city, and it was shifted from the hospital premises to a large house and compound on the river bank in the middle of the city.

That the work of the school expanded during this period was almost entirely due to the personal determination and efforts of Hinton Knowles. He wrote:

The school work occupied a good half of our working day during the past year, and not without reason. It has developed more than any other branch of the work here, owing to our being able to get a school building in the city, and to hire other suitable places in the district. We commenced the year with 80 scholars, and ended with 300 or more, two-thirds of them in our city school, and the remainder in the district school of Islamabad, an important town in the South-East end of the valley, about thirty miles from here.[17]

M   161

He expressed his future objective by concluding that 'our desire and intention is to bind Kashmir with a girdle of mission schools. It will be a very expensive business, and already we are spending from our own slender store, but we are determined to go on, assured that He who has opened wide the door, will furnish us with the means. We put our trust in Him'.[18]

The outcome of all their efforts was not very encouraging. The dreams remained, in a sense, unfulfilled. A meagre Rs. 200 were added from the local funds of the Punjab Committee to the general grant. As early as 1883 it was resolved 'that every effort be made in all our Punjab medical missionary stations to obtain grant-in-aid from municipalities and in Kashmir from the native Government'.[19]

In Kashmir this bore no fruit until 1900. It was in this year that a grant of Rs 1,800 was made towards mission educational work for the first time, though in the Punjab mission schools had received grants after 1854.

The reasons why State aid was thus delayed are manifold. Kashmir was a feudatory state. Consequently, neither Macaulay's Minute nor Wood's Despatch could be applied there. The steady growth of education in India was not accompanied by parallel development in Kashmir during this period. Three factors served eventually to modify this situation—missionary activity, political reforms and other reforms after 1885. These were followed by a growing demand for education, stimulated by the desire for Government jobs for which a knowledge of English was a prerequisite. This demand was further greatly increased by the building of cart roads between India and Kashmir, bringing Kashmir more closely into touch with developments in India.

THE IMPACT OF MISSIONARY ACTIVITY

During the growth of the CMS school it changed in most respects, but in one it remained the same—it was monopolized for a long time by large numbers of Pandit boys.

The reasons for the predominance of Hindus were primarily economic. Wealth in Kashmir was largely concentrated in the hands of the Pandits. They were the masters of the land. Regarding their prosperous economic condition, Lawrence says, 'the Brahmins, known as Kashmiri Pandits, had seized all power and authority, and the Muslim Cultivators were forced to work to keep the idle Brahmin in comfort'.[20]

Thus they had time to spare to go to school. The Muslims were, generally speaking, poverty-stricken. The lot of the majority of them from boyhood was hard manual labour and they seldom had either money or leisure for education. The Pandit minority had both. They possessed a long tradition of learning, and there was the incentive provided by the prospect of Government employment, the key to which was a knowledge of English. Since Government jobs were barred to the Muslims they lacked this powerful incentive. The cumulative effect of these factors was that for a long time the schools of Kashmir were almost entirely monopolized and dominated by the Pandit minority.

Though the classification of pupils was introduced quite early on, the process of westernization was necessarily slow. For some years there seems to have been no regular school vacations. The school used to open at 11.00 a.m., but pupils did not attend till midday, punctuality was not insisted upon because it was not the rule in the indigenous school which the State had started. The holidays were the holy days of the Hindu boys. Knowles, while explaining the nature of his work and difficulties, wrote '. . . we cannot give regular holidays here as the Maharaja's school does not'.[21]

The schools increasingly took on the aspect of English public schools. The notion of the school as an instrument primarily for training the character was adopted, and chief among the means for the achievement of this goal were games and the study of the Bible. The native emphasis on academic subjects was replaced by the ideal of an all-round education. In the details of school organization, the pattern of the West was followed. Even the incentives were those of which Arnold would have approved and among them the Speech Day occupied an honoured place.

The problem of staffing the schools was not too great, in spite of the special need for language teachers. The Central Committee's opposition to the employment of non-Christian teachers could not be maintained in view of the straitened financial circumstances of the society, and in a sense the staffing policy was thus determined by the internal economic condition of the society.

Thus by 1894 the major external difficulties to the educational work of the missionaries had been overcome, or at least sufficiently solved for teaching to be carried on and the scope of activities to be expanded. Up to this point expediency had largely determined the organization and content of the work in the schools. The firmer foundation and the growing scale of the enterprise provided an opportunity for reconsideration and reorganization. The sacrifice of the ideal in favour of the possible ceased to be necessary and the way was opened for new developments. The occasion of this change was the succession of Knowles, who had been primarily an evangelist, by Biscoe who was primarily a teacher and an educationist.

Biscoe takes over

The conditions which Biscoe inherited together with his own convictions and background prompted him to embark resolutely on a policy of westernization in the school. A new and fairly clearly defined phase in the history of the Kashmiri school thus began.

After 1894, although external difficulties remained they were relatively less important than the internal opposition which the new policy encountered. To practically every essential feature of a western school there was opposed some custom, attitude or belief of the Kashmiri pupils. Opposition from among his own scholars was Biscoe's greatest problem and he sought to solve it through a combination of tact and firmness. In this task his greatest asset was an unwavering conviction in the rightness of his aims and in the moral and intellectual benefits which would result for the country.

How and what to teach such pupils presented an immediate problem to Biscoe. Before embarking on any new plan, he tried in every way to know and to understand about Kashmir's people. This study revealed to him that the state of corruption, oppression and superstition had taken away from the people their very spirit, they had lost their self-respect. Biscoe sought some explanation of this state of affairs; he decided it was 'because they happen to live in one of the most beautiful countries on earth, and therefore other peopled had coveted it. Kashmir had been conquered and reconquered by invaders, who have murdered, oppressed and enslaved their ancestors, and so ground the life and heart out of them that their better selves have been crushed'.[22]

To these unfortunate people he was determined to give an education which would revive their spirit, which would help them develop character and become active citizens. The goal was, 'to produce good citizens, imbued with the spirit of serving the universal Father by following the example of Christ in serving their fellows who will thus be able to help the people of their country to cast aside the reproach which has been put upon them by their neighbours, until they become in character a worthy complement to their most beautiful country'.[23]

At this stage of the school's development the majority of the boys were Brahmins, sons of the ruling class, or holy caste. Many of them were twenty years of age or more and married and were, therefore, fairly set in their ways. It was an extremely difficult task to convince them that change was desirable and prepare them for it.

Biscoe's first action was to introduce regular hours of instruction and to insist upon punctual attendance by the pupils. He substituted holidays on the western pattern. Previous practice had been to close the school for the holy days.

All this was opposed at first. It was an unprecedented innovation in Kashmir. No other school in the country was thus organized. To enforce the new rules those who were absent were fined and a system of visiting the homes of the boys was devised, so that there remained no room for a pretence of sickness. Even so the lesson was not lightly nor quickly learned as Biscoe's school report for the year 1918 showed:

. . . We start our school day by being punctual, or at any rate teach the boys that it hurts in several ways and various parts if they are not. I need not say that we did not teach this virtue in a day or without pain.

Roll-call is a great opportunity for reading faces. For instance, spotting those who are ill in body or mind, discovering the reason, and then applying the remedy. Also ascertaining those who are absent, and why. We possess a smart man with a thermometer, a most useful instrument; for most of the absentees are sick! This instrument is a bit of a little devil, if not the very devil to some absentees, though a godsend to others. Many of our students hate the man who invented this instrument.[24]

Thus, through firm policy and determined action a transformation took place over the years. Not only did the mission schoolboys learn to be punctual and to enjoy regular periods of rest and vacation but the boys of the State school joined them. Indeed, any change which took place in the CMS school was followed by the State schools.

The next reform which Biscoe brought into the school concerned cleanliness. Its introduction was very difficult, not because of the dress or climate, but because of the attitude of the pupils. Brahmins firmly believed that they were the cleanest possible persons on earth. Biscoe points out that 'if by any chance one of the European staff should touch them, they would squirm in utter disgust at such defilement'.[25] So before they could become clean they had to learn that they were dirty. To this were added three more great enemies—parents, custom and public opinion.

The parents held that if a boy looked clean and tidy then the devil might take a fancy to him and run off with him. Personal cleanliness was further intimately connected with economic and social factors. At the economic level, a person who was clean and tidy had generally been more highly taxed even from the days of Afghan rule since the Government had based its taxation scale upon the rather simple assumption that anyone who was clean was also rich. Lack of cleanliness was thus a protection not only against the rigours of the Kashmir weather but also against extortions by the State. The beauty and fair skins of the women of Kashmir were known throughout India and they were in consequence often carried away and sometimes, even, sold. The system of purdah arose as a precaution against this danger, and a lack of cleanliness was also some safeguard against it. In the fullness of time by a simple process of reasoning it came to be argued that any woman who was clean was deliberately inviting some such fate and she tended to be regarded askance by her sisters whose respectability was in direct proportion to their lack of cleanliness. Thus in demanding cleanliness, Biscoe was crusading against more than mere lack of washing, he was attempting the extremely difficult task of changing the attitude of his pupils from their deeply rooted social opinions.

Against all these difficulties he went ahead. In carrying through this reform some harsh methods were used, but without their use success would not have been possible. Not only were bathing and washing programmes carried on in the school, but also as he explains in his annual letter, 'we have been able to raise the standard of our cleanliness to a degree that I never thought possible two or three years ago; we not only fine the dirty boys, but their form masters also are held responsible for the uncleanliness of the boys'.[26]

The third reform was of dress. At the time Biscoe took over the school, the dress of his pupils was as follows: (1) Pheran; (2) Nose ring; (3) Heavy earrings; and (4) Pair of wooden clogs.

This dress made any vigorous action impossible. To Biscoe, boys who could neither run, play nor walk fast, were strange indeed. All this demanded change. Before embarking on a plan of reform, he justified his determination to alter dress: '. . . the school is not intended to Westernize the boys, and wherever the habits of the people are harmless or commendable, they are encouraged to preserve their national customs and dress. But wherever the customs have harmful effects every means is employed to try to alter them'.[27]

The method which he employed to bring about this reform was the introduction of games which were made compulsory.

In one of his school reports he described how games served to emphasize the need for changes in dress. The nose ring and earrings were found to be a painful accessory when boxing was introduced. The pheran disappeared because of the horizontal bars. Wooden clogs were hardly serviceable for playing football[28]

Before the arrival of Biscoe the CMS school was virtually just another indigenous school with seven classes. It was raised to a status of high school under Biscoe, and in 1890 it sent its first batch of pupils for matriculation at the Punjab University. Besides the requirements of the Punjab University in considering the content of the education for the school, Biscoe was influenced both by a respect for the traditional western pattern and by the need to train the boys in his charge in body, mind and soul for a full life of service to their community. To this end he drew up a curriculum which contained not only academic subjects but also subjects which gave training in physical skills such as games and manual instruction. To these were added religious instruction, in which not privilege but service was stressed. The lessons of the classroom were in this respect emphasized by practical work in the neighbourhood which made the school a pioneer in social work in Kashmir.

But though intelligent and eager to learn there were some difficulties in getting these boys to accept certain information. As already mentioned, the boys were nearly twenty years of age with their own well-defined views. They had, moreover, a belief that as Pandits, whatever they knew or had learnt from their *gurus* was correct. For example, 'they knew the earth was flat'. So convinced were they of this that it was useless to tell them otherwise. Even the local staff believed this. Biscoe reports that in an examination the boys were asked 'what is the shape of the earth?' 'The earth is round (so Mr. Biscoe says)', was the answer.

Social service

The bold introduction of social service had a double aim. By this means, Biscoe sought to mould the character of the boys by impressing upon them that greater privileges and opportunities carried with them increased responsibilities to the less fortunate. From this point of view of the community as a whole the need for such work was great. The various activities on which the school embarked brought invaluable aid to a land where widespread poverty was unrelieved by any welfare organization and where no official steps were taken to mitigate the effects of the frequent natural disasters such as fire, flood or epidemics. In starting this work the school set an example which the State was not long able to ignore.

It was great and courageous work which Biscoe had undertaken. Undeterred by the formidable hostility from outside the school and prejudice within it, he pressed resolutely on to a goal which he believed justified all the efforts which its realization demanded. Success, amidst so many obstacles, came gradually. Social change, and it was not less than this that he was attempting, is even in the most favourable circumstances a plant of slow growth. His own determination, enthusiasm and self-sacrifice were of incalculable importance in the achievement. The results, however, were commensurate with his labours. He initiated change not only in the whole pattern of education in Kashmir but by the example of his school roused to a more lively sense of its responsibilities a Government long insensible or indifferent to the miseries and privations of its people.

The place of women

The position of women in Kashmir, originally one of dignity, honour and learning had declined by the nineteenth century to that of being unwelcome at birth, untaught in childhood, enslaved when married, accursed as widows, and unlamented when dead.

The missionaries set out to mitigate this deplorable situation.

The task was not easy. By the early half of the nineteenth century customs which had arisen amid the perils of the sixteenth century had become deeply embedded in the culture of the country. Practices which owed their origins to the predatory lusts of the Mohgul Emperors and subsequent conquerors had in the passage of time acquired dignity and sanctity. In the struggle to ameliorate the lot of the unfortunate Kashmiri women the missionaries employed every weapon at their disposal. Among these education was but one. At the legal level they campaigned successfully against *suttee*, the neglect of female children they opposed with improved medical services, and through founding schools they sought to penetrate the ignorance in which Kashmiri women passed their lives. Though complete success was impossible, they made substantial progress and in so doing stimulated the local State and private authorities to make some provision for the education of girls.

From the very beginning the missionaries realized that to approach Indian women was possible only through women. Duff urged that Englishwomen should be sent out to work among the Zenanas of India. This idea was at first opposed and Bishop Wilson's answer to it was 'I imagine that the beloved Persia and Tryphena and Tryphosa remained in their own neighbourhood'.[29] But the missionaries were not dissuaded by this; the work in the beginning was carried on through their wives, until a change came and two active women's societies began to work in India during the latter half of the nineteenth century. These were the Church of England Zenana Missionary Society (CEZMS) and the Zenana Bible and Medical Mission. Both co-operated with the CMS. The Zenana Bible and Medical Mission also collaborated with other Protestant societies in India. The Church of England Zenana Missionary Society was an offshoot of the Zenana Bible and Medical Mission Society. It started its work separately in 1880 under the title. To avoid overlap the societies divided the Indian field between them.[30] The Punjab and the Sindh came under the CEZMS, Kashmir being the branch station of the CMS (Punjab and Sindh) also came into its area.

This mission commenced its work in the beginning of 1888 by appointing Miss E. C. Hull, who was in the same year joined by Dr. Fanny Butler[31], followed by Miss Rainsford and Miss E. Newman.[32] Medical work and a willingness to proceed slowly in the face of

opposition finally overcame resistance to the education of girls
and by 1910 there were six schools for girls in Srinagar.

Conclusion

It is possible to view the history of education in Kashmir from
many angles. Some attempt might be made, for example, to analyse
the role of education as a determinant of social change and to see
whether educational reform has perhaps sometimes promoted
social and political reform there instead, as is the case in most
European countries, of following it. Again, the story might be seen
as illustrating the extreme difficulty of predicting and controlling
all the by-products of any programme of educational reform. The
missionaries came to Kashmir with an aim which was primarily
evangelical. They thought of education merely as an instrument to
that end. In the face of the conditions which they found not only
were they obliged to give education a much more prominent
position in their programme but they were also compelled to
change their conception of the kind of education which ought to be
provided. While the native rulers could with some justice denounce
literacy and Christianity as subversive and disruptive, medicine
could not be so opposed. The result was a change in missionary
policy, so that in the schools which subsequently developed
academic instruction was blended with practical social service to the
community as a whole. This in its turn raises further speculation
of some interest.

The break in educational continuity which occurred in Kashmir
between the fifteenth and seventeenth centuries, for example, was
regarded as an unqualified misfortune by the missionaries and by
native patriots alike. Viewed from the mid-twentieth century,
however, there are grounds for questioning this assumption. At
its peak indigenous education in Kashmir was widespread, highly
regarded and deeply engrained in the lives of the people. The
philosophical basis of this system was, however, mystical, and
advocated, as the highest virtue, the ideal of non-involvement. The
prime instrument of progress was the projection into immortality
of the individual soul achieved by a process of contemplation and
best conducted in solitude. Such an ideal could, when most
successful, produce a rare elevation and calm of mind in individual
disciples but it was incapable of stimulating any sort of scientific
enquiry or of producing any theory which involved a concept of

society. The missionaries inherited an intellectual desert. They came to a people for whom the harsh struggle for survival had created a preoccupation with material conditions which was essentially alien to their philosophical traditions. These factors combined to produce a climate favourable to the acceptance of a system of education whose aim was to view the world objectively. The method it used was service to the community. Self interest and prejudice created opposition to the aims and methods of the missionaries. When these had been overcome the missionaries were at least spared the problem of ideological dissension.

Indeed, when, as occurred in the fullness of time, their efforts led to a revival of indigenous education, the latter did not revert to traditional models and aims but followed closely the customs and institutions which the missionaries had introduced. Modern education in Kashmir is thus a continuation of missionary work. Its inspiration and the lines of its development stem from characteristically western concepts.

NOTES

1. Younghusband, Sir Francis, *Kashmir* (London 1909), p. 170.

2. Moorcroft, W. and Trebeck, G., *Travels in the Himalayan Provinces of Hindustan . . . from 1819 to 1825* (London 1841), vol II, p. 129.

3. Remarks of R. Clark which are published in the *Intelligencer Journal* of the CMS (1855), p. 84.

4. Sherring, M. A., *The Indian Church during the Great Rebellion* (London 1855), p. 355.

5. Letter extract from original letter of R. Clark. Box G. 2/14/06. (1854) (CMS archives).

6. Clark, M., *Robert Clark of the Punjab* (London 1904), p. 190.

7. *Ibid.*, p. 191.

8. *Intelligencer* (1863), p. 169.

9. From the original record of Minutes of a meeting of the Punjab Committee for the Medical missions held at Lahore on 21 Jan. 1864 (CMS archives).

10. Original letter of Rev. J. Hinton Knowles, No. 151 (1890), p. 1. Box No. G 2/14/06 (CMS archives).

11. Biscoe, E. D. Tyndale, *Fifty Years against the Stream, The story of a School in Kashmir 1880–1930* (Mysore 1930).

Biscoe, C. E. Tyndale, *Tyndale Biscoe of Kashmir, an autobiography* (London 1951).

Biscoe, C. E. Tyndale, *Character Building in Kashmir* (London 1920).

12. James Hinton Knowles of Pentonville. He joined the Punjab and Sindh mission of the CMS on 16 March 1881—working during that year in Kangra, and from 1881–3 in Hazara and Peshawar. From 1883–94 he was in sole charge of Kashmir mission except its medical branch. In 1894 he gave up its educational side, and continued only evangelisation work. He is author of *Dictionary of Kashmiri Proverbs and Sayings* (Bombay 1885); and *Folk Tales of Kashmir* (London 1893).

13. Cecil Tyndale-Biscoe was educated at Bradfield and Cambridge, where he took his M.A., coxed the Jesus College boat in the head of the river race for three years, and coxed the Cambridge Eight to victory in 1884. He joined the CMS Punjab and Sindh Mission, Kashmir branch in 1890, as a teacher. In 1894 he became the Principal of the CMS school in Srinagar and supervised its various branches for fifty years. For these fifty years he gave Kashmir of his best. The traditions of selfless service which he built will never die. The tribute in a foreword to his *Autobiography* paid to this great teacher by the Sheikh S. M. Abdullah, former Prime Minister of Kashmir, throws light on the work and influence this great personality exerted. He writes: 'Canon Biscoe came here at a time when Kashmiris were steeped in ignorance and apathy which are generally attributes of a backward community. A callously unsympathetic system of administration lasting for centuries on end, had reduced them to barbaric conditions of living which stultified their imagination and brought about their intellectual stagnation. Amidst this darkness, Canon Biscoe set out to kindle a spark of enlightenment and liberal knowledge, and immediately came up against prejudice, superstition and social taboos. He was misunderstood by many and these reactions at that time were natural. But he did not feel discouraged by these initial setbacks. He had an inspiring way of winning the people whom he had come to serve from across the four seas, with sympathy, love and understanding he associated himself with them and shared in their joys and sorrows and thus overcame one prejudice after another, till in the end he succeeded in creating for himself a place in their hearts.' His students are proud to be known as 'Canon Biscoe's boys'. The most notable ones are a Prime Minister of Kashmir, Bakshi Guhlam Mohmad, and an Education and Health Minister, Guhlam Mohmad Sadiq.

14. *Proceedings of CMS in Africa and East for the year 1884–1885* (London 1885), p. 122.

15. *Fifty Years Against the Stream*, p. 1.

16. Original letter of J. Hinton Knowles dated 22 Aug. 1883 (CMS archives).

17. Annual letter extract for years 1889 and 1890 from J. Hinton Knowles, p. 237.

18. *Ibid.*

19. Proceedings of the 21st Conference of the CMS missionaries in the Punjab, held at Amritsar, 14–18 Dec. 1883. Original manuscript, p. 7. Box. No. G 2/14. Years 1882–3 (CMS archives).

20. Lawrence, Sir Walter Roper, *The India We Served* (London 1928), pp. 126–7.

21. Extract from original letter of Rev. J. Hinton Knowles which he wrote to R. Clark on 3 March 1890 from Srinagar, Kashmir, p. 1 of the letter. No. 151 G. 2/14/06 (1890) (CMS archives).

22. Gervis, Pearce, *This is Kashmir* (London 1954), p. 309. Quoted by Pearce Gervis in C. E. T. Biscoe's book, *Kashmir in Sunlight and Shade* (London 1922), p. 79.

23. *Fifty Years Against the Stream*, p. xv.

24. School Report of 1918, *A School in Being* (CMS School, Kashmir), p. 10.

25. *Ibid.*, p. 11.

26. Annual letter-extract of C. E. T. Biscoe (1898) (CMS archives).

27. *Fifty Years Against the Stream*, p. 3.

28. School Report of 1920, *Still Pegging Away in Kashmir* (CMS School, Kashmir).

29. Andrews, C. F., *The Renaissance in India* (London 1912), p. 35.

30. Latourette, K. S. *History of the Expansion of Christianity* (London 1947), vol VI, pp. 143–4.

31. Dr. F. Butler. Born at Chelsea in 1850. Was the first student enrolled at the London School of Medicine for Women, in days when a teacher who started an elementary physiology class for her girls received the following note: 'Mrs. S. asks that my Mary Jane did not go again to these lessons where they talk about their bodies, first which it is nasty, and second which it is rude'. Women doctors in the popular view were rough, unwomanly and somewhat incompetent. In 1874 she offered herself to the Female Normal School and Instruction Society, but before her training was finished there had branched off from this a new society— The Church of England Zenana Missionary Society—on 20 October 1880. She left England as the first woman medical missionary sent to India. This was five years before the Countess of Dufferin, inspired by Queen Victoria herself, took the first steps towards the formation of 'The National Female Medical aid to the Women of India'. For six years Dr. Butler worked at Jubbulpur, Calcutta and Bhagalpur. In 1888, she joined Miss Hull in Srinagar, Kashmir.

32. Elizabeth Mary Newman. She was born on 27 April 1855 in London. Received nursing training in the years 1875 to 1878. In the

year 1887, she was matron of a nursing home in St. Leonards. It was at St. Leonards that Dr. Fanny Butler visited her and persuaded her to join her as a missionary to Kashmir. So we find them both in Srinagar, in 1888. She worked from 1888 to 1893 in Srinagar, and in 1893 returned to England. In 1901 she again went to Kashmir permanently. After six years of hard labour, she was able to open and build a hospital for women in Srinagar, Kashmir, in Rainawar, which is still flourishing in Kashmir and called and remembered after her name. She worked in this hospital up to 1928 when she retired from active work.

6

MISSIONARY WORK IN EGYPT DURING THE NINETEENTH CENTURY

Jack Sislian

IN 1825 the first missionary to start a school arrived at Alexandria. The period from then until 1863 coincides with the reigns of the first three rulers of modern Egypt: Mohammed Ali, Abbas I, and Said. The year 1863 marks the end of Said's rule, the decline of British missionary educational activity, and the accession of the francophile Ismail to the Egyptian throne. Consequently, after 1863 French missionary educational activity developed considerably. American missionary work began in 1863.

Pioneer work in education was done by British and French missionaries. The British included the Methodists, 1823–35; the CMS, 1826–63; the Church Missions to Jews (CMJ), 1847–68; and the Church of Scotland, 1858–64; the dates coincide roughly with the opening and closing of the mission schools. The French, as Catholics, represented religious orders rather than independent churches. They began their work in 1845 and for the reason given above their work will be considered up to 1863.

The first real contact Egypt had with the modern west was military, when Napoleon defeated the Mameluke warlords in 1798 on Egyptian soil. Egypt was then a far-flung province of the crumbling Ottoman Empire where lawlessness and internal chaos were rife. The appearance of Nelson at Aboukir, off Alexandria, made matters worse. The Turkish Sultan at once sent an army to restore peace in one of his richest provinces, but one of the army officers, an Albanian, Mohammed Ali,[1] had plans of his own. He turned his back on the Sultan, fought the French, defeated the British, literally massacred the Mameluke hordes, and by 1811 had made himself the undisputed master of Egypt. Turkish attempts to defeat this rebellious officer failed utterly. The first problem to receive his undivided attention was to remodel his army along European lines. His admiration for European superiority coupled with the desire to introduce western methods into his army, indirectly prepared the ground for European missionary educational work. The missionaries were regarded as representatives of the superior west, and their schools were European models, however imperfect, which the Egyptians could study at close quarters.

Mohammed Ali's ambition was to 'civilize' Egypt.[2] By this he meant 'Europeanize'. The mission schools reflected the encouragement he gave to persons who wished to introduce European institutions. In the special schools he opened, European staffs and directors trained his army, engineers, doctors and top administrators. He favoured Christians of any nationality who would help him to strengthen Egypt militarily, economically and culturally. But apart from his immediate associates the two and a half million people over whom he ruled were not quick to share his zeal. To an Englishman he said regretfully that he could find very few to understand him and carry out his instructions, that he knew that he was often deceived, and that as a result he had been almost alone the greater part of his life.[3] To another Englishman, years later, he said that when he had come to Egypt it had been barbarous—and it still was. He hoped his efforts had made the country somewhat better than it had been and that Europeans would not be shocked to find none of their own civilization.[4] To a French contemporary he complained about the laziness and ignorance of the Egyptians, of their bad faith, and the compulsion he had to use to make them work. His policy was to change them into efficient workers.[5]

Mohammed Ali hoped to achieve these aims during his lifetime. He decreed a strong and well-disciplined army and navy, and established schools, factories, and industries. Force was needed to make people work in his factories, to make people join his army and navy, and to make children attend his schools. His 'men hunters' were empowered to kidnap suitable men and children for his new establishments and institutions. He was fully aware of his dependence on Europeans, especially the French and the British, for a number of his reforms. Rosetti, Bokti, Cérisy, Campbell and very many others were friends from whom he acquired most of his new ideas. He himself acknowledged his indebtedness to them.

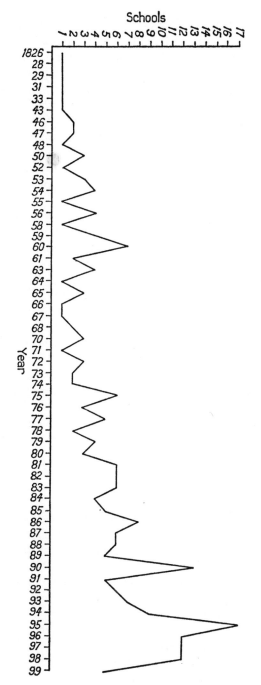

MISSION SCHOOLS, BRITISH, FRENCH AND AMERICAN,
OPENED IN EGYPT IN THE NINETEENTH CENTURY

N

For instance, to Colonel Sèves he owed his army, to Cérisy, his navy, to Clot-Bey his medical schools.[6] He was very anxious to maintain his friendship with the English, and to a British consul in Egypt he said he could not undertake anything important without England's permission, and that wherever he turned she was there to thwart him.[7] The attitude of the Muslim Egyptians to Europeans was one of traditional deep-rooted distrust if not hatred, and this was incompatible with his policy of 'Europeanization'. Mohammed Ali's own liberal example was obviously not followed in dealing with non-Muslims. These in their turn were not slow to exploit their new and secure status.[8]

In line with this general policy the ruler did everything possible to inspire confidence in Europeans by action rather than mere words.[9] To the growing English congregation at Alexandria he gave a site for their church. Missionary societies were granted free land and buildings as a token of approval of their educational work. They were allowed to travel free on trains and their personal effects and equipment for their schools were permitted to enter Egypt duty-free.[10] Comparing the status of Christians in the Ottoman Empire a missionary in Egypt who later became Anglican Bishop at Jerusalem wrote as early as 1826, 'Egypt is the most tolerant nation of the Turkish Empire'.[11] The missionaries made use of this rare opportunity in a Muslim land. It promised 'a harvest' and they came to Egypt with hopes of success through either persuading Muslims to embrace Christianity (Methodists), or reviving the Coptic Church to an evangelical faith (CMS), or converting the Jews to Christianity (CMJ), or teaching and preaching Catholicism combined with a love of France.

In order to carry out his missionary work the first step the missionary took was to open a school where boys and girls would learn religious and secular subjects but which offered him the practical possibilities of getting in touch with the pupils' parents and with the local community. The early nineteenth-century missionary was almost entirely cut off from the community by language, culture and temperament. Undoubtedly, sartorially, his European appearance was a sorry sight to the Egyptians until they got used to it. Then, again, with some exceptions, the Muslims were not eager to hear him talk about his or their religion. The Jews appear to have been willing to discuss and argue about Judaism and Christianity, but hardly any became Christians. The

Copts, the missionaries thought, were superstitious and fanatical. Compared with the adult population who were hard to move the children were quick to respond to the missionary's efforts. The schools were places where native helpers could be trained to work as preachers and teachers outside the walls of Cairo and Alexandria, but they should not, of course be considered distinct from the general missionary aim of world-evangelization. Missionary educational activity, like medical work, is a department of general missionary work, although the missionaries did not set out primarily to establish a national educational system in Egypt. During the course of their work, however, they tried to ameliorate the appalling poverty, disease, and ignorance around them, and to inspire in a few people the desire for a better education and a fuller life. And, in the event, they did much to promote education.

METHODIST EDUCATIONAL SOCIETY 1825–35

The Methodist Society was the first British missionary society to start educational work at Alexandria or in fact in Egypt. A group of Moravian Brethren had worked in Egypt from 1752–74 but opened no schools and perhaps the influence of these Moravians was limited to the lives they touched. An English Moravian, John Antes,[12] was among them and his account of his experiences depicts some social aspects of Egypt at that time. Another group of missionaries, the Franciscans, had a church in the native Muski quarter of Cairo in 1732 and through the assistance of their consuls seem to have started a school where Catholic children were taught Arabic and Italian by monks: probably the first school in Egypt where a western language was taught.[13] But such missionary educational efforts in the eighteenth century were ineffective compared with those of the nineteenth and twentieth centuries. Although the Methodist Society was the first to leave Egypt its contribution should not be underrated. The society's first representative introduced himself to the various Christian communities at Alexandria and facilitated subsequent mission contacts. John Wesley's concept of his parish[14] afforded the main justification to Methodists to begin work outside England; because of it they started to establish missionary stations in several Mediterranean countries in the early part of the last century. A quick glance at this society's mission and personnel in Egypt serves as background to its educational work there.

Purpose of the mission
The magnet which attracted the Methodists to the Mediterranean was Palestine, the Holy Land; other Methodist stations in places such as Greece and Egypt were considered as points to be occupied prior to the achievement of the ultimate goal. A permanent mission was to be opened in the Holy Land but this did not take place[15] doubtless because of the turbulent times through which the Ottoman Empire was passing at the beginning of the nineteenth century. Anti-Christian fanaticism on the part of the Muslims was encouraged by the Porte, and in 1824, one year before the first Methodist missionary arrived in Egypt, the Sultan of Turkey passed a firman forbidding the import of any Christian scriptures into the Turkish dominions and ordering copies to be burnt.[16] Further, the Turkish declaration of war on Russia in 1827 could hardly have helped the missionaries to begin work in Palestine. In this declaration among other things it was stated 'as is known to every prudent person, every Muslim is by nature the mortal enemy of infidels, and every infidel the mortal enemy of Muslims'.[17]

Some groups within the society were not unmindful of economic possibilities. With the fall of Napoleon and the establishment of English naval supremacy from Canada to Hong Kong English traders were searching for commercial openings.[18] A number of missionary subscribers offered suggestions about what should be done to further English commercial activity in the Mediterranean and they pressed them enthusiastically on the Methodists.[19] (Economic interest in missionary work in the early part of the nineteenth century was also apparent in the CMS; at least one-third of its first committee in 1801 were bankers, merchants and brokers.) Egypt's growing commercial activity with England had already led many Englishmen to live in Alexandria and the society felt it could help them religiously through permanent, active missions which would also bring the Gospel to lands connected with Egypt. Soon after this belief had been expressed in England the first missionary left for Egypt in 1825.[20]

The mission
There were in all three Methodist missionaries in Egypt—Donald

Macpherson, James Bartholomew and R. Maxwell MacBrair. They were ordained ministers. The first man to arrive at Alexandria was Macpherson who remained in Egypt from 1825–9; the second was Bartholomew, who stayed from 1830–4, and the last was MacBrair, who remained only one year in Alexandria from 1834–5. Altogether the work of the Methodists lasted some nine to ten years. Their aim was to win Muslims over to Christianity. They failed utterly because they were ignorant of Muslim traditions. On the other hand official British policy never ceased to urge them to desist from their 'extremely indecorous, impudent, improper, and highly dangerous work'. Consular authorities repeatedly warned the missionaries that if they got into trouble with the Muslim authorities they would not be accorded British protection. Lack of success—not even a fraction of what was hoped for—the constant friction between the missionaries and the English consuls in Egypt regarding proselytizing, and a series of personal shortcomings and unpreparedness for the task, put an end to the mission in 1835.[21]

Methodist schools

In view of official British policy the missionaries were cautious about preaching Christianity openly to the Egyptians. It was easier for them to turn their efforts towards the Greek community at Alexandria, which had certainly heard of the Methodist schools in Greece and in the Ionian Islands (the latter were then part of the British Empire). In these lands Methodist activity had the support of the British Government and Lord Guildford, Lord High Commissioner of the Ionian Islands in 1827, praised the efforts of the Methodists and encouraged the education of the Greek youths in English. Official British policy towards missionary work was, however, consistently negative when missionaries tried to convert Muslims. But in a country like Greece, overwhelmingly Christian, Methodist missionary activity hardly presented the British with a 'dangerous situation'. On the other hand the revolt of the Greeks against the Turks was received with enthusiasm in England and led to the establishment of the independent kingdom of Greece. It was expected to provide a stepping-stone for missionary work in the Holy Land. Obviously the Greeks in Alexandria responded favourably to the Methodists' proposal to start a school for their children. Macpherson lost no time in visiting the Greek patriarch in 1825.[22] He discovered that the Greeks could not afford their own teachers, and that the patriarch preached in Arabic as well as Greek because many of the Greeks had already become assimilated and knew no Greek.[23] The Greek patriarch heartily approved the idea of a school and sanctioned it.[24] So the first British mission school in Egypt was opened at Alexandria in December 1826.[25] This was the Greek school which for the most part accepted children of the Christian denominations and shortly after an Arab school was opened for Muslims and Copts.[26] A few Muslim boys did attend but by 1834 there were none.[27] The languages taught to the Arabs were their own and the East Mediterranean *lingua franca*, Italian. The books used were *Genesis*, the *Psalms*, the New Testament and Watt's catechism—all in Arabic.[28] Under the circumstances no alternative was possible for the Muslim parents other than to withdraw their children from the school. To the Muslim mind any attempt to equate Islam with Christianity is a contradiction in terms, and to try to replace it by Christianity is blasphemy.

Several native 'teachers', Christians such as Syrians and Copts, were engaged by the missionaries and were supervised by them. But with rare exceptions these teachers were unsatisfactory. They were lazy and dishonest, receiving a salary from the missionary as well as fees, secretly, from the children's parents, when the schools were free at the beginning of the mission's work. Attendance fluctuated with the change of teachers, with the introduction or abolition of fees, and with the extent to which the missionaries gave presents and money.[29] On the average there were throughout the years of the mission's activity some thirty pupils in monthly attendance. The schoolrooms were in a cellar without window or opening to admit light or air, and no sooner had the children come in than their breath made the place intolerable and many of them suffered from bad health as a result.[30] Bartholomew introduced writing, reading and arithmetic into the schools and he generally attended in the morning to listen to the children read the Bible in Arabic, Italian or Greek. No English was taught in Methodists' schools.[31] The Methodist Missionary Society's endeavour in places such as Greece, Palestine, Egypt, and Malta during the early part of the last century has been acknowledged to be disappointing by the society itself:

Missions seem to have been the product of a devout imagination rather than of a well-balanced judgement. Greece, Egypt, and

Palestine were names to conjure with and the sentiment they aroused seems to have been both to the Committee and to the Church at large the determining cause of the enterprise.[32]

Apparently the missionaries failed completely to convert Muslims. The schools which they opened, it was thought, would attract them and thus facilitate conversion. No child was accepted who was not willing to learn the Scriptures as well as the other subjects—a fair *quid pro quo* from the missionary point of view. The question whether one should Christianize to civilize, or civilize to Christianize, is still a moot one. But the consistently negative policy of the British Government together with Muslim traditions discouraged the missionaries so strongly that the last missionary said he had not the least faith in the scholastic plan of converting souls.[33]

Language was a great problem. Macpherson tried to learn Arabic but must have found it very difficult. In his manuscript letters to the Mission's headquarters in London are found here and there words written in Arabic, proof of his intention, but misspelled. Bartholomew spoke of his desire to learn Italian and then Arabic.[34] A year later he complained of the difficulty of learning Arabic and gave up under the strain.[35] MacBrair had to engage a dragoman in whom he had no confidence but he could find no one better.[36] The lack of conscientious native teachers for the schools was another problem which made them short-lived.[37] A contemporary visitor to Egypt said not unjustly that the failure of the Methodists' educational work was due to their lack of knowledge of Arabic and to the employment of translators in their schools. Since they knew no Arabic they had to rely on native teachers with whom they talked through the services of interpreters. Under such circumstances the Methodists' influence on their pupils was small and too indirect to produce any useful results.[38]

Evaluation

From a purely proselytizing angle the missionaries failed. But the fact that they took an interest in the children of the Alexandrian Greeks at a time when this community had no schools of its own, encouraged it some years later to give special attention to the education of its children. The provision by the Greek community of Greek schools from about 1840 onwards was educationally an immense step forward. The impetus was given by the Methodists' schools. It was especially remarkable because Greek was not understood by the patriarch's community as a whole. One result was that the Greeks gradually acquired a sense of belonging to a distinct community with its own language and culture. All those who felt themselves to be Greeks became part of one influential, organized Christianity as early as the middle of the last century. It was influential financially because the ruler supported those who furthered Egypt's commerce and because many of its members were enterprising. The political independence of Greece also contributed to a sense of national pride among the Egyptian Greek community. In other parts of Egypt a similar drawing together at about this time of other Christian communities, such as the Armenian and Coptic, was undoubtedly inspired by the Greek example.

This chain reaction among the various Christian communities of Egypt inevitably led them to become linguistically and culturally distinct. Since these communities were moving ahead, each in its own way, a rift widened firstly between the Muslim native population, and secondly between the Christian communities themselves, thus making it virtually impossible for Egypt to become, culturally, a united nation in the long run. The lack of a national system of education in Egypt and the traditional distrust of the infidel added sharpness to the contours of the various distinct Christian communities.

This ethnic and cultural consolidation naturally became more and more pronounced as time went by since the Egyptian authorities could not easily interfere with the process as they were not in a position adequately to replace the educational and cultural achievements of each of these Christian communities. This policy of non-interference lasted for about a century after the Methodists began their tentative educational experiments. But at the Montreux Convention in 1937 it was made clear to the world that Egypt was determined not to allow the country to become a conglomeration of non-Muslim nations within a Muslim land. At this Convention it was stipulated, among other things, that Arabic, Egyptian history and Egyptian geography must be taught in all foreign schools—whether missionary, non-missionary or community ones. A group of inspectors of education, called Inspectors of National Culture, under the Egyptian Ministry of Education, was appointed as a result of the Convention. Their special function was to see that private schools did not undermine the loyalty of Egypt's Christian citizens to Egyptian culture and aspirations. When the régime changed from a kingdom to a republic, the importance of these inspectors grew quickly because the national aspirations of a united Egypt had to be stressed. Perhaps the educational work of the missionaries, begun by the Methodists during the first six or seven decades of the nineteenth century, contributed to the present-day problems of building a united and unified Egypt.

CMS, 1826–65

The second missionary society to start schools in Egypt was also British. Unlike the Methodists, who concentrated on the Muslims, the CMS directed its attention towards the largest non-Muslim community, the Copts. Of the four British missionary groups discussed, the CMS alone remained educationally active in Egypt for some twenty years. By 1824 the CMS was showing a great interest in the Eastern Churches in the belief that any revival in them would affect the Muslim world.[39] The society hoped that 'As these Churches shall reflect the clear light of the Gospel on the Mohammedans and Heathens around, they will doubtless become instruments of rescuing them from delusion and death.'[40] Consequently, an attempt was made to evangelize the Coptic Church from within. To achieve this young men were needed for the Coptic priesthood with new ideas about religion and life. To train such young men the CMS started its schools in Cairo, where the Coptic Patriarch resided.

Earlier, in 1815, the society had appointed the Reverend William Jowett to collect information about the state of religion round the Mediterranean. His headquarters were in Malta and he was to enquire into the best methods of spreading Christian knowledge, since very little was known about these matters in England.[41] Thus the first contact Egypt had with the society was in 1815 through Jowett who went there to look into the condition of the Coptic Church and to confer with the Coptic Patriarch, Peter VII (1809–54). The Patriarch was genuinely anxious to raise his Church and people from their 'melancholy condition', but the formation in 1741 of a Coptic Uniat Church by Pope Benedict XIV[42] and the activity of the Catholic Church in attracting Orthodox Copts away from their church had understandably made the Patriarch sus-

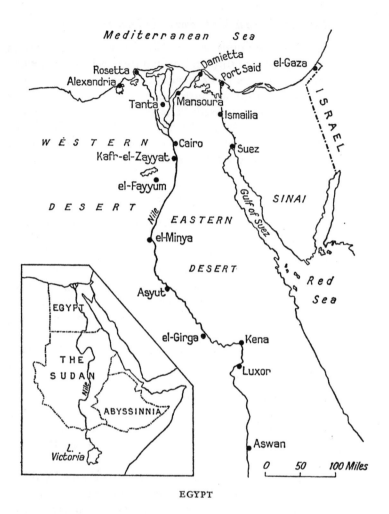

EGYPT

picious of western influences.[43] Apparently he obtained assurances from the CMS that they were not going to proselyitze because he helped the missionaries. For instance in 1843, he attended in person the first public school examination of the mission, a gesture which was rightly interpreted by the missionaries as support for their educational work among members of his community.

The missionaries serving with the CMS in Egypt were all Germans from the Basel Protestant Seminary, Switzerland, no English missionaries being then available. Their names were Samuel Gobat, who later became Bishop of the Anglican Church in

Palestine, Mr. and Mrs. John Rudolph Theophilius Lieder, Mr. and Mrs. Theodor Müller, Mr. and Mrs. William Kruse and Mr. Christian Kugler. They arrived in Egypt in 1826. Macpherson of the Methodist Society welcomed them at Alexandria and observed that in contrast to the cool reception he had received, the English Consul Mr. Salt, 'received them in a most hearty manner but they had a letter from Mr. Canning, Secretary of State'.[44] To obtain a general picture of the country the missionaries travelled by boat to places in Upper and Lower Egypt along the Nile and the canals linked with it. These served both as the principal means of communication and as an irrigation system.[45] Gobat and Kugler later left for Abyssinia to discover what possibilities there were for missionary work. Kugler lost his life in a shooting accident there.

There were about 200,000 Orthodox Copts in Egypt in the early part of the nineteenth century, 6,000 of whom belonged to the Roman Catholic Church and Coptic Uniat Church.[46] About one-fifteenth of them lived in Cairo, the rest being scattered about Egypt, particularly in Upper Egypt and the Fayyum area. The great majority of the Copts was Orthodox or Jacobite[47]—so called to distinguish them from the Greek or Melkite Church from which the Orthodox Copts had seceded in the sixth century.[48] The Copts were the surveyors, the scribes, the arithmeticians, the measurers, the clerks, in a word the 'learned' men of the land. Although they had numerous elementary schools, conducted on similar lines to the Muslim Kuttabs, there were none where the higher branches of knowledge were taught. Comparing the education of the Copts with that of the Muslims, Bowring, who was sent by the British Government to report on conditions in Egypt, said, 'Though education among them (Copts) is more diffused than among the Arab race (Muslims), their reputation for probity and veracity is very low'.[49] Apparently not even the Coptic monks undertook any kind of serious study. Peter VII's predecessor, Patriarch Marcus VIII, had written scrolls dealing mainly with religious subjects; one of these was *On Mercy*, another *Concerning those who speak impolitely in churches*. Sonnini, an observer in Egypt, described one of the Coptic convents thus:

Here, too, they keep their books, written in the Coptic language, which is compounded from a mixture of the Greek and the remains of the ancient Egyptian. Though they never read them, though they let them lie in heaps upon the ground, gnawed by insects, and smouldering in the dust, they are not to be prevailed upon to part with any of them.[50]

The missionaries also found drunkenness among the clergy.[51] Again, if a Copt fell sick he sent for his priest who came with the Four Gospels in one hand and a pair of scales in the other. On one scale the priest put the Gospels in heavy manuscript and on the other scale a vessel containing water. According to the weight of the Gospel the patient had to drink water to be cured.[52] Undoubtedly the missionaries found the ignorance and superstition more shocking than the practice. Religious meetings for the Copts were started by the missionaries. The meetings were sanctioned by the Patriarch who observed that it was better to read the word of God than to drink brandy and commit sin.[53] At times these meetings disappointed the missionaries; on one occasion for example a discussion on whether angels had wings or not lasted seven days.[54]

The CMS missionaries also found it very difficult to gain the confidence of the Coptic clergy. The missionaries therefore concentrated on educating the young Copts as one way of reviving the Coptic Church from within.[55] Success was difficult. Towards the end of his life after working among the Copts for some thirty-five years Lieder gave his verdict: 'It is painful to think that we can see none of those spiritual fruits which our eyes desire to behold'.[56] The mission closed with his death in 1865. He died of cholera and was the only surviving member of the mission in that year, the rest having died or returned to Germany.[57]

The missionaries had many other difficulties to overcome. In the course of their travels they found that although the Coptic Patriarch had received them well[58] it was difficult to enter the Coptic community which had scarcely had any contact with Europeans.[59] Another problem was that the Catholic priests in Egypt threatened to excommunicate Catholic Copts who had anything to do with the CMS missionaries. In one case at Alexandria in 1828, the Catholics who attended Müller's meeting were all excommunicated. The Catholic priests openly warned non-Catholics, Orthodox Armenians and even Turks not to have anything to do with them.[60] Three years after his arrival in Egypt, one CMS missionary complained that the greatest hindrance to the mission's work was the fear of excommunication on the part of Catholics.[61] One friendly Catholic

Copt was compelled by the Catholic priests to write a letter to be posted on the gate of the Catholic Church stating that he had allowed himself to be seduced by the English and that he was repenting. The man agreed in order to get back his wife who had been taken away from him. A young Syrian, also a Catholic, told the missionaries that he had been informed by a priest that they were Freemasons and that they had relations with the dead.[62] One reason for connecting Freemasonary with the missionaries was perhaps because from 1816 to 1830 the CMS Annual Reports were delivered at the Freemasons' Hall, Great Queen Street, London. People also feared the missionaries because a Roman Catholic, Hanna Bochari, was in charge of all oriental Christians in the service of the Pasha and there were rumours that he would induce the Pasha to expel the missionaries. The English Consul, Mr. Barker, gave assurances to them that the Pasha would not do such a thing.[63]

Again, some Egyptians thought the missionaries were political agents or spies sent by the British Government to explore the country and prepare the way for the English.[64] The 'Arabs could not conceive that Christians in England should do all this only for the glory of God, believing that England must have worldly designs'.[65] Visits up the Nile to the Delta region and to the south gave the missionaries the chance to assess the possibilities of initiating work they intended to carry out, and one result of these visits was that they established as many contacts as they could with the local clergy and laymen. They also distributed tracts and religious literature to schools and to adults. On visiting the Delta in 1828, Gobat reported, 'the people would scarcely allow me to return, from their wish that I should establish a school among them. Though they are in general very poor and ignorant still they wish more or less except the Roman Catholics to read the Bible'.[66] During the day the missionaries worked as colporteurs and in the evening they kept open house for visitors: 'No day hardly passes away without visits of Arabs, Italians, Frenchmen, Germans, Englishmen, and so forth'.[67]

The materialistic outlook of the Copts presented problems too. The Muslims' Arabic[68] impressed Lieder more than that of the Copts. He preferred their 'chanting' the Bible to the reading of it by the Copts because the Arabs 'read it purely and full-sounding according to the grammar as they read the Koran. Whereas even the best educated Christians read it and can read it only in their broken corrupted dialect'.[69] The rudeness of the Copts vexed him too, 'I can scarcely leave any school of the Copts without being greatly afflicted at the excessive rudeness both of the boys and adults',[70] and 'in the afternoon several Mohammedans called on, who behaved very well, so that I am grieved to say they surpass in manners and education most of the Christians here'.[71] The Copts' ignorance of the Bible surprised the missionaries.[72]

On surveying the situation in Egypt, Kruse and Lieder found little to encourage them to begin work, because the Copts were indifferent to the Holy Scriptures and because of the greater poverty and degradation of the community compared with the Muslims.[73] The missionaries faced a dilemma: to help them spiritually the young Copts had to read and write, but the missionaries feared that the boys would use their knowledge to earn a livelihood in the business world and neglect the propagation of the Gospel.[74] This was no doubt a naive belief which at first invited failure in their work; later, however, they became reconciled to the view that the material aspect of life was important, so much so that they offered their pupils clothing, food, and protection. The missionaries found the adult Coptic population indolent, lazy and indifferent even to their own language.[75] Nevertheless they cherished hopes for the rising generation.[76]

The missionaries found it difficult to obtain a teacher from among the Copts.[77] Kruse spoke about starting a school to the Coptic Patriarch, who gave his consent and promised to send a priest to look for a good schoolmaster. The Patriarch was also prepared to allow one of the best houses belonging to the Patriarchate to be used as a school. The missionaries were content until a priest asked them whether they would give the children food and clothing. On showing surprise Kruse and Müller were told by the priest that the English missionaries in India were doing it and that it was expected of the missionaries in Egypt too. The missionaries at first refused to comply but later changed their minds.

Prejudice regarding western influence had to be overcome. It was alleged, for example, that the Coptic custom was to have two masters at a school, one of whom had to be blind because he was better able to teach the children what had to be learned by heart and had to remain all day with the children to keep them in order.

The other master, a priest, would teach the boys to read and write Coptic and Arabic. The missionaries obviously were to pay their salaries. This plan disappointed the missionaries and they began to visit Copts in the higher social classes to find a suitable person as teacher. Problems and difficulties of this sort often depressed and discouraged the missionaries, who soon learnt that the educational outlook of the Copts and Egyptians in general was unlike that of north-west Europe.

One missionary visited Coptic schools run by priests in Cairo with his Arabic teacher. He found that in the Coptic quarter of the city there were seven schools with 220 boys, the largest contained 52 and the smallest 16. Two of the schoolmasters were blind.[78] E. S. Appleyard and MacBrair who knew Egypt fairly well confirmed that the Coptic teacher was usually blind.[79] No doubt it was thought that if a blind man could not be profitably employed he could at least teach children.

The missionaries were perplexed by the lack of response from the Copts. Apparently they were not aware that their dogmatic attitude contributed not a little to their disappointments. The feelings of the missionaries were no doubt known to Jowett in Malta, and in January 1828, he wrote to the mission in Egypt that it was time to consider what could be done in the way of schools. A new spelling-book in Arabic with a variety of lessons in it was being printed in large quantities to meet needs

from Alexandria to Aswan and farther. But a Central School as a Model conducted so far as circumstances would permit on the plan of Mutual Instruction would be requisite; it would demand all, namely all the time of Mr. Kruse, and a diligent application of all his powers and he ought to have at his disposal for the purpose of liberally paying a good Master under him and regularly rewarding Monitors or meritorious scholars not less than 200 dollars per annum. When the Patriarch and the Copts thus see it is for their interest they will probably in a tacit way sanction the proceedings.[80]

Mrs. Kruse's idea to open a girls' school as well at this time was dropped temporarily for health reasons.[81]

CHURCH MISSIONARY SCHOOLS AND SEMINARY

In 1828 the CMS opened its first school or the first British missionary school in Cairo. Lieder, who had been to see Macpherson's school at Alexandria compared his boys with those of Macpherson and reported that he had found there a great number of promising boys, an advantage which his school in Cairo was not able to boast.[82] The boys' school was opened in the Coptic quarter of Cairo and was put in the charge of a German, Kluge, who, though not a CMS missionary, was given the task because of his abilities.[83] He gave religious instruction to the 26 boys at the school.

Müller discussed with an Arab doctor in 1828 the CMS intention of opening a girls' school under Mrs. Kruse. He was told that the Christians would not send their girls to the school for fear that once they could read and write they would do nothing but write and receive letters. A Negress and ex-slave, Mrs. Dussap,[84] wife of a French doctor in charge of the Pasha's Army Medical Service at Aswan,[85] advised the missionaries that the Arabs would send their daughters to the girls' school if the girls were taught sewing and knitting as well as other subjects.[86] On 24 January 1829, the first girls' school in Egypt was opened by the CMS missionaries in Cairo.[87] Parenthetically, Young is mistaken when he says that the first girls' school in Egypt was opened in 1856 by an American mission.[88] Mrs. Kruse reported that she had tried in vain for a long time to start a girls' school, but only after the boys' school was opened were the Arabs (having observed what was being done elsewhere) inclined to send their daughters to her school. Mrs. Kruse's school consisted of ten girls from five to seven years of age, eight of whom were Copts and two Muslims, all of them so poor that they were hardly able to clothe themselves adequately. Only the two Muslims brought their own bread.

At first the girls enjoyed learning the alphabet but one girl told Mrs. Kruse that her mother was opposed to her learning to read.

> I replied, 'All those who will to come here into my school must learn to read the Bible; whoever will not do this, I cannot receive'. Hearing this she was immediately willing for the sake of learning to sew, to learn also to read.[89]

Lieder says that this school was an important step forward in the society's missionary work in Egypt.

> For reading alone no girl would come to school, as their parents cannot yet perceive what use they can derive from this acquirement, and therefore they only learn to read in order to learn sewing at the same time. But if once they perceive the great benefit which reading affords to them, they will consider the latter as secondary.[90]

Lack of space made it necessary to move the boys' school in May 1828 to a larger house which could hold 60 to 80 boys. The children belonged to various Christian denominations including Catholics. As a rule the missionaries only clothed poor Copts. In less than six months the school had gained solid ground despite threats of excommunication by Catholic priests. 'By our school,' wrote Kruse, 'we are growing more and more in public reputation. People of all denominations come to know what we are aiming at.'[91] Some educated Egyptians thought highly of their work[92] whereas others interpreted it as a cover for political activity.[93] By 1830 the average attendance at school was 40 to 55, the objects of the school were to give the poor children an opportunity of learning to read and write, and to instruct them in the way of salvation. The most important task of the school was to train promising children to become schoolmasters, so that wholly Christian schools might be organized throughout the whole country. The younger boys were taught from Watt's catechism and the older boys were made to learn six or more verses from the Scriptures. 'My most happy hours were spent with the boys,' wrote Kruse, 'and they themselves rejoiced in it and were very attentive and eager to hear me speak to them upon religion; and there was seldom one who could not recite all the verses.'[94]

During the summer of 1830 cholera broke out in Egypt and at the beginning of October after the epidemic only 20 boys remained at the school. Some of the boys had died and others, especially the older ones, had left to help their parents financially. By the end of November, the number had again increased to 70. Many were now orphans because of the epidemic. Kruse was disappointed when boys whom he had been training to become schoolmasters or translators left the school unexpectedly. The moment the boys could use the knowledge they had acquired at school to earn money their parents expected them to help them. Since the missionaries could not fail to see unspeakable poverty around them it is hard to accept Kruse's assessment that:

> Almost every boy from the beginning whom I had admitted had been delivered to me by his father or his mother, with the words—'This boy is your son, do with him as you like'. But I have now had proofs enough that their promises are but vain words.[95]

The seminary which was opened in 1833 was for the sole purpose of training boys to become schoolmasters. It was also a boarding school. The opening of this seminary caused a sensation among the Copts, since it will be remembered they had no institution of higher learning. Ten boys showing general promise were selected from the boys' school which now became the CMS day school, to start the seminary. The day school was intended for younger boys who received religious instruction. The importance of the seminary was that not only religion was taught but also literature. This new institution engaged a superior teacher who taught students classical Arabic, reading and writing, composition, arithmetic, and geography. The Bible and Church history were taught by the missionaries. Pupils were also to have an hour's instruction in English daily. This would enable them to understand their own grammar more thoroughly, and would later make it possible for them to read English tracts and books. Where a pupil showed some ability in translation he would receive special attention. The aim of the missionaries was to influence the Coptic Church through the Copts at this seminary. The greatest emphasis was given to making the seminarists true Christians, otherwise it was felt the work would be in vain. To ensure that they were truly converted the seminarists were supervised very strictly during their work and leisure hours.[96]

Attendance at the day schools was irregular and the missionaries found it extremely difficult to convey any lasting religious knowledge. For instance, on the occasions of the many Coptic feast days children were often kept away from the school for long periods. They tended to forget everything they had learnt at school. Another problem was military service. When the Pasha's army required soldiers young boys were kidnapped to fill his military schools, and later to be enlisted in the Egyptian army. During such periods school attendance increased but once the danger was over it declined. If pupils could prove to the officials in writing that they were attending British mission schools they were not taken away.

> In the newly erected school we had the same experience as in the older ones, viz., that many children attend only till they have got a covering for their body, and an attestation that they are scholars of our school, by which means they generally escape the grasp of these men-hunters, and then they stay away.[97]

If the parents of such children had a permanent dwelling the teacher usually went to ask for the certificate, but since many parents frequently moved from place to place like gypsies the teacher's task was well-nigh impossible. Madden, a British doctor in Egypt during Mohammed Ali's reign writes, quoting Clot-Bey, the Pasha's private physician, that parents had been seen to mutilate their children to prevent them from being entered in the Pasha's military schools.[98] The parents knew the Pasha's motives in kidnapping the children and his schools were abhorred. To evade conscription young men would blind themselves in the right eye, mutilate their right hands or pull out their front teeth to make it impossible for them to bite the cartridges and handle muskets.[99] An English mechanic reported in 1838 from Cairo that a *fellah* 'would rather lose a limb than be taken for a soldier: on my way to the cataracts I observed that almost all the natives were blind of the right eye, the nerve of the first finger of the right hand cut across or the teeth of the right side of the jaw extracted; and this done by themselves that they might not be seized for the army'.[100] Evidently the Egyptians resorted to such measures because at the beginning of the last century they were unable to think in terms of a nation state or appreciate the political value of an army. Boislecomte remarked that when a young man became a soldier in Egypt he was considered lost by his family, and there was resistance to the Pasha's compulsory recruiting campaign in even the poorest provinces. Consequently villages in Upper Egypt had a large number of inhabitants who had voluntarily mutilated themselves.[101]

Müller visited Asyut, Upper Egypt, in 1830. He was well received by the Coptic Bishop there, and though the Bishop was grateful that the mission desired to start schools in his diocese he told Müller that the people did not yet understand the object of free schools and that they were afraid that the English would educate their children in order afterwards to carry them to England as slaves. Moreover, the country people were so poor that their children had to help their parents make a living at an early age.[102] The missionaries also found themselves in a difficult situation over preaching and charity.

> On the other hand, if we do not cover their nakedness, and satisfy their hunger with bread, neither are we able to instruct them, nor they to receive our instruction: for how can we teach the naked and starving children to deal bread to the hungry and when they see the naked to cover him, and not to hide themselves from their own flesh? But if in a measure, we endeavour to exemplify Christian charity to them by giving them the most necessary clothing and food, they snatch it away, as a hawk does its prey, and off they are. They cannot be brought to believe that the benefactions they receive from us are acts of charity, proceeding from the love of God; but measuring our actions by the standard of their own corrupt hearts, they suspect that we use them as means to get them into our net, and make them slaves or the like.[103]

In May 1835 a plague broke out and the schools were closed, but not the seminary. The missionaries themselves moved to an island in the Nile for safety.[104] Müller wrote that before this catastrophe there were four schools in the quarter where he lived with ten or fifteen boys in each. His own and a Coptic school survived but 'perhaps one half of the present rising generation has been quickly snatched from time to eternity'.[105] Kruse did not close the seminary despite the pressure brought to bear on him by teachers and pupils because he thought that he would never again be able to start since the Pasha was filling his factories with survivors of the plague. Müller started his school again with two boys instead of the eighty he had had previously. The girls' school was reopened with very few pupils.[106] Cholera, epidemics, and bubonic plagues were a constant source of terror and interfered with the educational work of the missionaries. The Europeans shut themselves up in their quarter while the Muslims, who were fatalists, took little heed. To prevent epidemics and plagues in the Ottoman Empire a firman of the Sultan addressed to the faithful at about this time ran:

Though to shun the evils with which God visits us would be to pretend to immortality, it is allowed us to fly from the house we inhabit if that house be threatened with an earthquake; it is allowed us to pass rapidly by a wall which is about to tumble down; so ought we to preserve ourselves from the danger of the plague; for according to the spirit of the noble law (the Koran) the plague is like a fire which destroys what it touches. The body of the Ulemas have proclaimed in council that as Allah sends evils so Allah can remove them, and there is nothing opposed to the divine law in man's attempt to rid himself of them.[107]

The cholera outbreak of 1831 caused 9,000 deaths in Cairo and 1,500 at Alexandria, the populations of these cities were then 300,000 and 90,000 respectively.[108] These figures incidentally are bound to be rough estimates because of difficulties in Muslim law and tradition. Bowring observed that Mohammed Ali himself failed to ascertain the number of people in Egypt, despite assurances from the authorities and governors that the census was harmless. Not only did the 'lower classes' combine to resist the authorities but even persons of distinction connected with the court opposed the census. Every harem was inaccessible.[109] In 1834-5 the plague carried off 200,000 people and in the 1835 epidemic complete returns were not possible because the mortality rate exceeded the power of registration.[110] The figures show how disease and poverty constantly interfered with the smooth running of the mission schools.

Economic opportunities also detracted from the missionary success. No sooner were the boys confident that they had acquired 'a smattering of Frankish science' than they left for employment as clerks, usually in the Pasha's administration. This disheartened the missionaries because they felt that the boys would forget their Christian teaching. Some boys showed a talent for teaching but they would not become teachers if the missionaries had no work to offer them.[111] But not everything was in vain for sometimes news would reach the missionaries that their pupils were 'manfully fighting with their friends and contending for the Gospel's faith'.[112]

By 1839 the educational work of the CMS had recovered from the serious interruptions caused by cholera and plagues. As planned, the seminary was more important than the boys' and girls' schools since its aim was to train teachers. Heyworth-Dunne is mistaken when he writes that the CMS missionaries did not encourage their pupils to become schoolmasters.[113] Their main object was, in fact, to prepare Coptic youth to teach. At about this time there were 96 boys and 114 girls in the mission schools. Apparently the girls' school had a higher reputation than the boys' because a number of girls came from influential Coptic families. Marriage affected the attendance of girls who often became engaged between the age of nine and eleven. 'Once behrothed,' wrote Lieder, 'or married a girl is no longer allowed to appear in public. In consequence of this custom we lost last January no fewer than eleven of our most helpful pupils.'[114] Even as late as 1883 Lord Dufferin suggested in his Report on Egypt (Parliamentary Reports, Egypt, No. 6) that early marriages among Egyptian students was one of the main obstacles to higher education. Another aspect of this attitude was noted by Bowring when he visited the CMS girls' school in 1840:

> Had it been known that a European Gentleman had any intention of penetrating, I was given to understand, that the greater number of girls would have absented themselves. A few Mohammedans were among the majority of Coptic girls studying Arabic, a task in which they less willingly occupy themselves than in needlework, especially embroidery, which is the favourite employment and in which they are all particularly eager to engage themselves.[115]

The deep interest the girls took in embroidery and needlework was not surprising since the tradition in Egypt was that they were taught only to girls of the middle and upper classes. The use of the spindle was taught to poorer girls. Since most of the girls at the mission school were poor, needlework and embroidery appealed to them greatly. Finished articles[116] were taken to the market by a *dallalah* or female broker to be sold. Doubtless parents and daughters saw the commercial value of the needlework and embroidery taught in the CMS school.

The possibilities of raising the position of women in Egypt were of interest to the CMS women missionaries. They taught the daughter of the Pasha and a number of his harem.[117] Bowring saw great value in their visits to the palace harem and reported that the work in the Pasha's harem excited much curiosity. He considered it a first step in raising the position of women, which would promote a higher form of civilization in the East. The introduction into the harems of elementary instruction would create an appetite for education. All first impressions of infancy and childhood were received in the harem, so that the importance of intelligent early instruction within it could not be overestimated. If education could once be carried out in the harems it would follow more easily beyond its walls. Hekekyan Bey, who had received his education in England, was Director of the Polytechnic School, and was a key-figure in the Pasha's educational programme, had helped to direct attention to female education. It was impossible to estimate the beneficial results which might follow from the attempts by the women missionaries to educate women in the higher classes of society. There is room for a more detailed study of the role western women played in raising the position of eastern women.

In 1839 the Egyptian Minister of Public Instruction, Adham Bey, with other Egyptian officials visited the CMS schools and were very pleased with the work being done in them. They took notes and made enquiries about the Lancasterian system because they intended to start such a school for the Government.[118] Spelling books and atlases printed in Malta[119] were given in large numbers to the Egyptians for use in their schools. The Malta Press set up in 1827 by the CMS[120] played an important part in printing books for the use of missionaries. The number they distributed throughout the Arab East and their possible influence on aspects of life in the Eastern Mediterranean have not yet been investigated.

Evaluation
The missionaries appeared to be making no headway in their attempts to regenerate the 'fallen' Coptic Church. When convinced that they could not restore that ancient church to its 'primitive vigour' the missionaries planned to help train Coptic priests. The Patriarch approved and a committee of Coptic churchmen and lay-men was formed to remove any suspicion that the missionaries would teach anything beyond Christianity. This new native Christian institution[121] could not be started immediately because the CMS had not enough money and Mohammed Ali was politically entangled with the Great Powers, especially Great Britain, in

1839–40. The missionaries had to wait for this storm to abate. The Copts were also very cautious as a result of their experiences in an overwhelmingly Muslim country. The political storm blew over, the money came from the SPCK through the intervention of the Archbishop of Canterbury, and in 1843 this new institution took in seven priests, learning Church history, literature, Arabic and Coptic at an advanced level.[122] English was introduced in 1844, stress being laid on conversation. But again no improvement was seen. The hope, patience and funds of the missionaries were running out. Lieder reported:

> I am fully aware and keep carefully in view, in the execution of my duties in this Institution that no prescribed course of study or preparation however judiciously chosen and wisely administered, can of itself secure success in educating those entrusted to my care for a truly evangelical or efficient Ministry.[123]

Since this new plan was costly and not achieving its purpose, the institution was closed in 1848.[124]

As for the other schools, the Patriarch continued to encourage them, so that by 1857 the girls' school was still open and was apparently, the only institution of its kind in Egypt.[125] The boys' school and seminary closed in 1847 due to lack of funds. The former reopened in 1850, then closed again for good in 1852, also for financial reasons.[126] Since their opening in 1828 some 1,530 boys had received instruction at the seminary and boys' schools.[127] Many former pupils were employed in the Government as clerks, copyists, and accountants but the CMS felt that these youths had failed to benefit from the Scriptures. A contemporary mentioned that although the Pasha's schools provided him with administrators and executives, over 200 students in his offices had been trained by the missionaries.[128] One reason for the general lack of success of the mission schools was the poor quality of the pupils who came to them.[129]

From a purely evangelical point of view it could be said that the missionaries failed. This verdict would not be as accurate if applied to their educational and social work. Like the methodists the CMS missionaries failed in a religious sense. Lieder, who survived all the other CMS missionaries in Egypt, working there for over thirty-five years until his death in 1865, attributed the mission's failure to the Coptic priests' 'profound ignorance, gross superstition and rabid fanaticism'.[130] Sound reasons account for lack of educational success. Those trained in mission schools refused to teach because the pay was poor[131] and the title of *effendi* acquired as soon as they became clerks gave a social prestige coveted more than wealth. 'This defect,' wrote Bowring, 'pervades the whole of Oriental society.' The mission schools failed to destroy the prejudices of caste (but succumbed to them)[132] or to convey instruction downward among the people.

Two influential Coptic Church personalities attended the mission schools. One of them, Andraus, was appointed Bishop and Metropolitan in Abyssinia[133] and the other, Daud, became known as Cyril IV, the Reformer.[134] The latter took a great interest in the cultural welfare of his colleagues and is said to have started a centre where they could discuss religious and literary problems. He opened a school at Bosh, near Cairo, where Bible instruction and English were taught along the same lines as those at the CMS seminary where he had been as a young man. Daud, as head of the Coptic Church, established new types of school for boys and girls— a turning point in the cultural history of the Copts.[135] His untimely death in 1861 put an end to these reforms. His successor, Demetrius, was very conservative.

Politically, Cyril the Reformer's proposal made to Khedive Mohammed Said (1854–63) that the Copts should be allowed to take part in local government and be eligible for promotion was a very modest beginning which resulted, at the beginning of the twentieth century, in a Copt's becoming the Egyptian Prime Minister. Egyptian Muslim nationalism naturally made it impossible for an infidel to exercise such power and Botros Pasha Ghali, the only Coptic Premier of Modern Egypt, was shot.

Doubtless the spirit which increased communal feeling among the Greeks also played its part in consolidating the Copts culturally, religiously and ethnically. In what follows the educational attempts of two other British missionary societies to convert Jews will be discussed. It is significant that here too one result of the missionaries' educational work was the beginning of a stronger communal consciousness.

CHRISTIAN MISSIONS TO THE JEWS

Two British missions directed their efforts to the Jews in Egypt. One was the Church Missions to Jews (CMJ)[136] and the other the Church of Scotland. The educational activity of the former began in 1847 and ended in 1868, that of the latter lasted from 1858 to 1864. Information about the Jews living in Egypt for the period under review is scanty. The exact number of them is not known because official statistics are not available; the Turkish State Archives have material giving the number and distribution of Jews in the Ottoman Empire but only provinces under direct Turkish rule are mentioned, such as Palestine and Syria. The whole of North Africa, Egypt and most of Iraq are not considered. Egyptian Hebrew sources if extant and accessible might help, but the author has not yet come across such records. It is certain, however, that the Jews formed a very small community compared with the native Egyptians. The majority of them lived in the two big cities of Cairo and the busy port of Alexandria. There were also tiny communities in Rosetta, Damietta and other places in the Nile Delta. Cairo had a Jewish ghetto but, strictly speaking, Alexandria had none. This was in accordance with the general pattern for ghettos: namely, that wherever the native population is unfriendly ghettos exist to offer the Jews a better chance of survival. Cairo was inland and therefore provincial, not having experienced the civilizing process afforded to ports such as Alexandria. Mohammed Ali resided in Alexandria and took pride in saying that it looked very much like a European port.

The aim of the CMJ was to propagate the Gospel wherever the society felt such truth was unknown.[137] The missionaries held that as Christians they were obliged to take an interest in the welfare of the Jews, because they realized that it was through the Jews that the streams of revelation had flowed to the Gentile world; 'every prophet was a Jew, Jesus Christ, the Saviour of the World, was a Jew, all the apostles were Jews'.[138] For these reasons some English Christians felt they should help to meet the spiritual needs of the Jews. Of the other Christian mission societies, none directed its efforts solely to the Jews. For instance the SPCK (founded 1698) and the SPG (founded 1701) were primarily intended for the British Colonies and dependencies; in 1792 the Baptist Missionary Society, later called the London Missionary Society, was founded; in 1799 the CMS and the Religious Tract Society came into being. It was not until 1809 that the CMJ was established and it is now the oldest and most extensive missionary organization of its kind.

Who were these Egyptian Jews the society wanted to approach? A number of them had been keepers of wine-taverns in the ghetto. Al-Jabarti, the Egyptian chronicler, writes that Abdar-Rahman Katkhuda al-Kasdughli, a pious seventeenth-century Muslim reformer, closed these wine-taverns in the Jewish quarter. A number also occupied posts in the customs and finance departments as secretaries, clerks and accountants; there were medical men among them, as well as goldsmiths and silversmiths, moneylenders and merchants. They had synagogues where Hebrew was taught to their children mainly for religious purposes. Vocational education which the children received was taught through the system of apprenticeship.

The man who set out to prepare the ground in Egypt for the missionaries of the society was Dr. Joseph Wolff, who is known as the 'great pioneer missionary'[139] of the society and seems to have been a somewhat eccentric person. He was born at Weilersbach, a small village in Bavaria, in 1795. His father was a rabbi of the Levi tribe and brought him up as a strict Jew. He was converted to Christianity in Prague, became a communicant of the Roman Catholic Church and went to study at the College of the Propaganda. In 1819 he arrived in England and applied for membership of the Church of England and asked to be employed as a missionary. The committee of the London Society for Promoting Christianity amongst Jews decided that he should go to Cambridge to study theology, Persian, and other oriental languages, and be trained as a missionary at the expense of the society. Wolff remained at Cambridge for two years and instead of waiting for an appointment from the committee, secured a liberal patron, Mr. Drummond, whom he had met in Rome while a student. After obtaining letters of recommendation from the president of the society, Sir Thomas Baring, he began his career as a missionary. He left England on 20 April 1821 to visit Egypt and other Mediterranean countries.

Wolff visited synagogues in Egypt in 1821 distributing tracts and copies of the New Testament among the Jews in Cairo and Alexandria. With Mohammed Ali's permission he preached in the open air but the Pasha later asked him to leave the country:

Wolff, the mad missionary, was suffered readily enough to preach in the streets in an Arabic that no one could understand, but, when he placarded Cairo with too legible inscriptions then indeed the Pasha requested his departure since nothing could be done to protect him from a chance attack.[140]

After this incident the society waited till 1847 before sending further missionaries to Egypt. J. B. Goldberg and C. L. Lauria[141] were sent to Cairo. Hardly any information is available about the first. Lauria had been a rabbi in Palestine and was later converted to Christianity. He went on missionary journeys to Alexandria, Rosetta, Damietta and other places in the Delta where the Jews lived.[142] There were in Egypt European and Native Jews, the latter were in the majority and very ignorant.[143] As a result of the distribution of Bibles and tracts a *cherem* or solemn proclamation was read in the synagogues which prohibited the reading of missionary books by Jews.

The popularity of a book called *The Old Paths* by Dr. McCaul was one main reason for the *cherem*. According to the missionaries this solemn proclamation not only failed in its purpose but made the book so well known that the Jews compared its author[144] with their great rabbi. The book, of about 470 pages, first appeared in 1836; its full title was *The Old Paths; Modern Judaism with the Religion of Moses and the Prophets*. Its opening chapter dealt with 'Rabbinism not a safe way of Salvation'; there were also chapters on 'Intolerance of Rabbinic Prayers', 'Rabbinic Magic', 'Rabbinism Oppressive to the Poor', and so on. The book relentlessly and destructively criticized Judaism in an attempt to replace it by Christianity. Today, as the secretary of this society explained to the author in 1955, the present policy of the society was no longer 'destructive' but was based on the belief that Christianity was being built up as an edifice on Judaic foundations. Over a century ago the situation was different. The missionaries reported that they were well received. But there were dangers for the Jews. Several of them expressed to Lauria a desire to become Christians but the difficulties and the utter destitution to which they would have been reduced by their own community made them suppress their wishes.[145]

These fears are understandable when it is remembered how few Jews there were. When Wolff reached Alexandria in 1821 he was told that there were 200 of them in the city whereas in Cairo the number was estimated to be 300 to 2,000, among whom were 60 Karaite families.[146] These small numbers were attributed to the plague. He considered the Jews at Alexandria to be 'the most honest in the Levant, because they were expecting the Messiah very much'. He mentioned visiting two synagogues at Alexandria which were at least 600 years old and two out of the ten synagogues in Cairo.[147]

The Jews had no real ghetto in Alexandria but lived among and mixed with other peoples—especially the Greeks. By 1841 the Greeks were steadily purchasing land from the Turks whose position had become insecure because of strained Egyptian-Turkish relations. To raise the purchase price the Greeks borrowed money at an interest of twenty to thirty per cent a year[148] from the many Jewish *sarrafs*, money-lenders and bankers.[149] Another reason was that European influence had helped to extend home and foreign trade in which Jews definitely shared. Individuals prospered and Jews gradually emerged from their quarters to mix with other Christian communities. This process was certainly much quicker in Alexandria than in Cairo and it is of interest that Jews and Christians imitated European sartorial habits and customs long before the Muslims.[150] Although the Jews in Alexandria were easy to approach it was difficult for the missionaries to find them.[151] 'Most of the young Jews', wrote Lauria, 'study to remove every mark of the Jew from their countenance and dress. They shave their beards, clip their *paioth* (hair curls) and wear either the European costume or Egyptian white turban.' The rabbi felt that in ten years' time Jews would be unrecognizable in Alexandria. The Alexandrian Jews, because they mingled a good deal with Christians, did not have the same hatred for them as the Jews in Cairo who preferred to live in or near their ghetto which was known as Haret-al-Yahoud.[152] By 1847 the number of Jews in Cairo had grown to about 5,000 and they were generally fairly well off and easy to get in touch with.[153] The European Jews, of whom there were about 100 from all over Europe, looked down on the native Jews as ignorant, superstitious, and illiterate, which they probably were since they had very few schools. Egyptian Jews were always very slow to open their own schools. When they emerged from their quarters they valued the schools run by Christians and sent their children to them. Indeed one observer said that wealthy Jews lacked public spirit and failed to provide more schools for their children, and that they were intent on breaking off contact with their own community and integrating themselves into the European communities.[154]

The European Jewish immigrants to Egypt had nothing to do with the native Jews who, in fact, considered themselves to be orthodox.[155] It was difficult for wealthy Jews to settle in Cairo's ghetto for, while the city was acquiring modern roads and streets, the Jewish quarter remained as it had always been with over-crowded homes, narrow lanes and untidy shops.[156] Diseases, fever, plagues, and especially trachoma were prevalent.[157]

Initially there was some official Jewish opposition to the mission from the start, and it quickly grew stronger. As early as 1864[158] the committee of the society in London were anxious about the future of the mission in Egypt and four years later[159] it closed. Probably the missionaries felt they were making no headway. It was not until 1890 under the British that large numbers of Jewish refugees sought shelter in Egypt from the Black Pogroms in Russia. The society then reopened its mission.[160]

About 1847 the orthodox Jews in Cairo had six schools, each attended by between 25 and 40 children. Unfortunately there is no evidence as to the proportion of Jewish children attending these schools, but it may be conjectured that it was small because of the relative success of the mission schools. The teachers at these Jewish schools were badly paid, some fathers giving as little as 2*d.* a week as school fee.[161] The result was that the schools were 'miserably conducted, very dirty and disorderly'. Jewish schools were usually held in the court of the synagogue. One such school was visited by missionaries who found a few children under a rabbi who was ignorant of Hebrew and spoke Arabic. When the missionaries remarked to him that the children ought to be well educated he told them, 'No, no! they ought not to know more than their fathers'.[162]

One school run by Jews from Europe was outstanding. It was conducted on European lines. The teacher was a European Jew and the school was open to pupils of any denomination. Among the boys attending it were Greeks and Armenians. There were over 100 Jewish children who were learning Hebrew, Arabic, and French. No religious teaching was given to the pupils without their parents' consent. The annual expenditure of this school was 1,200 dollars, the greater part of which consisted of donations from Jews in Europe. This school enjoyed the support of the chief rabbi but his successor was not favourably disposed towards it.[163]

In the interests of efficiency a school for Jewish children was opened in Cairo in the autumn of 1850. Only two boys came to it but in about a fortnight the number increased to eight. Three of the boys were children of influential Jews. The chief rabbi was alarmed and preached against the school in the synagogue and 'would have fulminated an excommunication but for a rich Jew whose son attended the school prevented it by telling him that he would consider it a personal insult to himself and withdraw his support in future'. The rabbi urged the congregation to 'put away the strange gods among you', meaning the Christians, to burn their books, to attend the synagogue, and to send their children to Jewish schools. In opposition to Lauria's school a school was opened afterwards in the Jewish quarter. The warning had no effect and the mission school grew and benefited the mission both directly and indirectly.[164] In 1852 the school was teaching the boys English, Arabic, arithmetic, Biblical history, grammar and geography.[165] In 1853 there were 17 boys and the number jumped to 24 in the same year. One of the boys was the son of a Jewish schoolmaster.[166]

On Saturdays Lauria's house was full of Jews who came to see the school—one way of bringing them into contact with Christianity. In spite of Jewish ecclesiastical opposition some of the 24 boys attending the mission school attended church services. In 1855 Lauria left the mission in Egypt for health reasons and was succeeded by the Reverend H. C. Reichardt.[167] In 1855 there were as many as 95 boys at the school.[168] Probably because of this success the committee opened a girls' school in 1856[169] in response to requests from Jewish parents to admit their daughters to the boys' school. Mrs. Reichardt was in charge of 50 girls the year the school opened, and a year later 40 girls were acquiring great fluency in Italian and Arabic.[170] One reason for the success of these schools was the Jewish parents' desire to have their children taught English.

In June 1857 official Jewish opposition to the mission schools became fierce.[171] The chief rabbi was very bitter because his own school (where his son was headmaster) lost pupils to the mission school. His son's salary was thereby affected.[172] Opposition came from parents, too. They objected to the missionaries' teaching the

New Testament to their children. Several parents withdrew their children for this reason.[173] In opposition to the mission school for girls the chief rabbi opened a girls' school.[174] By 1859–60 there were 128 children attending the mission schools (average daily attendance being 50 to 60) where, in addition to the usual branches of instruction, every opportunity was taken of acquainting them with the Bible.[175] By 1861 the mission schools were flourishing and could boast of 178 children in attendance.[176] The missionaries reported, 'Our school is considered the best,' and that the Bible still formed the basis of instruction.[177]

But in the long run the relentless opposition of the Jewish ecclesiastical body to the mission and its schools in particular succeeded. By 1864 the missionaries were anxious about the future of the mission.[178] Attendance at the schools dropped from 178 in 1861 to 70 in 1866[179] and two years later the mission closed.[180]

THE CHURCH OF SCOTLAND MISSION, 1858 to 1864

Scottish interest in the conversion of the Jews stemmed from a revival of religion during the early part of the nineteenth century. The Church of Scotland was very active and between 1828 and 1841 over 200 churches were built in Scotland. Lord Cockburn remarked at the time that 'religion is certainly more the fashion than it used to be'. Other more enthusiastic observers commented on the revival of interest in religion and missionary work. This kind of spirit had inspired the formation in 1796 of two Scottish missionary societies whose aim was to spread Christianity throughout the world. It is hardly surprising that there were a number of people who thought particularly of the needs of the Jews. Indeed the fact that the Scottish Christians and the Jews shared many characteristics encouraged the former to hope that they could convert the Jews.

By 1840 the Assembly of the Church was of the opinion that the Holy Land presented the most interesting and attractive field for missionary work among the Jews. In fact the Church of Scotland commenced its mission in Safad and Tiberias in the northern part of the country. A number of societies were formed in Scotland at about this time to undertake work with the Jews. A Ladies' Association on behalf of Jewish females was established in Edinburgh in 1840. These ladies recruited teachers and raised funds for overseas work. Then the Scottish Society for the Conversion of Israel was formed in Glasgow in 1845 and in 1857 offered its missions and its agents to the Church—an offer which was readily accepted. That same year the Church of Scotland took over a very small mission at Alexandria. No further information is available about this society.[181]

When the first representative of the Church of Scotland, the Reverend James W. Yule, a foreign missionary from Calcutta, arrived in Alexandria in March 1858,[182] a hulk called *Margaret* was put at his disposal by a Captain Ryrie[183] (no doubt a member of the Royal Navy) as a floating chapel where services for the British sailors visiting the port of Alexandria were held.[184] Later another store-ship called *Bethel* was used for the same purpose. Some of the Scottish residents in Alexandria were pleased at the prospect of having their own form of worship. Yule was told that several Scotsmen working on the railways were living an almost 'heathenish' life and so he intended to visit them.[185] Because of the flourishing state of the cotton industry in Egypt the number of Scottish and English residents was increasing rapidly. They were employed in the ginning (the process of extracting cotton-seeds from the cotton fluff) factories[186] and on the railways since no Egyptian experts were then available. Thus the British were mingling increasingly with the natives and Yule felt that there was the danger of the Scottish and English residents 'going native' since it was '. . . impossible to get men to speak of or to listen to anything but cotton and money'. Ships were loaded and unloaded even on Sundays so that the crews had no time for worship and '. . . owners who at home would not dare thus openly to violate the commandment of God have no hesitation in a place like this to trample it underfoot'.[187] In this connection it is of some interest to recall that Richard Parker, the ringleader of the North Sea Fleet mutineers voiced one grievance, 'that they were not allowed to keep the Sabbath day holy, and that the fiddler had been ordered or permitted to play to them on Sunday'.[188] This kind of situation made Yule write home: '. . . you would do me a great favour if on hearing of anyone coming to this place you would give them letters to me so that I might come in contact with them before they became lost in the crowd'.[189]

Yule, who was superintendent of the Church of Scotland mission at Alexandria for about six and a half years,[190] shared the aim of most missionaries. The diffusion of Christianity was more important than secular instruction and it was hoped by the Church of Scotland that '. . . our schools shall yet be the means of diffusing in this region of darkness the light of the glorious Gospel of Christ'.[191] This was no doubt in the mind of Yule when he wrote that '. . . it is my humble prayer that many of them may through our means be led to think of Jesus as alone able to deliver them from the guilt and power of sin'.[192] Christie, another Scottish missionary at Alexandria wrote, '. . . most of these boys are progressing favourably and whatever effect their education may produce they are at least being put in possession of a knowledge of the truth which few of them could have otherwise had'.[193]

Secular instruction was one way of getting to know the parents and friends of the pupils since contact with the people was the main difficulty experienced by the missionaries.[194] 'It is of great importance especially in a missionary school to intermix secular instruction as much as possible with religious teaching. Lessons given in this way are generally inoffensive and and not always without effect.'[195]

In spite of this religious emphasis the list of materials required by the Scottish missionaries as needed in their schools reveals the Scottish traditional love for learning. Apart from Scriptural texts, they requested from home mechanical, zoological and astronomical diagrams for the walls; a magic lantern, a stereoscope with scientific slides and a small galvanic battery.[196] The range of subjects which the Scottish missionaries had in mind was more comprehensive than that proposed by the other British missions. The languages which had necessarily to be taught were Italian, Arabic and English.

> The Jews, Greeks, Copts, Armenians and Italians, all speak and do business in the Italian language and English is desired as a means of carrying on traffic with the British. A new language, or rather new languages, have now to be acquired for there seems to be no end to the number of tongues spoken in Alexandria.[197]

The Church of Scotland opened its first school in July 1859, with 4 pupils, 4 were added in the course of the month and in August 12 more; by October there were 28 pupils in all.[198] Its slow start was attributed to the fact that it opened in the hottest season of the year; fees were also thought to account for the small number of pupils.[199] Success came slowly but was not sustained. The boys were found to be gentle and interesting and within a year they were reported to be very diligent and all of them better disciplined 'than when they were first entrusted to our care'.[200] In 1861 Yule reported that the boys' school was growing:

> I go to it on the forenoons of Tuesday and Thursday and revise the English lessons. The charge of it is chiefly devolved on Signor Bolignini who not only teaches the Italian classes but takes a general superintendence of the other studies.[201]

By October of the same year new premises were acquired for the school as the number of boys had increased. Christie says that there were 39 names on the roll and 37 in attendance, 8 of whom were taught free because they were poor.[202]

By 1863, however, the Church of Scotland felt it was not making much headway in converting the Jews and made it known that if parents were unable to pay the school's fees their children would be accepted free of charge: a policy which fully indicated that the school was opened primarily for the Jews.[203] But the latter had anticipated the threat and had taken steps to counteract it. Yule wrote in 1859:

> During the past year the Jews themselves have been very zealous on behalf of Judaism—they have opened schools for rich and poor boys and are very watchful over all. I have twice visited the school for the poor. There are more than 100 boys in attendance, with Hebrew, Italian, and Arabic masters. The education is free and parents are commanded, under pain of excommunication[204] to send their children to school. One good thing connected with the school is that the books in use are those prepared by the Beyrout missionaries which are full both of Old and New Testament truths.[205]

Yule's school was in a rented house in Alexandria and he engaged a French teacher to give lessons in it.[206] At the same place a school of a 'superior' kind, that is fee-paying, was also opened under Mr. James Christie, a student of divinity. There were thirty-eight pupils, half of them Jewish.[207] Within a year an annual examination was held, the parents of many children were present and 'the greatest satisfaction was expressed with the progress the children had made'.[208] The 'superior' school was based on the principle that the pupils received the education which as far as possible met the needs of the place. What these needs were the missionaries unfortunately did not say. The school fees were raised from twelve to sixteen shillings per month. The 'inferior' school was free so that the poor 'were not excluded from the benefits of Education'. At first both schools were small. The majority of the Jewish youth in the 'superior' school came from respectable families.[209] Yule recorded in 1861 that the boys' school had seven Italian Jews, three Arab Jews, two Greeks, four Syrian Catholics, one French Catholic, one German Catholic, one Italian Catholic, four Italian Protestants, one English Protestant.[210]

When Christie left Alexandria for Scotland in 1861 his school was placed under Signor Bolignini[211] who was to teach Italian and junior English during Christie's absence. Bolignini refused to teach for more than six months and it was proposed that a Mr. Gooby should replace him, but the Church of Scotland declined the application on the ground that 'he knew none of the necessary languages'.[212] Mr. Gustav Stern was then put in charge of the boys' school but in 1863 he withdrew because of his health and the school was left in charge of the assistant teacher. About this time the lease of the schoolhouse expired and the school transferred to the native quarter of the town. It was then expected that poorer Arab and Jewish children would be more likely to attend. It was also thought necessary that the teacher should have a working knowledge of Italian and French.

Stern was replaced by the Reverend George Brown who had been a teacher for several years at Newington School. He had been sent to France for a month 'with the view of perfecting himself in the pronunciation of the French language', and took up his new post in Alexandria in 1863.[213] In less than a year Miss Ashley sent a letter to Yule, who was then in England, informing him that Brown was ill and that the doctor had ordered him to return home.[214] The boys' school closed down in July 1864, because no suitable successor could be found.[215]

There was some possibility that the Church of Scotland would start a school at Ramleh, near Alexandria. The residents were anxious to have a school and guaranteed Yule against loss, but it was never started,[216] probably for want of a teacher. Another proposal by Yule for young Jews in distress came to naught. This institution was very probably intended to help 'Christian' Jews to earn a livelihood since as a penalty their community would not offer them any work. It was also to serve as a Christian educational centre for very poor Jews who were willing to learn about Christianity and acquire a trade. The trade the missionaries had in mind was shoemaking because all the materials needed for it were available locally: shoemakers were rare, and shoes, although cheap to make were obviously expensive to buy.[217]

No sooner had the boys' school opened than Yule felt '. . . our mission will never be rightly organized until we have both'[218]— that is boys' and girls' schools. Consequently a suitable woman teacher was needed to start a girls' school at Alexandria.[219] Success was short-lived. When he arrived in Alexandria in 1858, Yule had met a Dr. Philip[220] who ran a Jewish girls' school, the expenses of which were defrayed by the Ladies' Association at Paisley. This Association sent out a teacher from Paisley for the school in Alexandria where the number of Jewish girls increased daily; there were eighty girls in attendance of whom about seventy were Jewesses. But the health of the teacher failed and she was obliged to return home. The Association had no funds to send out a successor. The ladies at Paisley, however, promised Yule that they would support a teacher for the sewing department and meet her incidental expenses. It is probable that the teacher engaged was an Egyptian. She managed to keep the school going since, although the number of scholars decreased, the school did not close. 'At present,' wrote Yule in 1858, 'the number of scholars is not great but the field appears to be a promising one; at the same time, we must keep in mind to cultivate it properly will be attended with considerable expense.'[221]

It was not until the autumn of 1861 that Miss Ashley (mentioned above) took charge of the girls' school in Alexandria. She was sent as the agent of the Glasgow Ladies' Association for the Education of Jewish Females. She reports that the school made slow and steady progress.[222] She had thirteen fee-paying pupils. Of these one was a Jewess, four were Catholics, one a Greek, one a Protestant and one was the daughter of a Turkish Bey. Miss Ashley soon acquired Italian, and was reported to be indefatigable in her efforts to promote the highest interests of the school.[223] In 1863 she retired,[224] probably with the intention of returning home, due to ill-health.[225] But apparently she stayed on, for the records show her still running the school in 1866. In 1863 Yule reported that under

Miss Ashley's care the school was flourishing,[226] and by 1864 there were seventy-five girls,[227] eight or ten of whom were Jewesses, the same number of Greeks, thirty-two Roman Catholics, while the remainder was Protestant.[228] Again, on 5 July 1864 the Reverend Thomas McKie who had visited some of the Church of Scotland mission stations in the east to report on them, told the members of the acting committee of that Church about the girls' school at Alexandria: 'I had very great pleasure,' he stated, 'in spending a forenoon in the numerously-attended school taught by Miss Ashley where I found the girls I examined well versed in Scripture, History and in the leading truths of the Gospel.'[229] A year later the Church of Scotland Report for 1865 echoed McKie's words almost exactly:

> The female school under the superintendence of Miss Ashley has been vigorously sustained this year. On an average about sixty pupils have been in attendance and have made very great progress in their different studies. In Bible lessons their attention has been directed to the chief doctrines of the Gospel; and though we do not see much at present of what is called fruit yet we hope and believe that the word of God read and taught will not be in vain.[230]

Although the school was supported by the Glasgow Ladies' Association and charged fees[231] in addition, there was a possibility that it would have to close for lack of funds.[232] However, £100 was handed over to Miss Ashley by the Association to meet expenses. At the meeting in 1866 the question of finance was discussed and it was resolved to make a rigorous attempt to continue supporting the school by recruiting more lady collectors in the several congregations of the city of Glasgow.[233]

Perhaps the Scottish missionaries' urgent need for money made the Church of Scotland decide in 1861 to request the Viceroy of Egypt, Said Pasha, through the intermediary of the British Consul-General and Agent in Egypt Mr. R. G. Colquhoun, to grant land for 'an institution in which instruction in all branches of education might be communicated to the children of Europeans and all classes of His Highness' Subjects'.[234] Said paid a visit to Queen Victoria in June 1861, and was approached by the Church of Scotland for help. Said reacted favourably and on his return to Egypt granted the Alexandria Scottish mission a large piece of land outside the city valued at £3,000 with the proviso that the Church was at liberty to sell the land to buy a site in the centre of the city.[235] This ground was to be used as a building site for church and schools.[236] The Church received £14,000 in cash when it sold the land—the balance after paying for the site in the city centre.[237]

The Church was so impressed by the Viceroy's gesture that its Convenor, James Macgregor, in the Report for 1862 said:

> Perhaps the highest tribute to the eminent success of the Mission was the encouragement and assistance which it received from His Highness Said Pasha. The Church has never thoroughly appreciated the significance of this notable fact that a Mussulman prince shrewdly alive to the progress of the times recognized the advantages which accrued to his people from a well conducted Christian Mission; and as a tangible token of that recognition, not only presented it with a floating chapel (*Bethel*), fitted up at his own expense with library, reading room, dwelling for a missionary and place of worship, but last year with a princely munificence which attracted the attention of the country gave a grant of land of the value of £3,000. That liberal grant was expressly made with a view to the erection of much-needed Mission premises.[238]

Other sources of income came from the sale of Bibles and religious books by the missionaries, contributions mainly by British residents, collections at services, and money granted to the mission by the British Government under the Consular Act[239] for carrying out religious services among British seamen in the Alexandrian harbour. The following entry was made in one of Yule's reports on the sale of Bibles and religious books during 1862 and the early part of 1863:

> Visits paid to Shipping 1895; Tracts distributed 9274; Bibles sold 96; Religious Books sold 200; services held 66; attendance at these 3163; also the following particulars for the first quarter of the present year—visits paid to Shipping 690; Tracts distributed 2368; Bibles sold 41; Religious Books sold 122; services held 19; attendance at these 1686. The sum of £136 has been contributed during the past year by British subjects and others residing in or resorting to Alexandria for the purpose of the Harbour Mission and the sum of £127 19*s*. 1*d*. has been

received from the Government under the Consular Act for the same purposes.[240]

In general the Jews were prepared to send their children to the mission schools provided no proselytizing took place. But since this was the express purpose of the CMJ and of the Church of Scotland they had little choice but to withdraw their children from these schools, which were eventually forced to close.

One result was that the Jews who previously had made very little educational provision for their children began to build schools. The keener awareness of their community corresponds to the *esprit de corps* developed among the Greeks and the Copts. Thus the cultural differences of another non-Muslim community in Egypt became more sharply delineated because of missionary activity among the Jews. It became virtually impossible for the country to attain cultural and national cohesion.

But the picture would hardly be complete without some awareness of the attitudes of Abbas I (1849–54) and Mohammed Said (1854–63) who reigned for the greater part of the period when the CMJ and the Church of Scotland were active. One historical tradition has it that Abbas was a reactionary of the worst type—an anti-European who closed schools because he felt they were impious and unnecessary.[241] Another is that Abbas is blamed for many things he did not do. It is argued that he simply gave the *coup de grâce* to an Egyptian educational system which in 1840 had already received its death blow during Mohammed Ali's reign. It will be remembered that this date marks the start of Mohammed Ali's decline as a result of his involvement with Great Britain. Schoelcher, who visited Egypt in 1844, wrote that

> les écoles n'étaient pour Méhémet-Ali que des instruments de guerre; il y renonce aujourd'hui que son rôle d'aggresseur est fini, et qu'il a dû perdre l'espérance de conquérir le trône du Sultan. Il n'a plus besoin d'armée, il ne veut plus d'école.[242]

Undeniably many schools were closed down by Abbas and indeed, Said's attitude to education and the enlightenment of the Egyptians is well summarized in his own words, 'Why open the eyes of the people, they will only be more difficult to rule'.[243]

From 1848 to 1863, when the pro-European Ismail came to power, little seems to have been done for education in Egypt.

Indeed, most of the institutions begun by Mohammed Ali gradually disappeared. Nassau Senior once asked Hekekyan Bey (mentioned above) what had become of the public instruction established with such a flourish in modern Egypt, 'The Council of Public Instruction, 1836, was abolished by Said,' was the reply. Of the primary schools which were spread over all Egypt? 'Abolished by Abbas and Said.' Of the preparatory schools? 'One exists, the other was abolished by Abbas.' The polytechnic school? 'Abolished by Said.' The school of languages? 'Abolished by Abbas. Shepheard's Hotel in the Ezbekeeyeh was built to receive it. Mr. Shepheard and his waiters are the successors of the Professors of Arabic, Persian, Turkish, French and English.' Of the cavalry school? 'Abolished by Abbas.' The infantry school? 'Abolished by Abbas.' The artillery school? 'Abolished by Abbas.' The veterinary school? 'Abolished by Abbas.' The medical school? 'Reduced by Abbas. The pupils remaining there when Said came to power (about 100 instead of the 150 whom Mehemet Aly left there) were all taken and sent by him to serve as privates in the army. These were young men who had given five or six years to the study of medicine or surgery, every one of whom would have diffused not only health but knowledge over the country.' What then remains of the great provision made by Mehemet Ali for public instruction? 'Nothing except one preparatory school. Abbas and Said, though they differ on every other question, agree in their hatred or their contempt of knowledge.' Senior visited the public library in Cairo, and there found the shelves empty, and the rooms occupied by the clerks of the War Office.[244]

It was against such an educational background that the missionaries maintained their schools for as long as they could. It is perhaps not fanciful to suggest that to some extent their educational activity kept the desire for learning alive, at least in non-Muslim communities, until, under Ismail, education once more began to move forward in Egypt.

With the Church of Scotland's work British missionary educational activity in Egypt came to an end for the period under review. Meanwhile, the French had been active, not in a military sense this time, but by spreading their language and culture first among the Catholics and then among the Egyptians generally.

FRENCH MISSIONARY EDUCATIONAL ACTIVITY (1845-65).

Information about the French missions is rather scanty. They came to Egypt about a quarter of a century after the British, and their reports are not as full. For example, one French missionary, Piolet, complained that the reports of his brethren left out almost entirely matters of local interest, and unlike those of the British missionaries concentrated solely on somewhat factual information.

Perhaps the policies of the French during the period 1840 to 1860 should be compared with those of the British rather than the extent to which each group provided schools. The French missionaries adopted a dual role—Catholic and *culture française*. Each of the four British Protestant groups had a purely missionary aim. The British schools were not intended to spread a love for England. The French schools, on the other hand, were centres designed to spread French culture.

Nevertheless, some mention of the scope of the French missionary educational work is desirable. Unlike the British who started schools for boys the French first opened schools for girls. The first of them was started in Muski, Cairo, on 6 January 1846. It was a free girls' primary school called the *Maison du Bon Pasteur*. In the same year at Alexandria another girls' school was opened by the *Soeurs de la Providence*. A year later two boys' schools were established at Alexandria—one was fee-paying, the other free. The free school was opened on 1 July 1847, by the Lazarists as the *École Gratuite des Frères*, but the teachers were *Frères de la doctrine chrétienne*. The fee-paying school was called the *Pensionnat des Frères*.

Two more schools were opened in 1850; one in Alexandria for girls under the *Filles de la Charité*. This school also helped orphans in 1860 when refugees came to Egypt from the Lebanon as a result of the Druse–Maronite disturbances. The other was a boys' school run by the French Franciscan Fathers in Negada, Upper Egypt. The same Franciscan order started a similar school in Girga, Upper Egypt in 1853. The *Pensionnat du Bon Pasteur*, a fee-paying school, started work in Port Said in the same year.

On 15 February 1854, the *Frères de la doctrine chrétienne* opened an *École gratuite* in Cairo which had a free as well as a fee-paying section. Another school, the *Pensionnat Saint-Joseph* started in Cairo in the same year with eight teachers. This school was in Shubra, then a suburb of Cairo, and was transferred to Khoronfish, probably because the *frères* wished to be nearer the centre of the city.

In 1853 the Franciscans opened a boys' school in Mansourah, Lower Egypt, and a year later another in Damietta, and in 1856 yet a third in Kafr-el-Zayyat, Upper Egypt. In 1858, 1859 and 1863, they started boys' schools in Rosetta, Suez and Port Said, and another in 1863 in Kena, Upper Egypt.

The background of this activity is of some interest. The Lazarists prepared the ground for it. In 1840, Abbot Etienne, a general-procurator of the Lazarists, was sent by Guizot, the French Minister for Foreign Affairs, on a political mission to Mohammed Ali. During his three weeks' stay he was told by Cochelet, the French Consul at Alexandria, that the Catholic population of the city had been asking since 1836 for Lazarist missionaries to establish a college in Alexandria, and for the 'Daughters of Charity' to run a European hospital.

The Abbot was in favour and Cochelet followed the matter up by going to Rome to obtain the permission of the Prefect Cardinal of the Propaganda. Guizot asked the French ambassador to the Vatican, le Comte de Latour-Maubourg, for help. Talks went on longer than was expected but on 3 April 1843, at the request of the holy congregation of the Propaganda, it was decided to send Lazarist priests to Alexandria to teach young boys. In addition, a number of 'Daughters of Charity' were to go to care for the sick and to teach young girls.

One reason for the decision was that the efforts of the Franciscans to meet the needs of the Catholic population were no longer adequate. By 1844 Alexandria had between six and seven thousand inhabitants and was growing fast. Muslims and Christians came to Egypt from many parts of the world expecting to make a fortune. Many were disappointed, but once having settled the thought of educating their children kept them there. The influx of new Christian communities and the growth in the Catholic population partly explain the arrival of the Lazarists and the Daughters who left France during the first days of 1844 and arrived in Alexandria on 29 January 1844. There were five missionaries—three priests and two brethren—and seven 'Daughters of Charity'.

They all received a warm welcome from de la Valette, the Consul of France. The Daughters stayed with the Pastre family from where they went to the hospital to set to work immediately. The Lazarists were offered an old fortress by Mohammed Ali and given permission to buy up the surrounding lands—a further example of the Pasha's religious tolerance. The 'European' hospital which they ran was so called because it received the support of France, Austria and Italy. Four of the sisters were permanently attached to the hospital and the other three lived there temporarily and taught and cared for the Arabs in an adjacent building.

In 1846 the Daughters founded the *Maison de la Miséricorde*. After receiving a large piece of land from Mohammed Ali its work grew and an orphanage and a boarding school were added to the already existing dispensary and day classes. Cholera, for the time being, put an end to the *Maison's* work in 1848 because, while caring for the sick the sisters were unable to devote themselves to school-work. When the epidemic was over the day-classes, the boarding school and the orphanage resumed with larger numbers of children than previously.

In 1847, while waiting for their college to be built, the Lazarists asked their general-superior for several brethren to teach in their free school housed in one of the Franciscan buildings. Their superior was a Frenchman, l'Abbé Bel, who was assisted by five other French Lazarists. By 1852 they had seventy pupils, the majority of whom came from the first European families to settle in Alexandria. In 1860, the school was turned into an orphanage for the children of the Levant, whose parents had been massacred in the Druse–Maronite crisis. Bel died and was buried within the precincts of the college. During the British Campaign of 1882 in Egypt, the Arabs burnt it down. The Lazarists applied to the British for compensation, and received it.

An *Orphélinat de Saint-Vincent de Paul* was founded in Alexandria in 1860. The purpose of this school was to receive and teach young boys who, for one reason or other, had no parents and no financial support. Here the boys were taught elementary subjects, principles of religion and ethics rather than academic subjects. This school was intended to prepare craftsmen or tradesmen. At the end of the course the boys could either leave to work outside or, if they wished, in the school. They received a remuneration according to the work they were doing. The priests made it clear to the boys that there would always be a place for them in the workshop of *St.*

Vincent de Paul if they wished to return. The boys were all under twenty years of age. Unfortunately no information about the teaching methods used in these schools is available except for some general observations made by visitors to French schools.

In 1859 six *Soeurs Franciscaines* opened their Maison under Sister Marie-Cathérine, in Rue Clot-Bey, Cairo. The aim of this establishment was to purchase Negress slaves, teach them and release them as free women. Some fifty Negresses were bought yearly until 1882 when the Maison's work ceased when Father Dom Verri, who brought the slaves, died. He was not replaced.

The Lazarists also co-operated with the *Frères de la doctrine chrétienne*. In 1847, Monseigneur Perpetuo Guasco, Apostolic-Vicar and delegate to the Holy See in Egypt, wanted to establish a Christian school in his episcopal city. He therefore met the Lazarists and the *Frères de la doctrine chrétienne*. The former agreed to pay the latter to teach in their school. The school was opened by Brother Adrien de Jésus, on 1 July 1847. There were three pupils at first but later the number increased to 120. A noviciate school was also started at Alexandria by Brother Adrien de Jésus in 1861 but shortage of Brethren prevented it from prospering at first. Brother Gémél-Marie was in charge but as he was also in charge of a class at the College de St. Cathérine (a boarding school opened in 1853) he could not devote much time to the noviciate school. When Brother Adrien de Jésus died in 1879 the school was transferred to Ramleh, near Alexandria, and Brother Gémél-Marie took over. Brother Gémél-Marie died in 1884, and Brother Jouannet-Marie, who was in charge of a school in Midi, France, succeeded him. By the end of the nineteenth century this noviciate had eight teachers and thirty-six noviciates recruited from French as well as Armenian, Syrian and Egyptian youth.

In 1856 the Catholics built a church in Kafr-el-Zayyat, Upper Egypt, with a boys' school attached to it with thirty-three children. The very few Catholics in Rosetta built a small church for themselves in 1861 and dedicated it to the Holy Family.

This account of the early French mission schools has been taken in the main from two important, if not virtually the only sources: Guérin[245] and Hilaire de Barenton.[246] It is intended to serve as background to important aspects of their educational policy. These very modest beginnings were to assume phenomenal proportions later in the century. The chart shows the rapid growth of mission schools in Egypt, including those of the Americans. The French schools were far more numerous than those of any other nation in Egypt during the nineteenth century. The framework of French missionary educational activity was political and religious. French politics served as a *raison d'être*. In fact, it would be hard to distinguish between the educational work of the French Catholic missionaries and their conscious effort to establish a belief in the superiority of French 'culture' and 'civilization' over those of Russia, of America and especially of Great Britain.

It appears that the advice given by Louis XVI's brother to Savary, in 1774, when the latter was to leave for Egypt for the purpose of study, had been forgotten by nineteenth-century missionary proponents of French culture and catholicism. The advice was:

Jeune homme, vous allez à une terre étrangère; vous verrez des hommes nouveaux. Observez l'influence du climat, l'empire de la religion, la loi impérieuse des usages antiques, et l'action que le despotisme exerce continuellement sur les faibles humains, et vous y trouverez l'histoire de leur vices et de leur vertus; pour faciliter cette érude, apprenez les langues de l'Orient; conversez avec les Grecs, les Turcs, les Arabes; vivez avec eux. Pour les voir tels qu'ils sont laissez en France vos préjugés. Tâchez de peindre d'après nature les peuples que vous verrez. Que le Turc ressemble à lui-même et n'allez pas représenter Paris au grand Caire.[247]

Nevertheless, such views probably in some way influenced Napoleon's declaration in 1799, on Egyptian soil, that he was the Defender of Islam. Between 1803 and 1807 events forced the French out and their threat to British control of the route to India was averted. France's political interest in Egypt remained and the mission schools served as one way of asserting it.

Almost a quarter of a century after Napoleon's withdrawal General Belliard, in a letter dated 29 October 1824, wrote to his colleague General Boyer, 'Les intérêts du pays (Egypt) que vous allez habiter sont tellement liés avec le notre que bien servir l'un c'est les servir tous les deux'.[248] The French knew perfectly well that if England did not hold Egypt she would see to it that France did not succeed, yet despite their own withdrawal the French could not accept the idea that England had come to stay. Circumstances eventually made this quite clear to them.

Thiers thought that 'It was in Alexandria that France had to seek and establish her true influence over the Mediterranean',[249] but in Nelson's opinion, 'an English victory on the sea would ensure the security of Egypt',[250] although it was 'England's policy not to interfere with the internal affairs of Egypt',[251] it was important to the security of the route to India. The same note was struck during the Second World War by the British who felt they had saved Egypt from the invasion by Nazi Germany; but Egypt thought that the British action was simply to safeguard her own interests.

During the nineteenth century Anglo–French rivalry was based on the question of who had the greater stake in Egypt. Because of her Empire, Britain had a direct political interest:

> The small amount of our military force with the enormous extent of our empire, must be counterbalanced by abundant means of communication, and extraordinary rapidity of transport.[252]

France, on the other hand, sought to acquire prestige and influence by the diffusion of French culture through missionary education. The British felt that the French 'have never, since it (India) was consolidated, failed in their efforts to secure, either by arms or influence, a footing in Egypt'.[253] 'Who has a greater interest at stake in Egypt than England?'[254] the British asked. Forty-three years later Lord Milner, as British High Commissioner in Egypt, said much the same thing: 'Great Britain is, by virtue of its enormous direct trade and still more enormous transit trade, the most deeply interested in Egypt'.[255] The British belief that 'A rapid means of communicating between India and Malta through Egypt would multiply tenfold the resources of Britain and secure the defences of our possessions from Canada to Hong Kong',[256] further emphasized the point.

In Britain's view France had no business in Egypt. She could develop the lands she already possessed.

> Let France keep her Algiers; let her develop its resources; let her make it an India within three days' voyage of her ports. All we want of Egypt is a road; and if she does not mean to retrograde among powers, to give up what she now enjoys, and yield

the best part of the fruits for which her sons have bled, then, we say, that road she must have.[257]

Both countries used political and military pressure to influence Egypt but, whereas Great Britain worked through diplomatic channels, France used both official diplomacy and the mission schools. It will be remembered how the British representatives made clear to the Methodist missionaries that their Government was strongly opposed to any proselytizing among the Moslems in Egypt. The French thought otherwise.

France claimed the right to protect the Catholics in Egypt, irrespective of nationality, whereas British policy extended protection only to natural-born Britons and not to those who had been converted by the missionaries—a policy regarded by some British missionaries as uncooperative, and obstructive. The following incident between the Church of Scotland and the Foreign Office illustrates the state of affairs.

According to Nathan Davis, the Church of Scotland missionary at Tunis, Jews who had embraced Roman Catholicism enjoyed the protection of the French Consulate if they were persecuted. The question arose as to whom could converts to Protestantism apply for shelter if not to the British Consul.[258]

The Church of Scotland committee felt that as far as native Protestants were concerned the decree of the Sultan of the Ottoman Empire giving complete liberty of conscience and civil protection to subjects of every creed had become almost a dead letter. Russia enforced the decree where members of the Greek Church were concerned and France did so when the case was that of the members of the Church of Rome. Already about the middle of the nineteenth century the CMS missionaries were mentioning in their reports to London that Orthodox Copts did not feel abandoned in a Muslim country as Russia had made known her intention to protect them. She was sending the Grand Duke, Czar Nicholas I's brother, to Egypt as a token of this support. The visit did not take place and the Turkish Pasha in the provinces discovered that the Protestants could be persecuted with impunity.[259]

The Foreign Office made its position clear in a letter dated 24 November 1848, stating that '. . . if British Societies wish their missionaries abroad to be placed under the protection of British officers, they ought to employ natural born British subjects'.[260]

Davis, therefore, did not enjoy consular protection as he was a Tunisian Jew by birth and a convert to Protestantism.[261] When the committee of the Church of Scotland received the letter it addressed two issues to Lord Palmerston on 8 February 1849. These were whether immediate instructions would be sent to the official at Tunis to do everything in his power to protect converts and whether his Lordship was prepared to give an assurance that if the committee sent out another missionary he could depend on British protection for himself and his converts.[262]

In reply the Foreign Office said that all the British Consul-General could do with regard to the Jewish subjects of the Bey of Tunis who might be converted to Christianity was to give them his unofficial protection. For these good offices to be effective it was necessary that the conduct of the missionary should not give offence to the Tunisian Government.[263]

The following letter represents official Foreign Office policy:

Foreign Office
March 20th, 1849

Sir,

I am directed by the Viscount Palmerston to acknowledge the receipt of your letter of 3rd instant. . . . A missionary who is a British subject will of course be under the protection of the British Consul-General but such missionary must conform to the laws of the country and if he is to succeed in his endeavours, he should be careful not to offend the prejudices of the nation.

With regard to Jews who may be converted to Christianity, H.M. Government cannot claim any right by treaty to take such Persons under British Protection but the good offices of H.M. Consul-General would on any proper occasion be exerted un-officially on their behalf.[264]

In his official capacity as head of a French diplomatic mission to Egypt, Boislecomte referred in his talks with Mohammed Ali to the Catholic interest in France's *protectorat religieux*. His recommendation to the Pasha was that 'les intérêts des catholiques de Terre Sainte protégés par la France'.[265] As a result the Catholics repaired and built churches, undertakings which had been forbidden by the Porte before Mohammed Ali came to power.

One French authority, Piolet, was inclined to include the Franciscan Fathers' mission among the French missions, but he hastened to add that this mission was not truly French but international and universal, because although Catholic, it did not, on feast days, hoist the tricolour but the red cross of the Holy Land.[266] Chateaubriand could hardly have included the Franciscans among his missionaries, since he held that: 'La maison au sommet de laquelle vous verrez flottez le drapeau de la France, c'est la demeure du missionaire'.[267]

Speaking of the love that impelled the French Catholic missionaries to sing among 'les peuples sauvages de l'Orient', Hilaire de Barenton asks what was the song which the missionaries sang, and replies, 'C'est le chant de ceux qui connaissent le Christ; c'est l'amour de l'Eglise romaine et l'amour de la France'.[268] The two loyalties to be inculcated in the oriental's mind were 'l'amour de la France d'abord,' and 'le second amour que le missionaire cherche à faire pénétrer au coeur de l'Oriental c'est l'amour de l'église romaine, et celui-la prime l'autre'.[269]

The success of these endeavours can be measured in terms of the extent to which the French language spread and replaced Italian. Even as late as 1826 the only widespread European language used in the Eastern Mediterranean lands was Italian. In that year General Boyer, who was in Egypt at that time, complained that 'la langue française est à l'indexe'.[270] Even in 1857 when the *Frères de la doctrine chrétienne* came to Egypt the French language was almost unknown.[271] Only by 1900, through the tireless and relentless efforts of the French missionaries for over half a century could it be claimed that the French language had replaced 'ce mauvais jargon italien' in the Levant.[272]

Several British missionaries, such as the Methodists and the Scottish, attempted to learn Italian in order to teach it to their pupils. The French missionaries, however, made no such effort. On the contrary Guérin reported in 1889 that on entering a boys' class in a French missionary school he was acclaimed with shouts of *Vive la France*, and considered that as it glorified France, it was an expression of educational success.

There is evidence that this policy persisted throughout the nineteenth century, and with greater intensity after the reappearance of English missionary educational work in Egypt in 1882—a date coinciding with the British Campaign.

Speaking of a Jesuit college in Egypt, called the Saint-François Xavier, Guérin wrote:

Ce collège prepare à la France, dans les jeunes générations qu'il forme, de nouveaux et futurs auxiliaires de son influence et de sa suprématie morale, intellectuelle et civilisatrice dans une contrée ou nous avons à reconquérir beaucoup de terrain perdu à la suite des funestes événements de 1882.[273]

The *funestes événements* was the British occupation of Egypt in 1882. In 1885, the Jesuit Fathers established themselves in Cairo, and at the request of the Propaganda annexed to their College of Sainte-Famille a seminary for the Copts. Some years later they settled in Miniah, Upper Egypt.[274] Of the work of the Jesuits Guérin wrote:

... les RR. PP. jésuites du Caire travailleront sur une échelle bien plus large à la diffusion de la langue et de la civilisation française, non seulement dans cette capitale, mais dans le reste de l'Egypte; car dans quelques années leurs seminaristes coptes seront à même d'ouvrir des écoles dans la plupart des villes ou des villages de la haute Egypte, écoles où ils enseigneront le français, la langue de leurs maîtres, ce qui fera aux écoles américaines et anglaises protestantes une concurrence puissante et éfficace.[275]

Whatever the kind of school, the oneness of Catholicism and France was never forgotten. 'Qui dira', wrote Louvet, 'l'influence que la pratique constante de ces oeuvres de charité nous donne en Egypte dans le double intérêt du Catholicisme et de la France?'[276] Against this dual purpose the British Campaign in Egypt in 1882 was considered to be a blow. 'C'est la substitution de l'influence anglaise à la nôtre, au grand détriment de catholicisme et de ses oeuvres,' and referring to the increase of English and American Protestant schools in Egypt, Louvet continued, '. . . et tous ces enfants emporteront, au sortir de l'école, la haine du catholicisme et le mépris de la France'. Furthermore, he maintained that political intrigues were the reason why the Orientals failed to embrace Catholicism. Russia was also involved. On learning that the Russian Czar had offered the Copts protection the French Consul urged the Catholic missionaries to hasten the return of the Copts to Catholicism. The non-Catholic European nations, the French held, were not interested in church dogma but their aim was '. . . tout simplement d'arracher à la France sa clientèle catholique pour substituer l'ascendant de la Russie et de l'Angleterre au nôtre'.[277]

About 1889, R. P. Wellinger, in a message to the French Minister for Foreign Affairs, emphasized France's role and duty in helping the four newly created *préfectures apostoliques* in Egypt to construct several buildings where agricultural subjects would be taught to the young fellaheen:

> Cette situation, toute nouvelle, impose à la France de nouveaux devoirs dont l'accomplissement sera largement récompensé. . . . Le peuple des campagnes, qui compose les cinq septièmes de la population et qui, a tous égards, est le plus intéressant, car c'est sur lui qui repose la prospérité de l'Egypte, avait toujours été complètement négligé, et personne ne s'était jamais occupé de lui . . . la plupart des principaux villages de la basse Egypte seront pourvus d'écoles qui répandront dans les masses rurales l'usage de notre langue et l'amour de notre pays . . . qu'un pareil établissement [where agricultural subjects would be taught] serait l'instrument le plus éfficace pour rendre sa prospérité à l'Egypte et y faire aimer la France. . . . Il est également évident que les élèves de l'établissment choisis parmi les jeunes fellahs orphélins les plus intelligents et recrutés aussi dans les familles des chefs de villages, assureraient à la civilisation occidentale des propagateurs d'autant plus puissants, qu'ils auraient toute la population rurale sous leur direction immédiate . . . à demander à ce sujet [that is the starting of agricultural schools] l'appui du gouvernement français et de tous ceux qui veulent non seulement conserver à la France l'influence qu'elle a toujours possedée sur les bords du Nil, mais encore l'étendre et la rendre à jamais inattaquable, en l'enracinant, pour ainsi parler dans le sol même de l'Egypte.[278]

Hilaire de Barenton wrote of the slow decline of French economic activity towards the end of the nineteenth century. One consequence of this decline was that French culture was gradually replaced by that of the English and the American. 'Notre commerce se trouve partout évincé, nos colons se font de plus en plus rares,' and 'L'Angleterre partout y [that is in the Orient] sème son or, ses bibles et ses écoles.' According to the French missionaries, the English and the Americans understood the peoples of the Orient well and they approached them with gold and science. Further, they exploited the massacres of the Armenians and indulged in the widespread trafficking of souls.[279]

On a dit souvent que l'ésprit oriental, fait tout entier d'amour et de respect pour les traditions anciennes et pour l'authorité ne se laisserait jamais entrâmer par l'esprit de Luther et de Calvin. On avait compté sans la puissance de l'or, sans le prestige de la science et de la force.[280]

The Americans established themselves in Assuit, Upper Egypt, in the heart of the large Coptic population. In this connection the French remarked, 'Assiout est un centre actif de propagande protestante; . . . Ils [the Americans] n'ont reculé devant aucun sacrifice d'argent pour asseoir là solidement leur oeuvre'.[281] An important Catholic contemporary, Paul de Règla, noted the influx of certain nations but indicated that although these nations were replacing France in the Eastern Mediterranean yet French genius was still able to assert its cultural superiority.

N'est-il pas douleureux pour nous français de voir des nations comme l'Italie, les Etats-Unis et l'Allemagne, . . . 'implantés victorieusement dans tous les lieux, où jusque à ces dernières années la France avait maintenu intact le drapeau de la civilisation et du progrès? . . . Et pourtant, étrange contraste qui prouve la supériorité du génie français sur celui des autres peuples, notre langue, nos habitudes et nos moeurs progressent en raison directe des échecs subis par notre diplomatie.

and

Nos écoles se multiplient au fur et à mesure que notre influence diminue; notre langue devient accessible à tous et entraîné par l'intelligente propagande des membres du clergé français. . . .[282]

In an attempt to outline clearly French missionary educational policy in Africa and the Orient, Guérin's words at the end of his book come to mind:

Pour que notre pays conserve en Afrique et en Orient la prépondérance politique et le prestige dont il y jouit encore, il faut d'abord et avant tout qu'il y maintienne avec soin son protectorat religieux, et que tous ses agents s'y montrent les zélés défenseurs des catholiques et des congrégations enseignantes et hospitalières. Autrement si, dans la personne de ses représentantes, il devenait, je ne dis pas hostile, mais seulement indifférent à la grande cause catholique dont il a été jusqu'à présent le patron séculaire et officiel, il verrait aussitôt les catholiques étrangers tourner leurs regards, leurs espérances et leurs sympathies vers une autre nation protectrice qui ne manquerait pas de se charger avec empressement de la mission que nous aurions, pour notre malheur, honteusement abandonée.

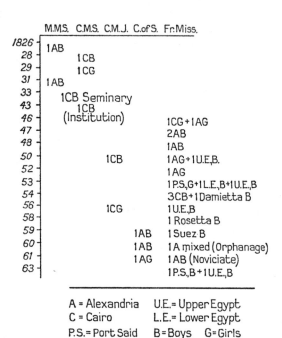

	M.M.S.	C.M.S.	C.M.J.	C.of S.	Fr.Miss.
1826	1 AB				
28		1 CB			
29		1 CG			
31	1 AB				
33		1CB Seminary			
43		1 CB			
46		(Institution)			1CG + 1AG
47					2AB
48					1AB
50		1CB			1AG+1U.E,B.
52					1AG
53					1P.S,G+1L.E.,B+1U.E.,B
54					3CB+1Damietta B
56		1CG			1U.E.,B
58					1 Rosetta B
59			1AB		1 Suez B
60			1AB		1A mixed (Orphanage)
61			1AG		1AB (Noviciate)
63					1P.S,B+1U.E.,B

A = Alexandria   U.E.= Upper Egypt
C = Cairo   L.E.= Lower Egypt
P.S.= Port Said   B=Boys   G=Girls

BRITISH AND FRENCH MISSION SCHOOLS
IN EGYPT, 1825–1863

He went on,

Tout nous fait donc une loi impérieuse de persévérer, sous peine d'une déchéance prompte et inévitable, dans notre politique traditionnelle à l'égard des diverses populations catholiques de l'empire ottoman, et comme ça sont nos congrégations religieuses qui contribuent le plus à nous attirer leurs sympathies avec celles des musulmans êux-mêmes par la diffusion de nos bienfaits, de notre langue et de nos connaissances, nous ne saurions trop les encourager dans leurs efforts, qui tendent à la fois à la gloire de Dieu et à celle de la France.[283]

In comparison with the British the French missionaries carried out their work in a more organized way and more methodically. Their educational influence in Egypt began at about the middle of the last century when the British missions were about to close down. Since then French schools have grown in number and influence.

The social work of the French missionaries, through orphanages, dispensaries and craft and trade schools, was carried out on a wider scale than that of the British. The Catholics organized charitable works. New attitudes were promoted. Apparently many men, women and children flocked to the dispensaries—a new tradition for thousands who had formerly been fatalistic or superstitious about health and illness.

The French missionaries must also be given credit for starting schools in Egypt and carrying on the tradition of western instruction, at a time when there was practically no real educational provision in the country. Many people, undoubtedly, benefited materially or culturally from these schools. Perhaps one reason for the growth of French mission schools is that they had the official backing of France, unlike the British. But undoubtedly the gradual transformation of Egypt is due partly to the work of the French and British missionaries who introduced many aspects of western education.

NOTES

1. The leaders of the Egyptian Revolution of 23 July 1952 believed that Mohammed Ali's dynasty symbolized foreign domination in Egypt and that with the dethronement of King Farouk and the proclamation of Egypt a Republic—putting an end to the Albanian family—foreign domination in all its various forms for over 2,000 years had come to an end. See *The Scribe* (Cairo 1955), No. 1, p. 4.

2. Douin, G., *La Mission du Baron de Boislecomte* (Cairo 1927), p. 146.

3. Quoted by Dodwell, H., *The Founder of Modern Egypt* (Cambridge 1931), p. 38 from Puckler-Muskau, H. von, *Egypt under Mehemet Ali* (London 1945), vol I, p. 195.

4. *Ibid.*

5. Douin, pp. 98–9.

6. *Ibid.*, p. 118.

7. Dodwell, p. 105.

8. Douin, p. 108.

9. 'The *great* game of improvement is altogether up for the present,' in a letter by the British ambassador, Stratford de Redcliffe in Istambul in March 1851. Quoted by Lewis, B., *The Emergence of Modern Turkey* (Oxford 1961), p. 113 from Temperley, H., 'British Policy Towards Parliamentary Rule and Constitutionalism in Turkey 1830–1914' in *Cambridge University Journal*, vol IV, 1932–4, p. 242.

10. Church of Scotland, *Home and Foreign Missionary Society* (Edinburgh 1859), vol XVI, p. 134.

11. *Missionary Register* (1827), p. 253.

12. Antes, J., *Observations on Manners and Customs of Egyptians* (London 1800). See also Watson, C. R., *In the Valley of the Nile* (New York 1908).

13. Heyworth-Dunne, J., *An Introduction to the History of Education in Modern Egypt* (London 1939), p. 90.

14. 'I look upon the world as my Parish.' John Wesley.

15. Findlay, G. G. and Holdsworth, W. W., *The History of the Wesleyan Methodist Missionary Society* (London 1921–4), vol IV, p. 421.

16. Stock, E., *History of the Church Missionary Society* (London 1899), vol I, pp.230–1.

17. Dodwell, p. 240.

18. Anon., *On Communications between Europe and India through Egypt* (London 1846), p. 7.

19. Findlay and Holdsworth, vol IV, p. 422.

20. *Ibid.*

21. The text is based on manuscript letters of Macpherson, Bartholomew and MacBrair. The original MS Letters of the MMS dealing with the society's Mediterranean mission are stored in the archives in a strong room of the MMS Library.

22. Macpherson, D., 24 April 1826 (MMS archives).

23. *Idem.*, 27 Dec. 1825 (MMS archives). Of this degree of the Greeks being well-nigh assimilated linguistically reminds one of similar instances in other parts of the Turkish Empire. Many sermons in Armenian churches in Southern Turkey and Cyprus as recently as 1920 were delivered in the Turkish language to Armenian congregations, as certain sections of the Armenians who had been completely surrounded by the Turkish community for centuries had gradually forgotten, in the absence of Armenian schools, their own language. It is interesting to note that although the language of the Bible in these churches was Turkish, yet the script was modern Armenian, the Turkish language having been transliterated into the Armenian.

24. Macpherson, 6 June 1826.
25. *Idem.*, 12 Dec. 1826.
26. *Idem.*, 1 Feb. 1827.
27. MacBrair, R., 12 May 1834 (MMS archives).
28. Macpherson, 21 March 1827.
29. MacBrair, 9 June 1834.
30. Macpherson, 2 July 1827.
31. Bartholomew, J., 19 June 1832 (MMS archives).
32. Findlay and Holdsworth, vol IV, pp. 420–2.
33. MacBrair, 19 May 1834.
34. Bartholomew, 11 June 1831.
35. *Idem.*, 17 Sept. 1832.
36. MacBrair, 2 May 1834.
37. Quoted by Heyworth-Dunne, pp. 280–1 from MacBrair, R., *Sketches of a Missionary's Travels in Egypt, Syria, Western Africa, etc.* (London 1839), pp. 88–9.
38. Olin, S., *Travels in Egypt, Arabia, Petraea and the Holy Land* (New York 1843), vol I, p. 118.
39. Stock, vol I, p. 222.
40. *Ibid.*, pp. 225–6.
41. *Ibid.*, p. 224.
42. *The Catholic Encyclopedia* (London 1907–14), vol V, p. 356.
43. Butcher, E. L., *The Story of the Church of Egypt* (London 1897), vol I, p. 394.
44. Macpherson, 15 April 1826.
45. *Parl. Papers* (1840), vol XXI, p. 193.
46. *Ibid.*, p. 4.
47. Fowler, M., *Christian Egypt* (London 1901), p. 189.
48. Butcher, vol IV, pp. 322–34.
49. *Parl. Papers*, pp. 7–8.
50. See Heyworth-Dunne, p. 87.
51. *Missionary Register* (1829), p. 164.
52. CMS *Record* (1833), p. 108.
53. *Ibid.*, pp. 104–5.
54. Watson, pp. 123–4.
55. *Ibid.*, p. 119.
56. *Ibid.*, p. 126.
57. *Ibid.*, p. 130.
58. Watson, p. 121.
59. *Parl. Papers*, p. 8.
60. *Missionary Register* (1829), p. 235.
61. *Ibid.*, p. 73.
62. CMS *Record* (London 1828), p. 390.

63. *Missionary Register* (1829), p. 584.
64. CMS *Proceedings* (London 1829), p. 231.
65. *Ibid.*, p. 234.
66. CMS *Report* (London 1829), p. 72.
67. *Ibid.*, pp. 72–3.
68. See Heyworth-Dunne, p. 279.
69. CMS *Record* (1831), p. 155.
70. *Ibid.*
71. *Ibid.*, p. 154.
72. *Ibid.*
73. Watson, p. 122.
74. *Missionary Register* (1827), pp. 586–7.
75. *Ibid.*
76. *Ibid.* (1828), p. 239.
77. *Ibid.*
78. *Missionary Register* (1828), pp. 239–40.
79. See Appleyard, E. S., *Eastern Churches* (London 1850).
80. Missionary Register (1825) pp. 239—40.
81. *Ibid.*
82. CMS *Proceedings* (1829), p. 164.
83. *Ibid.* (1828), pp. 63–4.
84. Macpherson, 15 April 1826.
85. See Heyworth-Dunne, pp. 113 and 124.
86. *Missionary Register* (1829), p. 234.
87. *Ibid.*, p. 308.
88. Quoted by Boktor, A., *School and Society in the Valley of the Nile.*
(Cairo 1936). p. 133 from Young, G., *Egypt* (New York 1927), p. 28
89. *Missionary Register* (1829), p. 308.
90. *Ibid.*
91. CMS *Proceedings* (1830), pp. 73–4.
92. *Ibid.* (1829), p. 231.
93. *Ibid.*, p. 234.
94. CMS *Record* (1832), pp. 112–13.
95. *Ibid.*
96. *Missionary Register* (1834), pp. 223–5.
97. *Ibid.* (1835), p. 330.
98. Madden, R. R., *Egypt and Mohammed Ali* (London 1841), pp. 77–8.
99. Cameron, D. A., *Egypt in the Nineteenth Century* (London 1898),
p. 149.
100. *Parl. Papers*, Appendix C, p. 196.
101. Douin, pp. 116–17.
102. *Missionary Register* (1831), pp. 144–5.
103. *Ibid.* (1835), p. 330.

104. CMS *Record* (1835), pp. 141–7.
105. CMS *Proceedings* (1835), p. 29.
106. CMS *Record* (1837), p. 11.
107. *Parl. Papers*, Appendix F asterisked footnote, p. 213.
108. Dodwell, p. 234.
109. *Parl. Papers*, p. 5.
110. *Ibid.*, Appendix F, p. 214.
111. CMS *Record* (1839), pp. 78–9.
112. CMS *Proceedings* (1838), pp. 48–9.
113. See Heyworth-Dunne, pp. 279–80.
114. CMS *Record* (1839), pp. 179–85.
115. *Parl. Papers*, p. 138.
116. *Ibid.*, p. 194.
117. *Parl. Papers*, pp. 137–8.
118. CMS *Record* (1840), pp. 103–4.
119. *Ibid.* (1836), p. 11.
120. International Missionary Council Joint Committee of Foreign Missions, *Christian Literature in Moslem Lands* (New York 1923), p. 50.
121. *Missionary Register* (1841), pp. 380–1.
122. CMS *Record* (1840), pp. 103–4.
123. *Missionary Register* (1845), pp. 246–50.
124. CMS *Record* (1848), p. 89.
125. *Ibid.* (1849), p. 155.
126. CMS *Proceedings* (1852), p. xvi.
127. CMS *Record* (1850), p. 105.
128. See Heyworth-Dunne, p. 280, footnote 1.
129. CMS *Record* (1849), p. 89.
130. Madden, R. R., *The Turkish Empire in its relations with Christianity* (London 1862), vol I, pp. 87–8.
131. Olin, vol 1, p. 119.
132. *Parl. Papers, op. cit.*, p. 137.
133. CMS *Record* (1849), pp. 107, 155–6.
134. Butcher, vol I, pp. 396–7.
135. Fowler, p. 131, *et seq.*
136. See *The Annual Report Minutes of the Church Missions to Jews* (the London Society for Promoting Christianity amongst the Jews), in manuscript, unpublished, 1890—still in use today. Vol II folios not yet numbered.
137. *Jewish Intelligence* (March 1846), vol XII, p. 94.
138. *London Society Report* (1851), 43rd Annual Report, p. 41.
139. See Gidney, W. T., *The History of the London Society for Promoting Christianity amongst the Jews* (London 1908), pp. 101–12.
140. Dodwell, p. 240 with footnote reference to Barker, E. B. B.,

Syria and Egypt (London 1876), vol II, p. 142. One of many instances of Mohammed Ali's spirit of religious toleration.

141. The pathetic story of Lauria's sufferings as a result of his becoming a Christian is found in the monthly accounts of the *Jewish Intelligence* for the years 1845–47.

142. *London Society Report* (1849), 41st Annual Report, pp. 44–5.

143. Gidney, p. 261.

144. See *Jewish Intelligence* (Aug. 1847), p. 326.

145. Gidney, p. 261.

146. The Karaite Jews usually come from the Crimea; the Ashkanazim from Poland and Germany, and the Sephardim from Spain.

147. Gidney, pp. 102–3.

148. *Parl. Papers, op. cit.*, p. 162.

149. See Heyworth-Dunne, p. 92, whereas Barker, vol I, p. 304 says that the 'sarrafs' in Syria and Egypt were also Greeks or Armenians.

150. *Ibid.*, p. 283, quoted from Ibrahim, Khalil, *Misbah as-Sari wa Nuzhat al-Kari* (Beyrut 1272), p. 20.

151. Gidney, p. 119. Dr. Dalton, too, who called at Alexandria in 1824 on his way from England to Palestine to work as the society's medical missionary there, mentions his visit to a synagogue where he was favourably received by the Jews who accepted his tracts.

152. *Jewish Intelligence* (May 1847), vol XIII, pp. 277–9 and Gidney, p. 262.

153. Again in the absence of official statistics for 1847 it is difficult to assess the exact number of Jews in Egypt for that year. Gidney, for example, p. 261, says that there were 5,000 Jews in Cairo in 1847. The rabbis' report to Lauria, on the other hand, for the same year, and for the same city, was 1,200. This number rose to 2,000 in 1849, whereas 'The Journal of a Deputation to the East by the Committee of the Malta Protestant College' gives the number of Jews living in Cairo in 1849 as 3,000. *Jewish Intelligence* (June 1852), vol XVIII, p. 306.

154. Heyworth-Dunne, p. 283.

155. *See* e.g. Boktor, p. 71. See p. 87 'In a sense similar . . .'.

156. This description of the Jewish quarter, Haret el Yahoud, still holds good today.

157. *Jewish Intelligence* (Nov. 1847), vol XIII, p. 164.

158. *London Society Report* (1864), 56th Annual Report, p. 105.

159. *Ibid.* (1868), 60th Annual Report, p. 70.

160. Gidney, p. 566.

161. *Jewish Intelligence* (May 1847), vol XIII, pp. 165–6. *Parl. Papers*, cit. pp. 193–5. See p. 88 'A notion of the smallness . . .'.

162. *Jewish Intelligence* (Nov. 1847), vol XIII, pp. 165–6.

163. *Ibid.* (Nov. 1847), pp. 164–5.

164. Gidney, pp. 305–6.
165. *Jewish Intelligence* (June 1852), vol XVIII, p. 212.
166. *Ibid.* (June 1835), vol XIX, p. 205.
167. *London Society Report* (1856), 48th Annual Report, p. 78.
168. Gidney, pp. 305–6.
169. *Jewish Intelligence* (Oct. 1856), vol XXII, p. 328.
170. *Ibid.* (May 1857), vol XXIII, p. 152 and *London Society Report* (1857), 49th Annual Report, p. 83.
171. *Ibid.* (June 1857), p. 207.
172. *Ibid.*, pp. 56–7.
173. *Jewish Intelligence* (March 1855), vol XXI, pp. 74–5.
174. *London Society Report* (1859), 51st Annual Report, p. 96.
175. *Ibid.* (1860), 52nd Annual Report, p. 106.
176. Gidney, p. 387.
177. *London Society Report* (1861), 53rd Annual Report, p. 105.
178. *Ibid.* (1864), 56th Annual Report, p. 105.
179. *Ibid.* (1866), 58th Annual Report, p. 91.
180. *Ibid.* (1868), 60th Annual Report, p. 70.
181. McDougall, D., *In Search of Israel* (London 1941), *passim.*
182. *Church of Scotland Manuscript Minute Book* (1863–9), vol VI, folio 135; *Church of Scotland Home and Foreign Missionary Record* (1858), vol XIII, p. 103. The *C of S Manuscript Minute Books*, unpublished, which are stored in the archives in a strong room at the C of S offices, are referred to as *MS Minute Book*; also the *Home and Foreign Missionary Record of the C of S by Authority of the Committee of the General Assembly* and the *C of S Home and Foreign Missionary Record* (*New Series*) are found in Tolbooth, St. John's Library and referred to as *Home and Foreign.*
183. *Home and Foreign* (1858), vol XIII, p. 137.
184. *MS Minute Book* (1863–9), vol VI, folios 53–4.
185. *Home and Foreign* (1858), vol XIII, p. 103.
186. *Ibid.* (*New Series*) (1864–5), vols III & IV, p. 13.
187. *MS Minute Book* (1858–62), vol V, folio 137.
188. McDougall, pp. 16–17.
189. *Home and Foreign* (1858), vol XIII, p. 137.
190. *MS Minute Book* (1863–9), vol VI, folio 55.
191. *Home and Foreign* (1860), vol XV, p. 294.
192. *Ibid.*
193. *Ibid.*, p. 302.
194. *Ibid.*, p. 32.
195. *Ibid.*, p. 249.
196. *Ibid.* (1859), vol XIV, p. 294.
197. *Ibid.* (1858), vol XIII, p. 293.
198. *Ibid.* (1859), vol XIV, p. 293.

199. *Ibid.*, p. 294.
200. *Ibid.* (1860), vol XV, p. 249.
201. *Ibid.* (1861), vol XVI, p. 53.
202. *Ibid.*, p. 292.
203. *MS Minute Book* (1863–9), vol VI, folio 310.
204. The influence of the rabbis was a reality that could not be ignored. The C of S missionary at Tunis wrote in 1846: 'The fearful sentences of excommunication which are pronounced against all who have incurred the displeasure of the Jewish Rabbis—dread which *these* (underlined in original manuscript) produce upon the minds of the people—and the severe persecutions to which converts to Christianity are exposed from their brethren have led some who are thoroughly persuaded of the truth and excellence of the Gospel, and who appear in a certain degree to feel its power to conceal their religious convictions and impressions.' (*MS Minute Book* (1847), vol I, folio 305); and in Constantinople in 1864 the Chief Rabbi of the Spanish Jews, the Sephardim, pronounced a *cherem* respecting Jewish children attending the C of S school in that city and as a consequence all the Jewish pupils withdrew in a single day. (*MS Minute Book* (1863–9), vol VI, folios 44–5.)
205. *Home and Foreign* (1859), vol XIV, p. 273.
206. *MS Minute Book* (1858–62), vol V, folio 78.
207. *Ibid.*, folio 133.
208. *Ibid.*, folio 134.
209. *Ibid.*, vol V, folios 144–5.
210. *Ibid.*, folio 219.
211. *Ibid.*, folio 170.
212. *Ibid.*, folio 177.
213. *Ibid.* (1863–9), vol VI, folio 28.
214. *Ibid.*, folio 81.
215. *Ibid.*, folio 134.
216. *Ibid.*, folio 137.
217. *Home and Foreign* (1861), vol XVI, p. 292.
218. *MS Minute Book* (1858–62), vol V, folio 145.
219. *Ibid.*, folio 134.
220. Biographical Notice: The Rev. Dr. Hermann Philip found his health affected by the heat at Alexandria and asked the Church to remove him to a cooler northern climate. His wish to go to Leipzig to work among the Jews there and among those who came to the annual fair at that city was agreed to by the Church. However, after acquainting himself with the situation he was convinced that there were few Jews in Leipzig whereas those who came to the fair made it known that they were too busy to trouble about religion. Dr. Philip then found himself

without occupation and as a result the Church dispensed with his services. See McDougall, pp. 72–3.

221. *Home and Foreign* (1858), vol XIII, p. 103.

222. *MS Minute Book* (1858–62), vol V, folio 205.

223. *Ibid.*, folio 220.

224. *Ibid.* (1863–9), vol VI, folio 32.

225. *Ibid.*, folio 136.

226. *Ibid.*, folio 15.

227. *Home and Foreign* (*New Series*) (1864–6), vols III & IV, p. 13 mentions 70 pupils in Miss Ashley's school.

228. *MS Minute Book* (1863–9), vol VI, folio 55.

229. *Ibid.*, folio 78.

230. *Ibid.*, folio 134.

231. The school fees received for 1864 by the school were £180. *MS Minute Book* (1863–9), vol VI, folio 55.

232. *Ibid.*, folio 108.

233. *Ibid.*, folio 184.

234. *Ibid.* (1858–62), vol V, folios 176–8.

235. *Ibid.* (1863–9), vol VI, folio 16.

236. *Ibid.* (1858–62), vol V, folio 257.

237. *Ibid.* (1863–9), vol VI, folio 32.

238. *Home and Foreign* (*New Series*) (1862), vol II, p. 10.

239. See Consular Act 6 George IV, Chap. 87.

240. *MS Minute Book* (1863–9), vol VI, folio 54.

241. Boktor, p. 7.

242. Quoted by Heyworth-Dunne, p. 230, from Carre, J. M., *Voyageurs et écrivains français en Egypte* (Cairo 1932) (2 vols), I, p. 290.

243. Malortie, C. von, *Egypt: Native Rulers and Foreign Interference* (London 1882), p. 69.

244. Education Department, *Special Reports on Educational Subjects 1896–7* (H.M.S.O. 1897), vol I, pp. 617–18.

245. See Guérin, V., *La France catholique en Egypte* (Tours 1889).

246. See Barenton, St. Hilaire de, *La France catholique en Orient* (Paris 1902).

247. Savary, C. E., *Lettres sur l'Egypte* (Paris 1785) (2 vols), I, p. 2.

248. Douin, G., *Une Mission militaire française auprès de Méhémet Ali* (Correspondances des Généraux Belliard et Boyer) (Cairo 1923), p. 1.

249. Madden, p. 109.

250. Douin, G. and Fawtier-Jones, E. C., *L'Angleterre et l'Egypte* (Cairo 1928), p. vi.

251. *Ibid.*, p. v.

252. Anon. *On Communications*, p. 8.

253. Anon., *The Present Crisis in Egypt in Relation to our Overland Communication with India* (London 1851), p. 5.

254. *Ibid.*

255. Milner, Lord, *England in Egypt* (London 1894), pp. 15–16.

256. *On Communications*, p. 7.

257. *The Present Crisis*, p. 24.

258. *MS Minute Book* (1850), vol II, folio 109.

259. *Ibid.*, folios 138–9.

260. *Ibid.*, folio 114.

261. *Ibid.* (1845), vol I, folio 274.

262. *Ibid.* (1850), vol II, folio 141.

263. *Ibid.*, folios 147–8.

264. *Ibid.*, folios 168–9. No signature appears at the end of this copy letter in the the *Minute Book*.

265. Douin, G., *La Mission du Baron de Boislecomte*, p. 17.

266. See de Barenton.

267. *Ibid.*, p. 302.

268. *Ibid.*

269. *Ibid.*, pp. 302–4.

270. Heyworth-Dunne, J., *Select Bibliography on Modern Egypt* (Cairo 1952), p. 22.

271. Guérin, p. 164.

272. de Barenton, p. 14.

273. Guérin, pp. 28 and 72.

274. Louvet, L. E., *Les Missions catholiques au XIXe siècle* (Lille 1898), p. 278.

275. Guérin, p. 166.

276. Louvet, p. 276.

277. *Ibid.*

278. Guérin, Appendix.

279. de Barenton, p. 11.

280. *Ibid.*

281. *Ibid.*, p. 12.

282. *Ibid.*, p. 14.

283. Guérin, pp. 233–4.

7

CHURCH AND STATE IN THE DEVELOPMENT OF EDUCATION IN CYPRUS, 1878–1960

P. K. Persianis

IN Cyprus the conflict between Church and State was quite different from those discussed elsewhere in this book. In the other cases the Church was established by missionaries some time after the colonization of the country. In Cyprus the Greek Orthodox Church had been established in A.D. 45[1] and this long life had given it not only a rich tradition but a strong determination to fight for its independence and a great faith in the soundness of its dogmas and tenets. Consequently the conflict took place between an ancient institution which had the support of the vast majority of the population and a foreign government which ruled Cyprus as a colony for some eighty-two years.

The most important characteristic of the Cyprus Orthodox Church was the temporal authority of the Church leaders which arose as a result of history. For example, for a very long time during the Frankish occupation (1192–1489) the Orthodox bishops were forced to take an oath of allegiance to the Catholic Archbishop of the island and the Holy See. The result was the birth of religious fanaticism among the Orthodox clergy most of whom fought openly against this violation of their faith, and some of them paid with their lives.[2]

In A.D. 488, after a long dispute against the Patriarchate of Antioch, the Cyprus Church was officially granted its autocephaly (independence) through an imperial decree of the Byzantine Emperor Zeno.[3] By the same imperial decree the Archbishop was endowed with three privileges, i.e. to wear a purple cloak at Church festivals, to carry an imperial sceptre instead of a pastoral staff and to sign in red ink. These privileges were an implicit 'recognition of temporal authority . . . and have had frequent repercussions down to the present day'.[4]

During the Turkish occupation of Cyprus (1571–1878) the temporal authority of the Archbishop increased considerably. The Turkish Government tolerated the Orthodox Church and its leaders as long as they were prepared to be loyal subjects of the Ottoman Empire. To this end the Sultan found the Archbishop useful. He granted him temporal power by declaring him Ethnarch, i.e. representative of all the Greek people of Cyprus, and restored the Orthodox Church 'to its ancient dignity and privileges'.[5] In return the Sultan expected the Archbishop to use his influence to persuade the Greek people to remain faithful and loyal subjects of the Turkish Empire.

Real political power was given to the Archbishop after 1660.[6] To check the flight of inhabitants from the cruelty and rapacity of the local Turkish governors, the Sultans endowed the Archbishop with the power to represent the Christians of the island before the Porte. The Archbishops accepted the new duty and 'appeared boldly in person before the Grand Vazir, stating their complaints and asking for a diminution of the taxes paid by the *rayah* (Greeks) and begging for help and support in other necessities'.[7] The Christians of the island looked upon the Archbishop as their spiritual protector and political supporter. In this way the Archbishops obtained great power and for a period in the eighteenth century actually governed the island.[8] It must be added, however, that their position was dangerous since they easily became the victims of the intrigues of their opponents or of the Turkish Governors.

Their political capacity was ensured by the processes of election. The Ecclesiastical Council (Holy Synod) and the people took part, through their lay representatives, in the election of a bishop or archbishop whose name was immediately reported to the Sultan, who, after receiving from him the proper amount of money, sent him the *Berat*, an official document conferring all the rights granted to him and his Church.[9]

These rights were economic, judicial and political. The churches and monasteries were safeguarded against probable destruction or economic exploitation by the local Turkish Governors. They paid no taxes. The bishops had the right to collect their customary dues from the Christians and were provided with executive power to enforce the collection of these fees.

The Archbishop had judicial power over his suffragans and the lower clergy. In the case of debt, transgression and ecclesiastical offence the Archbishop was the only judge, while in the case of a criminal offence his consent was needed before a clergyman could be arrested. For a very long time during the Turkish occupation the bishops were outside the jurisdiction of the commissioners and the provincial courts and councils of the island. Their cases were tried at Constantinople.[10]

The political rights of the Archbishop, a result of practice and custom rather than legislation, were more important: he was ex-officio member of the Great Council which shared in the administration of the island and the bishops were ex-officio members of the District Councils.[11]

During the Turkish occupation the Greeks enjoyed, as a rule, considerable freedom in their community affairs. District councils presided over by the bishop of the diocese and a Central Assembly presided over by the Archbishop dealt with the affairs of the Greek community, public works, health, public institutions and education. In this way the Church was in fact the 'sole institution for religion, education and politics'.[12] The Archbishop was regarded both by the people and by the Turkish Government[13] as the head of internal self-government.[14]

However, in July 1821 the Archbishop of Cyprus, Kyprianos was hanged and the three other bishops of the island, together with some prominent laymen, were beheaded on the charge that they were implicated in the Greek revolution which had started in March that year and which the bishops were leading. The Turks suspected that what had happened in Greece might be repeated in Cyprus. In fact, Archbishop Kyprianos was initiated in *Philiki Etairia*, the underground Greek organization, which prepared the revolution against the Turks, and he promised it financial support.[15]

Archbishop Kyprianos became a legend as one of the first Archbishops to sacrifice himself on the altar of his fatherland. His death placed a grave responsibility upon future Archbishops. No one could think of betraying or was allowed to betray Kyprianos' cause.[16]

The death of the Archbishop not only kept the Greek and

Turkish communities apart but aroused among the Greek population fear of new slaughters, sowed in their hearts a love of freedom and created the first nationalistic feelings. Their thoughts suddenly turned towards Greece fighting at that time for her independence. The apostles of the *Philiki Etairia* talked secretly to the people about the Great Idea—the wish to revive the Byzantine Empire as a sovereign power of the Hellenic Kingdom. Cyprus was to become a part of the Kingdom, since the majority of her people spoke the same language and had the same religion as the inhabitants of Greece. The schools that were established in the next few decades cultivated the Great Idea assiduously. The curriculum of the schools consisted mainly of the study of ancient Greek authors. Greek culture was revived and the Greek traditions, which had never been extinguished, raised morale and oriented the people politically. An emotional attachment grew eventually into a kind of political credo for the majority of the Greek population in which the love of independence became more concrete; it was their wish to be united with another country, which they regarded as the motherland.

The drive of the Greek Cypriots for freedom became as mystical as the aspiration of the Jews for the Promised Land. The people had experienced similar sufferings, not in exile as the Jews, but in their own country. They begged God for their own Moses, who could be no one other than one of their Archbishops—a belief strengthened by the role of the clergy in the revolt against the Turks in Greece.[17] This revolution thus acquired a religious character which distinguished it from the revolutions in America and France which took place towards the end of the eighteenth century.

Things were similar in Cyprus. The more the people were oppressed, the more they looked up to their Archbishop, whose influence increased daily. The Church became the Ark of Salvation, and regarded as the only powerful protector against the rule of a Government, alien both in nationality and religion and indifferent to the preservation of the religious and national sentiments of the people.[18]

This was the political situation with which the British were confronted when they took over the administration of the island in 1878. The political orientation of the Church was stressed to the first High Commissioner of Cyprus, Sir G. Wolseley, by a bishop, who in his address of welcome made clear that the Greek Cypriots welcomed the British as an intermediary step towards Union with Greece.[19]

When the Church leaders realized that the British Government was not prepared to repeat in Cyprus what it had done in 1863 in the Ionian Islands, they turned against it and stirred up political agitation. In this propaganda against the Government the schools and the teachers were a most effective instrument.

Another reason for Greek Cypriot dissatisfaction with the British Government was its unwillingness to recognize some traditional Church privileges, on the grounds that they were contrary to the correct conception and administration of justice.

These two factors should always be remembered when trying to understand the conflict between Church and State.

U.K. AND AMERICAN MISSIONARY SOCIETY SCHOOLS

Cyprus, as a rule, was not a country in which missionary activity could flourish. Except for a small Muslim minority of Turks the great majority of the people were Greek Orthodox, who were very proud of their faith, very attached to their spiritual leaders and, at the same time, fanatically opposed of any form of proselytism.[20]

Consequently missionaries coming to Cyprus were always careful not to offend the religious feelings of the natives. They restricted themselves to the establishment of some missionary schools where influence on the pupils was indirect.[21]

In some cases they avoided even this. For example, in the two elementary and one high school established in Larnaca and maintained by two members of the American Lutheran Church there was no wish to use these schools for proselytism. The Americans appointed Greek Orthodox teachers and visited the schools once a month to enquire about the children's progress.[22]

The Anglican Church was very sympathetic towards the Orthodox Church. In 1890 at a congress held in London under the presidency of Princess Helena (Princess Christian) a resolution was passed stressing that it was the duty of every member of the Anglican Church to work for the improvement of religious and secular education in Cyprus.[23] Some members of the Anglican Church wanted the two Churches to come closer together and, if possible, unite. A zealous promoter of this cause was the first Director of Education, the Reverend J. Spencer, an Anglican clergyman. He believed that 'friendly and intimate relations' with the Orthodox Church of Cyprus could be cultivated if clergymen of the Church of England were prepared to work as teachers in the high schools of Cyprus.[24] Spencer's activities were open to misunderstanding, however, and, as will be explained later, created very considerable political and educational difficulties for the Government.[25]

Policies of the Home Government

Up to 1910 it is very easy to follow the British Government's policy—or lack of it—as far as education in Cyprus was concerned. After 1910 the analysis is made more difficult because access to Colonial Office papers is forbidden by law. Guesses based on the attitude and actions of the High Commissioners and Governors of Cyprus are possible since none of them could effectively act without specific orders from the Home Government whenever major policies were to be decided and adopted.

On the basis of this assumption three major educational policies of the Home Government can be identified. A policy of *laissez faire* was more or less followed during the first fifty years of the British period between 1878 and 1931; a policy of integration and assimilation of the communities of Cyprus was introduced immediately after the 1931 riots when Greek Cypriots demanded Union with Greece; a policy of partnership between the two major communities of Cyprus, the Greek and the Turkish, was introduced at the peak of the revolution of the Greek Cypriots against the British but had no time to succeed.[26]

Laissez faire was in some cases a deliberate, well prepared and well defended policy. In other cases it was the result of doing nothing that was different from what had been done previously— a state of affairs which showed both an unwillingness and an inability on the part of the Home Government to take firm action.

The policy was introduced by the Earl of Kimberley as Home Secretary for the Colonies during the first years of British administration in Cyprus when he decided not to interfere with the education of Greek Cypriots. Influenced by the denominational arrangements in England made by the Education Act of 1870, Kimberley ordered that the administration of Cyprus schools should be similar. In the Orthodox Church of Cyprus he saw a religious institution, which, like the religious groups in England, wanted to control the schools and the teachers to protect its flock's faith against Government intervention.[27] He ordered the High Commissioners diligently to avoid any interference with Church schools, but indicated that the Government could and should financially support these schools.[28]

Later, however, when reports from the High Commissioners indicated that the schools were being used by the Church leaders and indigenous political leaders as agencies of pan-Hellenic propaganda the Home Government faced a very painful dilemma. On the one hand it did not want to abandon its liberal policy on the grounds of principle and also because it was afraid of the opposition such a change might arouse in England and Cyprus. On the other hand it realized that such propaganda was very harmful to the British interests.[29]

The Home Government drifted along for a considerable time in this way. Nevertheless the policy of *laissez faire* was gradually abandoned and measures were taken to counter the political pressure of the Church leaders, the schools and the teachers. In 1899, for example, the Home Government failed to approve a plan sanctioned by the Legislative Council to employ priests as teachers in order to relieve them of manual work and to raise their status. The Home Secretary for the Colonies, Joseph Chamberlain, did not approve because of the 'political activity of the Bishops against the Government' and made it clear that priests were 'undesirable as teachers', because they could thereby control the village schools and strengthen the political power of the Church.[30]

Again, in 1909, when a resolution of the Legislative Council to increase the annual appropriation for elementary education was submitted, the Secretary of State for the Colonies replied that he was not prepared to sanction any increase unless the Government was given some control. He also demanded an investigation into the whole question of education in Cyprus. The implementation of this policy, however, was delayed for many years.[31]

Perhaps the Home Government wavered because it lacked an objective, and a correct picture of the Cyprus problem. Colonial Office papers show that for a long time the officials could not decide whether Cyprus was Oriental or European and therefore they could not make up their mind what methods to adopt. They felt that a liberal constitution could be introduced and liberal methods adopted only if Cyprus was a European community.[32]

The same confusion prevailed in the minds of the Home Secretaries as far as nationality in Cyprus was concerned. The reports of
the High Commissioners divided the population on grounds of
religion instead of nationality.[33]

For example, Kimberley's suggestion to establish only one
Education Board to administer both the Greek and Turkish
schools shows how ignorant he was of the actual political conditions
in Cyprus.[34] The High Commissioner, Sir R. Biddulph, explained
to him that one board was impossible, because the two communities differed not only in religion, but also in language, habits and
systems of education.[35] He was not, however, perspicacious
enough to understand clearly or bold enough to report things as
they really were. Nor—with only a very few exceptions—were the
other High Commissioners.

The 1931 riots of the Greek Cypriots demanding union with
Greece opened the eyes of the Home Government. Its alternatives
were either to quit the island or adopt a new, illiberal and undemocratic policy in order to check hostile propaganda and
political agitation. It preferred the second. Complete control of
elementary schools and their teachers was established, the teaching
of Greek history was virtually eliminated from the curriculum,
considerable control over secondary schools and their teachers was
achieved and great efforts were made to assimilate the different
national communities of the island and orientate the people
politically towards Britain. Most of the Church leaders were
expelled in 1931 and a systematic effort was taken to eliminate the
Church influence on the schools and the teachers.

The results were not encouraging. Political agitation was increased daily and culminated in 1955, when an armed revolt
started against the Government. Church leaders, school teachers
and schoolchildren were the most active members of the underground organization responsible for this revolt.

Policies of the colonial governors
The colonial governors of Cyprus can be placed into three classes:
the liberal-minded, the illiberal and the colonial-minded. In the
first category could be placed Sir W. Sendall, Sir King Harman and
Sir Ronald Storrs, in the second Sir H. Smith and in the third Sir
G. Wolseley and Sir R. Biddulph.

The colonial-minded governors were men who had served

previously in British colonies in Africa and Asia and continued to think in the same terms in Cyprus. In this way they unwittingly created misunderstanding which could have been avoided had they appreciated the extremely different conditions of Cyprus. Sir R. Biddulph's suggestion, for example, to substitute English in the place of Greek language in higher education may be due to the fact that he thought of Cyprus in terms of India.[36]

The illiberal governors were extremely intolerant of pan-Hellenic propaganda disseminated by Church leaders, the schools and the teachers and were keen to find drastic ways of checking it. For them British interests were much more important than the preservation of a liberal institution or the need to respect the traditional rights of a people. In 1902 Sir H. Smith asked the Home Government for permission to overrule the constitution of Cyprus and independently of the Greek Education Board which was the Legislative body for Greek education frame grant regulations for the Greek schools. According to these regulations teachers and schools participating in political agitation would not be eligible for Government grants. He also made the suggestion that these grants should be used to establish a 'few model schools' manned with teachers working 'on proper lines'.[37]

The Home Secretary for the colonies, Joseph Chamberlain, refused to allow this on the grounds that such an action would 'tend to stimulate the agitation it is directed to check' and it would be interpreted 'as a blow struck on education'.[38] There is, however, evidence that the High Commissioner tried behind the scenes to do what he was prevented from doing lawfully. He brought pressure to bear on the teachers to stop advocating the union with Greece.[39]

The liberal-minded governors, known also as philellenes, followed Kimberley's *laissez faire* policy. Sir W. Sendall, for example, was present in 1893 at the inauguration ceremony of the Pancyprian Gymnasium, the biggest and most renowned secondary school of Cyprus, which was established through the efforts and the financial contribution of the Archbishop Sophronios of Cyprus.[40] Speaking at the ceremony the High Commissioner promised financial and moral support for the Normal School, which was to constitute a part of the school. The annual Government grant was fixed at £100.[41] In 1896 he infuriated the Home Government by increasing it to £200.[42] The Government recognized the certificate of the Normal School as a sufficient qualification for teachers to become eligible for Government grants.[43]

Sir King Harman was the first High Commissioner who accepted the Greek Cypriots' demand from the Government to call their schools 'Greek Christian Schools' and not simply 'Christian Schools'.[44]

Sir R. Storrs, as he himself contended, a lifelong opponent of anglicization or dehellenization' was 'strongly averse to diminishing the study of the Greek language and classical traditions'.[45]

After 1931 no governor followed a pro-hellenic policy but one of integrating and assimilating the several communities of Cyprus into a Cypriot nation oriented politically towards Britain. Thus in 1933, after the dissolution of the Legislative Council in 1931, the governor enacted a new Education Law placing the control of elementary schools in his hands.[46] In 1935 the Government suspended the grants to the Normal School of the Pancyprian Gymnasium and the Phaneromeni Girls' Normal School and in 1937 it established a teachers' training college at Morphou, which catered for candidates from all communities of Cyprus and which used English as the medium of instruction.[47] The 'Secondary Education Law, 1935', gave the Government indirect control over the secondary school curriculum and the teachers. Under this law a teaching licence from the Director of Education was necessary for everyone prior to his appointment in a secondary school. This licence might be refused or cancelled for 'a good cause, subject to appeal to the Governor in Council'.[48] Moreover the school committees had to supply regular information regarding their pupils and the curriculum. At the same time the Government withdrew its grants to bring pressure to bear on the schools. Under the new law only those which were prepared to change their curriculum and use English as the medium of instruction were eligible for Government grants.[49]

These decisions came at a time when the Church could offer very little opposition because most of the Church leaders were in exile and those left had their hands tied by the emergency regulations of 1931. Moreover the financial needs of the Greek secondary schools were more than the Church could meet due to the considerable growth in the number of Greek secondary school pupils after 1925 and a consequent increase in expenditure.

The Government's efforts in 1935 to control secondary education failed but it continued its efforts in three ways: by establishing Government schools, mainly agricultural and technical, and trying to attract pupils with promises of low fees and a large number of scholarships;[50] by undermining the respect of the people for the classical schools[51] and by putting forward attractive salary scales for secondary school teachers who would accept work in the public-aided schools.[52]

At the same time the Government tried to recruit secondary school teachers other than those who had studied in Greek Universities. In 1956 £240,000 was allocated to the Education Department for scholarships to study in British Universities and later work as teachers in Government schools.[53] Moreover in 1954 the Government notified the school committees that they could employ as teachers people who had only a pass in the Cyprus Certificate Examinations.[54] This was a very low qualification and it was interpreted by the Church leaders as another attempt to encourage the school committees to employ people other than those who had studied in Greece.

After 1953 the Government took very drastic measures to check the flow of political propaganda from the Greek secondary schools. In 1953 the Governor deprived a Greek headmaster of his licence, because the pupils of his school had staged an anti-British procession.[55] During the school year 1955–6 the governor struck five secondary schools off the register because their pupils had taken part in the EOKA armed revolt against the British.[56]

Policies of the Church leaders

The Orthodox Christian religion as a system of beliefs had had little influence on Greek education in Cyprus because, compared with Protestants, Orthodox Christians have never regarded the study of the Bible as very important. Christian charity, on the other hand, provided an incentive to establish schools. For example, the church committee of St. Lazarus started an elementary school in Larnaca in 1858 in order to educate and take care of the poor children who wandered aimlessly about the town.[57] In this way the example of Robert Raikes of Gloucester, who started, for philanthropic reasons, one of the first Sunday schools, was followed in Cyprus. Philanthropy did not play as important a role there as it did in England in setting up a system of elementary schools.

The Greek Orthodox Church of Cyprus was induced by political conditions there to regard education very highly. Influenced by the ideals of the French revolution its leaders regarded education as a human right and a sacred trust, which spread 'light' to the people.[58] Some of the bishops devoted themsevles completely to education.[59] During the first thirty years of the British period most of them, before being ordained as bishops, worked as teachers in Greek secondary schools.[60]

At that time ecclesiastical posts were the highest paid to which educated people could aspire. Later, after a legislative council had been set up and political posts created, the educated people strove to become politicians rather than bishops. Even some of the bishops hoped to become politicians and three of them and one abbot were elected to the Legislative Council. In this capacity they conducted the most bitter anti-British campaign ever carried out against the Government. At first the British Government was most tolerant,[61] but when the situation worsened and the demand for independence led to the 1931 riots it dissolved the Council and deported the bishops.

In fact during the nineteenth century the majority of Greek schools in Cyprus were Church foundations. In the early part of the twentieth century the communities became responsible for the establishment of new schools. But neither the Church-founded nor the community-founded schools were ever secularized. The Church leaders continued to stress the importance of education and encouraged the people to establish more schools and support them financially. Only the Orthodox religion could be taught in them and the teachers had to be exclusively Orthodox Christians. The situation did not change in spite of the diminution of Church control especially during the periods 1900 to 1910 and between 1931 and 1946. The schools were never laicized. On the contrary, religion and education were regarded both by laymen[62] and Church leaders as 'closely allied'. No one could ever imagine as possible an education devoid of religious influence.

This belief was a powerful weapon in the hands of the Church leaders striving to maintain control over the schools and teachers. As ecclesiastical and national leaders they regarded themselves as the highest authority on clerical and secular education.[63] And they used their position to strengthen their control over the appointment of teachers, over the appointment of inspectors, and over the curriculum.

On the first point it was held that because education was 'closely allied' with religion teachers had to play the role of priests in Greek schools and, therefore, care had to be taken that suitable persons, i.e. persons belonging to the Orthodox religion, were appointed. The appointment of teachers ought to be, therefore, the responsibility of the Church because 'to tell them that their school teachers would be appointed and dismissed by a heterodox Government was equal to telling them that their priests would be ordained by bishops of a different religion'.[64]

Again the Church leaders believed that the teacher's duty was not only to teach religion but also to make sure that children attended church regularly. As in scholastic matters an inspector was needed, therefore, to see how far teachers were performing their duty.[65] Furthermore, an inspector was needed to ensure that no teacher taught 'materialism or the follies of the evangelistic sect'. For these reasons the Church leaders claimed that an Orthodox Greek should be appointed as Inspector of schools. They were not afraid that an English inspector would interfere with the teaching of religion, but that he would be indifferent to it.[66] When, in 1901, the Cyprus Government appointed as inspector of schools a clergyman of the Church of England, the Bishop of Kition described it as 'a plot against the religion and language of the people' and supported a motion to reduce the education vote by a sum amounting to the salary of the inspector.[67]

As for the curriculum the close alliance of education and religion justified the insistence by the Church leaders that the Greek language, which had already been the language of the Orthodox Church, should be taught. For this reason according to them, the inspector of schools had to be an Orthodox Christian and a Greek with a thorough knowledge of the language.[68]

In summary, the Orthodox Church was strongly opposed to any attempt by foreign churches to proselytize. It mistrusted missionary schools and discouraged Greek Cypriot parents from sending their children to such schools on the grounds that attendance at them would endanger both their faith and their national feelings.[69]

The Church leaders also mistrusted the Government and were nearly always suspicious of its plans. Bishop Kyprianos of Kition, for example, warned the Greek members of the Legislative Council not to give 'the Government the power to interfere in (their) educational affairs'.[70] Again in 1903 the new Bishop of Kition, Cyril, speaking in the Legislative Council against a Government education bill, likened such bills 'to a flower bed under which snakes were hidden' and contended that he was always 'the first to approach these flower beds with a stick in his hand'.[71]

Policies of the local political leaders
During the Turkish period the bishops were the only indigenous political leaders. With the coming of the more liberal British new lay political leaders emerged but during the whole of their period of administration the Church was the strongest 'political party'. Indeed in some instances rival political parties were formed from the supporters of rival bishops. For example, during the period 1900 to 1910 the people of Cyprus were divided into those who supported the Bishop of Kyrenia (Kyrenia party) and those who supported the Bishop of Kition (Kition party) as candidates for the archiepiscopal throne.[72]

The lay political leaders followed the same nationalistic policies as those of the Church leaders. They all grew up and were educated in an atmosphere of fervent nationalism and realized that their political influence depended upon promoting union with Greece. Since in the minds of the people the Church represented something sacred, no politician could risk (even if he had wished to do so) opposing the Church and what it stood for. At the same time nearly all of them were educated in Church schools or in schools over which Church influence was considerable. They had been taught to appreciate the great contribution the Church had made to the preservation of the Greek nation, its culture and its education. Consequently nationalistic lay politicians were grateful to the Church.

ÉLITISM IN EDUCATION

For fifty years the Government's focus of attention was completely different from that of the Greek Orthodox Church of Cyprus as far as education was concerned. The Church was more interested in preparing an intellectual élite than in the common people. Consequently it favoured secondary education for the clergy and the laity and gave less importance to elementary education.[73] Compared with Roman Catholic policy the emphasis on secondary education was not very great but the rationale behind the policy was similar in both cases. The secondary schools could train leaders who would become teachers in the elementary schools and would also preach the glory of Greece. They would be the store-houses of Greek culture and the revivers of national awareness.

Consequently, Church policy was to use most of their money to support and maintain secondary schools, to press the Government to allocate a considerable part of the grant-in-aid to secondary schools,[74] and to establish as many of these schools as possible. In fact the more nationalistic the bishops were, the more secondary schools they tried to set up in their dioceses. Most of them were established between 1916 and 1922,[75] during a period of fervent nationalism resulting from the triumphs of the Greek national army.

Even through the lay schools the Church hoped to reach pupils and the people and guide them towards God and the glory of their fatherland. Some of the schools were theological seminaries and they had another role to play. Their graduates became priests, preachers or teachers, and after the Government took over control of elementary school teachers in 1929 they organized catechetical schools and taught the national history of Greece. Emphasis, in short, was on the preparation of leaders.

The Government, on the other hand, favoured elementary education as the best way of improving the backward social and financial conditions of Cyprus.[76] Hence it used the greater part of its grants to expand and improve elementary education. Its interest in secondary education was restricted to teacher training in the form of normal schools. From these it hoped to recruit elementary school teachers.

Eventually the Government realized the political importance of the secondary schools and, as has been said, tried by various means to bring them under its control.

English versus the vernacular
As was to be expected the teaching of English in the Greek schools of Cyprus soon acquired political significance and led to very fierce disputes between the Church and the Government at all three levels of education, i.e. elementary, secondary and higher.

The Church leaders did not object to the teaching of English as such, nor did they consider it unnecessary. They wanted, however, Greek children to study English after they had learnt their own language.[77] In fact, from the first year of the British administration, English was introduced in the Nicosia High School, which was governed by a committee presided over by the Archbishop, without any pressure from the Government.[78] The trouble started as a result of proposals made by the second High Commissioner, Sir R. Biddulph, and the Inspector of Schools (formerly Director of Education) the Reverend J. Spencer. In 1881 these two officials proposed to the Home Government that English should take the place of Greek in higher education. In their report they insisted that their advice was based on purely educational grounds and had nothing to do with politics.[79] Spencer went even further and made three specific proposals to reorganize Cyprus education. They were: the establishment of English schools, the introduction of the teaching of English in the native schools; and the payment of an increased salary to English-speaking people and graduates of the English school to encourage them to become teachers.[80]

When these suggestions became known in Cyprus they created uneasiness and gave rise to a considerable wave of protests. They were interpreted as a threat to the national language and conscience and as an attempt to dehellenize the people.[81] To demonstrate how opposed they were to these plans many village school committees. refused to accept Government grants.[82] The situation was saved only when the Earl of Kimberley rejected Biddulph's proposals and spoke in a flattering way about the Greek language.[83] But unrest was again provoked in 1899 when the High Commissioner, Sir H. Smith, suggested ways of making English the main language of the island.[84]

Until 1935 English was not, as a rule, taught in elementary schools. There were, nevertheless, some cases when teachers were encouraged through increases in pay to learn English and teach it in the schools.[85] In 1935, however, English was forced into the large elementary schools and became 'an integral part' of the curriculum in the top two classes.[86] At the same time steps were taken to man the schools with teachers who could teach English. According to a regulation of 1935 no candidate was to be accepted after 1938 in the teachers' training college unless he had passed the English Distinction Examinations.[87]

Compulsory English in the elementary schools, contrary to the advice of the educational experts,[88] was part of the Government's new political policy designed to integrate the different communities into a new English-speaking nation, the Cypriot nation. The Church leaders angrily rejected this policy. Their arguments were pedagogical, religious and political. It was not sound pedagogical practice, according to the locum tenens, to introduce a foreign language into the curriculum of elementary schools and over-stretch the minds of young children. Moreover, the learning of English would prevent them from mastering Greek and would consequently be detrimental to their religious life, because the Gospel and the sacred writings were all written in Greek. Finally the introduction of English and the consequent restrictions on the teaching of Greek would break the precious intellectual links binding Cyprus to Greece.[89] Church opposition had no practical results. On the contrary, the teaching of English was expanded in newly established model schools[90] and the situation persisted until the end of British rule in 1959, when the newly established Greek Education Council abolished the teaching of English in the elementary schools ostensibly on pedagogical grounds.[91] However, that there were political reasons behind this decision, is suggested by the burning of English textbooks by elementary school boys in protest against British rule.

Government policy on the teaching of English in secondary schools was very similar. Until 1935 the Government encouraged the teaching of English through grants[92] based on the number of teachers of English, the periods devoted to the teaching of English and the results obtained.[93]

In 1935 the grants were withdrawn and the Government declared that they would be given only to those schools which were prepared to change their curriculum and use English as the medium of instruction. In this way through the expansion of English teaching the Government hoped to meet the need for English-speaking teachers in the newly reorganized elementary schools.

No Greek school accepted English as the medium of instruction. Three schools, however, changed their curriculum by expanding the teaching of English to such an extent that it became the most important subject. The other schools rejected the offer and continued to be maintained on fees and Church contributions.[94]

The Government schools, however, i.e. the Apprentices' Training Centre and two technical schools, from the beginning used English as the medium of instruction. Two reasons were given; firstly, multilingual classes and secondly, the shortage of satisfactory textbooks and trade journals in other languages.[95]

The same arrangement was followed by the Government Teachers' Training College for the same reasons. The Church leaders resented the international character of the college and its adverse influence on the national spirit of future teachers.[96] Later on the Church leaders deplored the low standard of Greek among the elementary school boys and attributed it to the lowered standards of Greek among the teachers resulting from the use of English as the medium of instruction.[97] The Government rejected these accusations and countered that the college helped intending teachers to become tolerant and broadminded.[98]

During the revolt (1955–9) the Greek students of the college went on strike to force the Government to use Greek instead of English as the medium of instruction. Within two months their demand was fully met.[99]

Liberal versus vocational education

In the early 1950s the secondary schools of Cyprus fell into two hostile camps, the communal schools which were under Church influence and the Government schools. The former were mainly classical schools imparting a liberal and humanistic education. The latter were mainly technical and agricultural schools. Each of the two camps did its best to attract pupils by extolling the virtues of the kind of education it was imparting. The bulk of the pupils, however, attended the classical schools—(*Gymnasia*) only one per cent of the pupils attended the Government schools (three technical and one agricultural).[100]

There were two reasons for this imbalance: an old preference of the Greeks for liberal education and a reluctance to attend Government schools on purely political grounds.

Both the tradition and the epistemology of the Greek people encouraged intellectualism and liberal education. They remembered that the ancient Greeks despised manual work as something for slaves. Greek epistemology supported the view that people with a liberal education were capable of successfully undertaking any kind of job provided that after their studies they had a very short course of specialization.

Economic conditions also encouraged this kind of education. Cyprus was mainly an agricultural island which did not encourage scientific or technical subjects. The poverty and the hardships of the peasants made them desire a white-collar job for their children because it ensured a higher salary, less hard work and greater status. Greek education, moreover, was influenced by French intellectualism so that its aim was to train the intellect and make it capable of finding the truth. Learning through experience was not respected and experiment was hardly ever used in Greek schools.

The above situation was true both of Greece and Cyprus because conditions were similar and the Greek schools of Cyprus followed the pattern of those in Greece.

But in Cyprus the classical schools were popular because of a spiritual and natural idealism cultivated by Church leaders who believed that only the classical schools could efficiently propagate Greek ideals of virtue and freedom. Cyprus needed idealists who would be ready to sacrifice themselves for the cause of freedom. Sometimes the fight against materialism was identified with the fight against the British Government. To the British argument that union with Greece would impoverish Cyprus, they replied that their ancestors had never fought for material gain but to preserve their ideals and especially the ideal of freedom.

Government schools were established very late, i.e. after 1946. Previously during the sixty-eight years of British rule, there had been no technical education at all. As the two educational experts Talbot and Cape, who visited Cyprus in 1913, characteristically remarked, 'the only provision made in the island at present for any form of technical education is to be found in the Government Prison at Nicosia, where juvenile offenders are instructed in shoe-making and tailoring'.[101]

Most of the bishops did not object to vocational education as such. Some of them, in fact, realized the need for technical and vocational education and tried to meet it.[102] Others opposed them on the grounds that only classical schools could strengthen the national feelings of the people.[103] All the bishops, however, discouraged parents from sending their children to Government schools because they objected to Government control and the threat to national feeling.

After 1950 some of the larger Greek secondary schools introduced some differentiation in the top three classes. Children of fifteen had a choice between the classical, scientific and commercial branches.

Bible studies versus classical literature

Bible study and Christian literature were never prominent in the curriculum of the Greek elementary and secondary schools, nor was any great effort made by the Church leaders to appeal to the children's religious feelings. In contrast to the Protestant Church the Orthodox Church never regarded Bible studies as necessary to the salvation of the people. Tradition and faith were much more important, so no schools were established with the sole purpose of enabling children to read the Bible.

Ancient Greek literature has been always the most important subject in the secondary schools' curriculum. Even in elementary schools it was taught a good deal. For the Greeks it was a matter of national pride to teach about their ancient ancestors, and a matter of belief that ancient Greek literature would keep alive among the enslaved Greek people the ideal of freedom. Thus, even before the British period, the Church leaders themselves had more knowledge of ancient Greek than ecclesiastical literature. Codices[104] kept in the Archbishopric reveal the importance given to ancient Greek literature in the education of Church leaders.

An example of the appeal to national sentiment is found in the secondary school emblems. In contrast to English or American schools, whose emblems are usually derived from the Christian symbols, those of the Greek secondary school are drawn from ancient Greek history and mythology—for example, Hermes, the ancient Greek God of Commerce, the owl, the holy bird of Minerva, Zeno Citieus, an ancient Greek philosopher from Cyprus and so on.

EDUCATIONAL DEVELOPMENT

It is often argued that, in contrast to the Catholic or Presbyterian Churches, the Orthodox Church neither established an educational system of its own nor showed any interest in the education of its followers. Here an attempt is made to show that this view is not correct as far as the Orthodox Church of Cyprus is concerned. Indeed it took a considerable interest in education during the Turkish administration but was prevented from establishing an extensive educational system by political oppression, lack of funds and a shortage of teachers and educated people. During the final decades of the Turkish period, however, when the political and economic conditions of the island improved, a considerable number of schools was established and largely maintained by local churches and monasteries.

Interest in education increased during the British period. Meanwhile the Orthodox Church of Cyprus formulated an educational philosophy which said education was a good thing, something closely related to religion, and something which created good men and good patriots. The subsequent development of education in Cyprus can be understood in terms of these assumptions.

During the Turkish period and the first decade of British power there were two kinds of Greek schools in Cyprus: private schools and community schools.

The private schools can hardly be called schools. They were, in fact, private classes given by priests or monks inside the local church or in its precincts.[105] Reading and in some cases writing and sacred history were taught—in most cases very badly. Reading, for example, was usually taught 'after the fashion prevalent in the churches' and in some cases the pupils learned to read passages by heart without understanding their meaning.[106] The priests and monks were paid by the parents either in money or in kind with bread, cheese and wine. These 'Saturday gifts' were so-called because they were usually given on Saturdays.[107] Most of the priests were semi-literate. Very few monks, especially those coming from Greece, were sufficiently well educated to teach adequately.[108]

The community schools included elementary and secondary schools. The former usually had a six-year course and were run on the pupil–teacher method.[109] Their teachers were both laymen and priests, there were so many of the latter, in fact, that even today priests are addressed as teachers by the people.

The schools and the teachers were under the control of village committees, which, in most of the villages, were the local church committees. Money came from fees paid by parents and from local church contributions which were paid in proportion to the financial condition of the church.[110] Ignorance and negligence often made these committees inefficient. Very often they neglected to collect contributions, appoint teachers and pay them. Teachers consequently often left one village school for a better paid post in another village. The village schools were usually very short of teachers.[111]

The condition of the town schools was better. They were generously financed by the rich parochial churches of the towns under the direction of the bishops.[112]

Special care was taken of the secondary schools, known as Hellenic schools or Hellenomouseia. In 1880, soon after the British arrived, there were three of them—in Nicosia, Larnaca and Limassol. They were similar to schools on the mainland of Greece and in other cities with large Greek populations and strong Greek traditions such as Smyrna and Constantinople.[113] The first secondary school was founded in Nicosia in 1812 by Archbishop Kyprianos, who dedicated it to the Holy Trinity.[114] In 1893 the school became a *gymnasium* and its has since been known as Pancyprian Gymnasium and has performed an important service by educating a considerable number of laymen and Church leaders. Equally important was the contribution of this school as a normal school and a cultural centre.

The Orthodox Church established more secondary schools. In 1910 the Bishop of Kition opened a theological seminary, whose graduates became either priests or teachers.[115] But the period of greatest effect were the years 1916–22 when nearly ten secondary schools were established through the initiative of bishops and with the financial support of them, the local churches and the monasteries.[116] The drive was largely due to fervent nationalism. In October 1915 Cyprus was officially offered to Greece by the British Government 'on condition that Greece gives immediate and full support with her army to Serbia'.[117] The Greek Government rejected the offer, but news of it revived nationalism in Cyprus. Greece's entry into the war later on, the victories of her army in Constantinople and Asia Minor enormously strengthened nationalism and both in Greece and Cyprus there was hope that 'Great Greece' would shortly materialize.

In 1878, there was a decentralized system of administration. Actual control was in the hands of the village committees. District Committees and the General Assembly only co-ordinated the educational activities of the village committees.[118]

In response to the village committees' application for financial assistance in 1881 the Government started to offer grants to those committees prepared to accept certain conditions, such as the employment of qualified teachers, their regular payment and the submission of an annual report to the Director of Education.[119]

During the first three decades the Government's interest in the Greek schools was limited only to a natural desire to see that the money was profitably and properly spent.[120] It believed that its control over the schools could not be 'as effective as that which can be exercised by local bodies directly interested in and respon-

0 10 20 30 *Miles*

Kyrenia

Morphou

Nicosia

Famagusta

Kiti · Larnaca

Ktima

Limassol

CYPRUS

sible for their efficiency'.[121] The Government merely tried to help the existing schools financially, morally and educationally. As an English Inspector of Schools put it, the aim of the Government was 'rather to graft on the existing stock order and management in a spirit conforming to modern needs, leaving the actual control of the schools in the hands of local committees in each village than to introduce a new and ready-made system'.[122]

Evidence of the respect the British Government had for existing traditional rights is found in that the 1895 Education Law, which established a partnership between the Government and the Church in the control of schools and teachers did not apply to the town schools, on which traditionally the Church grip was stronger and where Government intervention might have resulted in fierce opposition.[123]

According to this law two major bodies were established, the Education Board, presided over by the Chief Secretary to the Government, and District Committees, which were presided over by District Commissioners. The Archbishop was an ex-officio member of the Education Board and the bishops were ex-officio members of the District Committees in their dioceses. No Government official sat on the village committees, which had executive power and were responsible until 1923 for the employment and the dismissal of teachers.[124]

Later on the Government reached the conclusion that it should interfere more drastically with the administration of education. Three reasons lay behind this decision: the persistent demand of the Greek community for increases in Government grants;[125] the political agitation which the teachers and the pupils caused, and the numerous abuses in the appointment of teachers by the village and district committees.[126]

The Government decided gradually to take over control of the elementary schools. The Education Law of 1923 deprived the village and the district committees of the power to appoint and dismiss teachers and vested it in the Education Board,[127] that of 1929 gave this control to the Governor,[128] and in 1933 a law deprived the Board of its power to lay down the curriculum and prescribe textbooks and vested it in the Governor.[129] The Board remained an advisory body with no actual power, a state of affairs which continued until the end of British administration in 1959.

Political consequences

Political conditions in Cyprus turned the Greek Orthodox Church into a political party. Its sole aim, union with Greece, gave great importance to education, the Greek language and the perpetuation of national feelings. Most of the bishops realized that the survival of the Orthodox religion depended on the achievement of these goals. Hence education had a double role: to embody the ideologies and aspirations of the Greek Orthodox Church and to promote its political aims by keeping alive the national feeling of the Greek Cypriots. Extreme nationalism later became the most important determinant of Greek education.

Nationalism was promoted through curriculum studies of ancient Greek literature and grammar. The schools acquired distinct Greek characteristics. Greek teachers were brought from

Constantinople, Smyrna or Athens. Books were brought from Greece. An educational link was established which strengthened the political move towards union with Greece, and indeed anticipated it.

The Church schools gave rise to far-reaching political consequences. They educated the first spiritual, political and intellectual leaders of the people who appreciated the great importance of these schools and were grateful to the Church for its educations efforts.

The Church itself was greatly helped by these schools. It recruited its high ranking members from among their graduates. In this way the Church leaders were sufficiently educated to enable them to remain popular leaders.

The political leaders on the other hand, having had a purely Greek education and having been initiated in the 'Great Idea',[130] had been trained to look to Greece as their motherland and to think of independence in terms of union with Greece. The importance of this generation becomes even greater, when we think that many of the graduates of these schools became the first teachers during the first years of the British rule. Gladstone's Liberal Government respected the school curriculum and its traditions and teachers continued freely to impart nationalistic education as they had been doing for over forty years. The pupils were taught that they were Greeks and should look forward to union with Greece. At the same time the teachers were the political agents in the villages, since they were the only educated persons there. They supported, rather than opposed, the Church.

Teachers were expected not only to support the cause of union with Greece but also to spread this policy in the villages where they worked. It is difficult to say what the results would have been had the British Government followed a different policy from the beginning and forbidden or limited the teaching of Greek. Lord Kinross insisted that 'had the British Government chosen at the outset to introduce an English system of education, and particularly an English University into the island, the Cypriots today would be English in speech and culture, and perhaps even in sympathy'.[131] Things would certainly have been very different had the British Government followed the policy advocated by Lord Kinross, but it is doubtful whether the results would have been so impressive. The roots of the problem were there long before the British arrived, because Greek culture and nationalism had been strengthened between 1830 and 1878. Perhaps the situation would have been different, had the British occupied Cyprus in about 1800 and immediately followed the policy advocated by Lord Kinross. English culture would have been welcomed because there would have been little organized opposition from the Church. It is no exaggeration to say that the years 1800 to 1880 were the most important in the recent political history of Cyprus.

Economic consequences

In every country the financial support of the schools has been always a most powerful weapon in the battle for control. In Cyprus control was at first in the hands of the Church, because most of the schools were founded and, until the British occupation, supported by it. The Turkish Government never concerned itself with Greek education. It used to grant £T500 annually for the Muslim schools, but never made grants to the Greek schools, although they were more numerous than the Turkish.[132] A heavy annual burden of £T400 fell on the Church out of £T700 needed to maintain four Christian schools at Nicosia.[133] No matter how poor the village and town schools were, the Church in fact met most of the cost. In a memorandum to the High Commissioner, Sir G. Wolseley, the Archbishop Sophronios and other bishops of Cyprus outlined the situation existing during the Turkish administration:

> Although the Christians contributed the nine-tenths of the Island's revenue, still not a penny could be found in the budget of the island for the education of the Christians; and this important need was always met as far as possible by the Church income . . . private contributions are small, because the people of both the towns and the villages are poor.[134]

During the British administration new factors reduced the Church's control. First, there was a substantial decrease in Church funds and property because the British Government, contrary to the Turkish Government, refused to help the Church leaders to collect their dues from the people.[135]

Under these conditions the Church was very reluctant to contribute generously to the maintenance of the schools. In one case a bishop closed down a school in protest against Government policy.[136] The Church leaders also refused to allow the Legislative

Council to fix an annual compulsory financial contribution by the churches and monasteries for educational purposes: they wanted these contributions always to remain voluntary.[137]

Secondly, there was a tremendous increase in the number of Greek elementary schools during the first thirty years of British administration. It was extremely difficult for the Church to assist these schools financially. No doubt the balance of power in education between the Church and the Government would have been different had the Church been able to keep pace with the increase in the number of schools. Government interference might have been prevented. The situation, however, made it necessary for the Church, except for the first three or four years, not to oppose Government grants-in-aid, and also made necessary the allocation of more and more State money for the maintenance of Greek schools. Money was needed to establish a Church college.[138] As was to be expected this financial policy weakened the Church's claim to retain control over education and after 1899 the Government in fact began to claim control over the elementary schools and the teachers.

The rationale was repeatedly stated in memoranda from the bishops and the Greek political leaders. Government grants, they said, came from Government revenue, raised from the indirect and direct taxation of people, four-fifths of whom were Greek. This money, therefore, belonged in a way to the people, and the Government was under an obligation to meet their needs without imposing conditions.[139]

Politicians and Church leaders demanded more and more money, but refused to accept Government control. They stated that 'they would sooner dispense with State aid altogether than surrender to an alien Government the control of the teachers which they had always possessed, alike under Turkish and British rule and which they deem to be vital to their political aspirations'.[140]

In spite of what they said, the Church and the school committees could not afford to dispense with State aid. In fact they needed more and more money, because the teachers, organized in a Teachers' Union, pressed for higher salaries. When the teachers realized that their demands could not be met, a considerable number of them claimed the right to become civil servants for the sake of better conditions.[141]

The administrative council of the Pancyprian Union of Teachers tried to check this move of teachers and urged the Church leaders to do their best.[142] In 1923 the Union drafted a bill to reorganize Greek education and submitted it to the Holy Synod. But the only relief the Archbishop and the Holy Synod proposed was to reduce the number of redundant teachers by limiting the number of training schools.[143] Evidently the Church leaders could not afford the money to solve the problem satisfactorily. Consequently teachers accepted the provisions of the Education Law of 1923 which put them under close Government supervision and the laws of 1929 which made them Government employees.

Things were different as far as secondary schools were concerned. During the first fifty years of the British period the number and size of Greek secondary schools was relatively small. The majority of the pupils came from rich families, and could afford to pay high fees. Subsequently the cost to the Church was not very great and it could respond quickly and effectively to the needs of the Greek secondary schools. This and the special interest shown by Church leaders in secondary education were the main reasons why the Government had little say in education at this level for a considerable period of time.

The situation changed in the late 1930s and again in the 1940s and 1950s. In the year 1933–4 there were sixteen Greek secondary schools with a total of 2,211 pupils. In 1935–6 there were twenty-one Greek secondary schools with a total of 3,038 pupils. In 1947–8 the number of secondary schools rose to thirty-five with 8,682 pupils. In the year 1954–5 the number of pupils rose to 15,401.[144]

These sudden increases reflected a deep social change and a rise in the standard of living in post-war Cyprus, but put a great strain on the Church's finances. To meet demands for higher salaries school fees were raised. An influx of poor children, who could not pay the high school fees, and the need for larger buildings increased the deficit enormously and the Church was asked to make a higher contribution. The Pancyprian Gymnasium offers an interesting case study. The school is the biggest *gymnasium* on the island and, according to the Church leaders, more than any other school deserved support since it had been one of the few to refuse Government grants and had remained completely free to choose its own curriculum. The contributions of the Church to the Pancyprian Gymnasium were as follows:

	£		£
1950–1	350	1955–6	9,250
1951–2	1,100	1956–7	5,500
1952–3	10,100	1957–8	21,103
1953–4	28,200	1958–9	5,500
1954–5	5,725	1959–60	6,766

In addition to these sums in 1952–3 the Archbishopric paid £42,000 to clear off a debt. Again seventy building sites, valued approximately at £150,000, were donated in 1958 by a local church to the same school for the building of a new school premises for girls.[145]

In other cases the Church contributed smaller amounts. In spite of its great wish to help, the financial needs of the Greek secondary schools grew beyond the ability of the Church to satisfy them. Nevertheless the school committees did not move over to the Government camp. They preferred rather to increase fees and equip the schools inefficiently than to surrender to the Government.

In conclusion, because of the generous donations made by the Church it managed to retain considerable control over the majority of the secondary schools until the end of British rule. Except for three schools, which in 1935 modified their curriculum in order to qualify for a Government grant and one which in 1952 accepted the status of public-aided, all the others remained independent of Government control in spite of financial difficulties. Some explanation of the modification of curricula in the three schools in 1935 is offered by the fact that the Church leaders were still in exile having been deported in 1931 and could not fight the Government's plans.

Social consequences

The schools had a considerable influence on the social structure of the Cypriot people, especially after the Second World War when the number of schools increased considerably. Then secondary school graduates had a better chance than previously of a white collar job either as teachers or as Government or bank employees. White collar jobs were always very attractive especially to farmers' children because farming was extremely tiring and unprofitable. The aspirations of all farmers were for a better paid and higher status job for their children: namely a white collar one.

These aspirations were encouraged by the schools. Greek secondary schools imparted a liberal education and despised agricultural and technical knowledge. The graduates, therefore, could not return to the villages. They had to settle in the towns and look for employment. Thus urbanization was encouraged and due to other factors increased after the war. With it there came profound social changes. The old conservative patriarchal family broke into small units. Moreover the old strict code of morality was questioned and new moral and social ideas began to creep in among the townsfolk.

The Church leaders and the Educational Council of the Ethnarchy, which was working under their auspices, were very apprehensive of the future of secondary school graduates in a country where the 'number of professional and business openings' was always limited.[146] They were afraid of the social repercussions that this new class of the 'proletariats of the intellect'[147] as they used to call them, might have on the social life of Cyprus.

Moreover, they resented the fact that many of these unemployed secondary school graduates might have to emigrate to Britain. In their despair they accused the Government, that it had not expanded Cyprus economically with the intention of forcing the Cypriot youth to leave the island and in this way weaken the nationalist movement.

NOTES

1. Acts XIII.
2. Hackett, J., *A History of the Orthodox Church of Cyprus* (London 1901), pp. 114–23.
3. Hill, Sir G., *A History of Cyprus* (Cambridge 1949), vol I, pp. 276–8; Hackett, pp. 13–32.
4. Hill, vol I, p. 278.
5. *Ibid.*, vol IV, p. 308.
6. Hackett, p. 197.
7. Kyprianos Archimandrite, *Chronological History of the Island of Cyprus* (Nicosia 1933), pp. 462–3.
8. Turner, W., 'Journal of a Tour in the Levant' in Cobham, C. D., *Excerpta Cypria* (London 1908), p. 447.
9. Cobham, pp. 470–4.

10. Parl. Paper C 2324, p. 10.

11. Memorandum of E. Fairfield, Parl. Papers C 3661, p. 83, Accounts and Papers (1833), vol 46.

12. Weir, W. W., *Education in Cyprus* (Nicosia 1952), p. 86.

13. Codex of Correspondence between the Archbishops, p. 72. The letter was published by L. Philippou in *Greek education in Cyprus during the Turkish occupation* (Nicosia 1930), vol I, pp. 173–4.

14. Zannetos, P., *Cyprus in the age of Palingenesia* (Athens 1930), p. 21.

15. Hill, vol IV, p. 124.

16. Sir R. Storrs, one of the colonial governors of Cyprus, mentioned in *Orientations* (London 1937, pp. 554–5) that it was rumoured that more than one Archbishop had 'been poisoned for refusing the behests of extremist or rival factions'.

17. Patriarch Gregorius V was hanged in 1821 because of his alleged implication in the revolution. A priest declared the revolution on the 25 March 1821.

18. *Salpinx* (Greek newspaper of Cyprus) Limossol No. 507, 17 Dec. 1894.

19. These were his actual words: 'We accept the change of Government in as much as we trust that Great Britain will help Cyprus, as it did the Ionian Islands, to be united with Mother Greece, with which it is nationally connected', Orr, C. W. J., *Cyprus under British rule* (London 1918), p. 160.

20. On 9 Feb. 1906 a group of Greek Christians in Famagusta attacked a member of the Reformed Presbyterian Church of North America and gutted his house because he had tried to proselytize Greek Christians (Despatch of the H.Cr. King Harman to the Secretary of State for the Colonies Earl of Elgin, 17 July 1906, C.O. 67/146).

21. The most important missionary schools established in Cyprus were two secondary schools; the first was established in 1845 by the French Missionary Society of St. Joseph and the second was established in 1908 by the Reformed Presbyterian Church of North America (Kyriazis, N. C., *Social Activities of the city of Larnaca-Scala*, pp. 22, 25; Weir, p. 204).

22. Philippou, vol 1, pp. 275–8.

23. *Manchester Guardian*, 4 June 1890.

24. Eastern Church Association *Report* for the year 1895, p. 9, C.O. 67/101.

25. See a more detailed discussion later.

26. This policy was introduced by the last Director of Education, W. B. Tudhope.

27. Conf. Despatch of Sir R. Biddulph to the Earl of Kimberley, C 3661, 1882, p. 93; Conf. Despatch 17 Feb. 1881, C.O. 67/18.

28. C 2930, pp. 136, 138.

29. Most illuminating are J. Chamberlain's, Home Secretary for the Colonies, comments on the situation in 1900: 'I am not at all sure that some measures may not have to be taken to stop the pan-Hellenic propaganda, though it is difficult to see how it is to be done. If children are educated in it, in a few years time it will become a very considerable and annoying force though less dangerous in respect of Greeks than in any other nationality. I think that this question wants very careful watching and, if necessary, control over education must be obtained by legislation or in the last resort by order in Council.' (Conf. Despatch, 4 Aug. 1900, C.O. 67/124.)

30. Despatch of the High Commissioner, Sir H. Smith, 24 Jan. 1899, C.O. 67/117.

31. C.O. 69/27, 1911, p. 461; C.O. 69/30, 1914, p. 229; Talbot, J. E. and Cape, F. W., *Report on Education in Cyprus, 1913* (London 1914), p. 6.

32. In 1900 a Colonial Office official suggested that the British could not 'introduce their western ideas into an oriental community like Cyprus'. (Conf. Despatch, 10 June 1900, C.O. 67/123.) But in 1904 another Colonial Office official warned the High Commissioner of Cyprus, Sir H. Smith, against any change of the liberal constitution of Cyprus: 'It does not seem to me to be practicable to adopt the legislation suited to India, an Asiatic country, conquered and held by the sword to a European Community like Cyprus. In that island three-quarters of the population are Greeks and hence by language and traditions attached to liberal institutions. This attachment is indeed a sentiment which it is impossible to ignore, if only on account of the corresponding sentiment which would be evoked in this country by any attempt to ignore it'. (Conf. Despatch, 14 June 1904, C.O. 67/138.)

33. Colonial Report for Cyprus, No. 1574, 1931 (London 1932), p. 5.

34. The Earl of Kimberley believed that, in the same way as in England, it would be constructive to make the two 'religious communities' sit together and discuss their educational problems; in this way, he believed, 'mutual criticism' would be very 'useful in restraining one-sided tendencies', C 3384, p. 14.

35. C 3384, p. 5.

36. C 2930, p. 28.

37. Conf. Despatch, 30 Aug. 1902, C.O. 67/132.

38. *Ibid.* and 6 Aug. 1900, C.O. 67/124.

39. In 1903 a Greek member of the Legislative Council complained against the Director of Police Force, Major Chamberlayne, who had told a schoolmaster to stop 'hurraying for Greece' if he wanted to be promoted (C.O. 69/17, 1903, p. 277).

The Inspector of Schools, Rev. F. D. Newham, reported also that some District Commissioners used to demand from him to transfer from their district teachers who were proved to be political agitators (30 Aug. 1902, C.O. 67/132).

40. The Pancyprian Gymnasium Codex, Document No. 1; Newham, F. D., 'The system of Education in Cyprus', in *Board of Education Special Reports on Educational Subjects*, vol 12, 1905, p. 421.

41. Correspondence between Sir W. Sendall and the Marquis of Ripon, 9 April 1894, C.O. 67/85; C 8076, p. 44.

42. C.O. 67/106, 6 May 1897.

43. Newham, pp. 441, 444.

44. Minutes of the Legislative Council, 1904, C.O. 69/18, p. 242.

45. Storrs, Sir R., *Orientations* (London 1937), p. 587.

46. *The Cyprus Gazette*, 29 May 1933, pp. 309–10.

47. *Cyprus—Colonial Report* (London 1937), p. 34.

48. *Report of the Department of Education for the school-year 1935–6*, p. 6.

49. *Ibid.*, p. 14.

50. *Reports of the Department of Education for the school-years 1942–5* (p. 18), *1947–8* (pp. 15–16), *1953–4* (p. 16), *1955–6* (p. 8).

51. Storrs, p. 549; *Report of the Department of Education, 1935–6*, p. 13.

52. *The Cyprus Gazette*, 29 Aug. 1952, pp. 331–2.

53. *Report of the Department of Education for the school-year 1955–6*, pp. 9–10.

54. Circular letter of the Director of Education to the Governing Bodies and Headmasters of all secondary schools, 24 Nov. 1954.

55. *The Times*, 4 June 1953, p. 4.

56. *Report of the Department of Education for the school-year 1955–6*, p. 3.

57. Philippou, vol I, p. 288.

58. *Minutes* of the Legislative Council of Cyprus, 1903, C.O. 69/17, p. 270; 1914, C.O. 69/30, p. 219.

59. An excellent example was the bishop of Kyrenia Chrysanthos, C 3384, p. 14.

60. Philippou, vol I, pp. 136, 140, 81, 209, 213, 286–7; Codex A of the Archbishopric, p. 190; C 2930, p. 32.

61. The H. Cr. Sir H. Smith recommended the disqualification of Bishops to be elected in the Legislative Council because of their intriguing character and 'in the spiritual interests of the Church'. The Secretary of State for the Colonies, however, had different views on the matter. He believed that 'Episcopal and other agitators . . . are much safer in the Council than out' because 'they can be answered and shown up in the

Council—a course which can hardly be taken with regard to outsiders'. (Conf. Despatch, 27 Feb. 1899, C.O. 67/117.)

62. *Minutes* of the Legislative Council, 22 May 1914, C.O. 69/30, p. 220.

63. Memorandum of the Locum Tenens to the Governor, 18 Nov. 1935; Myrianthopoulos, C. I., *Education in Cyprus during the British Administration, 1787–1946* (Limassol 1946), p. 118.

64. *Minutes* of the Legislative Council of Cyprus, 19 March 1895, C.O. 69/9; 22 May 1914, C.O. 69/30, p. 220.

65. Views expressed by the Bishop of Kition in the Legislative Council, 1902, C.O. 69/16, p. 260.

66. C.O. 69/17, 1903, p. 273.

67. C.O. 69/16, 1902, pp. 258–61; C.O. 69/19, 1905, p. 205.

68. C.O. 69/19, 1905, pp. 203–4.

69. Circular of the Holy Synod of Cyprus, *Eleftheria*, 18 Sept. 1948; Philippou, vol I, p. 275.

70. *Minutes* of the Legislative Council of Cyprus, 1909, C.O. 69/23, p. 202.

71. C.O. 69/17, 1903, p. 497.

72. *Minutes* of the Legislative Council of Cyprus for the years 1900–1909, C.O. 69/14; C.O. 69/23.

73. Conf. Despatch, 29 May 1885, C.O. 67/38.

74. Conf. Despatch, 18 May 1889, C.O. 67/60; 12 Aug. 1889, C.O. 67/62; 9 April 1894, C.O. 67/85.

75. *Eleftheria*, 6 Feb. 1917; 10 Jan. 1914; 1 April 1916; 15 Aug. 1917; Spyridakis, C., *The Greek Secondary Education of Cyprus (a historical survey and a report on the present conditions in the island)* (Nicosia, published by the Cyprus Ethnarchy Office, 1959), pp. 23–6.

76. Despatch of the Earl of Kimberley to High Commissioner Sir R. Biddulph, 10 June 1881, C 2930, p. 136; 18 May 1889, C.O. 67/60; 11 Feb. 1893, C.O. 67/79.

77. Speech of the Bishop of Kition in the Legislative Council, 10 April 1889, C.O. 69/12; 28 Oct. 1905, C.O. 67/143.

78. C 2930, p. 38.

79. *Ibid.*, p. 28.

80. *Ibid.*, pp. 81–2.

81. Myrianthopoulos, p. 34.

82. C 3661, p. 23.

83. C 2930, p. 137.

84. Conf. Despatch, 27 Dec. 1898, C.O. 67/114.

85. 15 Oct. 1900, C.O. 67/125; 27 April 1901, C.O. 67/127; 10 Feb. 1902, C.O. 67/130.

86. *Report of the Department of Education for the school-year 1934–5*, p. 8.

87. *Ibid.* for 1935–6, p. 5.

88. Talbot and Cape, p. 39.

89. Memoranda of the Locum Tenens Bishop Leontios to the Governor (Myrianthopoulos, pp. 116–25).

90. *Report of the Department of Education 1945–7*, p. 13.

91. *Eleftheria*, 30 May 1959.

92. The annual amount increased from £300 in 1899 to £7,124 in 1934 (31 May 1899, C.O. 67/118; 25 Jan. 1900, C.O. 67/122).

93. *Report of the Department of Education 1933–4*, pp. 10–11.

94. *Ibid., 1935–6*, pp. 14–15.

95. *Ibid., 1945–7*, p, 17.

96. Memorandum of the Locum Tenens Bishop Leontios (Myrianthopoulos, p. 122).

97. Circular of Archbishop Makarios III, *Eleftheria*, 5 Dec. 1951.

98. Myrianthopoulos, pp. 151, 163.

99. *Eleftheria*, 20, 21, 22 Feb. 1958.

100. *Reports of the Department of Education, 1949–50*, p. 15; *1951–2*, pp. 14–15.

101. Talbot and Cape, p. 38.

102. Such bishops were Archbishop Sophronios (9 April 1894, C.O. 67/85), Archbishop Cyril III (*Eleftheria*, 3 Feb. 1917) and Archbishop Makarios III (*Hellenic Cyprus*, Aug. 1955).

103. Kyprianos, the present bishop of Kyrenia is a characteristic example of this group (Minutes of the Educational Council of the Ethnarchy, 25th meeting, 4 Sept. 1953, p. 109).

104. See codices 47 and 48 (eighteenth century).

105. Philippou, vol I, p. 321.

106. C 2930, p. 32.

107. Philippou, vol I, p. 346.

108. C 2930, p. 33.

109. Philippou, vol I, pp. 214–15.

110. C 2930, pp. 31, 32.

111. C 2930, p. 31; C 3772, pp. 71–2.

112. C 2930, p. 39.

113. Philippou, vol I, pp. 189, 242, 274.

114. *Ibid.*, pp. 95–8.

115. *Cyprus—Colonial Report, 1932*, p. 33.

116. Spyridakis, pp. 23–6.

117. R. Hon. D. Lloyd-George, *The Truth about the Peace Treaties* (London 1938), vol II, p. 1217.

118. Philippou, vol I, pp. 164–72; Codex of correspondence of the Archbishops, p. 72; Big Codex of the Archbishopric, p. 250.

119. Newham, pp. 432–3.

120. *Minutes* of the Legislative Council of Cyprus, 1914, C.O. 69/30, pp. 207, 212–13.

121. C 2930, p. 136.

122. Newham, p. 411.

123. C 2930, pp. 83, 138.

124. *The Education Law, 1895*; Newham, pp. 434–7.

125. Talbot and Cape, p. 6; C.O. 69/27, 1911, p. 461; C.O. 69/30, 1914, p. 229.

126. Members of the Committees were accused of exacting money from teachers before they employed them (C.O. 69/37, 1923, pp. 150–2). The teachers were usually 'dependent upon the politicians for advancement' and they 'had to serve the political purposes' of their masters. There were also accusations of 'unsavoury inducements' by members of the school committees on 'reluctant schoolmistresses' (Storrs, p. 587).

127. 'The Education Law, 1923', in *The Cyprus Gazette*, 28 Aug. 1923, pp. 424–38.

128. 'The Education Law, 1929', *loc. cit.* 18 Dec. 1929, pp. 895–906.

129. 'The Education Law, 1933', *loc. cit.* 29 May 1933, pp. 309–24.

130. 'Great Idea' was the aspiration of modern Greeks to re-establish the Byzantine Empire.

131. Balfour, J. P., *The Orphaned Realm* (London 1951), p. 203.

132. Newham, p. 409.

133. *Ibid.*, p. 410.

134. The memorandum was dated 16 Feb. 1879 (Zannetos, P., *History of the Island of Cyprus*, Larnax 1911, vol II, p. 136).

135. Despatch of Sir G. Wolseley to the Marquis of Salisbury, C 2324, 1878–9, p. 5; C.O. 67/38, 29 May 1885; C.O. 67/41, 25 Jan. 1886; C.O. 69/1, 18 March 1886; C.O. 67/61, 1 July 1889; C.O. 67/113, 3 Oct. 1898; C.O. 67/117, 24 Jan. 1899.

136. C.O. 67/5, 16 July 1879.

137. *Minutes* of the Legislative Council of Cyprus, 1905, C.O. 69/19, pp. 43, 159, 169, 179, 234, 246, 338.

138. C.O. 67/123, 9 June 1900.

139. C 3384, p. 51; C 3661, p. 23; C.O. 69/30, 22 May 1914, p. 220; *Hellenic Cyprus*, Sept. 1952, No. 41, p. 141.

140. Talbot and Cape, p. 15.

141. Orr, C. W. J., *Cyprus under British rule* (London 1918), p. 132.

142. Myrianthopoulos, p. 42.

143. *Eleftheria*, 16 March 1923.

144. All the figures are taken by the annual Reports of the Department of Education, published by the Director of Education and printed at the Government's Printing Office, Nicosia.

145. All the figures are taken from the ledgers of the Pancyprian Gymnasium.

146. *Colonial Report for Cyprus, 1925*, No. 1313, p. 44.

147. *Minutes* of the Educational Council of the Ethnarchy, 12th meeting, 1 May 1952, p. 40.

Documents and Publications Consulted

Official Documents
Colonial Office Papers.
Annual Blue Books for Cyprus.
Annual Colonial Reports for Cyprus.
Annual Reports of the Department of Commerce and Industry.
Annual Reports of the Department of Education.
Census of population and Agriculture, 1946, published on behalf of the Government of Cyprus by the Crown Agents for the Colonies, London, 1946.
Parliamentary Debates—House of Commons.
Parliamentary Papers (1878–1905).
Ten-Year Programme of Development for Cyprus, Nicosia, 1946.
The Cyprus Gazette.

Church Documents
Big Codex of the Archbishopric.
Codex A of the Archbishopric.
Codex of Correspondence of the Archbishops.
Codex of Correspondence and other Documents of the Nicosia Schools.
Codex of the Kition Metropolis.
Minutes of the Educational Council of the Ethnarchy.
Statute of the Pancyprian Theological Seminary.

Other Documents
Records of the Pancyprian Gymnasium.

Newspapers
Aletheia (Nicosia).
Cyprus Mail (Nicosia).
Eleftheria (Nicosia).
Ephimeris (Kyrenia).
Paphos (Paphos).
Phileleftheros (Nicosia).
Phone tes Kyprou (Nicosia).
Salpinx (Limassol).
The Guardian
The Times.

Periodicals
Anamnestikon Lefkoma Pancypriou Gymnasiou, booklet published by the Pancyprian Gymnasium to mark the fiftieth anniversary from its establishment, Nicosia, 1943.
Annual Report of the Pancyprian Gymnasium.
Apostolos Barnabas (Nicosia).
Cultur (Nicosia).
Cyprus Review (Nicosia).
Cyprus Studies (Nicosia).
Hellenic Cyprus, edited by the Cyprus Ethnarchy.
Kypriaka Chronica (Larnaca).
Theologia (Athens).

8

SOME MISSION SCHOOLS IN EASTERN NIGERIA PRIOR TO INDEPENDENCE

Paul Inyang

NIGERIA claimed the attention of several British missionary societies. They came to propagate the Christian faith but as was the case elsewhere each of them made a significant contribution to the development of educational and medical services. Competition between them was at times sharp. Again the difficulties they had to overcome differed according to the region into which they attempted to move. Sickness, religious hostility and difficult terrain often stood in their path. Yet within a period of little more than a hundred years they achieved much. Some indication of these achievements is conveyed in this brief account of the way in which each of the missions penetrated further and further into the country to found schools, hospitals and churches.

This account will deal only with some aspects of the work of the Anglican, Methodist and Roman Catnolic missionaries. It is, moreover, confined to their activities in that region of Nigeria bounded to the west by the River Niger, to the north by the River Benue and to the east by the River Cross—until recently known as Eastern Nigeria. Some reference is made to the efforts of the missionaries to penetrate into the northern territories beyond the Niger and Benue rivers.

Evidently the pattern of development depended to a very considerable extent on communications. In the first instance places accessible to the coast could be reached with ease. Movement inland was possible along the rivers—the Niger and, to the east, the Cross. Later when railways were built missionary centres grew up around the towns thus linked. The first line ran from Lagos to

Ibadan and was started in 1896 and finished in 1900. The western line from Lagos to Kano via Kaduna and Zaria was completed in 1914 and the eastern line from Port Harcourt and via Enugu to Kaduna was built between 1913 and 1926. The limited possibilities of opening up the country help to explain the arrival of several mission societies in the same centres and the establishment there of competing schools and services.

Traders, missionaries and Government officials were all active in these centres. Macgregor Laird first organized the navigation of the Niger from its mouth to a point above its confluence with the Benue in 1832. For many years the United Africa Company operated in the region near the Niger from Lokoja at the confluence to the sea. Towards the end of the century officials took over from the traders the responsibility for political control. In 1885 a British Protectorate was established over the coast lands known as the Oil Rivers. The following year, 1886, the United Africa Company received a royal charter and became the Royal Niger Company. As such it negotiated treaties with several of the northern rulers. A transfer of political rights from the company to the Crown in 1900 was followed by a trial of strength between the Muslim powers and the British administration. Kano fell to the British in 1903 and in that year a large measure of control passed into their hands over the whole of the Northern Territories.

The gradual extension by each of the mission societies of their educational activity should be viewed against this background. The establishment of mission schools and medical services in the Eastern Region of Nigeria by selected societies will be surveyed prior to an assessment of the influence on Nigerian life of the education these agents of Europe provided.

The CMS began its work in West Africa and in 1841 an expedition to evangelize new territories was launched in Nigeria. It ended in disaster and was abandoned. The second expedition to open a mission on the Niger in 1854 was more successful and was followed by others. Earlier the Methodist Missionary Society had reached the country. On 24 September 1842 Thomas Birch Freeman, the son of an African slave, born of an English woman, landed at Badagry, then a hot-bed of the slave trade on the West Coast of Africa. To this pioneer, more than to any other, Methodist work in West African owes its existence. His work was chiefly in this region, Methodism in Eastern and Northern Nigeria had a different origin.

The Primitive Methodists began work in Fernando Po in 1870.[1] This island was the springboard from which the missionary society advanced to the mainland of Nigeria where work was effectively initiated in 1893.

As for the Roman Catholics, although the early Portuguese priests in Benin must have done some work in Calabar and when the Primitive Methodists arrived Roman Catholicism was the State religion of Fernando Po, the advent of Catholicism in Eastern Nigeria and ultimately in Northern Nigeria is of recent origin. In the late nineteenth century there were two prefectures in these regions, both named after the Niger. The first stations were established in the 1880s.

The scene was set for competition between the various mission societies for the allegiance of the people of Nigeria. Their first aim was evangelism, even though in practice it succeeded best through education and the giving of medical aid. The extent to which each of the missions succeeded depended on the region in which they were working. The complexity of the situation when independence was achieved is revealed by a more detailed account of the educational work of the various mission societies in one of the major regions of the country.

THE SPREAD OF METHODIST STATIONS IN
EASTERN NIGERIA

Fernando Po was the base from which the Primitive Methodists worked. In 1869 the Captain of the barque *Elgiva* landed there during August. He discovered a number of people previously won over by the Baptist Church whose ministers had been expelled by the Spanish authorities of the island. The converts had been left for eleven years without a minister, but they still kept their faith. Hands, the ship's carpenter, collected a few of the Protestants together to listen to his preaching and soon the number rose to some 150 or 200. On reaching England Captain Robinson wrote to urge his Church, the Primitive Methodist, to send missionaries to Fernando Po. The sequel of this was that the Reverends R. Burnett and Henry Roe, pioneers of the Primitive Methodist mission to West Africa, arrived on 21 February 1870 to 'evangelize as they educate'.

The mission faced tremendous odds. For many years the Spanish

Government in Fernando Po refused to grant the society permission to open schools. Not until 1923 was it made possible by a Royal Order from the Spanish Government. There were other obstacles. Lack of buildings, funds and teachers were formidable handicaps and a suitable school was built only in 1927, when a certificated teacher was posted from Europe to take charge of it.

The revolution in Spain during the thirties had social and educational effects on the island. The 1939 Annual Report of the Methodist Missionary Society (MMS) reported that work had suffered very severely from the Spanish wars. It became difficult for the Methodists to continue an independent mission in Fernando Po, hence 'under the circumstances it has been deemed wise to unite the Fernando Po mission with the larger and stronger Eastern Nigeria District'.[2] The work of half a century was virtually destroyed. By 1940 only four of the many Sunday schools (with thirty-four scholars) which had belonged to the Methodists remained. Government policy, a by-product of the Spanish war, seems to have been to create a situation which would make it impossible for the Protestant mission to continue on the island, cunningly causing the mission to remove itself from Fernando Po. However, the matter was reported to Lord Halifax, who brought pressure to bear on the Spanish Government, and the situation improved.

In 1946 the Methodists on the island had four churches and forty-five other preaching places manned to one ordained British minister and eight catechists. The day school, which had previously been closed now had four teachers, and the Sunday schools, previously four in number with thirty-four scholars, now had 259 scholars taught by twenty-nine teachers. The only day school had 111 scholars. By 1950 things looked brighter for the Methodist mission in Fernando Po: the number of churches had increased to six, as had that of the day school teachers and the number of day scholars was 127.

There appears to have been a swing of members away from the Protestant Church and its schools to the Catholics in recent years. In 1956 the Methodists stated that 'in a situation of disruption, diversity and confusion, African people feel the stronger appeal of Rome's definite Claims and colourful pageantry'.[3] Unfortunately, records of the work of the Catholic Church on this island are not available in London.

On the mainland the Primitive Methodist Society (PMS) success-fully established centres on the western bank of the Cross estuary. Further west they had been less successful. Burnett, for example, had accepted an invitation to open a mission from King Jaja of Opobo,[4] a flat, hot, humid and in places swampy district of the Oil Rivers on the coast of Eastern Nigeria lying between Bonny and

SOME MISSION CENTRES IN EASTERN NIGERIA

Old Calabar. The king was, however, at loggerheads with the British authorities and the society was unable to start work until after the death of King Jaja.[5] The Reverend W. Holland, Burnett's successor, visited Opobo in 1893 and reported favourably on the possibility of opening a mission there. But the credit for doing so fell on the Wesleyans rather than on the Primitive Methodists.

The names of two Primitive Methodist missionaries are associ-ated with the establishment of mission centres. The Reverend R. Fairley served in Fernando Po for twenty-two years. One of his outstanding achievements was his journey into the Oil Rivers Protectorate when he obtained a promise from Chief Archibong to settle and set up a mission. Later in 1893 the Reverend F.

283

Pickering, who had begun his term of service in Fernando Po a year previously, visited Oron on the mouth of the River Cross opposite Calabar. King Artokoro was away on a trading tour but when he heard that Pickering had arrived hastened back to Oron to pay his respects. Pickering also paid a visit to Archibongville, previously visited by Fairley. At that time the chief had already employed a teacher for his children and would not have a missionary, but on the occasion of Pickering's visit he changed his mind and invited the missionary to stay with him and start a mission. The chief promised to give the missionary every possible help which was no mean pledge. According to Pickering:

> Archibong is a man of great power and for an African, of great wealth. . . . The town is under English protection, and Sir C. McDonald, Her Majesty's Commissioner, promised Rev. R. Fairley to assist us materially if we went there . . .[6]

Support from the British representative was important and so Archibongville was chosen as the first centre for the spread of Methodism in Eastern Nigeria. By the end of 1893 Fairley had in fact succeeded in drawing up an agreement with Prince Archibong III concerning the establishment of a mission in the town. The agreement was signed and registered in the British Consulate in Old Calabar in the presence of Sir Claude MacDonald, Her Majesty's Commissioner. It is reproduced verbatim in the PMMS *Records* of proceedings. Under it Fairley secured a 'large and eligible site of land' in Archibongville and the prince commanded his people to prepare for the building planned by the missionary. Finally it was completed and the mission opened under the management of a Mr. Brown who was helped by a very reliable native catechist worker, Mr. Efa-Ekpe Esuk, and Mr. and Mrs. Knox from Sierra Leone.

In Oron work was started on a station on 22 July 1893, and later that year Pickering noted, 'before I left the place the framework of a house with a frontage of 38 feet containing three rooms of 12 feet each were erected and the bamboo rods on the roof. They could not have shown greater willingness than they did.'[7] The PMMS was really faced with a choice, however, between Archibongville and Oron as the centre of operations. By the end of 1893 Fairley hoped to transfer this centre from Oron, then in German hands, to Archibongville, hence his negotiations with the prince.[8] In 1901, however, Oron and Archibongville were exchanged, the latter came under German control while the former went to the British. The Methodist headquarters was transferred to Oron where they still remain. This exchange was perhaps fortunate because Oron was in a healthier region and the villages around it could be reached by a network of creeks and rivulets.

From Archibongville and Oron visits were paid to the surrounding villages and towns to negotiate the founding of new stations and schools with the chiefs. In this way Chief Ekanem Esin's town was opened. Of him Fairley wrote:

> Fortunately we found the chief at home and were hardly prepared for the degree of intelligence and comfort we witnessed. He received us most kindly and soon had a very enjoyable meal prepared. [9]

Jamestown, some thirteen miles nearer the mouth of the river was the first station set up by the society but by 1901 Aqua Effy, Idua Oron, Ikot Ntika, Uda, Oroko, Esuk Oron, Afaha Eduok, Eye Abassey and Urua Aye had been opened or visited. By then Jamestown, under the management of the Reverend Boocock reported thirty members, and the Reverend G. H. Hanney who had done so much for Oron reported two members at Urua Aye and sixty at Idua Oron.

Between 1901 and 1908 the PMMS advanced north into Okobo country where at Ekeya they made their first contact with the Church of Rome. Against determined opposition from a well-established group of Catholics they succeeded in opening a school. A further advance brought them to the borders of Ibibio land where they established some stations notably at Adadia which was proposed as a centre and a base for a further advance into Nsit territory. Ebukhu, a few miles up river from Jamestown, and Oyubia some fifteen miles inland from Jamestown formed other centres. Each of them was surrounded by a network of stations where there was a school of some kind. By 1908, in fact, a large area had been covered and was divided into 'circuits' each containing some thirty or forty stations of school-churches.

After 1909 the advance was swift, and by 1920 nine new centres had been opened. In 1924 there was another northward advance into the Igumale and Idoma countries. And Port Harcourt in the delta area, a valuable seaport, was occupied. With the occupation of Oturkpo, the northern outpost of the PMMS, on the railway, the march of Methodism into Eastern and Northern Nigeria seems to have slowed down greatly. But by this time the educational framework of the Methodist mission both in Eastern and Northern Nigeria, had been properly set up.

Before closing this account of the spread of Methodism and mission stations in Eastern Nigeria a few words should be said about the transfer of certain areas from the Wesleyans in 1927 to the PMMS. The areas affected were Calabar, Opobo and the Ogoni district. This transfer was a mark of goodwill on the part of the Wesleyans, those die-hards of Methodism who believed in perpetuating clerical rule as opposed to the radical belief in rule by the laity which was held by the Primitive Methodists. All along the Wesleyans had been opposed to the idea of reunion until the 1920s, when it became evident that all factions of Methodism must unite if it were to exist as a creditable organization. Five years after the transfer the Primitive Methodist Churches of Eastern Nigeria were renamed 'The Methodist Churches'. But the scars inflicted by Methodism on itself and on the people of Nigeria as a result of this split in their ranks can still be seen, for example, in Calabar and the neighbouring towns.

Methodist mission schools

The work of the Methodist mission centred on Oron was evangelical and educational and was directed towards the Efik people— a tribe originating from the larger Ibibio group whose early trading contacts with Europeans and the Church of Scotland Mission Society, particularly in Old Calabar on the eastern bank of the Cross delta, helped make theirs the literary language of the area and persuaded them to accept many European customs.

The first notable contribution made by the Methodist Mission was the Oron Boys' High School, originally known as the Native Training Institute, Oron.[10] The first buildings were erected by the Reverend R. Banham and the Reverend J. W. Ward became its first principal. The Institute was formally opened for serious work on 18 September 1905. Ward's paramount purpose was the encouragement of religious life. The ethos of the school was that of an English public school, character training through religion receiving high priority. It was a boarding school too, all but three of its original sixteen students were boarders. Exercises such as the reading of set portions of the Bible as part of evening worship, scripture teaching for everybody gathered together in the day room, singing and the saying of prayers were intended to contribute to the achievement of the religious purpose. In the main an English curriculum was followed, the syllabuses were largely those of the local authority schools in England, the textbooks were the same and the teachers English. Education was mainly literary although 'industrial education' was not, in the first instance neglected. Mr. and Mrs. Knox in Archibongville were in charge of the industrial part of the school there and though there is no evidence of great success it is known that handicrafts were developed. At Oron agriculture rather than industrial education received attention but in neither place is there evidence that this aspect of education received high priority.

The Institute trained personnel for Methodist work. The more capable boys became teachers or native agents. As part of the programme of work students helped to evangelize the neighbourhood. From these humble beginnings there developed the Oron Methodist Boys' High School—one of the foremost secondary schools in Nigeria. One indication of its success in its chosen field of endeavour was provided in 1956 when General Certificate of Education candidates were 100 per cent successful. Also in Oron was established the Mary Hanney Memorial Girls' School, built in memory of the wife of one of the pioneers of Methodist missionary work. In 1943, its Jubilee year, the school had 105 boarders and 62 day scholars. By 1960 it had added a department for the training of women teachers.

Among the Ibo people, the largest tribe in Eastern Nigeria, Uzuakoli became an important centre of Methodist educational activity. It was linked by rail to Port Harcourt in 1915. A mission centre was not opened there until 1920 but from the start it held out great promise. In 1923[11] when the teachers' training institute was opened it became evident that it was to play for the Ibo Methodists the same role as Oron had for the Efik Methodists. It became the educational centre for the whole district. It had a primary school and by 1933 had sent over fifty trained teachers for the college and a high school department was added to it. The Second World War, however, left its mark, buildings were left unused, and in the college classes 5 and 6 were closed down. There was an acute shortage of European staff and there were too few local people who had been trained to occupy positions of responsibility. A further reason for the decline in educational work was the priority given to the Church rather than the school. In 1943 there were still 104 boarders in the Ovim Women's Training College which provided for Ibo women the kind of opportunities provided for the Efiks by the Mary Hanney Girls' School.

In Northern Nigeria[12] the achievements of the Methodist mission were much less evident than those in Eastern Nigeria but it had some evangelistic success. In 1953 the number of assisted schools of the MMS in Northern Nigeria was given as three[13] and there were forty-nine unassisted schools. In 1954 the northern region became separate, previously the North and East had been jointly administered. Since then a considerable expansion— religious and educational—has occurred. The obstacles are formidable, even when a predominantly educational approach is used. Apart from Muslim opposition the region is sparsely populated and the way of life is far too agricultural for them to be permanently influenced by spasmodic education. The cost of providing education as a way of spreading the Gospel is very high. In addition the Idoma and Igumale tribes speak many different dialects which increase the difficulties of the mission schools.

Methodist medical work

In 1921, some twenty-eight years after the landing of Fairley and Pickering in Eastern Nigeria the first trained medical contingent of the society arrived. Miss Shepherd, locally known as 'Mam' Shepherd, Miss Roberts and Miss Godfrey were the three nursing sisters assigned to this pioneering work. Miss Shepherd and Miss Roberts were given the task of starting a hospital not far from Oron at Ifa Ikot Okpon. Other hospitals were also opened but at times there was no doctor to supervise the work of the nurses. Dr. Scott, the first of them, arrived in 1930.[14] He had the difficult task of supervising three hospitals which were separated by long distances. His arrival marked the transfer of the hospital from Ifa Ikot Okpon to Ituk Mbang where the centre of Methodist medical work was established. Until recently control of the Methodist hospitals was exercised from Ituk Mbang where the hospital is one of the most up-to-date in the country.

A certain amount of specialization was intended. The hospital at Ikot Ekpene, inland from the Cross River, was used as a maternity hospital when it was taken over by the Government in 1949. Another was to specialize in child welfare, but the immediate needs of the local population and the shortage of doctors tended to make the hospitals general purpose institutions. One educative result was the influence on attitudes towards hygiene.

Evidently the Christian mission regarded its hospitals as a means of propagating the Christian faith. It was hoped that hospital service and nursing would provide the young African men and women with an opportunity of 'giving expression to their love of Christ'.[15] As for patients it was thought that Christian hospitals gave 'practical evidence of a love greater than that normally shown between individuals. Patients . . . return to their churches with a clearer conception of what Christianity means and with false impressions corrected'.[16] The real object of the women's training centre at Ituk Mbang was to 'teach African women to be makers of Christian homes'.[17]

The success of this aspect of medical work is not easy to assess. There was always the possibility of misunderstanding and misrepresentation arising from cultural contacts. Gossip and prejudice and failure to live up to expected standards of behaviour contributed to this situation. Moreover people were convinced that the missionaries were working hand in glove with the Government, especially an imperial one. Even so, given a choice between a Government and a Christian hospital many patients would undoubtedly have chosen the latter.

Of special medical and educational interest is the Uzuakoli leper centre located near the centre of the Methodist mission educational activity among the Ibos. In August 1932, the year the Methodists reunited, Dr. Brown of the MMS opened the colony. The local government[18] financed it while the mission was responsible for its staffing and for the religious and social work. A group of Boy Scouts from the Methodist college three miles away cleared what was in part the 'bad bush' to build the first temporary houses for the patients. In a fortnight about 200 patients arrived and soon took over the work from the Boy Scouts. The development of this settlement was so rapid that by the time Brown left in 1936 the excellence of its medical work was widely known and a great tradition had been established. He left 800 patients there.[19]

By 1937 the settlement could not accommodate the large numbers that flocked to it. The work of expansion had thus begun.

The British Empire Leprosy Relief Association sent their first worker to assist the doctor provided by the MMS to open a clinic in 1938. By 1945 many more clinics had been opened and it became possible for treatment to be given at sixty clinics. In all, 26,000 patients had come under supervision from the Uzuakoli settlement. BELRA sent out more lay workers,[20] and the Nigerian Government took over the responsibilities at the settlement formerly borne by the local government. Immediate increased financial support was possible. Medical work, and those engaged in it, now were the concern of the Nigerian rather than the local government. Workers were nominated jointly by the society and the Government. By 1945 the Colonial Welfare Development committee had initiated schemes for leprosy control. Another settlement was established in 1948. A teaching centre was also a joint effort. In time the Uzuakoli Leprosy Research Department discovered 'sulphonedrugs' and as a result of their use the disease is no longer regarded as incurable.

But in addition to this medical work evangelism and education found a place in the colony. Sunday schools, Bible readings and catechism classes were provided. In 1937[21] it was made possible to offer education to leper children in the settlement, and now they sit for the University of Cambridge Senior School Certificate. There is some form of adult education too. In 1960 there were over 1,000 lepers in a settlement where social life was well organized and the patients apparently happy. The most impressive feature of it seems to be the rapidity with which lepers were won over to Christianity. All the patients there now, with the exception of 120 Catholics, are Methodists. In short, the running of the institution is rooted in religion.

Some brief assessment of the difficulties the MMS faced in Eastern and Northern Nigeria suggests that geography, climate, paganism, polygamy and language created serious problems. One minister described how he spent several days planning and preparing to visit some of his stations which had not been visited for a long time. He and his companions had had to cross many streams and rivulets to reach the first series of stations. On two separate occasions, after careful planning of the route, they started out, travelled for three days, mostly in rain, crossing several streams swollen to torrents, and finally were confronted with an impassable river, and were forced to turn back home. On the second occasion, they had to turn back as 'the bridge was under water up to a man's neck'.[22] Another great problem was malaria. The missionary death roll was high. Primitive living conditions did not alleviate their tasks.[23]

Paganism, polygamy and the language also created problems. In 1930 reports from Opobo spoke of the revival of heathen influences. Ikot Ukpong was particularly affected. It is said that the church was burnt down and the mission compound sacked. A report from the Adadia circuit noted that:

> Sometimes the hydra of paganism lifts up a new head in the form of a misguided band of people calling themselves Christians and propagating a strange mixture of paganism and bastard Christianity.[24]

In fact, it would be quite reasonable to suggest that paganism might be gaining ground once again in some parts of Nigeria.

BISHOP CROWTHER AND THE CMS

The CMS, of course, was also interested in Nigeria. It began its work in West Africa during the early part of the nineteenth century. Out of this grew the Yoruba mission. There was also the Sierra Leone mission. Prior to 1841, however, although there were three bishops in West Africa none of the thousands of Negro Christians had been confirmed and only three Negro clergymen had been educated in England and ordained there. It is with one of these clergymen, Samuel Ajayi Crowther, that this account of CMS activity along the Niger is principally concerned.

In 1832 a British merchant, MacGregor Laird, had organized a navigation of the River Niger from its mouth to a point above the confluence of the river with the Benue. It was not until 1841 that 'The Niger Expedition was brought about to open up new territories to evangelization'.[25] This first CMS expedition ended in disaster. Crowther was one of the company and witnessed the great loss of life on the trip through illness. By the time a second expedition was made in 1854 he was the Reverend Samuel Crowther and there is no doubt that this journey's success owed a great deal to him.[26] The expedition consisted of a single steamer, the *Pleiad,* fitted out at the expense of Laird, commanded by Dr. W. B. Baikie. This time the trip was a success. The *Pleiad* was up river for 188 days without a single death reported; nor was there any report of serious sickness. It went 400 miles up the Benue, then fuel ran out and it had to return; but a vital channel for further mission work had been opened up. Indeed Crowther wrote to urge the CMS to open a mission on the Niger on the grounds that the people and the chiefs were quite ready to receive one. This suggestion led to the third expedition, based on an agreement between the Government and Laird reached in 1856.

The next year, on 18 July 1857, the *Dayspring* was steaming up the river. Baikie was again in charge. Crowther was 'commissioned by the Society to start the Niger Mission'.[27] His plans for the new mission were very bold. He hoped to post teachers at strategic points along the river and in territory under the Muslim Sultan. He chose Onitsha, 140 miles from the sea, as the best centre for the Ibo mission. Further up the river he was accorded a cordial reception at Idah and at Gbebe, a town at the confluence. Both towns granted sites for mission houses. The *Dayspring* proceeded to Egan and Rabbah. This was the first visit by a Christian missionary to Rabbah but the Muslim chiefs gave Crowther a hearty welcome: 'they have also given us full permission to teach the heathen under their government the religion of the Anasara (i.e. Nazarene)'.[28] Significantly they were not allowed to teach Muslims.

On 6 October, the day after Baikie and Crowther hopefully left Rabbah to steam up the river, the *Dayspring,* endeavouring to force a passage between the islands against a strong current, drifted on to the rocks and was wrecked.[29] The native canoes which were around came to the rescue of the crew and passengers and no one was lost. Here they had to wait twelve months for the arrival of another steamer. During this time Crowther had plenty of opportunity to study the situation in Rabbah and considered it an ideal centre for missionary work—a meeting point of trading caravans from North Africa and the Sudan. The *Sunbeam* arrived in October 1858 and took everyone back, but on reaching Onitsha Crowther remained behind and from time to time went up the river to perform his missionary duties.

In the summer of 1859 Laird again got in touch with Crowther who travelled to the confluence; there he received a message from Baikie then acting as the British Agent, saying that Rabbah was closed to missionary work. No reasons were given but it is likely that the suspicions of the Muslim chiefs had been aroused. This hostility continued but in other areas Crowther's influence spread. A school was built at Lokoja at the confluence and in time it became the headquarters of what came to be known as the Sudan and Upper Niger mission. A report in 1879 suggested, however, that nothing was being done at this centre at that time. Later in 1889 the Reverends J. A. Robinson (an Englishman appointed secretary of the Niger mission in 1887) and G. W. Brooke (who arrived in the Niger region in 1889) gained the approval of the CMS committee in London to attempt to penetrate further into the Muslim north. The proposal involved considerable reorganization. Work beyond Lokoja was to become part of the new mission. The Lower Niger and the delta area was to be a separate mission. Differences of opinion between the African and English members of the missions created difficulties. The suspension of ordained African agents led to the establishment by the CMS of a special Niger sub-committee to investigate the situation. Its recommendations placed Europeans in positions of authority in both the Sudan and Upper Niger mission and the Lower Niger and Delta mission and reduced the power of Bishop Crowther and his son Archdeacon Dandeson Crowther. These proposals brought to a head the rift between African and European workers and led to the temporary assertion of independence under Archdeacon Crowther of the Niger Delta mission. Shortly after the publication of the report in 1891 Bishop Crowther died.

Eventually a new bishop, Tugwell, was appointed to the Niger mission with an African as an assistant bishop, an act by which it was hoped to restore the confidence which the native agents and the people had lost. With the concurrence of the new bishop the CMS secretaries wrote and asked if Archdeacon Crowther and his clergy would like, although independent financially, to appear once more in the society's list of missionaries. The proposal was warmly received and in 1897 their names appeared again in the CMS Annual Report. Early in 1898 Tugwell ordained David Okfarabietoa Pepple, the fifth of the first Ibo native pastors to receive holy orders.[30] The delta pastorate prospered and by the time it returned to the ranks of the CMS a large congregation and many schools had been brought into the fold. In 1912 a theological college was opened at Brass as a memorial to Crowther. Mr. Aitken, Mr. Reeks and Mr. Proctor began work in the Ijaw and Sobo countries at about the same time.

Throughout this period two issues were important; namely the respective roles of the Europeans and the Africans and the extent to which in the conduct of affairs the men on the spot should have authority. One object of the 1841 expedition had been to advise the parent committee on possible locations where Europeans could work.[31] The death rate among Europeans was so high that it was regarded as hopeless to expect them to live and work in that part of the country. Consequently one object of the CMS was to establish an indigenous church and a native agency. But debates about the role of Europeans went on. In spite of a certain reluctance on his part Crowther was consecrated Bishop[32] in 1864. The CMS was probably guided when making this appointment by the need for agents speaking the same language and having the same thought forms as those with whom they worked.[33] Crowther himself stressed the need to know the vernacular if true meaning was to be given to the Scriptures.[34] On the other hand, he maintained before his consecration that placing a native in a position of authority over Europeans was premature. Later he made repeated requests for Europeans to help him but for many years without success. Doubtless health hazards dissuaded many, but race consciousness played its part in spite of the fact that the committee in London wished to give more scope to African initiative and administrative ability.

From the start of the Niger mission in 1857 it was difficult to get personnel, and for the time it was conducted entirely by Africans. They came from Sierra Leone and Lagos and were either redeemed slaves or children of them. They were as far as the people of the Niger countries were concerned foreign missionaries. Difficulties arose. For example, the Reverend Taylor, for many years in charge of Onitsha, had a hot temper and a strong will.[35] He was joined by two African clergymen, Messrs. Cole and Thomas. All three returned to Sierra Leone, unable to cope with the difficulties and hardships of a young mission, and painted the picture of the Niger mission so grimly that thereafter no clergyman offered himself for work on the Niger. Consequently Crowther 'had to be content with very inferior men in those early days, men of no education beyond being able to read and write, indeed some could scarcely write'.[36] Of these one was suspended for repeated drunkenness, another was dismissed for bad conduct, while a third was retired for inefficiency. He had to rely on local men. But they were surrounded by temptations of every sort. Their stations were so isolated that they were in need of supervision. Yet between 1857 and 1877 they were visited only once a year by the Bishop and the time of the visit was always known in advance. The Bishop wrote:

> As trade on the river increased another difficulty arose by the coming in of ungodly Europeans and professing African Christians, whose horrid evil lives became a great stumbling block to the converts and inquirers, and a very serious hindrance to the agents.[37]

He mentioned the case of 'an intelligent, well-educated Englishman conforming to the idolatrous practices of the heathen at Bonny, it is said, at a cost of £300 worth of goods'.[38] He also recorded that the Muslim chiefs thought it a great honour to present a visitor or stranger with a female or two to live with him, giving as their reason that it is not good for a man to live alone. Many Christian travellers yielded to temptation and Dandeson Crowther claimed that the examples set by Europeans created the most serious difficulties faced by Christianity.

The CMS at Onitsha and Bonny

Crowther's original plans for the mission had been ambitious. He hoped to post teachers at various points along the Niger to the confluence and beyond. He intended to travel from Rabbah some 300 miles overland to Sokoto to whose Sultan all the less powerful Muslim chiefs owed allegiance. He chose Onitsha as the best centre for the Ibo mission and the Reverend J. C. Taylor, from Sierra Leone, was put in charge of it. He was accorded a cordial reception at Idah up the river and at Gbebe at the confluence. Both towns granted sites for mission houses. After the setback at Rabbah missionary work was continued in Gbebe and Onitsha but soon Crowther returned to the coast to lay plans for the permanent occupation of the Niger districts. No ordained minister visited the teachers in Onitsha and Gbebe for two years.

In 1862 Crowther assembled a missionary party of thirty-three persons including wives, children and their belongings. After some difficulties twenty-seven of the party were taken up the river on a gunboat, H.M.S. *Investigator*. He reached Onitsha, passed on to spend a few weeks in Gbebe where he preached, organized and taught the people and improved his vocabulary in the Nupe language and translated part of the New Testament into it. He hoped to develop trade in cotton between England and Nigeria. His 'Industrial Institution' was established to purchase, clean and pack cotton for the English market.

In the delta region stations were opened at Bonny and at Brass. William Pepple, one of the chiefs of Bonny who had visited London and had been baptized there, wrote when he returned home to the Bishop of London, Dr. Tait, asking for a Christian mission. Tait sent the letter to Crowther who in 1864 went to Bonny to arrange with the king for an annual payment of £150 as half the cost of the proposed station. A Negro schoolmaster from Sierra Leone started work by opening a small school and 'keeping service' on Sunday evenings. The station at Brass was opened in 1867 at the request of the Chief who agreed to bear half the cost of the school and a house for the native teacher at his port, Brass-town. This mission was subsequently extended to his chief town, Brass-Nembe, thirty miles up the river.

After his consecration Crowther returned to Nigeria and took up residence at Lagos. From there he paid annual visits to his mission, since there was no regular steamer service up the Niger. While at Lagos he took steps to see that his staff was enlarged. He ordained one of his catechists a deacon. He also recruited catechists and schoolmasters from Sierra Leone, posting them to different stations, ordaining those who seemed promising. By 1871 he had ordained eight of his classmen in addition to his son. The vast area over which he had influence provided a poor environment for the spiritual life of his isolated agents.

It should be noted that all along the church followed the school. From time to time new stations were occupied, each with a school-church. Osamara and Asaba were opened. Kipo Hill, 350 miles inland in the territory of the Emir of Nupe, was also opened. In about 1870 the personnel of the Niger mission was increased and the areas were organized into the Upper Niger with Onitsha as its centre, and the Lower Niger with Bonny as headquarters. While Deacon H. Johnson took charge of the Upper Niger, Dandeson Crowther, the Bishop's son, superintended the Lower Niger.

The work grew outwards from these two main centres. It was the High Commissioner, Leslie Probyn, who directed the attention of Tugwell to Owerri some sixty miles east of Onitsha as a fertile field for missionary work. At the turn of the century it was a town of about 2,000 inhabitants. In 1903 J. T. Dennis was sent to open a station. Owerri today has a very good school. Four miles from Owerri is the town of Ebu with 21,000 inhabitants. Here Dennis settled in 1906. Soon a crop of outstations sprang up and the demand for teachers increased. Awla, some forty miles east of Onitsha, was occupied by S. R. Smith in 1904 and has grown into a very big CMS centre. At first the class of student evangelists was transferred there 'and in due course blossomed into a training institution'.[39] There are many outstations and schools around it now. From Awla an advance was made in 1917 to Enugu on the railway line. An Awla boy induced the people of Enugu to ask for a teacher of their own. Today the town has a flourishing mission.

Educationally the CMS accomplished much. A men's training centre was founded, as stated, in Awla in 1904. By 1958 theological training and women's teacher training were carried on at Umuahia in co-operation with the Methodist and Presbyterian Churches. In its first year Trinity College enrolled five CMS, six Church of Scotland Mission and three MMS students all of whom were embarking on a three-year course of training as ministers. There are two elementary training centres for men, one at Diobu and another at Oluh, in this part of the world. St. Monica's for women is near Onitsha. Onitsha, Okrika and Nkwere each has a secondary school for boys while at Elelenwan there was one for girls. The Dennis Memorial Grammar School is one of the first-rate secondary schools in Nigeria.

By 1952 the total number of colleges and schools was 826, with 100,000 children in the primary schools alone. There were 89,000 in Sunday schools. In 1957 there were 250 church primary schools and a total of 969 institutions, colleges and schools. Over 127,000 men and boys and over 55,000 women and girls were in attendance. The demand for teacher training was tremendous and the need for agricultural training was being met by having a school-farm attached to each school.

The CMS in Northern Nigeria

Throughout the nineteenth century the work of the Upper Niger mission continued. Political events furthered this activity. Two years after the capture of Bida (north of the Niger's western branch) in 1897, C. H. Robinson backed by the Hausa Association (founded in memory of his late brother, first leader of the Mission), journeyed into that country to discover suitable centres for missionary work. Prior to 1897 the Bassa country—some distance to the east of Lokoja—was pioneered by the Reverend J. L. MacIntyre and E. F. Wilson-Hill. Lokoja itself was becoming increasingly important. The abolition of the slave trade in the town had led to the disappearance of most Muslims from what used to be one of their centres. Missionary work thus became less difficult.

In the year 1900 the CMS efforts to penetrate Northern Nigeria were redoubled. Tugwell made the first attempt. He was quickly repulsed. At first he was very well received in the important railway town of Zaria, nearly 450 miles from the Delta. Dr. Miller, a CMS missionary, had a knowledge of the Hausa language which did much to allay fears. But when Tugwell and Miller reached Kano, 'a great centre of trade and commerce said to be older than London',[40] the Muslim Emir expelled them immediately. They were subsequently expelled from Zaria and obliged to return to Lokoja on the Benue. The party finally dispersed.

The murder of an English officer in 1903 and the Emir of Kano's offer of protection to the murderer led to the capture of the city by the British. With the capture of 'the great southern port of the Sahara' and Sokoto in 1903 the military conquest of Nigeria was complete. Earlier, Miller with the consent of the Emir had met with some success in February 1902 in his attempt to open up a station at Girku in the Zaria province. Bida was occupied in 1903 with the permission of the Emir and the Bassa country entered. 'At Bida in Nupe a model farm had been begun and a school where . . . Hausa and Nupe were taught in the Roman character.'[41] Towards the end of 1904 the CMS had five other stations, one in Nupe and one in the Kabba provinces and three at Bassa, in addition to that of Girku. In 1905 Miller's Hausa mission was 'transferred forty miles north to Zaria itself on the invitation of the Emir'.[42] This was a step towards establishing a school to the pagans of Zaria. It opened in February 1906.

Of some significance in the work of the CMS in the North was the Cambridge University mission. The first members appeared in 1907 to carry out extension work on the Bauchi Plateau. This group wished

to plant a mission on some place which had never been reached by the Gospel of Christ. It was to be inter-denominational, and to seek for support from none beyond themselves. The mission-ary members of the party were to be maintained if necessary by the other members of the band who were unable to go abroad.[43]

The CMS history notes that the ideal was noble but not very practicable. The group consulted CMS officials, became affiliated with the society and a district in the Niger mission was assigned to the party. Its missionaries were to be supported by the society, to be on the roll and under the regulations of the CMS. Only in special matters had the CMS to seek the approval of the Cambridge University Mission Party (CUMP) committee.

It should be said that theirs was not an easy assignment. The work in the district allotted to this little band was too difficult. Work began among the pagans of the Bauchi highlands, at Panyam. Soon work began at a second station at Kabwir, and Per was the next important town occupied by the members of the CUMP, and work commenced among the Seyawa tribes who were entirely pagans. Considering the small number of its members the influence of the Cambridge party has been tremendous. But for the fact that the CMS drew the little party into its ranks in time it would have increased the number of churches, already too many, in Nigeria. This would have made no contribution to the unity of the country nor would it have made for easy government.[44]

By 1952 the educational work of the mission in Northern Nigeria was still on a somewhat small scale. In all there were 634 pupils and students, apart from 434 Sunday school pupils. This represented the work of nearly half a century. Evidently Northern Nigeria was unfertile ground for missionary work. The natural antipathy of the Muslims towards Christianity does not easily yield even to educational progress. Considering the progressive attitude of a vast majority of people in Nigeria this presents a curious paradox. In 1954 there was a sharp drop from fifteen stations to three and from ninety-six outstations to thirty-four. The 1956 figures were still less encouraging. The apparent decline in the work of the mission in the north was probably due to adverse political influences resulting from a rise of nationalism here, and the reorganization of the society's mission for administra-tive convenience. Nevertheless, the picture was not entirely gloomy. There were some bright spots. Teacher training, begun some years previously at Wusasa, had by 1949 developed into a teacher training centre. Centred at Samaru close to Zaria it became a higher elementary training centre in 1953, and then known as St. Peter's College, Zaria. There is also a secondary school, St. Paul's, at Wusasa, opened in 1953. Both these institutions serve the northern diocese as a whole.

CMS medical services

The medical work of the mission in Eastern Nigeria is centred at Iyi-Enu and also at Nnewi. Both places are centres for training midwives for the diocesan maternity homes. The Oji River Leper Settlement was opened by the mission in 1936 as a centre for the treatment and prevention of leprosy and is now primarily the responsibility of the Government of Nigeria. As in the Uzuakoli settlement under the Methodists, the CMS is responsible for the religious, educational and social work. Although the Oji leper settlement is considerably smaller than that at Uzuakoli, yet it is doing tremendous work among the leper communities of this area. What is more, the educational value of this institution cannot be overestimated. The mission also co-operates with the Government, and other missions in the Queen Elizabeth II Hospital at Umuahia.

In Northern Nigeria an out-patient department and clinic have been built in Zaria city. The hospital at Wusasa was being rebuilt in 1951 and organized as a training hospital for midwives and nurses.

ROMAN CATHOLIC MISSIONS

Although the early Portuguese priests to Benin must have done some work in Calabar, yet the advent of Catholicism to Eastern Nigeria and ultimately to Northern Nigeria is of recent origin. Ellen Thorp reports for example, that

> in 1699, Barbot records that one of the Calabar Chiefs who he met 'speaks Portuguese and seems to have been instructed by Romish priests, who are sent over from time to time from Sao Tome and Brazil'. But some time after that, Catholic missionary work there came to an end as it did in the Benin region.[45]

It is probable that the work of these early priests was more extensive than is generally supposed. It was left to the people of other nations rather than the Portuguese (notorious for their cruelties) to promote Catholicism in Nigeria as a whole and in Eastern Nigeria particularly.

The Catholic mission in Eastern and Northern Nigeria in the late nineteenth century had two prefectures. The Upper Niger prefecture included much of Northern Nigeria and had its headquarters at Lokoja. It was pioneered from 1884 by Father W. Fiorentini[46] and was entrusted by the Holy See to the Society for African Missions of Lyons. The other, the Lower Niger prefecture, was in the hands of another French Missionary Society, the Holy Ghost Fathers. This missionary society had its headquarters in Onitsha and remains there still. Its work extends over a large territory in Eastern and Northern Nigeria.

The first missionaries, with Father Lutz in charge, Father Horne and two brothers, Hermas and John, arrived in the Lower Niger prefecture in 1885.

> On 21 November 1885 we reached the mouth of the Niger in the midst of a terrible storm. Long brilliant flashes of lightning, peals of thunder peculiar to equatorial countries, the fury of the waves, the violence of the wind and rain were frightful enough to suggest the idea that hell was visibly let loose upon us.[47]

The party had left Brass on 26 November 1885 and arrived at Onitsha on 6 December for the sole purpose of founding a mission, 'to the chagrin,' it was said, 'of the Anglican already long established there'.[48] But with the co-operation of Bishop Crowther the Fathers were able to obtain land and simple headquarters for the Lower Niger prefecture.

The second station to be opened after Onitsha was Nkwelle in 1888. This shows how slowly the mission established itself. Obosi opposite the town of Onitsha was shelled and burnt by soldiers of the Niger Company for refusing to keep peace with its neighbours. Father Lutz rode in alone on horseback to attend the wounded, and so had little difficulty in founding a station afterwards. Meanwhile the King of Aguleri sent frequent messages to Lutz inviting him to open a school in his town. In consequence Father Bubendorf, who by now had joined the small band, paid his first visit to Aguleri in February 1890. Although Aguleri was frequently at war with its neighbours a church-school was built. It became prosperous and was soon made a centre for two resident priests. A school, mainly attended by slaves was also opened at Edea.[49]

More and more pagans in Onitsha were being attracted to the mission, and so were Protestants, and the chapel already built in 1889 was too small to hold the congregation.[50] By this time two orphanages had been built, one holding fifty boys and another accommodating twenty-eight girls. A quasi-technical type of education was being offered, or rather there was vocational training as carpenters and cobblers in special shops built for the purpose. The work at this time seemed to be a struggle. Nevertheless, people were getting more interested in it. The Chief of Aguleri was converted and his conversion quickened the growth of religion and education in his town. The Chief of Oguta, a town of about 30,000 people and situated some sixty miles south-east of Onitsha, asked the Father to begin work in his town, on a plot of land reserved for that purpose. He had already sent two of his children to be educated by the Father and further increased the number by three. At Ossamori, fifty Protestants gave up their faith and became Catholics, thus forming the nucleus of Catholic work in this town.[51]

Another centre of activity was Calabar. Father Lejeune, Prefect Apostolic of the Lower Niger prefecture, had opened a station there, where the Church of Scotland was working, in 1903. On 13 September 1903 he wrote from Calabar:

Today I am leaving Old Calabar for Onitsha, after spending three months in the Capital of the colony. During my stay we built first: the church which is now being painted and which will be opened for public worship in three weeks' time. Secondly half of a house, and thirdly: a kitchen and shed. Up to now the authorities of this new mission have been almost exclusively occupied with the schools, but their efforts have met with extraordinary success. The actual attendance is 180 in one school and 70 in the other; there are 360 on the books. The High Commissioner summoned me a short time ago to discuss with me the foundation of an Institute in which 150 sons of chiefs should be educated. I agreed to this. After spending three or four years at this Institute, the students would be sent to a Government College where they would be trained as lawyers, doctors and the like.[52]

Calabar was then the capital of Southern Nigeria. The demand for education was increasing. With many Government Departments and commercial firms perching on hills overlooking the lovely natural harbour of the Calabar River, there were opportunities for a boy who could read or write. The chiefs and the people began to realize the advantages of education, and so the missionaries' difficulties were reduced. It is interesting to note that in a bid to capture the people's confidence the principal motive, the religious side of the mission, was ignored at first and for a fairly long time. The Catholics had to be cautious because a very strong Protestant mission, the Church of Scotland mission, had been in the town for more than half a century.

Father Lejeune did not neglect Northern Nigeria. He reported:

> The High Commissioner of Northern Nigeria is urging us to resume the management of the anti-slavery establishment at Ibi, now that peace has been restored in those regions. I intended to occupy myself incessantly, for some time to come, in carrying out the plans which we formerly made in connection with this work.[53]

It is clear that the Catholics proposed to start a mission at Ibi and open a school for freed slaves, which was also to be for bought slaves. The project was abandoned, probably because the people of Ibi did not like the idea of a school for slaves. This meant failure for Lejeune in his attempt to carry out plans which had received strong official support.

With the support of Mr. Linley, the President of the Province, he opened a station at Dekina. Linley entertained Lejeune and his companions with great cordiality and expressed the desire for a mission in his province. The chiefs readily granted the missionaries land. Unfortunately there was frequent trouble between the tribes around Dekina and neighbouring towns. They also came into conflict with the Royal Niger Company. Dekina was destroyed by Government forces. Of course, the mission was also destroyed and had to be rebuilt. Father Joseph Lichtenberger wrote from Dekina: 'The native quarters of the town is being rebuilt and the soldiers' Barracks are rising rapidly. But nothing, alas, is being done for our poor mission. I must begin everything from the beginning . . .'.[54]

In 1905 Father Shanahan succeeded Lejeune as the Prefect Apostolic of the Lower Niger prefecture and the whole policy of the mission was changed. Shanahan evolved a policy of conversion through the schools rather than through slave and charitable institutions. It was a turning point in the history of Catholic education in Eastern Nigeria. The confidence and respect of the chiefs and the people could be won. Success was soon evident. In the years 1905–18 there was a total increase of 48,161 in the congregation. The overall picture was that although most of the Christians entered the church through the schools it was nevertheless significant that greater numbers from the outside were entering the church year by year—a result of the influence of the schools upon the minds of the people. From a statistical point of view, at least, the policy was successful.

Work among the Ibos grew. In 1906 a station was opened at Nri, said to be the headquarters of 'Juju and voodoo and pagan priesthood for the whole of Iboland tribe'.[55]

> Although the King of Nri and chiefs of two or three nearby towns absolutely refused to allow any interference with pagan rites, they professed themselves quite pleased at the idea of their children 'learning book', and they even admitted that it would be good for them to learn what the Father had to teach them about God.[56]

At about this time also a permanent school building was erected in Ntedje and new stations were opened at Nsube, Isingwu, Iboro and 'Awba'; and at Uli, Ihieala and 'Okidja' each station had a school of its own. A central school at Ozubulu was opened and permanent buildings for a resident priest were erected in 1907. Normally the central school was a boarding establishment supported by several villages.

Further east work in the Efik country and Ibibioland was also being developed. During his tour of 1908 the Prefect reached the Ibibio country as far as Itu, from whence he went to Calabar and returned by motor cycle to Onitsha. It appears that some work had been begun some years earlier (1906), the Catholic missionaries in Calabar had already reached the borders of Ibibioland from Ekeya and had hoped to open stations in the Nsit Section of Ibibioland. Anua is mentioned, in the 1918 report, by the Prefect as one of the chief centres of the mission, having ninety-one outstations. In 1906 it was reported that over 400 Ibibios[57] went to the Catholic mission at Calabar to ask the missionaries to open missions among their people.

The opening of Ekeya stations, as that of many others in Ibibioland was largely the result of the people's invitation or initiative. In brief the chiefs sent people to ask the missionaries to come and work among them. The case of 400 people going at a time to the Catholic mission at Calabar is a fine example of this. Traders played their part. A certain Mr. Eyo of Ekeya, for example, during his trading excursions to Calabar, often attended, out of interest, the lessons in catechism given by the Fathers to the congregation there. On his return he assembled the chiefs and people of his town and spoke to them about the mission and his experiences. That was enough for them to ask Mr. Eyo to bring the priest to them. The latter left Calabar without delay and went with Eyo by boat to Ekeya. There the priest found the chiefs and the people waiting for him. The chiefs showed him a corrugated iron roofed building which was meant for their juju, but none given over to education. On the next day over 300 pupils gathered round the building—more than three times the number the building could hold. Only 100 pupils were selected to start with. No wonder that when the Methodist missionaries went there later they found it really difficult to begin a mission. Work progressed, at first rapidly, then somewhat slowly.

Successes were achieved during the first decade of the twentieth century in spite of great shortages of staff. This, coupled with the vast area to be covered by the few who remained (only ten in 1906—and some stations like Calabar and Onitsha were separated by hundreds of miles) was a great handicap to the growth of the Catholic mission and a drawback to its educational activities in Eastern Nigeria. In 1909 it was reported as follows:

Father Joseph is in Calabar, sick and unable to do much work. Father Robino has gone home in a sad condition. Fever got the upper hand of him. He is now in France awaiting patiently the last hour to come. Brother Eucher is going home by this boat very sick. Brother Armand went home at Christmas for the same reason. So it has been an awful year for us. As you know every departure means a big gap in our ranks and it means also a big hole in our poor purse already not so heavy.[58]

When one considers the fact that in the Onitsha and Ogboli schools alone there were 1,000 pupils it is necessary to add that there was too much work indeed for ten people. But had the priests no teachers to help them? If they had, what sort of teachers?

The usual type at that time was the teacher-catechist. Sometimes it did not matter much to the missionary whether or not the teacher did any school work as long as the catechism classes were kept going. Most of these teachers were in fact poorly trained. The early teachers were trained in Onitsha, the central station for the whole prefecture. From here other stations were supplied with teacher-catechists. But in 1913 a training college was founded at Igbariam, which aimed at forming 'a *corps d'élite*, ... a selected few who would undergo specialized training. These men would set the tone for the rest in discipline and devotion to duty.'[59] The college was very successful in its first few years. It finally closed on St. Anthony's Day 1919.

> The war laid a heavy hand on the resources of mission health and mission finances. From twenty-two [students] the number diminished to four to three, and even these had finally to be placed in charge of schools before the end of their period of training.[60]

It was hoped that when circumstances permitted the college would be reopened and would finally be transformed into a seminary for priests. In fact the college never reopened and so the prospect of a seminary was stillborn.

After 1910 there was a rapid expansion of education. Catholic educational centres could be found here and there in Iboland and Ibibioland. Ogboli had 28 outstations, Calabar 13, Emekuku 125, while Anua had 91. There were main centres each with many out-stations. In 1918 the discovery of coal and the resulting construction of a railway link with Port Harcourt on the coast tipped the scales in favour of rapid expansion. Coupled with this went the projected new industry in the midst of the Abaja clan. The Portuguese Father Correia, of the Holy Ghost Fathers, opened schools in and around Eke and through the influence of Chief Onyeama, the despot of that part of Iboland, it became the tenth centre of Catholic operations in Eastern Nigeria. Missions at Emen-Nike and Nike were opened; each had a school. By 1920 the number of school-churches had reached 700. The number of Catholic adherents had reached 70,000, half of whom were at school.

After the war the problem of staff became even more acute, and Shanahan left for Europe to look for helpers. It was during this trip that he was consecrated Bishop and his prefecture was raised to the status of a vicariate. At first his efforts to get helpers met with failure. But he finally got volunteers, and the total number of European missionaries increased to twenty-three for the whole of what was the Lower Niger vicariate. The relief reduced but did not remove the problem; for the work was increasing far too rapidly. Such was the pace that in 1922 Emekuku alone had 200 out-stations, and Anua 125, while in the whole vicariate there were only 1,000 teachers.

The opening of the Emekuku stations afforded an instance of the very important part Nigerian women everywhere have played in the educational progress of the country. The missionaries had made their first attempt to open a training college at Olakwo. This had met with failure. The second unsuccessful attempt was at Owerri. It was then moved to Emekuku. At first things went well. The people and the chiefs agreed to its establishment and a plot of land was given on which to build the college. It happened that the workers felled some palm trees during the process of building. This event was enough to destroy the goodwill that had existed. The owners were offended, and demanded compensation, as the felling of the palm trees, they said, was not part of the agreement. The Fathers turned down this demand and a deadlock was reached. They then issued an ultimatum that they would leave within twenty-four hours unless they were allowed to continue building the college without interference from the land owners. At the end of this time there was no change and they left. Just as they were about to depart the women intervened. Realizing that the Fathers would help their children they decided in their omu (women society) that they should stay.

'We cry with shame,' the women said, 'when we remember how foolish God made man. If Father wishes we shall cut down all the young palm trees ourselves. Then if any man in Emekuku objects we can all talk to him together.'[61]

The women won. A year later Father Dan Walsh came and made it his headquarters, pushing into the most thickly populated part of the Ibo world and laying the foundations of the faith in town after town. Emekuku became a great power house of Faith, sending out year by year relays of teachers to meet the needs of towns as far away as forty miles.

Prior to 1922 no special attention had been given to girls' education. There were thousands of them in school but the proportion of them was not high. This was probably due to the attitude of the people to mixed schools which predominated up to 1929. When separate schools began to be provided for girls the attitude towards their education changed fairly rapidly.

Between 1922 and 1930 Bishop Shanahan devoted much of his time to attempt to enlist the support of those women's religious societies which might render special service to the education of women. He obtained the services of volunteers, one of whom, Sister Magdalen, kept a girls' school at Calabar. On 7 March 1924 he founded at Killeshandra in his own country the Congregation of the Sisters of the Holy Rosary. The profession of the first group took place in February 1927 and the first band reached Nigeria in 1928. The first venture of the Holy Rosary Society was to build at Onitsha a convent which opened with 230 girls. From here the work spread over the years throughout the length and breadth of Onitsha, Owerri and Benue Provinces. The success of the school prompted many towns and villages to ask for girls' schools. Mother Mary Stanislaus, for example, noted: 'Almost immediately came petitions from other towns for Sisters to establish schools for their girls'.[62] If the people of Eastern Nigeria are enthusiastic about education, they are more so about the education of women. As a result the building of a girls' school is, more often than not, a community concern. In 1954 there were 150 girls' schools in the Onitsha and Owerri dioceses alone, catering for 22,000 girls. Since then many more schools have been opened. Side by side with them are marriage training centres in central stations. All teachers are Nigerians. The Sisters manage, supervise the work of teachers, and train more teachers. There are now modern well-equipped teacher training colleges for girls at Enugu, Adazi, Emekuku and Aba, with an annual output of more than 220 teachers. There are also two secondary schools for girls, one in Onitsha and one in Owerri. Besides offering a secular education they also give religious education to Nigerian women who have a vocation to enter a convent. By 1954 there were 120 Nigerian Sisters who will gradually replace the missionary Sisters. The prospect of universal primary education created great demand on the missionaries.

One final note before the account of the Catholic efforts in Iboland and Northern Nigeria is brought to a close. Since the second decade of the present century the rate of expansion has been continuous and rapid, if not evenly distributed. There is a grade II training college for women and another for men at Onitsha. The one previously founded for men at Igbariam is virtually defunct. Besides this there are about four more, one being at Emekuku. The mission also has a secondary school at Onitsha. Founded in 1934, Christ the King College is one of the pioneer secondary schools in the country. Besides its academic achievements it has a fine record in sports and games. There is yet another excellent Catholic secondary school in Enugu and a third in Owerri. The Catholics have also a theological seminary at Okpala. While the one at Onitsha is a junior seminary the one at Enugu is a senior seminary. The academic standards of this senior seminary are the same as those of a university although it is not yet recognized as one.

Work had been attempted in the Munchi country with little or no success. Here the country is sparsely populated. The inhabitants live in small villages spread over a wide area, agriculture being the main occupation. These farmers always require their children to work on the farms with them. A decision was taken to create a network of catechist-stations, and for this purpose the mission selected an outpost from which to operate. As a result Ogoja was opened by the Holy Ghost Fathers James Mellett and Bouvrey who left Calabar in 1912 for the purpose. Ten years later the two priests felt that they had failed in their objective. They wished to give up the venture for more rewarding work. But Bishop Shanahan decided against this. If more ground could not be broken at least what had been won must be kept. Father Bouvrey was recalled but Father Mellett was obliged to remain at his post.

St. Patrick's Missionary Society

In 1930 St. Patrick's Missionary Society took over from Bishop Shanahan in the provinces of Calabar and Ogoja.

> This young Society under the leadership of their founder Rev. Father P. J. Witney, set out resolved 'to send out priests to co-operate with Bishop Shanahan and his missionaries in the conversion of the pagans of Southern Nigeria'.[63]

Shanahan and Whitney met and agreed that Calabar and Ogoja in Eastern Nigeria should constitute the field of activity for the new

Paul Inyang

society. The arrangement was officially recognized when on 17 March 1932 the society was canonically accepted as a Catholic Society for Foreign Missions. In 1938 Calabar and Ogoja became separate prefectures.

School after school has been opened. In 1957 there were four secondary schools in Calabar managed by the Catholic mission and a fifth was to be opened. St. Patrick's College, one of the secondary schools, was the first to be opened in 1939 just before war broke out. It is one of the most modern secondary schools in the country and has already created records academically and in sport. It is one of the very few colleges in Eastern Nigeria which have developed a post-secondary course of two years. The Holy Family College, Oku Abak, was established as a result of Catholic action by the Ibibio Catholic League in the 1940s. Many graduates of the two secondary schools are already holders of British and American university degrees. Until 1953 there were only three training colleges, one for women teachers. Since then the rapid expansion of education and the demand for universal free education has necessitated the addition of eight more colleges, excluding preliminary training centres which offer a one-year course preparatory to entry into the training colleges. In Ogoja Province the mission has two secondary schools, four training colleges and a preliminary training centre (PTC).

With Whitney and his companions came three Sisters of the Holy Child Convent who were to attend to the education of women by helping Sister Magdalen in the convent at Calabar where she had laboured single-handed for nearly eight years. The schools of the Sisters of the Holy Child are among the best in the country and have a high reputation not only in the Federation of Nigeria but outside also. By 1955 their institutions at Uyo included one secondary school, three PTCs and over fifty primary schools. At Ifuho there was a training college for teachers, a PTC, a technical class specializing in needlework and included more than four primary schools. At Ogoja there was a marriage training centre, a PTC, beside a primary school and over twenty primary schools in the rural areas. Afikpo had a training college for teachers, a PTC and many schools around it. Since 1955 many more schools and training centres have been opened.

310

Catholic medical work

In addition to their purely educational work the Holy Rosary Sisters look after the medical side of the Catholic missions at Onitsha, Owerri and Benue Provinces. Their first hospital was erected at Emekuku in 1930. Since then there has grown under their care a network of hospitals, maternity homes and dispensaries throughout these provinces. The hospitals have clinics for the ante-natal and post-natal care of mothers, and midwives are trained and helped 'to break down the wall of prejudice and suspicion, thereby succeeding in sounding the death-knell of pagan practices and superstitions'.[64] These hospitals look after eight leper villages. In 1954 they cared for and treated 10,000 lepers with the new invention for the malady. In 1953, 574 leper patients were cured and discharged.

The medical work of the Catholic mission in Calabar and Ogoja is now entrusted to the Society of the Medical Missionaries of Mary, founded in 1937 by Mother Mary Martin. The work began in Nigeria in 1937 at Anua where there was in 1957 a modern hospital. It was always full. It trained nurses and midwives. With Anua as centre, other hospitals, maternity homes and clinics have sprung up. A maternity clinic, orphanage and marriage training centre was built in 1946 at Use-Abat; St. Mary's Urua Akpan is a maternity clinic and was founded in 1952. The society is also interested in the maternity clinic at Akpa Utong in Asutan Ekpe. In Ogoja there is a general and maternity hospital at Afikpo built in 1948, and another at Obudu opened in 1954. The society also opened many leper settlements in the leprous districts of the Ogoja Province.

AN ASSESSMENT OF MISSIONARY POLICIES

Each of the missionary societies mentioned attempted to raise an indigenous church. Their efforts seem to have been quite sincere. But they have met with varying difficulties arising mainly from the attitude of the missions towards Christianity in general, as well as local snags. There is the problem of training a minister. In the Anglican and the Methodist Churches it takes something like six years to prepare a minister of religion. In the Catholic mission it takes a rather longer time which makes the whole enterprise discouraging. The rule of celibacy is about the greatest single deterrent to entry into a Catholic ministry. With Nigerians in general childlessness is regarded as a great misfortune both to men and women.

As for educational policy, it is clear what type of Christian education each proposed and gave, though not quite in detail, to Nigeria. Although the three policies are not identical, they are similar. The three missions proposed, and have endeavoured, to cater for the spiritual and temporal needs of their flocks. They proposed to give the Nigerians an education which would give them not the type of mental emancipation imposed on the Bantus of South Africa but mental emancipation in the true sense of the word. But it does not seem that this was the original aim. At first the aim was to evangelize and educate. The quality of the education was not specified nor was there any other real purpose for educating the natives except to enable them to read the Bible for themselves. The Catholic mission only gave them the catechism, and had no intention in its early years of giving the Nigerian an education of any depth. An important point is, of course, that the missionaries transplanted the form of education with which they were familiar from their own countries to Nigeria with scarcely any modification to suit the Nigerian situation. The type of schools set up in Nigeria were modelled after English charity schools, and the pattern of subjects taught was European and mainly British, although this latter was flavoured by some Irish elements. It is not to be wondered at then that the system of schools run by the three missions under study has given birth to secondary schools, which approximate to the English grammar schools in every way. The point to make here is that the missions, in spite of the expressed desire of some, neglected to adapt their schools to Nigerian conditions even in the case of language. To conclude, it should be observed that the mainly literary form of education given by the mission schools to the Nigerian peoples has helped detach the literate Nigerian from manual occupations like farming and to create a rift between the literate and their illiterate brothers and sisters. This is a serious educational problem.

As for medicine there is no doubt that the three missions have achieved a great deal. If the whole matter had been left to the Government it is probable that hardly 25 per cent of the medical facilities Nigeria boasts today would have been available. But because of the influence of the missions the practice or culture of indigenous medicine and treatment has greatly declined. In some cases the medicine and method of administration, in themselves quite good apart from other paraphernalia which often accompany the African medicine-man, are lost to this generation and to civilization. The idea that the medical missionary institutions act as a means of conversion is controversial. That the medical missions have helped to break down some prejudices with regard to child-birth, twins and the treatment of some diseases like yaws and leprosy, is undoubtedly true. But this is only true in some places and not in all the places they have worked so far. This may in-directly—and only indirectly—bring about conversion. But direct conversion can only be attributed to the Church.

In general the influences which arise from the points on which the missionary Churches in Nigeria have been in agreement have been on the whole beneficial. But many people in Nigeria look at the future with some misgivings when they see the points of disagreement among the Churches and the consequent conflict of views. The Churches adopt different attitudes towards the in-stitution of marriage. Often in Nigeria different members of a family are known to profess many creeds, sometimes as many as four. In such a case all the views presented by the Christian Churches are likely to be represented in the family. Thus there is a tendency to disrupt marriage rather than to make it firmer. The Christian religion is at once associated with inconsistency. The different Churches adopt different attitudes towards the Bible and its uses. One of the most highly extolled principles regarding the use of the Bible is that of individual inspiration, and it is most probable that such an attitude towards the Bible has been the cause of the rise of so many sectarian mushroom Churches all over Nigeria, which to some people ranks as one of the greatest injuries Christianity has inflicted on the peoples of the country. It is not unusual to find in a village of about 200 people upwards of four prayer houses which pass under the name of church, each quite independent of the other and following its own prescribed rules as inspired by the Holy Spirit. At this rate, very much against the hopes of many, it is to be feared that paganism is reviving in new forms and taking unto itself the insignia of Christianity. Many a community has been known to be firmly under the grip of the influence that issues from these prayer houses, very much counter to the cause of Christianity and frequently that of education and general progress.

The moral situation of the country is made worse by the quarrel

and struggle of Church against Church, thus sowing seeds of dis-
cord and trouble in the community as a whole. It is more of a
struggle for territories for membership and for prestige and power,
rather than for the propagation of Christian knowledge and truth,
that gives impetus to a good many missionary movements in
Nigeria. Thus in a way the missions have helped to break down the
very standards which they set out to build by their poor examples.

The impact of missionary work on indigenous institutions
Some assessment of the influence of the missionaries can be made
by examining selected indigenous institutions, of these the religious
and political organization, the family, the secret societies, and the
languages of the country are of considerable importance.

The indigenous religion of the people is still a pagan one,
although the impact of Westernism and Christianity made it lose
many of its ancient forms, grim as some of them were. In many
respects it was not a humane religion. But it had a number of fine
institutions and ideas, which have been destroyed, partly by the
importation of European materialism, partly by simple neglect on
the part of the pagans themselves, and mainly by the wilful destruction of pagan institutions by the agents of Christianity. They
might not have succeeded unopposed had there been no political
umbrella to protect them from the rain of pagan anger. Certain
features of pagan religions are similar to some aspects of Christian
belief, and could have been utilized to better purpose by Christian
preachers. Unfortunately they were attacked, undermined or destroyed completely. To all intents and purposes politics and religion
in pagan Nigeria were closely intertwined.

In many cases the chiefs were the religious as well as civil heads.
And so most laws of the land had a religious basis. As such, a
breach of the civil law frequently meant an offence against religion.
Any attack either subtle or open, directed against the law of the
land or its institutions was ultimately against the authority of the
chief who, apart from his duty as head of state and religion was a
symbol of moral authority as well.

For the missionaries, however, Christianity and heathenism
cannot and must never co-exist. Heathenism must be destroyed
through its institutions, but the destruction of the fetish institutions
produced an adverse moral effect, to mention but one consequence,
on the social attitudes of the people. The tendency seems to be that

in any society the greater the permeation of Western ways the greater is the deterioration of traditional morality.

The situation was complicated by the presence of British administrative officers and political influence. The administrative authority was in the hands of Government officers. Religious and moral authority was accorded to the missionaries. This division was quite different from the traditional power which resided in the chiefs. The missionaries and the Government worked towards a change in the bases of power in the country. Undoubtedly the seeds of revolt were sown in many mission schools. Yet at the same time the training provided by the non-religious bodies and particularly through military training create possibilities of further divisions within the society.

The next vital institution which has been very much disturbed both by the Church and State is marriage, and thus, ultimately, the family. Needless to say, a Nigerian values the family very much and attaches great importance to marriage.

> Had the missions understood that the bride price had nothing to do with any economic transaction, that its function was not to enslave the woman, not to give her over as a chattel to her husband, they certainly would not have committed the capital mistake of prohibiting it, and thus would not have exercised an unfortunate influence on Native marriage and family.

In fact, the whole system was an attempt to stabilize marriage. Thus when the missions voted to abolish the bride-price they were surely endeavouring to defeat a principle for which they stood. In addition, the Government joined hands with the missionaries to stamp out polygamy. But they were not successful in this respect. The introduction of such laws, and the deliberate and open attacks by missions on the existing marriage custom naturally threatened the solidarity of Nigerian marriage. The threat to the old marriage customs and family life created by the missions, coupled with the incursions of Western materialism, has created serious educational problems which need enlightened educational planning if some of the consequent dangers are to be averted. Among the many institutions vehemently attacked by the missions was the fattening of girls, but in some respects this institution was an influence for good. The standard of sexual morality it promoted among the girls was very high, and this was higher than it is today despite the teaching of the Christian missions. The effects of the attack on the family structure and social life, and indeed moral standards have been serious.

These were by no means the only institutions which clashed with Western culture and Christianity. The part played by secret societies, some of which like the Ekpo and Ekpe were mainly political instruments, has not been mentioned. Both these institutions were highly anti-social and greatly opposed, directly or indirectly, to educational and social progress of the communities concerned. If this were the case, it need hardly be said how very antagonistic the attitude of the missions was to them and other kindred societies scattered all over the country. Although these two societies are still firmly entrenched, there is no doubt that the activities of the missionaries have done enough to shake the confidence of the members of both. However, the Ekpo and Ekpe societies were and are institutions of training for the few in government, and besides their political character they are religious institutions. Thus their clash with an alien culture has given rise to many social, political and moral problems. It was these societies, together with the fetishes, that established standards of moral, political and social conduct.

In Nigeria the language situation is very complicated, and there is no real indigenous tradition of writing. The codification of most, if not all, the Nigerian languages in Roman characters was solely the work of the pioneer missions. It was a great feat, indeed, for a foreigner who knew very little of a language to reduce it to a print which has through the passage of a century undergone very little or no modification. The CMS reduced the Yoruba and many other Nigerian languages including the Hausa to print. The Scottish mission did the same with the Efik language with later modifications by the Catholic mission. The CMS also did the same with the Ibo language, and so did the Primitive Methodist missionaries for the Idoma language. Into these languages the various Protestant missions translated the Bible. All translated their catechisms and prayer books into these languages, and consequently these became the classics of the various languages. It must be said that the missionaries did not always find it easy to reduce these languages to print. Sometimes the population was so mixed that it was not possible to choose a dominant language.

The main incentive of the missions was to create a means by

which their converts could learn about the mysteries of the Christian religion, so the various vernaculars were reduced to writing for that purpose. As long as a person could read and sometimes write the vernacular it was enough. This required about two or three years' study. Beside this, the vernacular was regarded merely as a means by which the teaching of English could be effectively done. As soon as a child could acquire enough English to construct a few sentences the vernacular was immediately abandoned. In some instances it was regarded as a serious offence to make use of the vernacular in schools. This view of the vernacular still largely obtains even in Nigerian mission schools today.

The missions and the Government

One phase of the work of the missions remains to be mentioned, namely the relations of the Government with the missions and the co-operation which existed and still exists between them. From their own experience in Britain, the administrative officers were well disposed to the educational activities of the missions. Official policy attempted to be impartial whether the mission was foreign or British, and this policy helped educational progress in the country and did much to lessen the jealousies and tensions among the missions. Government policy was at first one of indifference but changed rather slowly to one of active participation and co-operation.

Until 1900 there was no Nigeria as it is today. Lagos was administered conjointly with the other British territories on the West Coast. By the 1880s many mission schools had sprung up in Lagos and the Colony. So the Government of Lagos, the Gold Coast (Ghana), Sierra Leone, and the Gambia began to think of co-ordinating the educational efforts of these territories under one administration. The system the Government proposed to introduce was the British. The missions agreed to accept this. But they and the Government clashed over the vernacular policy. Mr. Sunter was appointed the first Inspector of Schools for the British West African territories in 1882. He referred to the desire of the missions for vernacular education in a report in 1884 that, 'The natives must and will know English in spite of all such well-meaning but diseased notions; it is the language of commerce and the only education worth a moment's consideration or attainable'. But he was set an impossible task. He had thousands of miles to cover annually, each territory being separated by hundreds, and in some cases by thousands, of miles. When one realizes how difficult and dangerous it was to travel on the coast in those days, his endeavours to create co-operation between the Government and the missions on the whole of the West Coast were admirable. In 1892, when Sunter died, the Education Department of Lagos was separated from that of the Gold Coast (Ghana) and Sierra Leone. A full-time Inspector of Schools was appointed for the colony of Lagos. In 1906 a radical change took place when the Lagos education system was merged with that of the southern provinces. The position in Northern Nigeria was quite different. For a long time the Government had forbidden the missions to enter that part of the country. At the amalgamation of the two parts of Nigeria in 1914 the educational work in the north was not very considerable, although an Education Department was founded in 1910.

Writing in 1925 Lord Lugard said, 'The relation of government towards mission schools has not seldom been marked by irritating interference, or by a patronizing attitude not less irritating', but noted that co-operation between the Government and the missions was beginning to take its proper shape. The educational development of this period reached its height when the Education Departments of Southern and Northern Nigeria were combined in 1929. The difficulties of the missions in north and south were much reduced as some educational laws which were passed were common to both parts of the country. Now the country has been divided into four self-governing regions, and education is a regional function.

Summary and conclusion
So far it has been stressed that the modern form of education was begun in Eastern Nigeria in 1842 by the Christian missions notably, the MMS, the CMS, the Catholic mission and the Church of Scotland mission. The work of this last society has not been recorded in this chapter, attention having been restricted to those missions which worked chiefly among the Ibos. It has been emphasized that the organization and supervision of education were almost entirely in the hands of the missionaries until the turn of the century when the Government joined the venture.

Each of the missions treated here has contributed tremendously in the field of education by helping to build hundreds of schools in which thousands of Nigerians have been educated. Each has added substantially to the medical facilities enjoyed in many parts of the country. Mission hospitals, dental and other clinics and maternities cover very extensive areas of the country. They all have done much in the field of social welfare, in the care of the aged and handicapped persons, in the care of children and the blind. For instance, the blind have been taught, in centres like the Oji River Settlement, how to earn a living through farming and handicraft, and even how to teach others. In all these aspects of development missions have so far done much more for the people than has the Government. But all these could not have been done without the political umbrella offered by the Government, even from the colonial days. For since the days of the British, Nigeria has enjoyed a fairly long period of comparative peace. Not only this; the spirit of freedom has generally prevailed through that length of time.

This spirit is so strong that it has been outwardly expressed in the constitution of the country. By the relevant portion of the constitution, 'Every person shall be entitled to freedom of thought, conscience and religion . . . belief in worship, teaching, practice and observance'.[65] The constitution also provides for the instruction of pupils of a community by that community or denomination in any place of education maintained wholly by such a community or denomination. This then makes much room for religious education in any form.

Long before the arrival of the missions, the Muslims of the north had Koranic schools which gave instruction in the reading and interpretation of the Koran. The Animists of the north and south had also their own form of education which laid stress on the building of physique, ritualistic training and initiation into one or other stage of life. Since the 1920s there has been an increasing regional and local government sharing in the provision and management of education, joined in recent years by private individuals. The point is that these old traditions still have a strong influence on the habits and educational thinking of the people, as will be shown shortly. Meanwhile, the operation of the law in each region in respect of education will be outlined here.

In Western Nigeria all grant-aided schools are controlled by the regional government through local education committees or authorities. Denominational schools still maintain their identities,

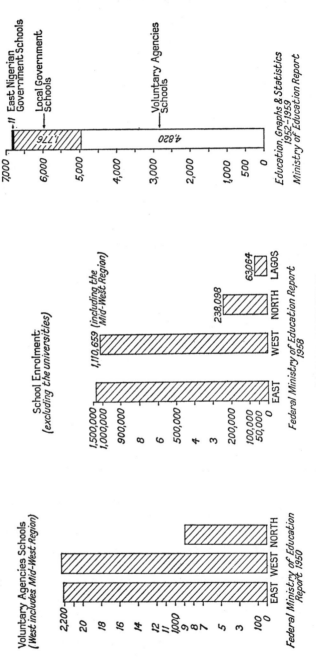

School Proprietorship
in Eastern Nigeria

East Nigerian
Government Schools

Local Government
Schools

Voluntary Agencies
Schools

11

1,776

4,820

7,000
6,000
5,000
4,000
3,000
2,000
1,000
500
0

Education, Graphs & Statistics
1952–1959
Ministry of Education Report

School Enrolment
(excluding the universities)

1,110,659 (including the
Mid-West Region)

238,098

63,064

EAST   WEST   NORTH   LAGOS

1,500,000
1,000,000
900,000
8
6
500,000
4
3
200,000
100,000
50,000
0

Federal Ministry of Education Report
1958

Voluntary Agencies Schools
(West includes Mid-West Region)

EAST   WEST   NORTH

2,200
20
18
16
14
12
11
1000
9
8
7
5
3
100
0

Federal Ministry of Education
Report 1950

EDUCATION IN NIGERIA

such as St. Paul's, St. Peter's, as is the case with the Muslim schools. Religious instruction is entirely optional. That is to say, a child of any religious creed can attend any denominational school without being obliged to practise the religion of the denomination which operates the school. The school gives religious education to any child but must not compel attendance at such classes. In the Western Nigerian Government and local authority schools, no form of religious instruction is allowed. This has been replaced by moral instruction. It seems that the Western Government has gone a little too far here. Also at registration, parents are expected to indicate whether or not they wish their children to receive any form of religious education. There is no religious restriction in the employment of teachers, although the missions always prefer those trained under them. In secondary schools the missions can hardly maintain this attitude without losing the services of excellent teachers. But some die-hard missions do not care.

In the East there are far more mission schools than other kinds —Government, local government, private—put together. Here one mission is sufficiently strong to have considerable impact on Government educational policies and when they all combine they sometimes have most of what they want. A strong point in their favour is that they are giving an efficient form of education. Besides, many Government ministers are likely to be practising Christians and like to have religion taught in schools. Even so, there is a great deal of religious tolerance and all the missions, particularly the Catholic admit pupils of other denominations to their schools and colleges. There are, however, a few exceptions to this.

Nevertheless, political consciousness has brought about a lively awareness, on the part of the Government, as to the supreme importance of education in the political structure and development of the State so that the tendency is for the Government to exercise greater control over education than ever before. This is the case with all the regional governments. It seems, however, that their slender resources have prevented them from taking over education. This spirit is evident in the attempts by the Eastern Nigerian Government to introduce educational measures similar to those provided by the British Education Act of 1944; otherwise they would be modelled along non-sectarian lines like the American educational system.

From its inception the British Government in Nigeria, as already indicated, had forbidden the Christian missions to operate in the north. (Even today, these missions still operate in rather limited areas.) The reason given was to prevent the Christian missionaries from offending the religious susceptibilities of the Muslims and so cause political unrest.[66] Besides, the Muslims regard all other Nigerians (both Christians and Animists) as *Kaferis*, that is, pagans and look on them with contempt if not with revulsion and long for the day they will become Muslims. This attitude no doubt, must be reflected in a Muslim controlled educational policy and can be evidenced in the fact that the Christian missions make very little headway in the north educationally and religiously. For, the letter of the law may be present but its interpretation and execution may be so manoeuvred that they make nonsense of the rights and privileges accorded Christians by the law.

However, there are not many mission schools in the north. Control of all schools is exercised by the Northern-Regional Ministry of Education through local authorities. Grants-in-aid, teachers' salaries, curriculum advice, outline of syllabuses, primary school leaving certificate examinations (as in the other regions), financing of secondary schools, all are under the control of the Regional Ministry of Education which inspects all the schools in its domain. But the internal administration still rests with the mission authorities. Strictly religious education is given in seminaries and the Koranic schools. Since the Government pays teachers it demands that there must be at least forty pupils in each of four classes for a school to merit approval. Strong control over schools by local bodies is limited to their own schools. Catholics admit people of all faiths to their schools and allow free practice of religion, but Protestants tend to enforce their own faiths. The Government wants to have more and more control over schools and to see people of all faiths admitted to any school. This allows for cultural diffusion. But whether the free practice of religion in Government owned schools is allowed is not very evident. Be that as it may, it has to be emphasized that the banning of Christian missions in the past from the north had created a near iron-curtain between that region and the rest of Nigeria, and that this division was further deepened by the wedge of different educational policies for the north and the south.

The Amalgamation of 1914 and the centralization of the education departments of both north and south were two great steps taken to break down the great wall and thus foster the unity of the country. When the Nigerian Constitutional Conference placed education under the regional government and in the hands of political and religious demagogues it was, in fact, reversing the march of the young nation towards solid unity. True, federalism has its blessings. But it also has its woes, one of which is its inherent tendency to tear unity apart. Where there are mature minds the problem of nursing unity in federalism is comparatively easy. But where such minds are lacking, unity is always tottering in the balance, as it is the case in Nigeria. One or two mature minds cannot do the job.

To return to our main point, Christian missions were admitted late to the Northern emirates; but such admission has not brought to the region educational facilities comparable to those of the east and the west, where the missions had worked successfully for decades. The result is that there are by far fewer educational institutions of all classes except the university in the north than in either the east or the west and, in fact, even the mid-west, the smallest of all the regions. The problem becomes enormous and even ominous of danger when it is looked at from the standpoint of population.

The north with the largest population has the least number of educational institutions. This educational gulf, together with the religious cleavage has further strengthened the dividing wall between Muslims of the north and the west, and the mixed groups of the country. Thus, the policy of Nigerianization—a policy which has already done enough to break the unity of the country. Had the Christian missions been allowed from the start to work in the north as they did in the south, the situation might have been different. Yet it is true, too, that the southern Nigerians under a free operation of the policy of Nigerianization would have overrun the public services of the north in addition to their own. In such a case a balance could be struck by allocating a specified quota of appointments in every segment of public activity to the north. This then would lead to a balanced policy of Nigerianization rather than that of regional or ethnic indoctrination, particularly through the schools.[67] A policy by which other Nigerians except Northern Nigerians, are treated worse than aliens in their own country; a policy by which inefficient Nigerians can be installed without question over those better qualified and more efficient in their particular jobs, yet a policy of separation cannot but create suspicion among most Nigerians, especially in the south, as the genuineness of the northern leaders' desire to build a united country. This policy is certainly inflicting nasty wounds on Nigerian unity before it has had time to blossom.

From the few points above it will be seen that the preservation of the ban on mission activities in the north, even to the first half of this century, has militated very seriously against the expansion of eduational facilities here and, therefore, against the provision for skilled educated personnel of northern origin. The result is that most Northern Nigerians feel cheated because the number of their sons and daughters employed in Nigerian public service is totally disproportionate to their population.[68] Even now, if the Northern Government continues to depend far more on its slender resources for educational expansion and either by omission or by design fails to encourage expansion of educational facilities by the missions it will still have many decades to catch up with the rest of the country in this respect. This would, indeed, mean a further obstacle to Nigerian unity. Also the Northern Government may find that a policy of banning Southern workers from the Northern public service may have similar effects to the ban on missions.

Furthermore, the attempts by the Northern Government to provide almost all its schools[69] in its recent programmes of expansion have a tendency to divert considerable funds from other fields of development. There is no doubt that the Government and certainly the peoples whom it governs, would stand to gain a great deal more by its vigorously encouraging the missions to expand their educational facilities. Although the north appears to be expanding educationally, much more rapidly than any of the other regions, the relative paucity of educational facilities is evident from the fact that in 1950 Eastern Nigeria alone had 17,000 primary and 900 secondary school teachers while the north had only 4,500 and 100 teachers respectively.[70] The disparity is still further increased by the fact that the north has at least twice the population of the east. Under the circumstances, the north should not discriminate against the expansion of mission schools.

Finally, it should be said that at the present state of the Northern Region's development it would be most unwise for the Government to adopt any policy which would exclude the missions from educational activities, or hamper them in this respect. There are times when the missions succeed in persuading the people far more than the Government. On the other hand, there have been some serious clashes over educational policy in Eastern and Western Nigeria. It seems that the era of partnership between Government and missions will pass and the Government will become a trusted educational agency of the people. During this period of transition it would be unwise for any of the four Regional Governments, overtly or indirectly, to place the missions in a predicament, or in fact take away the schools rather abruptly from them (an action which should not be recommended). The missions have still a great part to play in educating the Nigerian youth. In fact, leaving some educational responsibilities to the missions may, in the near future, even lead to the complete unity of the Christian Churches in Nigeria and closer collaboration with the Muslims, and there would be no greater glory to the country than this.

NOTES

1. Ching, Donald S. (Ed.), *They Do Likewise* (London 1951), p. 52.
2. *The Eighth Annual Report of the MMS ... for the year 1939* (London 1940), p. 37.
3. *Ibid.* (1956), p. 28.
4. PMMS *Records* (April 1892), p. 584.
5. See Burns, Sir Alan, *History of Nigeria* (London, 4th ed., 1948).
6. Pickering Report to the MMS. PMMS *Records* (1893), pp. 85–9.
7. *Ibid.*
8. *Ibid.* (Jan. 1894), pp. 119–20.
9. *Ibid.* (1895), pp. 9–12.
10. PMM *Herald* (1906), p. 121.
11. MMS *Annual Report 1937*, p. 92. See also Murray, A. V., *School in the Bush* (London 1939), pp. 104–5.
12. MMS *Annual Report 1954*, pp. 24–5.
13. Nuffield Foundation Report, *African Education* (London 1953).
14. Ching, p. 53.
15. *Ibid.*, p. 63.
16. *Ibid.*, p. 62.
17. MMS *Annual Report 1938*, p. 50.
18. *Ibid.*, *1935*, p. 95 points out that it was a Government institution.

19. Ching, p. 67.
20. *Ibid.*, p. 70.
21. MMS *Annual Report 1937*, p. 92.
22. Ayre, George and Wiles, George E., *The Weavers* (London 1930), p. 32.
23. PMMS *Records* (1893), pp. 85–9.
24. MMS *Annual Report 1936*, p. 58.
25. Stock E., *History of CMS* (London 1889), vol I, pp. 368 and 375.
26. *Ibid.*, vol II, p. 120.
27. *Ibid.*, p. 121; see also *West Africa* (London, 16 Nov. 1947), p. 1085.
28. Stock, vol II, p. 251.
29. Groves, C. P., *The Planting of Christianity in Africa* (London 1954), vol II, p. 76.
30. Stock, vol IV, p. 60.
31. Groves, vol II, p. 13.
32. See correspondence of Bishop Crowther to the Rev. Henry Venn (CMS archives). *Report of Special Niger Sub-Committee 1890* appointed by the minutes of the CMS Committee Correspondence of 30 Sept. and 4 Nov. 1890.
33. Groves, vol II, pp. 13–16.
34. Schon, J. and Crowther, Samuel, *Journal of the Niger Expedition of 1841*, p. 14.
35. *Report of Special Niger Sub-Committee 1890*, p. 9.
36. *Ibid.*, p. 9.
37. *Ibid.*, p. 10.
38. CMS *Intelligencer* (1879), p. 97.
39. Groves, vol III, p. 217 and Lewis, L. J., *An Outline Chronological Table of the Development of Education in British West Africa* (Edinburgh 1953).
40. Stock, vol IV, p. 73.
41. Groves, vol III, p. 263.
42. *Ibid.*, p. 263.
43. Stock, vol IV, p. 72.
44. *African Education*, p. 31.
45. Thorp, Ellen, *The Ladder of Bones* (London 1956), p. 170.
46. Walsh, M. J., *The Catholic Contribution to Education in Western Nigeria 1861–1926* (unpublished M.A. thesis, University of London, 1951).
47. Jordan, J. P., *Bishop Shanahan of Southern Nigeria* (London 1948), p. 14.
48. Groves, vol II, p. 190
49. *Annals of the Propagation of the Faith 1893* (BM), pp. 346–7.
50. *Ibid.*, *1900*, p. 211.

51. *Ibid., 1902,* p. 141.
52. *Ibid., 1903,* p. 67.
53. *Ibid., 1903,* pp. 153–5.
54. *Ibid., 1903,* pp. 392–3.
55. Jordan, p. 29.
56. *Ibid.,* p. 29.
57. *Annals, 1906,* p. 20.
58. *Ibid., 1909,* p. 252.
59. Jordan, p. 110.
60. *Annals, 1935,* p. 2.
61. Jordan, p. 113.
62. *The Capuchin Annual* (1955), p. 330.
63. *Annals, 1931,* p. 21.
64. *The Capuchin Annual,* p. 326.
65. Federal Ministry of Information, Nigeria, *Modern Nigeria* (Lagos 1964), p. 100.
66. Awolowo, Obafemi, *Path to Nigerian Freedom* (London 1947), p. 51.
67. *Daily Times,* front page of issues 8 and 9 June 1965.
68. *Daily Express,* front page of issue 10 June 1965.
69. *West African Pilot,* front page and editorial of issue 16 June 1965.
70. Buchanan, K. M. and Pugh, J. C., *Land and People in Nigeria* (London 1955).

NAME INDEX

Name Index

SUBJECT INDEX

Subject Index

Animism, Nigeria, 23, 319, 322
Anti-British activity, 35
  Cyprus, 245, 246, 248, 251, 252
  Egypt, 18
Antioch, Patriarchate of, 241
Anua, 304, 306, 307, 311
Apprenticeship—*see also* vocational
  education
  Bahamas, 69
  Cyprus, 257
  Egypt, 203
Aqua Effy, 285
Arabic language, 18
  Egypt, 27, 179, 182, 183, 189, 191,
    194, 198, 200, 204, 206, 207,
    210, 211, 217
  Kashmir, 158
Arabic schools, Kashmir, 158
Arabs
  in Egypt, 187, 189, 192, 211, 212,
    220
  in Kerala, 124, 125
Arawaks, 47, 48
Archibong Ville, 284, 285, 287
Arithmetic, 26
  Bahamas, 56, 62
  Ceylon, 78, 79, 98
  Egypt, 18, 182, 194
  Kerala, 126, 134, 136
Armenian language, 232 n.
Armenians, Egypt, 184, 206, 210, 221,
  228, 232 n., 236 n.
  Orthodox, Egypt, 188
Aro people, 23
Art Education, Kerala, 141, 145
Asaba, 296
Ashram, Method of Education
  Kerala, 143
Asia, vii, x, 16, 77, 113 n., 152, 248,
  262
Astronomy, Kerala, 128, 136
Asutan Ekpe, 311
Aswan, 191, 192
Asyut, 195, 229
Athens, 265, University, xii
Augustinians, Ceylon, 78

Badagry, 280
Baddegama, 37
Bahamas, xi, 5, 7, 8, 11, 14, 21, 40, 45 n.,
  47–55
  Associates' School for Free
    Negroes, 54, 60, 63, 64, 65, 67,
    68, 69
  Board of Public Instruction, 21
  Christ Church Parish, 63, 64, 65
  Constitution, 5, 49, 50
  Department of Education, 47
  Director of Education, 50

Educational legislation, 21, 49, 59,
  68, 70, 71–2
  Government High School, 49
  Institute of the British and Foreign
    Society, 21
  Legislation, 11, 14, 53, 60, 62
  Report on Education 1958, 47
  Training College, xi
Baptism, Ceylon, 101
Baptist Missionaries
  Bahamas, 61, 67, 72
  Ceylon, 27, 80, 82, 83, 91, 103
  Nigeria, 281
Baptist Missionary Society, xiv
  Ceylon, 36, 97, 113 n.
  Egypt, 202
Barbados, 73 n.
Basel Protestant Seminary, 186
Bassa, 298
Bauchi Plateau, 298, 299
Bazaar schools, Kerala, 29, 128
Beirut Missionaries, 211
Bell's System—*see* monitorial system
Benares, Hindu University, 143
Benin, 281, 300
Benue Provinces, 308, 311
Benue River, 13, 279, 280, 291, 292, 298
Bethel (floating chapel), 209, 215
Bhagalpur, 173 n.
Bible, the, 25, 27
  Bahamas, 48, 56, 61, 65, 70
  Ceylon, 83, 91, 93, 101, 102, 106
  Cyprus, 260
  Egypt, 180, 182, 183, 189, 190, 192,
    193, 194, 200, 204, 208, 210, 228
  Kerala, 125, 130, 131, 140
  Nigeria, 286, 294, 312, 313
  as a textbook, Ceylon, 93, 101
  Classes, Ceylon, 101
  New Testament, Egypt, 203, 208,
    211, 214, 215
  Societies, xv, 94
  study, 25
    Cyprus, 251, 260
    Egypt, 207
    Kashmir, 207
    Nigeria, 290
  teachers, Ceylon, 101
  translation of,
    Ceylon, 83, 94, 98, 101, 113 n.
    Kerala, 126, 131, 132
    Nigeria, 296, 316
Bida, 297, 298
Boarding houses, Kerala, 129, 130
Boarding schools
  Ceylon, 37, 81, 96
  Egypt, 194, 220, 221
  Kerala, 29, 128, 129
  Nigeria, 286, 304

Subject Index